Joy is the energy that allows a person to see with their own eyes. Consciousness moves from the level of imitation to imagination. . . . The joy of seeing oneself with new eyes after being released from unfocussed fear, anger, and sadness allows the spirit to sing.
— Winnie Tomm

Bodied Mindfulness

Women's Spirits, Bodies and Places

Bodied Mindfulness
Women's Spirits, Bodies and Places

Winnie Tomm

Wilfrid Laurier University Press

Canadian Cataloguing in Publication Data

Tomm, Winnie, 1944-
  Bodied mindfulness : women's spirits, bodies
and places

Includes bibliographical references and index.
ISBN 0-88920-269-9 (bound)
ISBN 0-88920-273-7 (pbk.)

1. Feminist theory.   2. Feminism – Religious
aspects.   I. Title.

HQ1190.T65 1995   305.4′01   C95-932855-6

Copyright © 1995
WILFRID LAURIER UNIVERSITY PRESS
Waterloo, Ontario, Canada N2L 3C5

Cover design by Leslie Macredie using an illustration created for this book by Sandra Woolfrey.

Photographs on page 66: The woman in the bathtub is Karma Tomm and the woman playing the cello is Jill Tomm.

Printed in Canada

Bodied Mindfulness: Women's Spirits, Bodies and Places has been produced from a manuscript supplied in electronic form by the author.

Contents

Acknowledgments

I WISH TO express my appreciation to the Social Sciences and Humanities Research Council of Canada (SSHRCC) for the grant I received from them to write this book. In addition, I want to thank my own university, the University of Alberta, for its generosity in providing me with grant money to present papers in countries, such as Finland and the Netherlands, which were associated with this book. As a result of working on this manuscript, I have had many opportunities to give papers in Canada and the United States. They have all facilitated the writing which was important to my own university career. Thanks are due to several people who have helped read the chapters and comment on their contents. During the writing of the first draft there were several people reading the chapters. They included Professor Terence Penelhum, Professor Leslie Kawamura, Professor Susan Wendell, Professor Petra von Morstein, Professor Karl Tomm, and our two daughters, Karma and Jill. In the later stages of writing there were four people who were very instrumental in giving me feedback. These are Mary Wright, Sharon Petkau, Karl Tomm, and Claire McMordie. I am grateful for their generosity in working on the book. In addition, I am thankful to the Calgary Institute for the Humanities for the space and facilities to complete the revisions. Thanks especially to Gerry Dyer and Jane Kelley for their kind support and generous spirit toward my scholarship. Most importantly I want to thank the Women's Studies students at the University of Alberta for their courage and their dedication to their beliefs. They have provided me with the confidence to go ahead with this work and get it out. I dedicate this book to them.

This book has been published with the help of a grant from the Canadian Federation for the Humanities, using funds provided by the Social Sciences and Humanities Research Council of Canada.

Preface

THIS BOOK IS the result of a search for a textbook for a course I was scheduled to teach at the University of Alberta. I couldn't find the kind of text that I wanted, so I applied for a SSHRCC grant and was successful in obtaining one. I was granted a study leave as well as some financial support over a period of three years to write the book. It was designed to relate insights from feminist spirituality and feminist social, critical analysis. During the period of writing the book, I travelled to various countries presenting papers and gathering information from those who heard the presentations. The book has provided me with a good framework within which I have developed my own thinking and have worked with students in stimulating ways. In 1994-95, I have been on a one-year study leave at the Calgary Institute for the Humanities, The University of Calgary. This has given me time to finish the revisions. My aim is to contribute to the developing literature on feminist spirituality in universities and outside them.

Growing up in the Cypress Hills

Introduction

IN THIS BOOK, I explore topics that have been central to my discussions with students in Women's Studies and Religious Studies for the past ten years. These topics include spirituality, women's bodies, cultural constructions of women's sexuality in language, sexual ethics, the sexual contract in politics and at work, and the relation between nature and culture. In this exploration, nature, culture, and social organization are considered to be inextricably related to each other. The purpose of the book is to bring together insights from a spiritual perspective and a social, analytical one in an attempt to contribute to feminist theory and practice that is directed toward greater social justice and ecological balance.

Several years ago I began a different book, out of which this one developed. The other one, which was not completed, was entitled "Human Nature, Woman, and the Relation between Reason and Emotion." I had just finished my dissertation on the relation between reason and emotion in self-development, using Spinoza's *Ethics*, Hume's *Treatise on Human Nature*, and a Yogacara Buddhist text, *Trimsika*, which I translated from Tibetan. My interest in the relation between reason and emotion arose from my own life situation. While the dissertation was a rigorous academic endeavour, it was motivated and sustained by my personal search for a greater degree of self-determination in my life. It was a search that began a few years earlier when I realized that for my own health and survival it was necessary to sort out how to *feel rationally* and *to think passionately* about what was important to me.

The dissertation had served as a sorting process. It was, however, a study of abstract ideas coming from men's realities. I did not learn anything specific about being a woman, even though I learned a great deal about theories of being a human being (from the perspective of males) in the abstract. Such abstract male knowledge was problematic for me. For example, I had given birth to two children and had spent several years raising them. None of the inspirational male authors whom I had been studying had anything positive to say about women, much less about having babies. As a woman, it was difficult to "get it together" with respect to the importance of giving birth and raising children in light of the alleged

Notes to the Introduction are on page 14.

greater importance of intellectual knowledge, which implicitly denigrated the unique contributions of women. (Fortunately, I was conscious enough to choose for the dissertation only literature which did not explicitly disempower women.) Experiencing the gap between an abstract understanding of human nature (as male nature) and ideals of self-development, on the one hand, and the concrete realities of my own life as a woman, on the other hand, motivated my search into the relation between ideals of human development and actual lived experiences of women.[1]

This book reflects a shift from the predominantly abstract theorizing of the earlier book to a more explicit attempt to connect theory with realities lived by women. Both the theory of spirituality and the social theory are grounded in experiences, including my own. I refer to spirituality rather than religion because it fits better with my focus on consciousness of the presence of the spiritual powers of nature in self-determination. I ground my discussion of consciousness in the Yogacara Buddhist doctrine of *pratityasamutpada*, a doctrine that posits the nature of reality (i.e., ontological reality) as a changing process of interdependent causality. The other Buddhist pillar that is central to my analysis is the doctrine of *sunyata*, i.e., emptiness or openness. Emptiness and openness refer to the same thing, namely, an absence of essential sameness in self-identity or identification of other things. Identity is grounded in the interactive process of continuously changing reality that is given meaning according to what is attributed to it by each person within their own cultures.

The terms 'spiritual' and 'religious' are sometimes used interchangeably. In my view, however, a spiritual way of living explicitly includes belief in the presence of life forces in nature by which we live. A religious view may or may not. It may regard god as the only spirit and as separate from natural phenomena. A spiritual consciousness is one which is, at least partially, constituted by awareness of immanent, creative powers that serve to integrate the life system. Experiences of spiritual power are sometimes referred to as mystical experiences. I wish to avoid the use of the term 'mystical.' It usually refers to 'other-worldly' or abnormal experiences. Such a view of spiritual experiences separates them from experiences of this world which are more likely to be considered 'real' or normal. I intend to show that spiritual experiences can reasonably be considered normal rather than abnormal and that, indeed, they often support one's social and ecological awareness. So-called mystical experiences, by contrast, are usually associated with isolation from society and are, therefore, often thought to be irrelevant to serious knowledge or lifestyles. I wish to emphasize the continuity between spiritual consciousness and historical consciousness, thereby broadening the scope of acceptable and reliable knowledge. Although spirituality is often associated with 'other-worldliness' and historicity with 'this-worldliness,' it is my aim to integrate the two from the perspectives of women's experiences and feminist theories.

Religion is too often concerned with other-worldly salvation while supporting unjust social practices in this world. Consider, for example, the widespread sexism as well as intellectual and social elitism in religion. Liberation theology is a notable exception. It is organized around resisting oppression in the hope of liberating the poor. Feminists working within the major religious traditions are beginning to alter the institutionalized sexism in the patriarchal traditions. Their work is also directed at liberating the poor rather than encouraging them to accept their oppression and expect liberation after their lives are over. Because women constitute the majority of the poor around the world, one cannot separate women's issues from issues of class and social poverty. Paulo Freire's (1970) belief that there can be no revolution without love guides the attempt in this book to connect the spiritual and feminist aims of social justice. The intellectual insurgency of bell hooks[2] and Cornel West (1991) carries on the tradition of Freire on behalf of Afro-Americans. Their work has been inspirational for me in my efforts to move beyond existing boundaries of knowledge and to incorporate material that has been excluded from the main body of literature that contributes to the new patterns of thought in feminist efforts toward social change. I agree with Freire, hooks, and West that the motivating force behind constructive social change must be love.

Spirituality is most importantly about locating our social consciousness in a network of connecting and supporting spiritual powers. From a spiritual perspective, our spirits, bodies, and the social and cultural places where we live our daily lives are part of an interwoven whole that is made healthy through participation, using spiritual creative energy that is intrinsic to life. Love is regarded here as the activity of listening and responding to oneself and others. It is energy that moves inwards and outwards simultaneously. Spiritual development is a spiralling, life-long task of self-determination that is motivated by the desire for expression of energy that moves us beyond skin-bounded egocentricity while, at the same time, stabilizing us in our own personal energy. Love is the energy that moves out from the stillness at the centre of a person's being to provide connectedness within a person and among persons. I believe that social change that is motivated by such energy is liberating for all the participants involved. I hope this book contributes something toward this process of liberation.

Although feminist spirituality has much in common with liberation theology, it is not a theology. Theology is about god language. Feminist spirituality is not about god language. It is not about a single god as the spiritual creator, usually symbolized by images associated with male power. Nor is it about including female symbols in traditional theologies. Including so-called feminine imagery in god language is, in my view, an activity that trivializes female power. Feminist spirituality is most importantly about women living as self-determining persons with spiritual creative power that is imaged predominantly in female symbols. Women's spiritual power, in this view, is integral to their existence as human be-ings. Their openness to it largely depends on the circumstances in which they come to know themselves.

Spiritual feminists are motivated by both an attitude of love and one of ethical outrage. It is difficult to separate the two in a context of social injustice. Love does not overlook oppression. It is often lived in conjunc-tion with an ethics that is characterized by principled disloyalty, i.e., tak-ing a reasoned stance against those to whom one is conventionally sup-posed to be loyal. In the context of systemic social restrictions imposed on women in general, or any particular woman, tough love is in order. In my view, spiritual feminists participate in the efforts toward improving social conditions for women because they live with a strong desire for justice. This desire is tied to equally strong beliefs about the right of women, as well as men, to actualize their spiritual potential in the process of self-determination in relation to the well-being of others.

There is no unifying agreement among spiritual feminists about the existence of spiritual powers external to individual consciousness. It is reasonably safe to say, however, that most spiritual feminists either reject or resist belief in a wholly external spiritual god or goddess. Some talk about spiritual experiences as exclusive to individual consciousness, with-out reference to an external reality. Others speak of encountering an in-teractive power that is both outside as well as internal to oneself and which is imaged in various ways. Regardless of which view is held, spiri-tual feminists share the belief that their own creative and self-determining power is an integrative motivating force in their lives that supports their personal authority as women. This belief strengthens an identity that is shaped by experiences of centred subjectivity and strong relationality. This experientially based belief is a significant form of personal strength within a social order in which women's authority is often undermined by a man's or by male-imaged creative power. An important social implica-tion that derives from acknowledging women as self-determining human beings, with their own creative power, is greater freedom from social op-pressiveness within personal relationships, within families, and among so-cial groups in various patterns of organization throughout the world. Feminist spirituality is liberationist in calling for social reorganization: women's spirits, bodies, and places are constructed in ways that facilitate women's self-determination and full social participation.

In Canada, the dominant secularism of our society also characterizes much of the feminist scholarship. Within academic feminism there is much the same degree of scepticism toward spirituality as there is outside of feminism. While feminist scholarship aims to ground claims of knowl-edge in experience, spiritual experiences are often rejected as sources of information. Because of this scepticism toward accepting spiritual experi-ences as sources of reliable knowledge, it is a challenge within the femi-nist scholarly associations in Canada to be openly spiritual, intellectual, and academic simultaneously. Fortunately, within the past five years there has been more opportunity in Canada to share ideas about feminist spirituality with other colleagues. Thanks to recent efforts of several colleagues at Canadian universities, a community of feminist scholars interested in spirituality is developing. I am happy to be part of that community of women. This is not to say that it is exclusively women who are interested in issues of spirituality and feminism. Rather that it is women, unsurprisingly, who have taken the initiative to organize around their own feminist spiritual interests and those of their students. I hope that this book will contribute to increased discussion about the relevance of spirituality to social transformation for women.

Feminists want major social change such as reorganization of power relations with respect to things like pay cheques, conjugal relations, social leadership, cultural constructions of meaning, and self-determination. Freedom from institutionalized violence in its various manifestations is required for the kind of social change feminists envisage from within their particular social contexts. The hidden thread that connects abuse in private relations with unjust social organization is acknowledged in the feminist slogan 'the personal is political.' Feminists have empowered women by showing how abusive personal situations can be explained in terms of larger cultural patterns that have normalized unequal power relations.

The study of power relations is a central focus of feminist research. A clear understanding of power dynamics is required for effective social action. I believe that such critical analyses and corresponding social action can be combined with the ethic of compassion that characterizes all spirituality. Consideration of the last twenty-five years of feminist scholarship gives a new meaning to the relation between self-love and benevolence. From my perspective, an ethic of care, without an ethic of justice, within a social context of dominance is neither coherent nor healthy. The mandate to care in our society is predominantly a woman's mandate. Women's work is often caring work, without pay. The labour of love is not counted in the national system of accounts. It commands little respect or authority. When women are gainfully employed there is often still the expectation that nurturing behaviour is their first responsibility.

Social expectations for women to nurture are reinforced in everyday experiences. For example in my pre-feminist days, I used to work in a place where there were two people named Winnie. One day a male co-worker thanked me for bringing cookies to the office. It was, I told him, the other Winnie who had brought the cookies. I went away feeling like I was at fault for not having brought the cookies. I do not think that my feelings were a consequence exclusively of prior feelings about what I should do to be a good woman. I believe those feelings were also reflected in the face of the man who was nourished by the cookies. I was left with conflicting feelings about my status as a woman colleague and how I should proceed with respect to bringing cookies next week. I had to evaluate the consequences of succumbing to social pressures to bring cookies so others will be delighted or developing a thick skin about being regarded as non-nurturing. An alternative would be to brush it off as nothing significant and forget it. That would amount to claiming to be free of social pressure. At the same time, however, it would be wasting energy denying the effect of social pressure on one's conscience. Because it is unrealistic to expect anyone to live entirely free of social expectations, it is important to change the expectations when they are disempowering. This is a feminist priority. It is facilitated by revisioning ourselves as women with independent creative power that can be actualized in healthy social structures in which an ethic of self-love and benevolence operates in a context of mutuality. Through the revisioning process, it might be possible to create new conditions in which women are no longer disempowered through their own goodness.

Benevolence, i.e., caring for another, needs new expressions for women. It might include, for instance, leadership qualities exercised in decision-making positions rather than making cookies for those in authority. Suppose qualified women were given opportunities as a matter of course to demonstrate goodness of character and greatness of mind (David Hume's criteria) as spiritual leaders. Suppose also that they were adequately nurtured by those around them. Then we might be able to point to a correspondence between ideals of self-determination and social realities where an ethics of self-love and benevolence would be beneficial to all concerned.

In the meantime, there is a need to minimize disproportionate power relations between the sexes in the private and public spheres that restrict the potential of women to exercise social authority. It is important, therefore, to revision our understanding of women as independent selves, to explore women's spirituality as it might be expressed through one's body; to see how language (interpretive meaning) is related to the body; to connect liberationist ethics to feminist spirituality; to revision socio-economic structures to reflect the ethics which are grounded in a spiritual understanding of human nature, with women as a normative form of humanity; and finally to connect culture and nature so that there is an orientation of living with the provisions of the earth. I shall explore these issues in the following chapters, connecting spiritual ideals with feminist social criticism.

Spirituality provides an integrative orientation toward social justice. It helps us to speak our truths from a disposition of compassion rather than from opposition. I do not claim, however, that social justice requires a spirituality of connectedness. For example, an Afro-American told me recently that he didn't care whether the waitress serving him in a restaurant loved him or not. He only wanted to be served his cup of coffee like everyone else. At the same time, as he pointed out, if the coffee is served in the spirit of person-to-person connectedness rather than out of obligation to legal rules or external moral prescriptions, the experience is qualitatively different. He strongly affirmed the connection between social justice and a spiritual consciousness which is about the spirit of connectedness, without claiming that an experience of connectedness is necessary for justice. An integrative spirituality, in which nature is experienced as a process of interdependency, is a strong basis for revisioning a more humane, natural social order. Buddhist theories of interdependency and emptiness/openness help to establish a framework of understanding that is without exclusionary categories. They emphasize the relational quality of differences. The same account of the interrelatedness of nature and culture and the corresponding ethical stance of respect is illustrated in the writing of Canadian Native author Marie Wilson when she says, "All people on this planet must dignify their existence by attempting to analyze their relationship to the rest of creation."[3] Human dignity and ethical social action are seen to be integrally related in this account of spirituality and feminist social analysis.

Widespread differences among women, even from within the same family (not to mention between social groups and diverse cultures), must be considered when working toward constructive social change. Every woman lives in her unique way. There is not a universal form of spirituality, nor is there a common human nature that is independent of the localized living conditions. I am not attempting to gloss over the multitude of differences that distinguish individuals and groups from each other. At the same time, I believe that it is possible to generalize across difference with regard to spiritual ideals of human development. This is an important assumption for the purposes of political solidarity among groups and action that is directed toward a common goal. Because we know that it is possible for persons from diverse cultures and social groups to actually communicate across differences and to organize collectively, it is reasonable to accept the category of 'women' as a place from which to work globally toward improvements for women. This is not, however, to forget that lived experiences are characterized by local diversity and that these diversities are multiplied by social categories and cultural variations. Individual, social, and cultural places provide the differences from which creative interaction among people occurs in the spaces between and within the particular places. My own theoretical perspective is intended to be one among many. I make no claims to a universal theory of self or social reorganization. Rather, my aim is to contribute to the growing number of feminist perspectives that are being articulated around the world.

My voice is located in Alberta, coloured by a rural background. Growing up in the Cypress Hills (in the southeast corner of the province) significantly shaped my interests in spirituality, even though the word was not part of anyone's vocabulary then. My childhood heritage includes horseback riding in solitude up and down steep hills that were covered by thick evergreen trees; peeling the bark off trees that were snaked out of the bush by a horse led by my mother; helping my dad load and unload power poles, telephone poles, rails for corrals, and fence posts; and howling with the coyotes in the long moonlit, winter nights. Packing coal, wood, and water were daily chores. Cleaning the soot off the lamps so we could play cards in the evening was a regular activity after supper. Each of us four children was encouraged by our parents to get an education so we could earn a living and at least have running water and electricity somewhere outside the Cypress Hills. With all the chores, there was very little time for intellectual pursuits. Reading was often interpreted as an attempt to avoid work. Taming wild horses in the rodeo arena across the fence from our barn had a higher priority than learning what a poet or novelist might have to say about the beauties of nature. The immediate demand was not for spiritual enhancement or intellectual speculation. I knew from a very early age that spiritual and intellectual activity without practical result is unappreciated by those trying to scratch out a living by working with their hands. I bear this in mind as I write this book. I also remember the encouragement in our family conversations to pursue ideas as far as I could. The seeds of my intellectual insurgency were planted in my consciousness as I worked on our place in the Cypress Hills, thinking about getting out of there and exploring new landscapes. My belief that intellectual insurgency is a necessary condition for social change and my experiences growing up in subsistence conditions in southern Alberta shape my consciousness with optimism and caution as I attempt to strike a common ground between speculative ideas and everyday matters.

The method used to strike this balance might best be referred to as 'experiential.'[4] Throughout the book I use personal experiences, as well as descriptions of others' experiences, to facilitate clarity. There are several reasons why I refer to my own spiritual experiences despite strong academic scepticism toward the practice. First, I benefit a great deal from reading about other people's personal experiences and believe that others do so as well. An example of a work that relates a personal experience in a powerful way is an article by Inés Talamantez in which she relates a dream where she met a Native American goddess, Isanaklesh.[5] In the dream she realized what her path in life was to be, namely, to do the work of the goddess. The power of Talamantez's own truth about what this means to her comes through vividly in her own words. She uses her spiritual experience to show the way in which the goddess spoke to her. There is no intention to impute a universality to her own personal spiritual truths. Rather she contributes to a growing body of knowledge about how spiritual experiences can be significant in self-determination and social participation. I discuss Talamantez's dream more fully in Chapter Two.

Another work that effectively utilizes personal experience to ground theory is Carol Christ's *Laughter of Aphrodite*. She combines personal narrative with philosophy and literature analysis. Her story of receiving

Aphrodite in a cave in Greece is graphic. Christ's description of herself standing tall (as she is) with her legs apart, her head flung back with hair flying while she laughs with the power of Aphrodite at patriarchal injunctions for women to be less than they are invites the reader to join her. Her narrative provides a concrete image to support Hélène Cixous's directive that "Woman must put herself into the text—as into the world and into history—by her own movement" (1991:224). This kind of empowerment is a good reason to cite personal experiences in the development of theory.

A second reason is that as we listen to each other we realize that our stories are not merely idiosyncratic, but rather that there are shared themes from different places. Each story has its own specific details, but individual experiences become part of a larger picture of reality. The cumulative effect is to see that the combination of different stories form an evidential basis for knowledge claims about reality. There is a truth value to this kind of knowledge that might be considered stronger than mere theorizing without such grounding. A greater reality is given to an experience when it is told to, and accepted by, others. Sharing personal experiences often has the effect of affirming those who have had them. Narrative identity is developed through sharing stories. In this way spiritual experiences enter the world through dialogue and become integrated with more everyday occurrences. As this happens it is likely that there is more integration between self-identity and cultural norms.

A third reason to ground theory in personal experience is specifically feminist. An explicit goal of feminist research is to build theories from lived experiences. Religious or spiritual theory development is no exception. For the most part the academic study of religion in Canadian universities eschews spiritual experience as a basis of knowledge except if it is done in an anthropological manner, that is, if it is a study by one person, or group, of another person's, or group's, experiences. Religious Studies departments are concerned with being accepted as academic. Their reluctance to include the personal, spiritual experiences of the researchers as valuable sources of information reflects the larger academic rejection of personal experience as a reliable source of knowledge in academic research. The reason behind the acceptance of anthropological reporting and not personal narrative is that the anthropologist is allegedly largely neutral in the observation of the subject, even if the method used by the researcher is participant observation. To observe one's own experience is often regarded as self-indulgent and fraught with blind biases. In contrast to the widespread academic emphasis on neutrality, many feminists encourage personal experience especially as part of their method. That is part of the project of bringing women into the world. I support that project and am applying the feminist principle of grounding theory in experience.

Another reason for reporting personal experiences is to open up space for others to speak about their own spiritual experiences. As I have discovered since beginning to talk about spiritual experiences as sources of important knowledge, many individuals have reported similar kinds of experiences to me. They are reluctant, however, to speak or write about them because of powerful social or academic pressures not to mention such experiences. Including personal spiritual experiences in this text is an attempt to normalize the reality of spirituality in everyday life. My hope is that in relating some of my personal experiences and theorizing about them, I will encourage others to do the same.

Probably the most important reason for me to refer to my own spiritual experiences is that they now inform my consciousness so thoroughly that it has become impossible to ignore them. My consciousness has been changed, and continues to evolve, because of them. An analogy can be drawn between my spiritual consciousness and the religious consciousness of John Hick, a British philosopher of religion who is a leader in the subject of religious pluralism. The analogy is based on both of us crossing over from one perspective to another. Hick moved from fundamental Christianity to a religious pluralistic position. He said that when he began to see the Christian claim to definitiveness as both groundless and unethical, he could no longer hold it. He had to develop a new way of thinking about Christianity as *one* of the world's religious traditions rather than the definitive world religion. His many books and articles on religious pluralism express his attempt to redefine Christianity as one response among many to consciousness of 'the ultimate reality.' Whether one agrees with him or not, it is powerful testimony to the fact that once one has "crossed the Rubicon" it is no longer possible to live with the old perspective. This is true for me in the sense of living with a changed (changing) consciousness as a result of my spiritual experiences. Living with these experiences is part of the process of self-determination. I do not believe this to be unique to me. Rather, from my perspective, openness and receptivity to spiritual energy is intrinsic to becoming more fully human.

The goal of a spiritual path, as I see it, is to increase one's mindfulness of everyday lived experiences. Developing theory that is grounded in personal experiences is an important way of paying attention to what is happening in one's life and to connect it with realities that can be shared by different people. I believe that a spiritual orientation to life is not restricted to one tradition or to one person's way of experiencing spirituality. There are as many spiritual orientations as there are spiritually minded people. I agree with Emily Culpepper (1991) that insights can helpfully be drawn from various traditions and social movements in the consciousness of a spiritual freethinker. My perspective is that of a spiritual freethinker and intellectual insurgent, i.e., a person who uses ideas to bring about constructive social change. I see spirituality and social change to be integrally related to each other. I believe that liberation efforts that are supported by spiritual experiences of integration promote human dignity as well as social equality.

Spirituality for everyone is mediated through a network of social relations in which each person participates. Sometimes these networks are affirming, leading to healthy self-regard and compassion for others. Too often, however, they are abusive. There are many forms of abuse that inhibit and virtually eliminate possibilities for self-love or compassion. These include psychological and intellectual bullying; sexual and physical violence; enforced economic dependency; and restricted access to social resources. The widespread abuse of women and children from all social categories, as well as men in marginalized groups, is closely associated with their lack of social privileges. Restricting privileges reinforces prejudices against the already underprivileged. This self-defeating cycle supports beliefs that those who live in severely restricted conditions are usually unworthy and deserve to be abused. This perspective overlooks the reality of organized social unjustice. Systemic discrimination against the socially underpriviledged is not readily acknowledged. Prejudices often become the alleged rationale for normalizing and enforcing violence and inequalities between individuals and groups of people. They are widespread against such social categories as Native people, people of colour, poor people, disabled people, old people, lesbians and gays, religious believers of various kinds, and those whose 'mother tongue' reflects an unfamiliar culture. Indeed, these abusive prejudices are sometimes invisible because they are so normal. Women and men in all these categories suffer discrimination in Canada.

I wish to acknowledge clearly that abuse is often experienced by people from marginalized groups more because of factors other than their sex. Gay men, for example, do not experience discrimination because they are men, but rather because they are gay. Lesbians experience discrimination because of their lifestyle as well as because they are women. The same dynamics of discrimination are relevant to, for instance, Native men and women. The men are discriminated against because of their identity as Natives and the women live with the interacting factors of race and sex. A lesbian Native woman would have a more pervasive network of limitations with which to live. Interlocking systems of domination affect all persons to different degrees and in various ways. Individual people experience lack of privileges or advantages according to local values regarding their various characteristics by which they are identified or by which they identify themselves. One person cannot speak for another about which issue is the most poignant.

Women often experience intense conflict between their identity as, say, an Afro-American person and as a woman. When one reads Toni Morrison's *Beloved*, it is difficult to imagine how her people can sit in the same room as white people. It is understandable that Black feminists often do not wish to identify with white feminists. In Canada, maintaining their minority culture frequently takes precedence over solidarity with white, English-speaking feminists. This is the case for many women like, for example, Chinese, whose ancestors were forced to pay a 'head price' to be indentured slaves on the railroad; and Japanese, whose families were interned in southern Alberta as 'enemies' of the country during World War II. There are numerous other groups of people who suffer abuse because they are categorized socially and are unwilling to join forces with the 'colonizers.' Women share common cultural identities with their male partners or relatives and may be aligned more with those men than with women from other social or cultural contexts. This is also true with regard to social class. Working-class women and university professors have to struggle to find common cause, sometimes without success. There is little doubt that it is difficult for women from different social and cultural places to work together collaboratively.

While acknowledging the sometimes unbridgeable differences between women from various social and cultural contexts, I believe there are some issues that cut across cultural categories. Women's low self-esteem, for instance, is a widespread phenomenon in Canada. A new sexual ethics is required in order to counteract the socialization of women into low self-esteem. Abstract theories of an ethics of self-love and benevolence, such as one finds in alleged gender neutral religious ethics courses, for example, do not translate directly into a path of self-determination for women. While it is helpful to have a visionary theory of self-determination and social ethics, it is important to take into consideration the reality of sexual ethics in societies that devalue women and privilege men's authority. A feminist analysis helps to locate an ethics of care within a context of social oppression where the mandate to nurture others is central to the low self-esteem experienced by women.

Low self-esteem reflects internalized, as well as external, forms of disempowerment, that is, limitations on self-determination. It indicates a notable lack of personal authority. Claiming one's own authority is required for the personal dignity that characterizes self-determination. I shall refer briefly here to an experience I had which illustrates some of the dynamics in which women's low self-esteem is reinforced despite attempts to speak with authority. I believe this example, like the others that I cite, has generalizable value and is not merely idiosyncratic. A group of us was sitting in a hotel lounge discussing ideas from a conference meeting. An important man (important in that group) was telling us what Spinoza had to say on a particular topic. The speaker's claims were inaccurate. At that time I was working on my PhD dissertation which focussed, in part, on Spinoza's works. I practically had memorized Spinoza's reasoning on one of the topics that was now being discussed. I asked him where he found the basis for his claims. He revealed that he had never read Spinoza. At that point I referred to textual citations that indicated Spinoza's view in his *Ethics* was inconsistent with this man's claims. He became red in the face, jumped up in front of the others and shouted obscenities at me. I left the group and was later criticized by my husband for speaking up the way I did and for "overreacting" to the obscenities. It was clear to the important man that I was not justified in my knowledge, but he perceived himself to be justified in both his mistaken beliefs about Spinoza and in his abuse of me. My initial reaction to being criticized for the spectacle that I had made of myself was to internalize the view of my husband. A later reaction, however, was anger as I realized that I had been doubly disqualified.[6] Following that incident, there was a determination to work toward better conditions in which women can speak and act on their own authority. An ethics of care has to be balanced by an ethics of resistance in abusive situations.

The existence of widespread hierarchical power relations between men and women does not mean that such dominance/subordinance is inevitable or that it invariably characterizes all personal relations and social structures that include women and men. There is evidence from different cultures, periods in history, and within our own contemporary Canadian society that indicates the existence of examples of relatively egalitarian relations between the sexes. The point is that, despite instances of egalitarianism, there are widespread dominant/subordinate relations between men and women in our society. Theories of self-determination cannot ignore disempowering social practices that unjustly limit self-determination because of systematic discrimination. Abstract philosophies that ignore power relations are not useful when applied to lived experiences. Power relations are constitutive of all social relations, with varying degrees of importance. A philosophical or spiritual view of self-determination must be cognizant of the social conditions that are necessary for self-determination.

Within the view developed here, an important component of any theory of women as self-determining subjects is the topic of women's subjectivity. In Chapter One, I explore a theory of self as spiritual from the point of view of experiencing oneself to be grounded in a reality of interrelatedness. In this view, knowing oneself includes living with a consciousness of one's unique individuality as well as the deep sense of living within a network of relations. In Chapter Two, the discussion of self is grounded in the body. Because I am developing a spiritual view of women as selves, I explore the relation between spirituality and women's bodies. This is done from the point of view of the inseparability of spiritual and body energy.

Chapter Three is an analysis of the construction of the meaning of female sexuality in language. By female sexuality, I mean simply femaleness or female sex-specificity. An underlying presupposition of this book is that social reorganization depends upon cultural changes that emerge through new symbolic representations of women's bodies and female sexuality in language. An important consequence of cultural constructions of female sexuality is the kind of sexual ethic that dominates social practices. This is discussed in Chapter Four. As is well known, the ethics that govern patterns of social organization in any society do not depend solely on the sex of the participants. They also depend on, for example, race, class, age, sexual orientation, and religion of the subjects involved. The social factors that determine how people are treated are limitless. Ethics and social justice have to do with all the possible social contingencies that affect any particular person's life. I do not wish to claim that sex-specificity is the only factor. Nevertheless, it is connected to all the others and it is the focus of this study.

Social norms, that is, approved-of social patterns of behaviour, are closely associated with political and economic realities in which people's identities are constructed. In Chapter Five, I examine, for example, how the persecution of women as witches was an important precursor of social contract theory, which excluded women from participation as full citizens, while institutionalizing asymmetrical power relations between the sexes as a normal and just form of social organization. An effect of social contract theory was to legitimize unfair pay and devalue women's work. The association of femininity with dependency corresponded with the prohibition of women's full citizenship and the trivialization of their work inside and outside the home. I discuss how the reconstruction of women's identities as spiritually and socially self-determining persons is a necessary part of social reorganization where women would have full citizenship and fair social rewards for their participation.

The book concludes, in Chapter Six, by connecting a spiritual view of life as a changing process of interrelated circumstances with personal, social, and ecological balance. Nature, culture, and social organization are brought together in a manner that connects a feminist theory of self as spiritual with the everyday concerns of women's realities, in relation to the pressing issue of global ecological balance.

Notes

1 Tsultrim Allione makes a similar point in the Introduction to her *Women of Wisdom* (1984). The discovery that the spiritual experiences of women had been omitted from Buddhist teaching was the stimulus for her own research.
2 bell hooks does not use capital letters in the spelling of her name. It is her professional name that she chose. Her birth name is Gloria Watkins.
3 Marie Wilson, an elder of the Gitksan nation in northwest British Columbia (1988:18).
4 I use the term 'experiential' in the same manner as David Young and Jean-Guy Goulet (1994). Their book, *Being Changed: The Anthropology of Extraordinary Experience*, is a helpful example of including personal experiences in the expansion of knowledge in academic scholarship.
5 See Talamantez (1989).
6 Fortunately my husband eventually did come to recognize the injustice in his lack of support and in his criticism of my actions.

One

Self as Spiritual

Buddhist Mindfulness

SPIRITUAL EXPERIENCE IS the basis for Buddhist theories of mindfulness. It is probable that every person's spiritual path includes the development of mindfulness, i.e., increased attention to what is happening at any moment. The level of mindfulness corresponds with the kind of reality that one experiences. There is a continuum from drowsiness to wide awakeness, from a state of inertia to one of fullness of being. I focus on Buddhist mindfulness because it was an important part of my own spiritual path and theoretical development. Buddhist mindfulness is not about the individual self in an isolated moment. Rather, it refers to knowing about reality (ontology) as a process of interrelatedness that is shaped by each person, according to their[1] ways of perceiving (epistemology). Mindfulness includes paying attention to how one feels in every situation and to how one wants to feel.[2] Mindfulness prevents self-loss and facilitates well-being. A goal of those engaged in the spiritual path of Buddhist mindfulness is to minimize confused thinking and distorted emotional reactions. This is a life-long process that is never completed but continually opens up new possibilities for greater connectedness to oneself, other people, and the natural world of animals and things.

To illustrate what I mean by Buddhist mindfulness, I shall cite an example where I relied on my training in mindfulness to work through a problematic situation with another person. When in the presence of the other person, with whom I was engaged in a work project, I felt a strong negativity directed toward me that undermined my sense of self-worth and my effectiveness in getting the job done. One night after work, I meditated on that day's encounter with that person, which I had found particularly difficult. My first aim in the meditation was to discover whether there was negativity being directed at me by the other person or whether it was merely me projecting my own negativity outwards. At any rate, I knew that I did not want to continue to engage with that person in such a disturbing way. As I concentrated my attention on the situation that day, images began to appear in my consciousness. They were images

---

Notes to Chapter One are on pages 62-65.

of weakness, such as a sick wolf lying down in front of me. I associate the wolf with providing outer protection. The image of the sick wolf led me to realize that I was not protected from external danger. I needed protection from the negative energy that was coming from the other person towards me. After becoming aware of the reality of the negative energy coming from the other person, I concentrated my attention on how to protect myself from self-loss in the face of such negativity. As I focussed my attention on that question, a pack of healthy wolves appeared in my consciousness. They were frisky and moved close to the weak wolf, nuzzling it and helping it to get up. Gradually it stood up and joined the others. They formed a circle around me. I felt protected and strong. Since this meditation, I have been able to work with the same person without experiencing the disruptive entanglement of previous encounters. In the meditation, I became mindful of the need for protection as well as how to protect myself from disempowerment by others. I have used the same technique in other 'chilly climate' situations. I cite this example to illustrate the applicability of Buddhist mindfulness in everyday situations. It is not merely a theory. Buddhist mindfulness is a practice based on a theory that can be connected to other spiritual orientations and to feminist theory and practice. I begin with Buddhism because my training in Buddhist mindfulness was an important turning point on my spiritual path. It was a turning point away from earlier spiritual beginnings, but it is connected to them.

I was raised in the Anglican Church, as much as one could say she was raised in any church when living in the Cypress Hills. Church services occurred about three times each summer. St. Margaret's Anglican Church is located at Eagle Butte, Alberta. It has been designated an Alberta Heritage site. Services are conducted there each summer by the son of the minister who came out from Medicine Hat when I was a child. It is likely that the church, located out in the lonely hills where eagles soar over miles of dry prairie, was an important part of my spiritual beginnings. I know that it is today, despite having left the church and gone on to explore alternative spiritual paths. The solitude of the hills and the vast stretches of untouched grassy lands brings one home to oneself in meditation. At Eagle Butte in the Cypress Hills, one feels very small. At the same time, there is an overwhelming sense of being special. There is a feeling of gratitude for being alive, for surviving in the vastness of the space around one. The feelings of being vulnerable to the snow storms, dust storms, lightning storms, hail storms, to ice cracking on the lake while crossing it, and to herds of wild horses stampeding across the prairie while riding alone on my own horse have never left me. I live with a sense of gratitude and still want to sing "How Great Thou Art," even though I rarely think in terms of god language.

An important Buddhist insight is the inseparability of ontological reality and epistemology. By ontological reality, I mean things, ideas, and events that are happening. I do not mean a metaphysical reality that is independent of what people are living with daily. Metaphysics, in contrast to ontology, usually includes belief in a separate reality that determines the way things go in the world. Metaphysics is dualistic. It separates a transcendent (spiritual) reality from an immanent (material) reality. It is part of god language. Because I reject the dualistic metaphysics entailed in it, I do not use that language. Ontology is about the study of being, of a reality in which transcendence and immanence are inseparable. Transcendence, here, is about going beyond linguistically constructed boundaries to experience reality as a process of interrelated and changing conditions. Intellectual insurgence is a form of epistemological transcendence. Epistemology is about ways of perceiving reality. Intellectual insurgence is about thinking in ways that go beyond existing styles of thought. The purpose of intellectual insurgence is to effect social change, i.e., to bring about a different reality. Reality means perceived reality. It is not possible to comment on the nature of reality except from a particular epistemological perspective that is shaped by each person's ways of perceiving. This is not to say that reality is exclusively a product of interpretation. Rather, it is to say that reality, i.e., what is there, is shaped by each person's participation in it. Reality is there affecting our perceptions of it and, at the same time, it is created through our perceptions of it. It has meaning for each person only according to that person's perceptions of it. Because the self is part of reality, it, too, is both there and is created simultaneously. That is to say, each person is uniquely real and is constructed socially as person-in-relation.

I shall describe an experience in which a change in perspective altered the way I perceived certain other persons and, simultaneously, changed my own way of being. My reality was transformed through the new perceptions that emerged in my consciousness during the meditation. I had been experiencing certain people as very intimidating and was afraid of them. I meditated on the question of how to overcome my fear of them. As I focussed on this question in meditation, their images came into my consciousness. They each were about two centimetres tall. I was much bigger than they were. It was like the dragon had turned into a tiny finger puppet. In the meditative experience, I proceeded to squash each of them with my thumb against the wall. Then I walked into another room, without looking back. As I walked into the adjoining chamber, the same people were there, along with several others with whom I enjoyed being. They were all their normal size. I walked around and shook hands with the people in the room, including the ones who had transformed into normal size from their earlier shrunken state. I no longer felt any fear of them. I could talk and laugh with them as I did with the others. The meditative experience was an experience of, first, claiming my own power in relation to them by seeing them as smaller and destroying their destructive power over me and, second, perceiving them to be normal-sized persons with relatively the same relationship to me as other persons with whom I can feel comfortable. Subsequent to this meditative experience, the reality of my relationship to them changed. Overcoming fear of them was part of minimizing self-loss when interacting with them. Without fear of self-loss in relation to others, it is easier to be more receptive and responsive to them. The meditative experience provided a change in perceptions of these people, as well as a change in the reality of my relationships with them. Consequent interactions have been more favourable, which has altered my perceptions of them and very likely their views of me.

A Buddhist view of the self includes both a strong sense of self-determination and a "deeply relational nature of identity" (Klein 1987:194).[3] The Buddhist view of self and reality discussed here is from the Yogacara Indo-Tibetan tradition of the fourth century C.E.[4] There are basic similarities with the other major Buddhist schools, especially those from the Mahayana tradition.[5] The view of reality as a process of interdependent conditions continuously coming into existence and disappearing is depicted in the doctrine of *pratityasamutpada*, i.e., interdependent origination. Reality is not a thing in itself. People's experiences of reality, such as seeing a rainbow, give meaning to the reality. The rainbow, for example, is there but the reality of the rainbow is different for each person, according to their experience of it. In other words, one's state of consciousness or awareness reflects the nature of reality for that person. Participation in Buddhist meditation is motivated by the belief that one can move from a less developed state of consciousness through stages to more expanded forms of consciousness. Deeper or higher levels of meditation (i.e., intensities) indicate the practitioners' degrees of mindfulness. The development of mindfulness is the process of moving from self-centred, distorted knowing and being to a centredness of self in which one's ontological connectedness is experienced. In the process of developing mindfulness, one becomes more conscious of ontological interrelatedness. Consciousness, in this view, is a matter of felt experience and reflection. It is not merely about intellectual reflection. It is also about body feelings. Knowing is also a matter of being. Buddhist mindfulness is a way of knowing and 'living with,' from a grounded centre. Buddhists, along with Socrates, could say that one cannot know one thing and do another. This is the basis for claiming that Buddhist ontology and epistemology provide an important orientation for egalitarian social action.

Meditation is practised with the purpose of developing a clear understanding of the nature of reality. The starting point for meditation is focussing on one's experiences of oneself. The task is to overcome a view of the self as the 'big I' and to come to know oneself more as a fluid process. The ultimate realization of the nature of self is reflected in the doctrine of *Sunyata*, emptiness or openness.[6] I shall use openness, as it reflects more clearly the view of the self as open to all possibilities for change, the permeable self. Emptiness, on the other hand, could imply nothingness in a nihilistic sense, although that is not what is intended in

Buddhist discourse. Emptiness, in the *Sunyata* sense, means reality is empty of the objectifying constructions, like labels, that we attribute to it through language. The doctrine of *Sunyata* is about fluidity of reality, of the self in particular. Meditation on the fluidity of the self is intended to eliminate nominal categories or labels attributed to oneself, others, and the world. Calmness of mind is seen as a result of awareness of things as they are in the process of interacting, free of society's prejudicial labels. Each moment is constituted by changing relations which might yield any one of a number of new realities. The self is a process of changing moments that are organized according to a set of perceptions, including patterns of body feelings as well as established ways of thinking.

In a Buddhist view, reality for each person is as it is perceived by that person. We are responsible for our ways of knowing. They characterize the nature of ourselves. Knowing and being constitute the process of self. This view of self largely as a socially constructed reality is humorously expressed by Myrtie Barker (American columnist, born 1910) when she quips, "The idea of strictly minding our own business is moldy rubbish. Who could be so selfish?" (Partnow 1977:13). There is a nice irony in a gossip columnist unintentionally employing a Buddhist notion of self to justify minding other people's business. Indeed, gossip (chatting about other people) is a major way of knowing that facilitates interrelatedness. When gossip is destructive, however, it is merely another form of egocentricity, from a Buddhist perspective.

Not all forms of knowing are considered of equal value in Buddhist epistemology. It is believed that there is a way of knowing reality that is more enlightened than others. An enlightened view is characterized by the wisdom of experiencing the interrelatedness of all that is, compassion for living reality, and gratitude for being part of it. In this view, the calm mindfulness of an enlightened view allows for the most effective interaction. The most developed way of knowing, i.e., concentrated mindfulness, is intrinsic to the best way of being, i.e., wise and compassionate. The inseparability of ontology and epistemology in Buddhism is captured by Anne Klein's claim that "certain ontological truths are available only to particular subjective states" (1987:195). The point of meditation is to develop subjective states that enable insight into the nature of things.

The path of increasing insight is the path of life. One never completes it. It is a winding and spiralling path, moving downward and upward, inward and outward. The path of increasing insight is largely about overcoming attachment to the self. As that begins to happen it is easier to accept others and the world in ways that are not characterized by excessive attachment or repulsion. In meditation, one's view of reality changes as a transformation of consciousness occurs. At a low level of awareness reality is characterized by "notional-conceptual" awareness. We think things correspond to our linguistic labelling. Buddhism is opposed to a strict correspondence theory of truth that claims there is a direct correspondence between perceptions and things. In Buddhism, perceptions and objects of perceptions (things) are believed to exist and are part of the reality of interrelatedness that is known in individual consciousnesses. Along with those two components of consciousness, there is a third, namely, interpretation. Consciousness is constituted by the interaction of perceptions, objects of perceptions, and interpretations of the perceptions of the objects. Each of the three components are affected by the interaction of one with the other. In that sense, reality is always in flux. There is nothing that remains unchanged, including self-identity. This means, among other things, that attachment to a fixed image of oneself is bound to be a mistaken view of the self and will lead to frustration. Frustration comes from inappropriate expectations, especially of oneself. Inappropriate expectations of oneself due to a mistaken identity are part of egocentricity. One takes oneself too seriously as though tied to a certain image and relates to others on that basis. Others are inappropriately objectified in relation to the mistaken "I." Social hierarchies of importance are established on the basis of such erroneous identities with respect to oneself and others. Hierarchies are seen to be a consequence of widespread mistaken identities that are part of "notional-conceptual" awareness.

Egocentricity with respect to oneself and the objectification of others characterizes this level of awareness. It is an individualistic view of the self with strong distinctions between self and other. Exclusion of the other is seen to be necessary for self-preservation. Social organization is constructed around this view of the self. From the Buddhist perspective, the "notional-conceptual' view of reality prevails in the consciousness of most individuals. Accordingly, social practices are usually organized around the notion of the separate self. If we are going to change social structures, we must first get over our attachment to the concept of self as separate individuals with strongly competing interests. The purpose of meditation is not to bring about calmness of mind for the separate individual to retreat peacefully from society. Rather, it is to develop insight into connectedness and, thereby, motivate compassion towards others. Wisdom and compassion are the two cornerstones of Buddhist epistemology and ethics.

Through meditation, one's consciousness is transformed so the individualistic nature of the "notional-conceptual" view of reality changes to that of "relationality." The focus is on meditative understanding rather than on conceptual analysis. Meditative understanding increases to the point where there is an intuitive way of knowing. That is the most adequate way of knowing in Buddhist epistemology. The idea of meditation training is to approach intuitive knowing through increased focussed attention. It is to move through different levels of interest which determines the attention one pays to whatever the focus of attention is. They are listed in the following way in the *Trimsika*:[7] (1) moderate attention, based on a desire to learn more about the subject; (2) a pursuit which increases the focus of attention; (3) sustained attention; (4) intense concentration;

and (5) total absorption, which is characteristic of the first transformation at the stage of liberation (*T.*, Vs. 10b,c and commentary*)*. There is a move away from scattered interest to single-mindedness. It is maintained that increased study and attention to what is good (in this case good means the three jewels—the Buddha, *Dharma* or teachings of the Buddha, and *Sangha* or community of monks) leads one to realize the dynamic interrelatedness of existing conditions, which is what constitutes proper seeing. Total concentration is believed to be possible with extensive focussed meditative practice. Progression from one level of attention to another increases one's awareness of the interrelatedness of reality and the truth of the Buddha's teaching.

Concentration on the nature of the Buddha involves increased understanding of the doctrine of *Trikaya*, the three bodies of the Buddha. Understanding the doctrine of the *Trikaya* includes understanding oneself in a particular way. The three Buddha bodies are the *dharmakaya*, *sambhogakaya*, and *nirmanakaya*. Body (*kaya*) refers to activities rather than concrete material body (King 1991:73). *Dharmakaya* is the basic transformative power which allows for freedom from attachment (insight) and the ability to be compassionate. It is considered the purity of being, which is intrinsic to all forms of being. The *sambhogakaya* and *nirmanakaya* are the emergent manifestations of the underlying *dharmakaya*. The *sambhogakaya* is the activities of wisdom, meditation, and compassion. Wisdom is "nondiscriminative knowledge"; meditation activity is about being in the world for the sake of others in the same way as for oneself, without dualistic perceptions of self and other; compassion is about removing suffering and establishing peace (King 1991:74). The *nirmanakaya* has the same three functions. A difference is that compassion for others is the central reason for its existence.

A central idea about the *Trikaya*, all three bodies as Buddha nature, is that practising meditation to develop these characteristics and corresponding social actions based on wisdom and compassion constitutes the main activities of human endeavour. Buddha nature is believed to be the nature of reality for all living forms. As the Buddha comes to be understood as a universal principle, there is a sense in which the Buddha principle is seen to be a part of the consciousness of each individual. Sallie King (1991:81) points out that, although there are levels of awareness of the Buddha nature (*dharmakaya*) in each person, everyone has the capacity to become aware of their own Buddha nature. Buddha nature is characterized by a consciousness that is fully aware of interdependent causality, without misplaced attachments or repulsions. Realization of one's own Buddha nature, i.e., potential for wisdom and compassion, enhances one's own self-regard and respect for others simultaneously. This view of the nature of self and the relationality of self has important implications for ethical behaviour and social organization. It is an egalitarian framework for social theory and practice. The connection between a spiritual under-

standing of the self and a liberationist ethics is intrinsic to Buddhist epistemology and ontology. Buddhism is not, however, a vehicle for intellectual understanding without experience. Its strength lies in its meditative
practices in which there is concentration on mind control. In Buddhist
meditation, one does not reach an end point, merely different starting
points: new perceptions of reality.

It is a Buddhist 'truth' that each person creates their own reality. At
the same time, their reality is integrally connected to the realities of others. It is believed that we each construct our own reality as we interact
with others who are also giving meaning to their experiences according to
their level of awareness. Insight into that process both within oneself and
among selves is coextensive with compassion for self and others. Recognition of one's own agency is inseparable, in this view, from recognition of
the agency of others. While the self is deeply relational, a goal of Buddhist
meditation is to develop one's own understanding and become free from
merely reacting to the authority of others. The Buddhists have an appropriate saying that reflects the priority of personal knowledge over that of
the expert. They say, "If you meet the Buddha on the road kill him." In
other words, claim your own authority. In the Buddhist view, claiming
one's own authority is to gain wisdom. This is only possible in conjunction
with compassion. Both are believed to develop through meditative practices focussed on understanding the causes of frustration and overcoming
egocentric attachments to dualistic perceptions of self and others.

Compassion and wisdom are regarded as two wings of the same bird.
Levels of insight increase as one becomes less attached to oneself as a separate entity, with an elevated distinctiveness. Egocentricity gives way to
centredness in clear awareness of changing interdependency. One could
say that self-centredness diminishes and centredness of self emerges. Centredness of self is characterized by knowing calmly and being grounded in
that way of knowing. It is knowing about interdependent causality. In
particular, it is knowing about the relation between emotion and reason
in consciousness. The psychology of Buddhist training is consistent with
compassionate social action. The development of greater awareness of the
relational nature of reality is seen to involve the development of eleven
positive mental qualities: trust, self-respect, decorum, non-attachment,
non-hatred, non-deludedness, diligence, alertness, conscientiousness,
equanimity, and non-violence (*T.*, Vs. 10d, lla,b,c and commentary). Each
of these qualities is related to the others, yet has it own distinctiveness.

Trust is having confidence in the value of the pursuit of virtue and the
corresponding desire to act on that trust. *Self-respect* is coextensive with
the confidence one has in the pursuit of virtue, and which is based on
one's faith in the value of it. Because of self-respect, one avoids doing
what is personally viewed as objectionable. *Decorum* means treating others with consideration, paying attention to the effects of one's behaviour
on another. *Non-attachment* means not clinging to changing situations as

though they were unchanging and not becoming disturbed because of thwarted expectations (violent males, for example, could benefit especially from some Buddhist meditation!). *Non-hatred* is associated with non-attachment, just as hatred is associated with attachment (trying to hang onto an image of oneself that is threatened). Hostility resulting from thwarted expectations is seen as the condition which promotes misery. Freedom from expectations based on prior conditions is a condition for release from hostility and corresponding misery. *Non-deludedness* refers to experiencing causal interrelatedness with respect to one's actions and their consequences. It includes taking responsibility for anticipating consequences of one's actions. *Diligence* is the pursuit of what is good and the avoidance of slothful behaviour. *Alertness* refers primarily to mental quickness and secondarily to physical agility. It is claimed that alertness derives from the power of the sutras (Buddhist sacred literature, as taught by the Buddha). *Conscientiousness* is contrasted with indifference. It is about being engaged with a respectful attitude towards the activity. *Equanimity* means tranquility, a balanced mind in which there is no excessive elation or depression. There is an absence of attachment and any of its consequent emotional disruptions. This does not mean an absence of passion. On the contrary, equanimity includes passion for life that is a consequence of gratitude. The passion, however, includes a mindfulness of the interrelatedness of personal desires with the well-being of others. It is a passion that is infused with wisdom and compassion. *Non-violence* involves compassion towards all living beings. Compassion means desiring the happiness of others and sharing in the pain of others. It will be discussed more fully in relation to eros and agapé in a discussion of spirituality and the body in Chapter Two, and to self-love and benevolence with regard to ethics in Chapter Four. All eleven positive mental qualities cited above are believed to require trust in the Buddha's teaching and relinquishment of attachment to the self through disciplined training of the mind. Cultivating a positive mind corresponds to overcoming basic negative characteristics in the pursuit of wisdom and compassion.

The six basic negative attributes to overcome in this view are: passionate attachment, anger, arrogance, lack of insight, being opinionated, and indecision (*T.*, Vs. 11d, 12a). *Passionate attachment* is mostly about taking the physical structure of the body as fixed. This has important implications for issues of disability.[8] We tend to have relatively fixed images of who we are in relation to our physical structures. Susan Wendell (1989) raises important issues about the ideal of perfection which guides our views of self-worth. Her own experience of becoming disabled significantly altered her philosophy of self. In Buddhist discourse one could say that she has become relatively free of expectations of what one should be. The ideal of perfection has lost its grip on her evaluation of a person's existential reality. Rather, there is appreciation of personal creativity according to existing circumstances. That is not to resign oneself to fixed conditions, but rather to use one's creative potential to open space within different contexts of ableness. Wendell sets an example of opening new spaces from what would normally be called a disadvantaged position. Her important work in the area of feminist theory and disability extends the boundaries of feminist research with respect to the ethos of striving for perfection. This issue of body consciousness has important implications for women, especially with respect to the obsession with slimness. I explore this further in the next chapter on spirituality and the body.

Anger is described as a hostile disposition and is inconsistent with the clear thinking of a calm mind. While this is axiomatic, a subtle point must be clarified. There is a difference between an angry orientation to the world and a justified anger at widespread or individual injustices. Freedom from an angry orientation does not imply withdrawal from action directed toward social justice (although it could result in that). Anger at social injustice or personal abuse is not inconsistent with clear understanding and compassionate action. The Dali Lama, for example, spends much of his energy working for social justice. He motivates many others to do the same. The anger is turned into a constructive strength and expressed through a positive orientation toward change. By contrast, anger as an orientation within one's consciousness is believed to be self-destructive because it blocks the positive energy that allows one to be creative. Meditation on letting go of destructive mental qualities is useful for women, or men, who have been victimized. Letting go of bitterness, however, is not to let go of the motivation for correcting social injustices. Rather it allows for the development of strong positive energy to apply toward changing social inequalities. Anger that can be transformed from a reactive, self-defeating energy to an active, self-determining one is a useful resource for political activism.

Arrogance is believed to arise from seeing the self as more than what it is; one imagines a permanency that is not there and then attributes qualities to oneself that do not exist. It is thought that one develops an inflated notion of an 'I' because one projects onto the psycho-physiological self a permanent status it does not have. In addition, it is claimed that one develops arrogant attitudes because of social class, knowledge, and wealth. According to the *Trimsika*, arrogance can be described as sevenfold: (a) thinking that my predication is more impressive than it is, in a relatively innocuous way; (b) thinking that I am great because I am like those who have similar alleged impressive histories; (c) thinking that I am greater than my colleagues because I am more ethical and skillful than they are; (d) thinking that I am as great as those who are, in everyone else's opinion, superior to me; (e) thinking that I am superior to those who are indeed superior to me; (f) thinking that I am only slightly inferior to the fully enlightened ones; and (g) thinking that my non-virtues are virtues, or that I am completely virtuous when I am pitifully deficient. All seven of the arrogant views involve an inflated opinion of the permanence and attributes of the self and characterize lack of insight, which leads to counterproductive action. Meditation on these qualities within oneself is a step toward overcoming them, to some extent. Release from the grip of arrogance allows one to laugh at oneself. Margaret Halsey (an American writer, born 1910) reveals her 'Buddhist' wisdom when she humorously comments, "Whenever I dwell for any length of time on my own shortcomings, they gradually begin to seem mild, harmless, rather engaging little things, not at all like the staring defects in other people's characters." The self-aggrandizement of arrogance is a form of distorted perception that blocks insight into the interrelatedness of causes and consequences.

The fourth basic negative characteristic of consciousness is referred to as *deludedness* (lack of insight). It is the inability to distinguish between the causes that produce disruptive mental states and those which produce tranquility. There is little or no understanding of interrelated causal conditions. A deluded understanding characterizes disruptive activity which is at odds with positive action. It creates the conditions for future offensive activity. In other words, when one lacks an understanding of the interrelatedness of causal factors, one cannot act effectively. More trouble is created without resolution of any existing problems. In practice, however, it would be unlikely that any one person would be entirely deluded. We are all somewhat deluded. When looking for a leader, the question becomes, Who is the least deluded? Practising Buddhists believe those who are most aware of causal interrelatedness are the least deluded. The same kind of evaluation of normative consciousness occurs in all religious traditions and spiritual orientations. I shall discuss the issue of expanded consciousness of interrelatedness with respect to shamanism and goddess spirituality in the third part of this chapter.

Being opinionated includes: (a) views concerning the self as a separate identity; (b) views that assume a fixed identity which is thought of from an eternalist perspective or a nihilist one; and (c) views of self which are based on assumptions from the two previous sets of opinions and are situated within a framework of causality that is explained by reference to universal laws of cause and effect. In other words, from a Buddhist perspective the Enlightenment notion of a transcendent, separate self is characteristic of opinionatedness. A theistic belief in a separate eternal god who is self-starting is also rejected. Such a view of ultimate reality is seen to support an opinionated, inflated view of the self as created in the image of god. In contrast to a view of reality in which ontology and epistemology are separate, the Buddhist view of their inseparability supports a relational view of consciousness. It reduces the likelihood of egocentricity that is central to the notion of self-sufficiency. Reduction of egocentricity is seen as a prerequisite for self-determination. Margot Fonteyn (English prima ballerina, 1919-91) illustrates the Buddhist point of view in her statement, "The one important thing I have learned over the years is the difference between taking one's work seriously and taking one's self seriously. The first is imperative and the second is disastrous." She is speaking from a position of power; others do take her seriously. If, on the other hand, one is disempowered through implicit or explicit trivialization, then the task of taking oneself seriously becomes an appropriate focus for overcoming negative consciousness. The difference between inflated egocentricity and a strong sense of self-worth as an important participant in a community are important to a discussion of self-consciousness. If a person's self-consciousness is dominated by a sense of worthlessness, owing to oppressive living conditions, it is of little use to devalue an already minimal ego identity. In such instances taking oneself seriously is likely the most important act one could perform. The same process of meditation is useful for both the egocentric person and the one who has little awareness of self-worth. In both cases meditation on disruptive feelings and their multiple causes can lead to a letting go of negative consciousness and the development of strong, positive self-awareness, free of egocentric attachment. It allows for responsible action with respect to attributing blame and praise where they belong.

The sixth basic negative mental characteristic is *indecision*. It is about harbouring two minds in believing in the Four Noble Truths (i.e., suffering is part of life, it is caused by attachment to the self, there is a way out, the way out is the eightfold path of meditation and practice) and the Three Jewels (the Buddha, *Dharma* or teaching of the Buddha, and *Sangha* or community of devotees). It is contrasted with a single-minded search for insight and compassion that is characteristic of total meditative concentration. Because a lack of trust signifies indecision, it is incompatible with wisdom. The Buddhist path of wisdom and compassion requires trust in the truth of Buddhist scriptures. There is no self-evidency about the truth of the scriptures. It is discovered through meditation, which is motivated by faith in the truth of it. Just as in other religions, basic assumptions of the existence of a certain reality lead to its discovery. It is a circular and closed process, without any possibility for establishing a basis for absolute truth outside the system in which the truth is considered absolute. In this case the test of truth is pragmatism, i.e., living a life of wisdom and compassion and experiencing freedom from negative consciousness.

Truth in Buddhism is not truth about fixed natures. There is, however, an essentialism intrinsic to Buddhist epistemology and ontology. Reality is essentially a process of changing objects, perceptions, and interpretations. Meditative experience is the basis of knowing the truth about the nature of reality for the Buddhist. Different kinds of consciousness characterize various levels of meditation.[9] Meditative consciousness is not restricted to separate times for meditation. Rather, as we see in the movie *Karate Kid*, everyday activities can be performed with a meditative consciousness. The point is to be fully awake regardless of the activity in which one is engaged. Just as catching a fly with chopsticks is a meditative practice, so is ironing, doing dishes, writing papers, talking with another person, and so forth. Paying attention to what is happening is a meditative practice that can be done anywhere. More focussed attention on a specific attachment which is causing disturbances in one's consciousness requires a more separate meditation. Disruptive attachments or repulsions are seen to be indicative of lack of insight into the multidimensionality of causal relatedness. Inappropriate causal power that is attributed to oneself or others and creates a form of deludedness overshadows one's view of reality. Such deludedness is traced to categorical essentialism of the 'notional-conceptual' level of consciousness, which mistakes the categories for reality. In other words the map is mistaken for the territory.

Vasubandhu outlines five basic qualities of consciousness which are intrinsic to being a person (*T.* Vs. 3c,d).[10] They are: (1) rapport, (2) feeling tone, (3) mental orientation, (4) focus of attention, and (5) a capacity to understand in a conceptual way. *Rapport* refers to the relatedness of subject and object of consciousness. One exists necessarily in a relational mode. Three aspects of rapport which are entailed in relatedness of consciousness are the subject's sense organs (the body), the sense organs (the body) of the other and the perceptual-cognitive interactive process. Consciousness is always an interactive and bodied activity. *Feeling tone* is about body feelings of attachment, repulsion, or easiness of being with the other. The feelings of the body are inseparable from the perceptions that are filtered through the interpretive process. Easiness of being characterizes an unprejudiced consciousness. Unprejudiced does not mean apathetic, but rather non-egocentric, accepting. It is constitutive of a consciousness that experiences reality from the perspective of non-conceptual interrelatedness. Strong attachments and repulsions are qualities of the "notional-conceptual" level of consciousness. The third basic mental phenomenon is *orientation or directionality of mind*. It is the inherent tendency in one to incline attention in one direction or another with reference to the input a person experiences. The mind moves "by the power of a magnet" (Tomm, 1984). The fourth constitutive quality of consciousness, as outlined by Vasubandhu, is the *capacity to focus one's attention* after it has been drawn in a certain direction. The mind "sticks" on things, positively or negatively, when one does not experience a flow of consciousness that reflects the changing nature of reality. It has a grip on one's attention that restricts one's flow of consciousness. Meditation on that "stuckness" is used to overcome it. Because of the difficulty of overcoming this kind of stuckness, it is easy to understand why reincarnation is included in the Buddhist path to wisdom and compassion. It is not likely attainable in one lifetime. The fifth essential constituent of consciousness is the *capacity to conceptualize*. The danger is to mistake the conceptualizations for reality. The conceptualized world becomes the only world we can acknowledge.

Categorical understanding includes the potential for the negative qualities of consciousness listed earlier.

The aspect of consciousness that permits escape from categorical understanding is the *alayavijnana*, the basic consciousness of Buddha nature which exists prior to the other qualities. One is born with it and it remains present in one's consciousness throughout life. It constitutes the source of enlightened consciousness and is developed through meditation. I believe that babies and young children often reflect this raw, undifferentiated consciousness which is not influenced by conceptualizations. Most of us marvel at our young children (and sometimes at the children of others). We can't believe how much openness and potential they have. Unfortunately it tends to disappear rapidly as children are socialized. We often lead our children away from a basic awareness of connectedness towards dualistic and oppositional modes of understanding. Perhaps if we believed in the existence of the *alayavijnana* we might train children's consciousness in the way of basic awareness of connectedness. The consequence could well be a less fractious existence. It is reasonable to claim that a spiritual consciousness of interrelatedness is a helpful orientation for revisioning a social order which might be freer of prejudices and structural injustices, as well as one that is more compatible with the continuation of life on the planet.

Normative and Historical Consciousness

The Buddhist view of the self and of the nature of reality is particularly helpful in these postmodern times when the category of self is being called into question and the nature of reality is said to be constructed exclusively within an "historical consciousness" that is allegedly independent of a spiritual consciousness.[11] A useful definition of historical consciousness is provided by Sheila Davaney (1986). She says that the historical determination of consciousness means that "individuals, communities, institutions, as well as ideas, symbols and myths, are all influenced and given shape by their locus in history and by the temporal and social setting in which they take place" (Davaney 1986:6).

Feminist theory is grounded in experience and is, therefore, committed to the influence of historical realities on personal consciousness. At the same time, feminists argue for a normative perspective, e.g., one that takes all women seriously. Although there is a wide spectrum of feminist perspectives that focus on different issues according to what is important to particular women, there is an underlying normative claim that women's status as citizens ought not to be subjected to men's. Feminist interests are centrally about women's realities. Particular women are located in diverse social places by which they are identified and by which they identify themselves, such as working class, Native, Black, Chinese, Japanese, Serbian, disabled, elderly, and so forth. Because of these differences in the uniqueness of persons, any feminist perspective is part of an analysis of a network of social factors affecting women.

Historical consciousness is invariably gendered consciousness. Women's experiences are historically constructed, at least in part, in terms of formal and informal gender codes of the particular place in which they are located. Knowledge from a feminist perspective is said to be more accurate than knowledge that excludes women's knowledge, trivializes it, or ignores it. It is more accurate because it is more inclusive. Feminism, from the perspective developed in this book, is a humanism. It is a new humanism that includes femaleness and maleness as normal forms of humanity with equal ontological and social value. Feminism is a humanism that is grounded in historical experiences. Felt knowledge of the body and reflective knowledge of the intellect are part of human consciousness that is formed from particular experiences in defined places. This is at least one of the reasons that historical consciousness is central to feminist theorizing and practice.

A conundrum that arises when theory is developed from experience is the difficulty of taking a great variety of different experiences into account while, at the same time, generalizing beyond the differences to say something normative that applies to women more generally. Feminist standpoint theory (e.g., Harding 1986 and Hartsock 1983) grounds feminist normativeness in class issues in a neo-Marxian manner. The underprivileged are more aware of injustices than the privileged. They see things to which the privileged are blind. This is unquestionably so. It is also the case, however, that every position is limited. It is false to claim that any one person, or group, stands on the Archimedean point outside the constraints of a local social and historical context.

This problem of generalizing beyond individual differences and formulating a theory that might apply across boundaries of differences is sometimes articulated as the search for foundations. It is particularly poignant within the discipline of religion and is relevant to any spiritual orientation because of an assumed natural, creative spiritual power that is intrinsic to a spiritual consciousness. It is generally agreed that historical consciousness is shaped by the living conditions of each person. Spiritual consciousness, on the other hand, is often associated with influences outside of history. An apparently irreconcilable tension exists between claiming that consciousness is always historically determined according to particular local conditions and, at the same time, that there exists a spiritual reality that provides a ground for shared consciousness across differences. Sheila Davaney (1987, 1986) put this issue on the table and pinned it down with a knife when she asked, How can we assume, on the one hand, that all consciousness is historically determined and, on the other hand, continue to search for foundations of truth? This is a question that we, as feminists, must address. It is even more serious for us who are theorizing about feminist spirituality. Davaney pushes the question farther and asks about the limits of the appeal to women's experience as sources of normative knowledge which we claim despite affirmations of historical consciousness. In feminist theory, women's experiences are often taken as normative in the sense that they reflect more accurately the principle of human connectedness than men's experiences of separateness. This is usually seen more as a function of gendered social conditioning than of natural gendered tendencies.

By normative perspective I mean that it is the preferred perspective because it is seen to be more 'real' than others. To say that one perspective is preferred over others is to assert its superiority. If its superiority were not assumed, then there would be no reason to prefer it over another perspective. Sheila Davaney poses the dilemma as a choice between totalizing claims to truth or nihilistic relativism. While I see her critique to be relevant to current debates about the limitations of universalizing and the importance of relativising knowledge claims, her articulation of the dilemma is situated within a dualistic framework that categorizes according to the logic of 'either/or.' This way of stating the dilemma as either eternalism or nihilism (absolutism or radical relativism) is precisely what the Buddhist philosopher, Vasubandhu, was criticizing, as I discussed in the previous section. Either/or logic is characteristic of the 'notional-conceptual' way of of knowing. Davaney's stated dilemma about historical consciousness (relativism) versus the search for foundations (eternalism) comes out of the kind of categorically structured thinking that characterizes the 'notional-conceptual' level of consciousness from Vasubandhu's point of view. In Davaney's account, either consciousness is historically determined or it follows the eternal laws of a metaphysical god or reason. Truth is either relative or it is absolute in this dualistic logic.

There have been attempts to soften the dilemma from within Western philosophy. For example, David Hume's 'soft determinism' is a notable example of an extended effort to temper a complete relativism with some kind of normative understanding of human nature, without reference to god or the superiority of reason.[12] In Hume's view, we are socially determined but that determination is influenced by tendencies that are allegedly intrinsic to human nature, such as benevolence and sympathy. He claimed that experience is invariably the source of not only all knowledge, but also of morality. According to Hume, all action is motivated by desire. Experiences are regarded as desirable in so far as they are pleasurable. Both action and knowledge are motivated by the desires to pursue pleasure and to avoid pain, in his view. Desire is mediated by understanding the relation between the object of desire and its social situation. Tensions between self-interest and benevolence (concern for others) are balanced through attention to their relation to each other. Each person is part of a system of relations. Hume uses the metaphor of a string on a stringed instrument to illustrate his doctrine of sympathy. Each string resonates with the others when one of them is plucked. One string on its own is of little consequence. It needs to be strung with the others in order to have this effect. In the same way, the interests of one person need to be expressed in relation to those of the community in order to bring about a satisfying expression of them. The satisfaction of expressed personal desires in relation to the shared expression of the community constitutes moral conduct for Hume. Knowing right from wrong is grounded in feelings of pleasure that one has from living in accordance with the satisfaction of desire for self-expression and benevolence towards others.

Felt experience is the main basis for knowing, in this view. Reason provides for considered action that follows from the felt motivation toward pleasure and avoidance of pain. It serves only as a guide toward the satisfaction of the desire for self-expression in conjunction with the desire to express benevolence towards others according to the tendency to sympathize with them. Hume claims that moral behaviour is natural, human behaviour. If people act morally only out of duty, they are acting according to external prescriptions and ought to reflect more on their own humaneness. He claims that while we are always determined according to the social conditions in which we are located, there is a natural humaneness that is intrinsic to self-determination. His view is characterized by a relativist position with regard to knowledge claims. All knowledge is relative to personal experience. At the same time, he claims that there are normative human characteristics that provide for a shared humaneness. Hume's 'soft determinism' is an example of integrating a relativist position, where truth claims depend on the experiences of particular knowers, with a universal claim about human potentials and tendencies. He rejects the notion of rational certainty in favour of reasonable probabilities based on repeated experiences. Repeated experience by credible observers provides the basis for probability in Hume's 'soft determinism.'

Probability versus certitude is the same issue as historical consciousness versus the search for foundations. Or is it? Perhaps it is necessary to shift the rules of logic in order to get away from framing the question in terms of either/or. Is the question of probability or certitude a matter of either historical consciousness or metaphysical foundations? I don't think so. Buddhist theory provides an alternative reframing of the dilemma. It is a theory about historical consciousness in which different kinds of consciousness reflect different realities. The radical historicity of Buddhism would logically lead into nihilism except for the assumption of a normative ontological reality that is characterized by continuous changing conditions. The alternative to nihilism is not eternalism provided by a transcendent metaphysics but rather living with a consciousness of normativeness that is relevant to a person's particular social and historical location. In the Buddhist view, different levels of consciousness correspond with different realities. There is no reality for any person apart from the way it is experienced by that person. There are, however, preferred ways of knowing reality: those which are increasingly free of egocentric understanding and distorted emotional reactions.

The test of which reality is preferred is pragmatic. Is a particular view of reality empowering or disempowering? Does it strengthen the possibilities for the actualization of human potential or does it restrict possibilities? Within Buddhist theory of truth, it is a pragmatism that has a normative basis to it: Buddhist scriptures. The truth of the scriptures is allegedly discovered through meditation. Logically, some form of normative basis underlies all forms of pragmatic evaluations. Each choice can be traced back to a more fundamental principle which authorizes the choice. Otherwise there would be no reason for decision-making. (I am including non-rational reasons such as intuition as well as those which can be articulated coherently.) At the same time, all decisions about the preferred good are relative to an historical consciousness. From a Buddhist perspective, the goal is to develop an historical consciousness that is consistent with the normative basis of truth discovered through meditation. It is believed that the development of an historical consciousness that is characterized by an enlightened view of reality provides the best basis for effective social action in any particular historical and geographical location of the participator. Effective social action is believed to be grounded in the consciousness of interacting causal conditions and an understanding of how to change them. Resistance to existing conditions is one step towards social change. Another step is effective action that constructively changes the conditions. Both assume an ethical view of the situation. This means that social consciousness entails social conscience, a standard regarding human decency and social justice.

To be outraged at a social injustice is to assume an a priori ethic, that is, a view of what is good and just that shapes one's reaction to a situation of injustice. Daphne Hampson writes of an 'ethical a priori' position in which "certain principles are held to be . . . a priori and not subject to qualifications" (1990:29). An example of an outrageously unethical act is put to us by Dostoevsky in *The Brothers Karamazov*.[13] A landlord is offended because a young boy who worked on his estate stepped on the hoof of one of his favourite horses. He wanted to punish the boy and set an example. The boy was locked in a shed overnight in cold weather. In the morning he was taken outside and stripped in front of the other workers who were commanded to gather around the shed. The landlord placed the mother of the boy directly in front of the ring of onlookers and then set the boy running with the hounds after him. He was torn to pieces in front of his mother's eyes. That was to be a lesson to everyone to be more careful with the property of the landlord.

Dostoevsky wrote the story as an argument against belief in a good god. The story was intended to reflect the contemporary ethos of class oppression in his country, nineteenth-century Russia. In his view, there is no justification for such evil. John Hick's (1966) influential theodicy (*Evil and the God of Love*) was written partially in response to Dostoevsky's indictment. Hick attempts to make sense of evil in the world, while holding a belief in the existence of a loving, all-powerful God. His basic answer is that many afterlives may be required for certain individuals (like the land-lord) to realize their full humanity.[14] For those who reject the notion of continued, singular identity through many lives or for those who, like Dostoevsky, judge the action from this side, Hick's theodicy has little per-suasive value.

The point here is that Dostoevsky's challenge is powerful because of the a priori ethical position of the author. The actions of the landlord were considered inhumane because of prior assumptions about what con-stitutes acceptable human behaviour. A priori positions are sufficiently similar among diverse communities of people for a shared reaction to a single experience such as that cited by Dostoevsky. It is an extreme ex-ample of inhumane action and therefore it elicits a widely shared negative response to it. Less extreme examples would elicit more diverse re-sponses, each grounded in a priori ethical positions which are moderated by different social and historical influences. Normativeness here does not refer to universal normativeness but rather to degrees of normativeness which approach universality at times, and at other times (in the event of less outrageously inhumane actions) reflect greater individual and social differences in response to situations of suffering.

From a Buddhist perspective, evil or suffering is a fact of life which is ex-plained fundamentally in terms of egocentricity. Attachment to the self causes negative qualities of consciousness and corresponding unethical behaviour. Human action which is motivated by attachment to oneself as though oneself were more special than others is characteristic of the 'notional-conceptual' view of reality. Categorical thinking arises in relation to the elevation of the self as a separate category with special privileges. A goal of meditation is to reach a view of reality that is less affected by egocentricity.

Davaney's challenge to normativeness in light of acknowledging the reality of historical consciousness and its intrinsic relativeness is framed within the same context that Dostoevsky framed his challenge to belief in the existence of a good god as the basis for ethics. Both conclude there is no reason to believe in a transcendent reality which informs human expe-riences. The reasons for the rejection, however, are different. Dostoevsky claimed that it is irrational to believe in a good god when such evil exists in the world. Davaney claims that acceptance of the relativity of knowl-edge from within historical consciousness requires rejection of knowledge with certainty. In her view, this is because certainty is grounded in the al-leged sure foundations of a transcendent reality. Both Davaney and Dos-toevsky reject a transcendental reality. Dostoevsky rejects it because of the historicization of faith in the interests of reasoned passion or passion-ate reason, while Davaney rejects it because of the historicization of rea-son and the historicization of experience. She claims that no experience can be considered normative if one accepts the relativity of historical con-sciousness.

The position I am developing is that normativeness is integral to consciousness, without the requirement of certainty and absolute universality or a transcendent reality such as god. This interpretation of normativeness has more to do with probabilities than certainties. The Buddhist position helps to work toward an understanding of normativeness without categorical rigidity. Analyzing consciousness from the point of view of different states or different views of reality facilitates a broader notion of normativeness. Normative consciousness is historical consciousness. It is not, however, radically historical in the sense of total relativism where any view is as valid as any other. Rather, certain states of consciousness, views of reality, are preferred to others. They are characterized more by responsible ways of knowing which 'are both useful and agreeable to oneself and others' (Hume's phrase). Fluidity rather than fixity is an essential quality of normative consciousness in this view.

Anne Klein aptly comments that "an expanded vocabulary of subjective states may be an important step in bridging epistemological and ontological areas of inquiry" (1987:193). Different states of consciousness are part of any serious religious or spiritual consciousness. In the next part of this chapter, I shall discuss altered consciousness in shamanic and goddess theory and practices. At this time, however, I would like to bring Baruch Spinoza into the discussion because his epistemology and ontology are connected in ways that make his view of consciousness and reality compatible with the Buddhist one.[15] His philosophy supports Klein's suggestion that an expanded vocabulary of subjective states of consciousness is important to getting beyond the dilemma of absolute truth and nihilism. Spinoza describes three levels of understanding reality: imaginative, scientific, and intuitive. The imaginative level is like Vasubandhu's 'notional-conceptual' level. It is characterized by reactive tendencies rather than actions based on an understanding of causal relatedness. Lack of understanding is coextensive with inappropriate or ineffective responses. The scientific level of understanding is based on laws of cause and effect which are intellectual without the actual felt experience of interrelatedness of the conditions of reality. This is the level of knowledge without wisdom. In the intuitive level of understanding, one experiences the reality of interrelatedness, of cause and effect as a process of interdependency. The linearity of thought which constitutes the scientific state of consciousness is transformed into multiple causality. Both Vasubandhu and Spinoza assume a normative state of consciousness which informs other states of consciousness. The goal of human endeavour is to achieve a state of consciousness that allows insight into connectedness that informs daily living in other states of consciousness. Meditative awareness is sharpest in the intuitive state of consciousness for Spinoza. It is not, however, restricted to that particular state, just as it is not restricted to the deepest state of meditative consciousness for the Buddhist.

When epistemology and ontology are not separated, the dilemma be-tween historical consciousness and the search for foundations dissolves. Foundational insight is historical consciousness par excellence. Foundational insight is not the authority of revelation of a transcendent, separate reality through scripture or the ecclesia of pre-Enlightenment history. It is not the authority of the Reason of the Enlightenment. Neither is it the authority of individual experiences in which perceptions allegedly correspond to a meta-physical reality that exists separate from perceptions. If we can expand our vocabulary to describe subjective states of consciousness in which percep-tions and ontology (reality) are intrinsically connected, then it is possible to circumvent the dilemma of historical consciousness and normative con-sciousness. I hope to be able to show in the next part how spiritual con-sciousness and historical consciousness are coextensive with each other as experienced in shamanic theory and practice and in goddess spirituality. In both shamanic and goddess spirituality, realities are experienced which are often considered inconsistent with reality as allowed for in our accepted symbolic schemas. I aim to show that it is not the experiences that are 'wrong' but rather that the boundaries of normative consciousness are too restricted. When perceptions in spiritual experiences do not match percep-tions of reality according to normative consciousness, perhaps it is reason-able to reconceptualize possible realities and include spiritual experiences as possible sources of reliable knowledge.

Spiritual Consciousness

By spiritual consciousness I mean mindfulness of the presence of creative power that alters one's perceptions of reality, especially of oneself. Spiri-tual consciousness is transformed in the process of encountering the pres-ence of spiritual, creative power. When I say that a person encounters a presence, I do not mean that the reality of this presence exists wholly sep-arate from the person. The encounter between a person and a spiritual presence is an interaction in which the person becomes aware of her-self/himself in a new way. The encounter is partly an opening up of one-self to what was already there, but of which one was unaware. At the same time, spiritual consciousness includes going beyond oneself to participate in a creative reality that is not limited to any particular person. While it is not restricted to individual consciousness, it is imaged from a personal way of knowing. The reality is given its meaning through the manner of imaging it and then of reflecting upon it. Our current symbolic system of meanings, i.e., language, is impoverished with regard to reflecting on ex-periences that constitute moments of heightened spiritual consciousness. That does not mean, however, that we should not try to develop a way of giving meaning to such experiences, but rather that our language needs to be expanded to allow for more adequate discussion of them.

I will recount briefly my first experience of encountering the presence of spiritual creative power in the form of an explicit image.[16] The image was that of three women's heads with a common bosom. They included an old woman (crone), a middle-aged woman (mother), and a young woman (maiden). This image appeared several years ago while I was meditating and has been the most important image of my spiritual guides since it first appeared. I do not take this image to be paradigmatic for anyone else besides myself. It was a foreign image to me when it first appeared. After having the experience I was interested to give it meaning. I began reading on women's spirituality and found that the three faces represented archetypal images in goddess spirituality, each reflecting different stages of a woman's life that interact in her consciousness throughout her life. My experience of encountering these women and going with them while, at the same time, remaining where I was, was a transforming experience. It was transforming in many ways. I experienced myself going beyond myself as I went with them, yet remaining centred in myself. Indeed, I felt very centred in myself while they were present in my consciousness. Even when I was conscious of going with them, I felt grounded where I was. This is one way in which my consciousness of myself as an individual person was transformed. My interaction with them provided greater awareness of the reality of myself as person-in-relation, simultaneously moving inwards and outwards. Another change in my consciousness occurred. It had to do with perceiving myself as a composite of the three women. The image is recurring. The presence of it in my consciousness reminds me that at each moment of my life these three aspects of myself are present. Life is not a single, chronological path. Rather it is a path spiralling inward, outward, forward, and backward. The presence of spiritual power, as imaged in the three women's faces, provides energy to live courageously during the spiralling journey. Mindfulness of this presence includes an attitude of gratefulness for it in everyday activities. In my view, the reality of such a presence is part of the ontological reality in which spiritual consciousness is grounded.

Spiritual consciousness includes awareness of the unity of perceptions and what is perceived. The diversity of images that emerge in each person's consciousness during spiritual experiences does not undermine the reality of spiritual creative power. It merely attests to the claim that reality and perceptions are constitutive of each other. It is not a matter of correspondence between the image a person has and the reality 'out there.' Rather, the reality 'out there' is only there for any person in so far as an image or some other kind of symbolic representation is present in one's consciousness. The reality of the perception is necessary for the reality 'out there' in the same way as the reality 'out there' is required for the perception. The dichotomy between inner consciousness and external reality is a false one in spiritual consciousness. Indeed, there is no experience of such a dichotomy within spiritual consciousness. Spiritual experiences have not been widely accepted as sources of reliable knowledge in Western culture largely because they do not include a separation between 'subjective' and 'objective' knowledge. The assumed dichotomy between perceptions and objects of perceptions (i.e., reality) is entailed in categorical thinking. A demonstrable correspondence between perceptions and objects of perceptions is intrinsic to scientific verification of claims about things in the world. Without such a demonstration, empiricists remain highly sceptical. Rationalists in theology and philosophy of religion resort to *via negativa* arguments for proofs of the existence of god, in the absence of any concrete object of perceptions. Their epistemological enterprises are framed within the 'notional-conceptual' level of consciousness that depends upon categorically separating perceptions from what is perceived.

Spiritual consciousness is developed from spiritual experiences in which images in a person's consciousness emerge within the presence of a spiritual creative power. Because of this, there is no reason to discuss whether there is a reference outside of one's consciousness to which the image corresponds. I am not debating the existence of the referent apart from perception of it. That debate belongs to a different epistemological framework, namely, the 'notional-conceptual' one, which does not reflect spiritual consciousness. On the basis of personal experiences and reports by others, I assume the existence of dimensions of powers outside a person's consciousness. I believe it is only in encountering those powers that one knows about them. In this view, spiritual consciousness depends upon spiritual experiences of creative power that is both intrinsic to each person and is there regardless of any particular person's awareness. The reality of it for any person, however, is in that person's experiences of it. I support John Macquarrie's view (1983) that a cumulative, anthropological argument for why spiritual or religious experiences ought to be taken seriously is about as good as one could hope for.

Spiritual experiences are intuitive experiences in the sense that one's consciousness is expanded beyond categorical reasoning. At times there is a leap even beyond one's imagination. During particularly striking spiritual experiences, foreign images emerge powerfully in one's consciousness. It is as though they burst into one's awareness. They can be integrated into the existing perceptions only after considerable time and reflection. Their initial appearance is often unsettling. One intuits that they are meaningful but cannot immediately discern their meaning. It usually helps to talk about these experiences with others who have had similar ones or who have some understanding of the possible meanings of various symbols. Intuition is a form of knowing that encompasses more than can be expressed through the system of meaning that is restricted to language. Spinoza's intuitive level of awareness, in which one's consciousness goes beyond the scientific level of understanding to experience the 'intoxication' of the presence of god in everything, is an example of spiritual consciousness. It resembles the Buddhist level of consciousness in which reality is perceived as a process of interrelatedness, without categorical objectification. Both Vasubandhu and Spinoza claim that ontology and epistemology are inseparable. This claim has important consequences for disentangling some philosophical knots that cause a great deal of debate in discussions about whether spiritual experiences are to be taken seriously and whether spiritual consciousness can be integral to historical consciousness.

Two questions dissolve in light of an assumed inseparability of ontology and epistemology. One question is whether there is something that one experiences in religious experience, that is whether there is an actual god, goddess, or an other spiritual reality to which one's perceptions refer.[17] A reflexive relation between consciousness and reality indicates an interactive process which creates both consciousness and the object of consciousness. There is no separate reality out there and yet it is not the case that there is no reality out there. This is particularly relevant to experiences described by shamanic practitioners and those who have experiences of goddess presence, as I shall discuss shortly.

The second question, as raised by Sheila Davaney, is about whether an historical consciousness can be compatible with a spiritual consciousness. She asked: Is an historical consciousness consistent with a search for sure foundations? The question assumes a separation of ontology and epistemology. The views she critiques (Schüssler Fiorenza 1983; Ruether 1983, 1985a, 1985b; and Daly 1973, 1978, 1984) make that assumption. Davaney is right to critique the attempt to use women's experiences as normative perceptions of god or goddess when it is agreed upon that all experiences are interpreted through lenses which reflect a social and historical context. In these postmodern times, as Davaney points out, reason is historicized, just as revelation and ecclesiastical authority were during modernity (the Enlightenment period). She concludes that it is a logical mistake to insist on the historical conditioning of reason, indeed of all consciousness, and continues to search for normative truth claims from experiences, including religious experiences. I believe her conclusion is correct within the dichotomous framework which posits either the relativity of historical consciousness or certainty about the nature of ultimate reality through metaphysical assumptions. There are alternative models in which to frame the discussion of historical consciousness and normative groundedness. It is axiomatic to say that when individuals make choices about how to act they do so more from underlying assumptions than from mere whim. Buddhist theory (as well as Spinoza's) shows us how choices are made according to ways in which we experience reality, and the ways in which we experience reality shape the reality in which we make our choices. There is a circular relation between reality 'out there' and 'in here,' which undermines both total sociological determinism and egocentricism. It supports self-determination and relationality through an analysis of interdependency of epistemology and ontology.

Discussion of the relation between what is 'out there' and what is constitutive of consciousness shifts with the introduction of the inseparability of ontology and epistemology. It does not shift, however, toward nihilism, that is, radical relativism where there is no basis for choice making. Rather it shifts to a discussion of expanding our vocabulary of states of consciousness and, accordingly, the nature of reality. The inclusiveness of ontology and epistemology is particularly relevant to shamanic and goddess spirituality where there is an emphasis on fluidity between external and internal spiritual powers.

Shamanism is centrally about altered consciousnesses in which journeying to other places and times occurs.[18] I believe that the Buddhist meditative practices that I learned several years earlier helped me to enter into an alternate consciousness in shamanic training. In addition, I had had several experiences of goddess presence while meditating before I began shamanic training. By the time I was introduced to shamanic healing practices, my consciousness was sensitized to radically different states of consciousness. Shamanic journeying is a practice that supports a theory of ontological interdependency, connectedness of various forms of life. The most important point to be illustrated is the reality of alternate consciousnesses of the self. Shape-shifting in shamanic rituals is a common experience. It includes taking on a different form or shape. One becomes conscious of one's body as something other than, for example, the human female body. I was receptive to what I would encounter on this journey to find my animal spirit power and was interested to discover it. I was instructed in a training session to enter the lower world and discover my animal spirit. The drumming started, I was lying on my back with a blindfold over my eyes. I had no expectations, just a sense of wondering what would happen. I had become familiar with entering into an alternate consciousness through drumming.

We were told to find a hole, a tree, a lake, or whatever served our purposes to go down into the lower world. We had to find an exit from this world. Shamanism has a three-layered cosmology: upper, middle, and lower worlds. We normally live in the middle world. One can live in the middle world, however, with a consciousness that has been informed by knowledge from the upper and lower worlds. The forms of discourse differ between Buddhism and shamanism but the relation of epistemology and ontology is similar. For the Buddhist, it is possible and desirable to live in the conventional, normal world in which egocentricity shapes the structuring of society, and to be more or less free of the beliefs and values of the society. That is, one can be in it but not of it. This allows for greater freedom to resist status quo expectations and to work for social restructuring which would have less egocentric power shaping its evolution. Just as a Buddhist practitioner draws on wisdom from meditation to expand normative consciousness, so a shamanic practitioner uses insights from journeys to other times and places to alter perceptions of this world.

On my shamanic journey, I entered the root cellar door into a hill be-hind our house where we lived in the Cypress Hills when I was a child. As I made my way inside the black dugout, I noticed a tunnel going off into the hill. I followed the tunnel and was tripping over roots sticking out of the ground in the darkness. A number of other tunnel entrances appeared before me. I was unsure about which one to enter. At that moment the image of three women's heads on a single bosom came into my conscious-ness. When I am conscious of this image, I experience goddess presence in a strong way. They simply took me down a tunnel which led to where I was supposed to go. As we proceeded, the tunnel got smaller. I could see the end of it by the lightness that shone through the dark. I felt no appre-hension when the women left and I turned into a snake. I was slightly smaller than the tunnel. I arrived in the lower world and encountered a huge snake at the entrance. It was coiled up like a gigantic rope so that the coils went to about my own height as a woman when I experienced myself as a woman standing before it. During my encounter with it, I was sometimes the small snake, sometimes my normal shape, and from time to time I was simultaneously both my normal shape as a woman and the big snake.

I had been instructed by the teacher to ask the animal spirit a ques-tion and had formulated the question before I encountered it. The experi-ences of being both the large snake and my normal self occurred when I was asking the question. On reflection, the meaning of the shape-shifting during the question asking could be similar to the Buddhist saying, "If you meet the Buddha on the road kill him." The idea that each person is their own authority is the meaning I take from the interchanging shapes. The snake is an animal spirit power of mine. The claim that a person has an animal spirit whose power is continuous with one's own is like the Bud-dhist claim that the Buddha nature is continuous with an individual's con-sciousness. The forms of discourse in Buddhism and shamanism are differ-ent. The theory and experiences, however, of interrelatedness of spiritual powers with one's consciousness is shared by both spiritual approaches. When I returned to this world from the journey I was exhausted. I slept for two hours on the floor. It was a powerful experience which continues to inform my understanding of myself and my ontological connectedness to the nature spirits, i.e., to the web of creative power that is integral to all of life.

Sceptics will ask: Where were you when you were the snake? One implication is that I was out of my mind. That implication is valid only if one assumes the exclusivity of a normative, categorical consciousness of the 'notional-conceptual' level of consciousness and rules out the validity of more extended forms of consciousness. I don't believe there is any way one can convince a sceptic. As cumulative evidence increases, it will be-come less reasonable to disregard experiences of alternative conscious-nesses, including out-of-body experiences and dreams, as well as other less explored forms of consciousness. The meaning of 'intuition' may change with an expanded vocabulary that reflects new ways of thinking about the inseparability of ontology and epistemology. It may assume a more respectable place among the sources for reliable knowledge.

On another journey, I went into the lower world on behalf of a person present in the room whom I did not know. Another woman and I selected each other from the members of the circle to be partners for this journey. We were each to discover for the other the animal healing power that she needed most in her life at that time. It was explained to us before the drumming started how we would know which animal was the right one. We would recognize the connections among the various manifestations of the same animal power. The animal would reveal itself to us through any or all of our senses. I thought I would not be able to recognize it and would simply come back without any information. I did not know anything about the person for whom I was journeying. I have never had much of an imagination when it comes to free associating. I believed that unless the animal power was represented very explicitly I would not be able to provide any assistance to the woman lying beside me. She told me afterwards that she had faith in my ability to do it but was sceptical about her own. We shared the same lack of confidence in ourselves and trust in each other. It turned out that we were both able to discover the animal power of the other and restore some of it to each other through the techniques we were taught. I have since experienced shape-shifting into the animal power that she discovered I needed for my health. Processing the information sometimes takes months or longer. Sometimes it fits so closely with existing consciousness that it is incorporated quickly. Regardless of whether the new perceptions have a high degree of coherence with prior ones or whether there is little coherence, prior perceptions are invariably altered through journeying.

Experiences of shape-shifting are examples of "cognitive relativism" (Harner 1980:xx): knowing in alternative ways. Cognitive relativism involves possibilities for moving beyond our limited cognitive organizing structures. It is not restricted to spiritual experiences. For example, Glenn Gould, in a conversation with John McClure of CBS Records in 1968, tells us about an experience which is an example of the integration of epistemology and ontology that is characteristic of spiritual experiences. He was on a concert tour and had to play on a piano that he disliked intensely. After about four performances, with about four still left to do, he went to a secluded spot and concentrated on his preferred piano in another country. After securing the feel and sound of the other piano in his consciousness, he went back to the concert hall and performed on it. The actual piano on which he was playing was superceded by the one in his consciousness, yet it was the instrument though which he conveyed his intentions.[19]

In this epistemology, cognitive relativism is not limited to mystics, geniuses, or eccentrics. Rather, it is intrinsic to human consciousness and

is realized on occasions when one's consciousness is open to new perceptions. A prerequisite is freedom from rigid, categorical thought patterns.
Michael Harner (1980) points out that cognitive relativism is analogous to
the more familiar cultural relativism. It is about pluralistic approaches to
knowledge and cultural practices. Just as there is a parallel between cognitive relativism and cultural relativism, so there is a similar relation between cognicentricism and ethnocentrism. Ethnocentricism is believing
that one's own ethnic perspective is the only one. Cognicentrism is the
view that one's way of knowing is the best for everyone. Shamanism illustrates cognitive relativism through alternate states of consciousness which
one experiences in journeying, while assuming an ontology of interrelatedness similar to Buddhism. Both assume a normativeness consciousness
which is inseparable from historical consciousness. The various forms of
consciousness are taken as different manifestations of the relatedness of
all of them. Shamanic journeys are about connecting with various spiritual powers for the purpose of healing. The use of spiritual powers for
negative purposes is understood as misuse. This view of cognitive relativism is based on the assumption that interrelatedness is the normative ontology and epistemology.

According to Sandra Ingerman, "The word *shaman*, which comes
from the Tungus tribe in Siberia, refers equally to women and men"
(1991:1). Shamanic journeying is part of many cultural heritages such as
"Siberia, Lapland, parts of Asia, Africa, Australia, and native North and
South America" (p. 1). Shamanism, like goddess spirituality, became marginalized with the rise of the priesthood and priestly castes in the countries where shamanism existed and continues to exist. In North America
shamanism among the Native people was denigrated by the conquering
Christian colonizers. It is important to respect Native teachings as a gift
from one people to another, not something to have as an appropriated
thing.[20] The teachings are to be lived with, just as one lives with art, music, good friends. 'Living with' one's spirituality is different from 'having' a
spiritual orientation in the way that knowing something is different from
having knowledge of something. When we live with the presence of something it lives inside us. My shamanic experiences are integral to my consciousness in the same way as are Buddhist meditative consciousness and
consciousness of goddess presence. Each of the three could have different
labels, or they could all have the same label. It is possible that they all
originate from similar earth-based spiritual communities in which dichotomous conceptualization of spirit and matter or spirituality and intellectuality did not dominate the interpretive schemas of those who had spiritual
experiences. Regardless of the history of the different traditions, the practices of the three orientations are commensurate with each other.

In shamanism, as in all knowledge based on spiritual experiences, the
truth of the theory is in the practice. That statement reminds me of the
English proverb, "The proof of the pudding is in the eating." Don McGil-

livray, a Canadian journalist, has noted that the saying remained the same for four centuries and then within the last generation changed to "The proof is in the pudding."[21] The proverb "The proof of the pudding is in the eating" could be restated as "The truth of the theory is in the experience." But what happens when it becomes "The proof is in the pudding" or "The truth is in the theory"? It could be argued that the academic study of religion has taken up the new version of the proverb. Theological truth claims and academic analysis of religious practices, rather than actual sprirtual experiences, become the proof in the pudding. Theoretical "truths" have largely replaced experiential "truths." Like most analogies it isn't perfect. Equating a pudding with a theory might not be acceptable to some. However, as McGillivary suggests, could it be that the intention is that the truth is hidden in the pudding? To find the truth one needs to eat the pudding. It is somewhat like finding a coin in the Christmas pudding. One feels slightly dejected when it isn't there, even though it is just a small coin. Its symbolism retains its lively importance despite its low cash value.

In Sheila Davaney's account of symbols she says religious symbols "are recognized as human constructions that function to focus the world-view of which they are a part, embodying the values embedded in . . . interpretive schemas" (1987:48). She says their "truth" lies in the effects they have on maintaining one's commitment to chosen values. In another place, Davaney writes that "religious symbols would be interpreted, along with the larger world-views or visions that they center, as solely the products of human imagination and the projection of human values and desires" (1986:23). Davaney seems to be looking at the coin's cash value without recognizing its liveliness in the creative consciousness of the one who treasures it. Her challenge to the referential capacity of symbols is an important one. But her proposed 'revitalized projection theory' leaves me, at least, devitalized. She claims that the value of a symbol is that which is projected onto it, as if it were an inert body. For many, symbols embody a liveliness that affects one's perceptions of it.

In my defense of the interactive process of meaning, I shall invoke Davaney's own criticism against normative stances and challenge her reductionist view of the symbolic meaning as exclusively projection. I agree with her that there is no sound basis for assuming the existence of a particular divine entity such as god or goddess apart from individual consciousness. Therefore, to claim that a symbol refers to such a deity is erroneous. That does not mean, however, that the only other alternative is that symbols are exclusively objects of projections. Another alternative, for example, is that found in Buddhist epistemology. There is invariably an interactive process taking place in consciousness. The interaction occurs between the object of perception, the sense organs of the perceiver, and the construction of meaning. The object, in this case a symbol, brings to the perceptual and meaning-giving process a lively reality which alters the perceptions of the perceiver. That is, at least, part of what distinguishes a symbol from an object which has little meaning for a perceiver. There is no sound basis for excluding the existence of creative powers in objects with which one interacts in a meaningful way. This view of symbols could be extended to all objects, thereby creating a sacred orientation to all of life. To say that meaning is projected entirely from individual and collective consciousnesses, without the possibility that the presence of symbols alter consciousness by evoking new and meaningful images, is to deny the experiences of people throughout history. Or is it a matter of reinterpreting other peoples' experiences for them from a perspective that misses the reality such symbols have for others? Scepticism with respect to the sacredness of symbols is reasonable. Outright rejection, however, is unreasonable.

Davaney's denial of the active participation of symbols in the creation of spiritual consciousness reminds me of an incident between Gilbert Ryle, a scholar of Western philosophy, and Ninian Smart, a scholar of Eastern philosophies and religions. Ryle reportedly told Smart that Eastern philosophy has nothing important to say to Western philosophy. Smart replied that one would have to know a great deal to say such a thing.[22] The same quip could be applied to Davaney's rejection of the liveliness of symbols within the consciousness of those who live with them as embodiments of a creative power. One would need to know a great deal to deny categorically the creative activity of symbols in the construction of meaning. In light of Davaney's "projectionist theory," one wants to ask where the spiritual or religious component is in her epistemology. The reduction of religion to psychology, however, is not unique to Davaney.[23]

In contrast to the exclusively psychologized status of symbols described by Sheila Davaney, Carol Christ provides a more spiritually creative attitude toward them. She does not, however, clearly commit herself to spiritual creative power apart from individual consciousness. Her attitude toward symbols is that they are not merely objects onto which perceptions are projected, but they also shape perceptions. She says that "religious symbols shape a cultural ethos, defining the deepest values of a society and the persons in it" (1987a:117). Christ's account of symbols occurs within the context of goddess spirituality. Her book, *Laughter of Aphrodite*, includes accounts of the author receiving goddess power in Greece at Aphrodite's shrine. Unless Christ is inconsistent between her account of symbols and her account at the shrine, it would seem that symbols of the goddess have referential capacity for her.

An implication of this discussion of symbols as creative tools with non-analytic meanings that contribute to alternate ways of knowing is that the symbol and one's perceptions are both part of the larger interrelated reality. The symbol can be said to refer to that interactive creative process. The snake, for example, is a symbol of the regenerative process: birth, activity, death, rebirth. The menstrual cycle can be understood as a sacred time, symbolizing the same regenerative process. The symbolic meaning is part of the process of reality. It refers to the process in which both the symbol and the symbolizer participate in the creation of reality. It is not accurate to say the symbol has or has not a referential capacity. It is possible, however, to say that the symbol is part of enlarging the consciousness with respect to the individual concerned.

Just as symbols change consciousness, so consciousness creates symbolic meanings. Normative consciousness refers to intentional consciousness and entails coherence among perceptions. It also refers to shared perceptions by groups. The distinction between normal and abnormal is generally made according to a community's understanding of where to draw the line with respect to coherence of perceptions in relation to realities that are perceived. Normative consciousness is about coherence of perceptions within an individual's consciousness, between individuals and, in both cases, between the sets of perceptions and objects which are perceived, as described in language. The limits of normality are established through consensus or they are dictated by those who occupy positions in which superior knowledge is assumed. Even when there is consensus, it very often reflects the interests of the powerful, with alternative forms of consciousness excluded from normal discourse.[24] New symbols, such as shamanic symbols, contribute to the development of alternative meanings. A shamanic consciousness is one in which symbols such as snakes, tigers, trees, energy waves, water, and so forth, indicate creative powers in nature and in one's consciousness. The belief is that as one's shamanic consciousness increases, all objects become symbols with sacred meaning. From a shamanic perspective one 'lives with' the spiritual powers of reality. They become normal and continuous with 'ordinary consciousness.' The claim here is that there are other forms of consciousness in addition to normative knowledge. Indeed, normative consciousness is regarded as only one of many alternative forms of consciousnesses. In this view, essentialism and constructionism are inseparable. Historical consciousness is coextensive with spiritual consciousness.

In shamanic journeying wolves, tigers, and snakes, for instance, represent presences of those spiritual powers. One encounters an animal power that one needs for healing. Or one meets one's animal power and learns about oneself through becoming the animal. Journeying always has a purpose, usually it is for the benefit of another. It is unlikely, though, that one person can journey for another without already having journeyed to heal oneself. Shamanic journeying shares the deep relationality of Buddhist meditation. It is healing and centring for the self. Self-healing depends on awareness of one's connection to other powers. The power of women's regenerative cycles, for example, is recognized as part of the regenerative power of nature. That close connection forms the basis for ecofeminism: caring for the earth as one care's for one's body.

Because I draw attention to the connection between women and the earth, I do not mean to exclude men from connection to the earth. We know from shamanism, for example, that men can be spiritual healers who live in relation to nature spirits just as women spiritual healers do. I mean to say that women's reproductive anatomy is designed for giving birth and for lactation. The engendering capacities of women are awesome in the same way as are the creative power of the seasons of the earth and the changing phases of the moon, affecting not only the earth but also the pull of the bodies of water. There isn't any good reason to deny the parallels. Is there? Many would argue to the contrary. It could be argued that such a view privileges women's position with respect to natural knowledge. Perhaps it does. Why wouldn't it? What are the implications of the claim that women's reproductive anatomy gives them(us) a leg up (so to speak) with respect to elemental knowledge? The implication for Mary Daly, for example, is that women's be-ing is characterized more naturally by connectedness than men's (1984). Her "elemental feminist philosophy" is likely the most sustained argument for the separate natures of women and men that exists in feminist literature to date. Luce Irigaray's work is another powerful effort to argue for the value of women taking themselves seriously in their anatomical differences from men. Recognizing women's connection to nature is not an end in itself, but it is an important strategy which helps us start where we are as women and begin to think in new ways.

One objection to closely associating women with nature is the fear that the meaning of women's nature and purpose will be reduced to their reproductive capacities. This objection/fear is understandable and fully justified in light of our patriarchal history in which women's 'being' is seen as largely complementary to men's 'doing.' Simone de Beauvoir's quip (in *The Second Sex*) that *women are while men do* haunts the consciousness of many of us. It is not surprising, then, that many women are reluctant to be associated closely with reproduction. In Alberta, where the birth rate has been declining, the government has not been persuaded that good daycare facilities might encourage more women to have babies. About three-quarters of women in Alberta with young children work outside the home.[25] There are not enough daycare facilities, never mind good ones. Many women choose to not have children. They will continue to work for pay outside the home for various reasons. One important reason is their right to do so. The fact that women have babies and have the right to work means that there is an ethical requirement to ensure adequate working conditions for women, as well as for men. Specifically, it means placing childcare facilities higher on the political agenda as well as restructuring the home-workplace relations for both parents. This means rethinking the relationship between nature and culture so that the social, political, and economic structures support women's subjectivity, as well as that of men, within a system of ecological balance.

Ecofeminism is a branch of feminist spirituality which has been emerging with considerable effectiveness over the past five years in Canada, longer in the United States.[26] In Chapter Six, I explore ecofeminist theory and practice in relation to new visions for economic restructuring and re-evaluating work. In addition to Buddhist meditation and shamanic journeying, goddess spirituality is helpful with regard to connecting personal subjectivity with the ecological network. It also provides a useful framework for social ethics that takes sexual difference into account in a way that empowers women as well as men.

Goddess spirituality, for me, is mostly about living with the presence of strengthening energy that is simultaneously directed at me and unleashed within me. My own spiritual experiences have included symbols such as white and red energy waves, rocks, snakes, a burning fire, a tiger, and a wolf as expressions of my identity. They are all part of my consciousness of goddess presence. It is not a matter of concern whether these symbols refer to something external. Their presence embodies the reality of spiritual power. The significance of spiritual symbolism lies in its power to transform a person's consciousness. The political importance of such transformation is that it provides an existential basis for believing in the possible relation of humans with each other and with the ecosystem. This belief is a strong motivator for social action directed toward social and ecological well-being.

Ajit Mookerjee (1988) claims that this is the Kali Age. Kali is the Hindu goddess of creation and destruction. According to Mookerjee, "India is the only country where the goddess is still widely worshipped today, in a tradition that dates to the Harappan culture of c. 3000 [B.C.E.] and earlier" (1988:11). He points out that Kali has regularly been negatively represented in patriarchy because of her supreme powers of creation and destruction. Patriarchal fear of female elemental power is projected onto goddess figures like Kali who are denounced as destructive. Death in patriarchal culture is often seen as defeat of the ego rather than accepted as part of an ongoing transformation of changing reality. The body is the exemplary symbol of change. Women's bodies often represent the kind of immanence that is to be transcended in the move toward immortality. Figures like Kali serve as a reminder of the reality of change, of death. When death is understood as 'letting go,' however, it loses its association with finality. As part of the cyclical regenerative process, death has a positive power of letting go of old ideas, patterns of behaviour which obstruct transformation into new ideas and actions. Kali represents the conscience reminding us not to get fixed in egocentric categorical thought and become stuck in static 'notional-conceptual' realities that prohibit transformation. Mary Condren describes the overthrow of women-centred power in Ireland. She says:

The Great Mother Goddess Macha vanished from the stage of Irish history following her downfall at the hands of the king and his warriors. The disappearance of
Macha symbolized the elimination of the possibility of any woman-centered social
system, philosophy, or religion. The Male Word, rather than the Female Womb,
would take responsibility for ensuring the continuation of the social order. . . .
With the arrival of Christianity in the fourth and fifth centuries any remaining
goddesses were destined to undergo a profound sex change. (1989:48)

All goddess representation did not undergo a sex change. In some cases it
was transformed from a virginal, independent power into a more sub-
dued, patriarchal feminine character where goddess power came to be
equated with nurturing power, the inspiration for male heroes on their
quest for immortality. The vestiges of goddesses, such as Brigit, became
saints and were tamed symbols of women's power. The virginal power
represented by earlier goddesses was not represented by Brigit the saint
or Mary the Madonna. Goddess virginal power is about power in their
own right, unto themselves. The notion of women's virginal power, as
represented by different powerful goddess images including Hestia,
Artemis, and Athena, was inverted in patriarchy. It is symbolized most
powerfully in the Christian tradition by the Madonna. As the Virgin Mother she is exemplary of male cultural engendering overshadowing female
body engendering. Her privileged status as a mother who has a baby
without sexual intercourse with a man is the supreme example for women
of the separation of their sexuality from their spirituality. Mary's sexuality
serves as the vehicle for the male god's self-expression. Her spiritual
power as mother of god lies in her sexual purity. In the Christian tradition, women's spirituality has come to us yoked to sexual purity, through
the image of the Madonna. The yoke began to strangle women as they
tried to break free of it in search of more adequate expressions of their
full humanity.

Goddess imagery as it is found throughout the world today, as well
as in prepatriarchal archeological artifacts and rare extant scripts, provide
women with sources of revisioning their humanity and a social order that
would create and support it.[27] Miriam Robbins Dexter has provided us
with an important survey of twelve countries in which goddess imagery
was important in the earliest extant myths and hymns. The oldest records
are Indic, while the Baltic folktales and folksongs "were recorded quite
late, but, nonetheless, both Baltic language and Baltic folklore preserve
very archaic vestiges . . . which show many parallels with those of the
Indo-European culture . . ." (1990:x). The life- and death-giving qualities
of the goddess in her various manifestations were symbolized most often
by bird and snake symbols. The earth and sky are represented by the
snake and bird. The representation of both the earth and the heavens in
female goddess imagery of Indo-European culture has shades of the same
themes found in Hopi mythology of America. Paula Gunn Allen says, "The
Hopi account of their genatrix, Hard Beings Woman, gives the most artic-

ulate rendering of the difference between simple fertility cultism and the creative prowess of the Creatrix. Hard Beings Woman (*Huruing Wuhti*) is of the earth. But she lives in the worlds above where she 'owns' (empowers) the moon and stars. Hard Beings Woman has solidity and hardness as her major aspects. She, like Thought Woman, does not give birth to creation or to human beings but breathes life into male and female effigies that become the parents of the Hopi—in this way she 'creates' them" (Allen 1986:14). Thought Woman is the mythological Creatrix of the Keres Indians of Laguna Pueblo, the community to which Paula Gunn Allen belongs.

An important point made by Dexter is that the power of the goddess of prepatriarchal Indo-European cultures was not restricted to fertility. The same is true of the early Native creation mythologies, as illustrated by Allen. Dexter's findings are based on a comparative study of linguistically related words from texts and archeological remains (mostly from burial sites) from twelve cultures in which Indo-European languages were used. She describes the decline of goddess powers with the rise of male-centred 'socio-religio' systems. Within patriarchy a three-tier 'socio-religio' structure emerged: priestly caste, warrior caste, and nurturing caste (farmers, homemakers, those who kept the community running). Goddess power was relegated largely to the nurturing caste. In patriarchy, women's natures and purposes are seen primarily in terms of reproductive capacities and inspiring the work of men as warriors or intellectuals. Their inspiration as mothers or lovers continues to be their central source of power. I have heard the term 'domestic goddesses' used in a self-referential way by women who do not work outside the home, or very much inside it. These women use the term within the patriarchal notion of goddess as a source of inspiration for men's creativity. They generally do not identify with goddesses such as Kali, the goddess of creation and destruction, who challenge men's authority as intellectuals, spiritual leaders, or men of war. Challenging men's authority is still often considered an act of subordination by men who strongly believe that they should be in charge.

It could be, as Condren and others have claimed, that it is fear of women's elemental power that keeps men struggling to control nature through culturally constructed symbols of male power. Before a partnership model of society can be developed in social theory and enacted in practice, it is necessary to go through the transition period of focussing on sex-specificity.[28] Goddess consciousness facilitates that focus. There is an emphasis in goddess spirituality on women's independent power as virginal power. This understanding of 'virgin' as a self-sufficient woman shifts the focus from a woman who hasn't had sexual intercourse to one who can stand with her legs apart, throw her head back and laugh at notions of women as the second sex. This view of women-centred power has considerable potential for releasing women from the yoke of patriarchy that ties them to concepts of inferiority. I do not think it is important whether one labels awareness of independent female power as goddess consciousness, shamanic consciousness, or something else. The important point here is that if knowledge is to be more representative of lived realities, then experiences of such power must be included as legitimate forms of knowledge.

It is also important that spiritual experiences of goddess presence are not trivialized through romanticization of so-called feminine power. I reject the view of goddess power as exclusively unthreatening. At the same time, I do not see it as necessarily oppositional to the power of a god. Goddess power represents for me, a spectrum of strengths that can be lived out by any particular woman. These include the more usual mother-child relationships, partner relationships, and nurturing activities that women are often mandated into. These forms of connectedness are relevant to men as well as women. The spirit of caring can be provided equally well through god and goddess symbolism. The romanticization of feminine spiritual power is constituted by focussing exclusively on this kind of goddess power. The broader spectrum includes women's power of social authority and their ability to resist oppression in their lives. This power of independence, i.e., virginal power, is required for women to live out their full humanity, if it is their desire to do so.

The distinction between feminist and feminine revolves around this point about the kind of power that women can express and still be culturally normal. It is a political act to take a stand for oneself as a full citizen with the right to social authority, regardless of one's sex. A feminist spirituality is a political spirituality. It is about claiming one's power as a person-in-her-own-right (i.e., as ontologically independent) and one who speaks from her own knowledge. This is about women claiming their own birthrights as persons in their own right. It is about women participating fully in cultural production and in the establishment of traditions of women's knowledge. It is true that knowledge is power. It is also true that knowledge is grounded in experience. Therefore, it is true that power is grounded in experience. Experiencing goddess power is learning about one's own power and its connectedness to other natural and cultural powers.

Permeable Self

I am indebted to Catherine Keller (1986) for her distinction of the separate and soluble self. The separate self is the transcendent self, as illustrated, for example, in Lawrence Kohlberg's sixth stage of moral development.[29] The emphasis is on self-sufficiency through reason. The soluble self, on the other hand, has no identity apart from the separate self. Indeed, the identity of a soluble self is that of dissolving into the other. The soluble self is characterized by dependency on the autonomous. The construction of the separate and soluble self has been part of widespread constructions of masculinity and femininity. It informs the gendered ethics of Kohlberg and others who have emphasized the importance of separation of boys from their mothers in the construction of their own identity. In Kohlberg's view, moral development is measured in relation to separateness of self. Moral dignity and social leadership are contrasted with an ethic of care, the ethic that is associated with femininity and the soluble self.

In the ontology of interrelatedness, the self is neither entirely separate nor soluble, rather it is more aptly conceived of as a permeable self. A separate self person has strong egocentric boundaries. People who live with a separate self model of themselves are those who like to be self-sufficient and emotionally independent of others. They like to make decisions by themselves and be regarded as leaders in whatever endeavours they are active. The separate self characterizes most cultural heroes. By contrast, the soluble self supports others in their endeavours, without maintaining adequate self boundaries. Soluble self people can disappear into separate self lives. They may or may not be recognized for their own value. The permeable self maintains a balance between separateness and solubility. As a permeable self, one is a unique individual without being disconnected from others, yet is connected without experiencing self-loss.

The soluble self is particularly relevant to women when femininity is constructed in terms of dependency. Being overly dependent can result in severe self-loss. A difficulty in preventing severe self-loss is the lack of awareness that it is occurring. There may need to be a moment of awakening.

During one period of my life, I was a full-time homemaker, a mother of young children, and a professional's wife. The work I did with the children was mostly very satisfying. The context of disparaging attitudes toward mothers in the home, however, had a demoralizing effect on me. This was not unique to my situation and it was not restricted to the 1970s. Many women in the 1990s who chose to remain in the home and raise their children also feel demoralized. Disempowering attitudes towards mothers in the home range from mild patronization to unequivocal derogation. Men in the home likely experience a variety of disempowering attitudes as well. Theirs will differ to some extent from women's experiences because their status as men is more closely associated with work outside the home. In the move toward equality, women have often bought into the belief that work for pay deserves more recognition than home management. The association of women with nurturing and men with earning money coincides with the fact that the vast majority of childrearing is done by women. The lack of monetary valuation of nurturing type work is at the heart of the trivialization of women's work in the home and outside of it. In my own case, as a woman who worked full-time in the home for over ten years, I experienced, along with almost every other mother in the home with whom I spoke, a lack of social status.

The relationship between a housewife and a professional husband is analogous to the relationship between maintenance and management in the paid labour force. It is largely a gendered relation in the home, just as it is in the office. Very often the same holds true for work in the community. Homemaking often goes hand in hand with community volunteer work. Society gets both for free. Most of this work is done by women who live often as soluble selves and experience self-loss. I experienced self-loss in this context. I shall relate some of the experience here because I have found that when I have told this story to other women, many of them could relate their own experiences to it.

During this period of self-loss, I read a number of Simone de Beauvoir's works which were recommended to me by a former female professor who urged me to read about other women's lives and to get on with my own. De Beauvoir claimed that a person needs two things to be happy: friends with whom to share one's joys and sorrows and meaningful work. I have always had good friends, but I could not think of what might constitute meaningful work. I was overcome by drowsiness and inertia. There was an inward spiralling of anger and sadness at a loss I could not name and a fear of the unknown that kept me where I was. Despite this foggy consciousness, a clear idea surfaced. I thought that if I could learn how to think, then I might imagine what I could do that would constitute meaningful work outside the home, since both children were now in school.

I made an appointment with a philosophy professor whom I had heard in a debate. I liked the way he formulated his thought. I wanted to learn to think like he did. He could present both sides of an argument with equal persuasion, leaving the decision-making power up to the listener. I was determined to study with him and develop my power of reasoning. I believed that if I could learn how to think like he did I could make my own decisions about what was meaningful work. A surprising thing happened when I met with him. I sat before him, without being able to say anything. I didn't want to tell him that I was the mother of children or the wife of somebody. I wanted to tell him something about myself, to recommend myself to him as a possible student in philosophy, however, I had nothing to tell him. I was a blank, a tabula rasa. This was a time of considerable self-loss, where I had no identity to describe. We sat in silence for five minutes. Then he quietly said, "You came here for some reason." There was no urgency in his voice. I felt safe. I looked up from my feet and said directly to him, "I want to learn to think." He didn't laugh at this outburst. Rather, he quietly asked how I planned to do this. It was the first time for many years that I experienced a person taking me seriously.

That was the beginning of eight years of study in philosophy and religious studies. My mind was simultaneously put into a strait jacket of linear thinking with formal logic, and opened up to lateral thinking with Buddhist studies and meditative experiences. Between the two extremes, there was a wonderful continuum of thoughtful views to study and from which to draw insights. Gradually, with much encouragement from the teachers, I began to think for myself and to give status to my own authority. That is not to say that I no longer listened to the authority of others, but rather that I could integrate it with my own. I learned to trust my own authority to make my own choices. This includes trusting my felt knowledge, i.e., intuitive knowledge that comes from places in my body. The integration of felt knowledge and reasoned knowledge provides a strong basis for trusting oneself, and is a condition for trusting others. The permeable self suggests a conception of a person that includes both self-regard and respect for others as the basis of receptivity and responsiveness. In this view, knowing how to think for oneself is part of being able to reach out to others and to connect with them without fear of self-loss. The strong feeling of gratitude toward the teachers who helped me in the recovery of myself continues to motivate me to work with women to help them to strengthen their thinking so they can be more self-determining in their own life choices.

The model of the permeable self is important from a feminist perspective because it begins with the assumption of the equal ontological and epistemological status of women and men. There is no first or second sex in this view. There is equality of the sexes that takes sexual difference into account. I am not arguing for sexual equality that ignores sexual differences. In my view, gender neutrality that does not address sex-specificity covertly perpetuates the hierarchical relation between the sexes. It does so because of the tendency to continue privileging so-called masculine traits, such as moral dignity and strength of character, in the notion of androgyny.

I wish to emphasize sex-specificity with respect to the notion of permeable self. I realize that economics and skin colour, as well as many other attributes, affect one's individuality and sociality. Sociality refers to the context of relatedness of each individual. Although individuality is shaped by many social factors, I shall concentrate here on the distinction of sex differences and the importance of sex-specific ontological claims with respect to the relation between autonomy and interdependency in the permeable self. I do not use autonomy here to mean separate and self-sufficient, as it is used, for example, by Kohlberg. I use it to mean self-determining. I find it useful when discussing self-determination in relation to women because of the lack of autonomy in the soluble self. In this view, autonomy has to do with freedom. It is about freedom from restraints and freedom to act as one chooses. An important aspect of freedom for many women is freedom from fear of sexual control in various forms, such as date rape, conjugal duties, being stared at, harassment at work, unhealthy representation of women's bodies in advertisements and the media, and other forms of sexual terrorism. Terrorism is characterized by fear. It is about fear of not knowing when or where the danger is. As Carol Pateman (1988) points out, the hidden cultural assumption of male sex-right, i.e., male access to women's bodies, makes many forms of sexual terrorism seem normal and unproblematic. Male domination of female sexuality is a consequence of the gendered model of separate and soluble selves.

The model of permeable self that takes sex-specificity into account, by contrast, provides an alternative model of connectedness. In this model, women's sexuality is not associated with the soluble self-image of femininity. It has to do with autonomy and interdependency. A theory of the self as both autonomous and interdependent, i.e., as a permeable self, supports social reorganization of the relations of the sexes so that women would have the freedom to work, to play, or simply to be without fear for their well-being, merely because they are female. This model of the self is supported by spiritual experiences in which goddess presence, nature spirits, and mindfulness of one's presence to oneself give strength to a person's subjectivity and connectedness. The ontological grounding of spiritual experiences provides an important source of knowledge for constructing the self as autonomous and interdependent. The ontological status of woman as a normative form of humanity that is experienced in spiritual experiences shapes the ways in which a woman knows herself as a person in her own right. She claims her birthright. It is a birthright that legitimizes her full participation as an autonomous (self-determining) and interdependent person in social organization and in the cultural production of meaning.

Within the dichotomous, gendered model of self as either separate or soluble, the issue of individuality in a discussion of self-determination has different implications for women than it does for men. As we know from feminist psychoanalytic theorists,[30] individuation (separation from one's mother) in early childhood is an ideal for boys while continued identity with the mother is the norm for girls. When we speak of individuality, ambiguity flourishes. A certain amount of anxiety is provoked with respect to the issues of autonomy and dependency. We have been conditioned to think in terms of either the separate or the soluble self. A permeable self, by contrast, is one which is neither entirely separated from, nor dissolves into, another. Rather, a person who lives as a permeable self expands through relationship, and at the same time, is grounded in subjectivity.

The Buddhist doctrine of *pratityasamutapada* (interdependency) is the cornerstone for this view of permeable self. The forms of spiritual consciousness represented by Buddhist meditation, shamanic journeying, and goddess spirituality reflect an understanding of self as permeable, i.e., as both private and relational. Relationality is integral to self-determination in the model of the permeable self. Spiritual experiences are means by which otherness is incorporated into the self-consciousness of a permeable self. A presupposition here is that recognition of differences in the constitution of one's own identity facilitates living with the differences of others as possibilities for creative interaction.

The view of the self as an interactive process is captured in the metaphor of jazz improvisation. The music is the process. Mary Catherine Bateson writes about "life as an improvisatory art" (1990:3). Rather than life being a quest from one end to the other, as often portrayed with respect to male heroes, it is a process of detours and happenings. Just as jazz improvisation is not predestined to follow a particular pattern, so one's life is shaped by the unexpected. For example, those whose lives include caring for young children in a serious way are familiar with daily surprises that take them away from other activities. I am dubious of the claim that it is not the amount of time one spends with one's children that matters, but rather the quality of time. I agree that quality time is important. It is important, however, all the time. Children don't wait for a designated quality time. They want, and deserve, as much of the time as they can possibly get. (So do adults.) Quality time is characterized by mindfulness. It might include sweeping the kitchen floor, washing dishes together, studying, or playing ball. Mindfulness is part of any activity between people when there is a respect for the individuality of each person and their contributions to the shared reality they construct together.

Paying attention to the realities of those around us is part of the improvisatory art of living. It requires openness to the other from within one's own subjectivity. Openness, however, does not mean availability for exploitation. Audre Lorde reminds us that "There is an important difference between openness and naivete. Not everyone has good intentions nor means me well. I remind myself I do not need to change these people, only recognize who they are" (1988:124). Mindfulness of different interacting intentions is central to this view of identity as composite. A naive approach to permeability is a recipe for subjugation. A Buddhist interpretation of naivete is deludedness, that is, lack of insight into the dynamics of the process. Self-identity that emerges through interaction requires a notion of permeable self that resists oppression and intrusion. It is supported by an orientation toward mindfulness of egocentricity and related forms of domination/subordination. Awareness of otherness in one's own identity is a step toward expanding self-consciousness to include the presence of others in their diversity.

An important way in which identity through otherness emerges is through spiritual experiences. Spiritual experiences are often kept secret because of their lack of acceptance as normal. When, however, identity is understood to be pluralistic rather than singular, then it is easier to see that various forms of consciousness, rather than merely one form, can be included as normal in a person's identity. Living in relation to one's own forms of otherness, as well as those of others, requires a kind of permeability that is based upon openness and receptivity as well as resistance to interference with one's own subjectivity.

Interdependency is characterized by receptivity of others and responsiveness to them. Ann Belford Ulanov (1981) helpfully distinguishes three aspects of receptivity: receiving oneself, receiving the other, and being received by the other. All three are considered necessary conditions for self-determination. While I find her psychological and theological analysis of the self applicable, it would be even more useful if it included more critique of power relations between women and men. The book is entitled *Receiving Woman*. If all things were equal, there would be no reason to be sceptical of the title. In light of the pervasive dominant-subordinate relations between men and women, however, the title tends to reinforce the problem. It could give the impression that the book is a defence of women as soluble selves, governed by a gendered ethic of care, despite the fact that it is about self-determination. The importance of it here is the emphasis on being receptive not only to others but also to the different dimensions of oneself. Self-identity within the paradigm of permeable self entails rejection of identity in terms of a single, essential feature in favour of diversity in identity.

The permeable self is characterized by connectedness of differences within one's own subjectivity and between oneself and others. Spiritual experiences that include shape-shifting and multiple images of spiritual powers, for example, facilitate receptivity of differences within oneself and others. Shape-shifting is an extreme example of the permeable self. The fluidity of self-identity experienced in shape-shifting, such as becoming a flame or a wave, is consistent with the Buddhist view of self as a process of changing perceptions, with no fixed self. My own experiences of shape-shifting into animals, trees, waves, and flames, and participating in imaged realities of diverse women, have been integrating rather than fragmenting. I did not experience a splitting off of parts of myself, but rather a more inclusive way of knowing myself and about being connected to other things and people. It was about my own permeablity with relation to my differences and those of others. These experiences are constant reminders of how it feels to be centred and related. Experiences of being strongly centred and outside myself at the same time are times of ontological and epistemological permeability. My various ways of being and ways of knowing inform each other.

Alternate ways of knowing experienced in spiritual consciousness helps us to move out of cognicentrism with respect to identity. Cognitive relativism is consistent with a pluralistic view of identity. The permeable self is a pluralistic paradigm of identity. One of the challenges of emphasizing a pluralistic view of the self is that of knowing oneself as a centred self, without becoming a separate self. Finding solitude in the self while remaining open to others requires considerable attention to balance. In other words, retaining one's subject position in relation to the subject positions of others requires taking oneself seriously. It is not helpful for those who experience themselves as soluble selves to be told that there is no subject position in which to locate the self.[31] It leaves them in danger of being constructed largely through the discourse of the other.

The importance of boundaries in conjunction with permeability cannot be overemphasized when there is a danger of the soluble self emerging as one's identity. The prevalence of gendered power relations makes resistance to self-loss an important issue for women in our society. Part of resisting self-loss is to be aware of one's own desires and the conditions for their satisfaction.

Desire

The underlying assumption about desire here is that it is intrinsic to every person's consciousness in two ways: there is a desire for connectedness and a desire for separateness. In this view, desire is not discussed exclusively in terms of the lack of something.[32] (It is usually the case that when we desire something we do so as a consequence of not having it.) I wish, however, to discuss desire as the motivational force both for connectedness to others and for a protected personal, subjective space. This understanding of desire is included in the view of self as permeable. The desire for connectedness motivates openness and receptiveness. The desire for separateness motivates resistance to 'space invaders,' other persons and things that intrude into one's private space. For women, the latter is a particularly important aspect of subjectivity, with respect to uninvited sexual intrusions. It is also directly relevant to an ethic that integrates care and resistance. To speak our truths from within a context of relatedness and caring while resisting subjugation is a goal of those concerned with a liberationist ethics. From my perspective, a liberationist ethics requires the two dimensions of care and resistance. Sometimes it is necessary for resistance to be more dominant. At other times, especially in more just circumstances, an ethic of caring can be exercised more explicitly without self-loss. A goal is to have the desires for connectedness and separateness experienced in terms of self-regard and benevolence towards others, resulting in social justice. John Macquarrie (1983), a British religious philosopher, and Jessica Benjamin (1986, 1988), an American psychoanalytic theorist, are two major sources of insight for this section. In addition, I draw on the work of Hilary Lips (1991), a Canadian/American psychologist, for her contributions to an analysis of power relations.

John Macquarrie claims that humanity is about persons-in-the-making. We know about humanity first of all from meeting people. Personal identity develops through encountering ourselves in reflections from others. The process of mirroring is constitutive of becoming human. To be human is to participate in the interactive process of perceiving and being perceived. It is to be subjected to the scrutiny of objectifying gazes as well as to be transformed through loving attention. Sometimes the two kinds of interaction are simultaneous and at other times they are distinctively separated. Macquarrie develops a philosophical anthropology in his religious understanding of humanity, albeit without attention to social differences and corresponding power relations. A feminist humanism to which I wish to contribute includes multiperspectival theories of humanity. Such a humanism cannot be captured by any one perspective. It can only be added to from various perspectives. I am advocating one feminist humanist perspective which may allow for connections among women and men living within diverse kinds of social and cultural conditions. Macquarrie's religious anthropology contributes to that aim through his attempt to relate egoity to sociality in an interactive process which is compatible with the view of a permeable self discussed in the previous section.

Macquarrie invites us to imagine a space in the centre of each person which is the place where one goes in the process of centring oneself. This is an ontological space at the centre of one's being. He says, "the empty space of freedom which I have called the metaphorical hole is a centre of creativity" (1983:12). Individual desire is shaped by intentionality toward egoity within the metaphorical hole and toward sociality through interaction with others. By egoity he means "the condition of being an ego or a self. This is the condition of every human being, even if he or she has never reflected upon it" (p. 38). Freedom, from Macquarrie's view, requires an ontological space from where intentional action might arise. He suggests that the metaphorical hole of freedom, i.e., the ego, is the "leading edge" (*hegemonikon*) of a person. It is "the conscious, rational, discriminating, unifying, purposeful element in the human being that leads us in one direction rather than another. It is this directedness that makes the difference between human action and mere natural happening, and that allows us to speak of freedom rather than randomness" (p. 38). For Macquarrie, desire is integral to egoity. Egoity is distinguished from egoism. Egoity is seen as inner subjectivity. Egoism, by contrast, is "a philosophy or ideology which puts the interests of the self before all others" (p. 45). Egoism, in Macquarrie's discourse, is similar to Vasubandhu's view of egocentricity, the central cause of social injustice. Egoism belongs to the notional-conceptual level of consciousness in which the self is seen as a separate category. Self-interest, from that level of awareness, is based on a desire to maintain the image of oneself as self-sufficient rather than interrelated. Egoity, by contrast, is the presence of self in the world as an intentional person, motivated by the ontological creative power that is integral to the person's consciousness.

Sociality is inseparable from egoity in Macquarrie's view of persons-in-relation. He says, "however impressive is the individuality of each human being, equally striking is the essential sociality of each one" (p. 85). He points out that

Individualist philosophers of the Enlightenment taught that society had been formed by individual human beings coming together and giving us some of their 'natural rights' in a social contract. But it seems more likely that individuals emerged from a social matrix. We become aware of the face of the other long before we see (and then only indirectly) our own faces. But perhaps it would be no more correct to say that society is prior to the individual in an ontological as distinct from a chronological sense, than to say that the individual is prior to society. Both the social and the individual poles seem equally original in the being of [humans] and their tension is there from the beginning as one of the factors contributing to the dynamics of human life. (1983:85)

Macquarrie's Christianity commits him to a view of the self as that which is created in the image of God. I do not agree with this account of the self. Rather, I assume an ontology of interrelatedness in which humans, animals, and the rest of nature are part of a continually changing reality. There is no fixed image of ultimate reality as God or any other single reality. The ontology that grounds my view of the self is reflected in the Buddhist doctrines of *pratityasumtpada* and *sunyata*. Reality is a process of interrelatedness that is empty of 'thingness' and open to new becomings. The similarity between Macquarrie's ontology of the self and my own is that we both take the self to be grounded in an integrative, creative power that is basic to personal desire and that shapes ethical action. Being present to oneself is to be conscious of the ontological creative power that is integral to one's identity. I agree with his claim that egoity and sociality are like the concave and convex sides of a dish. Each is required for the other. The interactive process of persons-in-the-making is shaped by the desire for centredness in egoity and connectedness in sociality. The paradigm of the permeable self allows for the twofold desire to shape intentionality towards integrative action while respecting the uniqueness of individuality.

Jessica Benjamin's suggestion (1986, 1988) that we use the model of intersubjectivity to discuss desire is helpful. As Benjamin points out, from the more traditional psychoanalytic perspective which she critiques, desire has been represented from within an intrapsychic schema (1988:125). Since Freud, psychoanalytic theories of desire have been presented from within the phallic interpretation, linking desire to social power, as symbolized through the phallus. An independent account of woman's desire, free from the phallic mode, has not been theorized. Within that framework, the phallus signifies power and desire. Identification with the father by the children is regarded by Benjamin as an expression of the desire to be powerful and separated in the outside, away from the relative powerlessness of mother. The powerlessness of the mother is connected to fear of one's own powerlessness through identification with her. Identification with the father, the survivor of battles, outside the home is perceived by Benjamin to be as strong in girls as it is in boys.

She aims to move from a phallic model of representing desire, which is intrapsychic, to an intersubjective model of desire. She says,

The phallic mode of representation really corresponds to what we have called the intrapsychic mode, which includes the whole constellation of using the father as a vehicle for separation, and internalizing him as the representative of agency and desire. Once phallic representation has developed, it organizes the processes of internalization and identification that make up intrapsychic life within. The intersubjective dimension, on the other hand, refers to experience *between and within* individuals, rather than just *within*. It refers to the sense of self and other that evolves through the consciousness that separate minds can share the same feelings and intentions, through mutual recognition. (1988:125)

This intersubjective sense of self "meshes with symbolic structures, but it is not, as internalization theory would have it, created by them" (p. 125). Benjamin explores possibilities for theorizing about woman's desire through the model of intersubjectivity. She starts off with the premise that

recognition of the other is the decisive aspect of differentiation. In recognition, someone who is different and outside shares a similar feeling; different minds and bodies attune. In erotic union this attunement can be so intense that self and other feel as if momentarily 'inside' each other, as part of a whole. Receptivity and self-expression, the sense of losing the self in the other and the sense of being truly known for oneself all coalesce. (1988:126).

The erotic union, as described here, closely resembles spiritual experiences of being simultaneously centred in oneself and in another. Desire is seen as "desire for recognition" (p. 126). It is a desire for the recognition of agency, one's creative power.

Benjamin uses the metaphor of space rather than symbolism to represent desire. Open space is a prerequisite for the expression of the desire to be recognized. Inner space represents the capacity to hold oneself. This is similar to Macquarrie's idea of the metaphorical hole within each person from where freedom of self-expression originates. Benjamin says the open space inside "allows us to feel that our impulses come from within and so are authentically our own" (p. 128). The difference between random drive and intentional desire is seen to come from "the ability to hold oneself" and, thereby, give an action its authority. Such authority through holding one's space inside gives an action "its purposefulness in regard to the other, its authenticity for the self" (p. 128). In Benjamin's view, "The significance of the spatial metaphor for a woman is likely to be just this discovery of her *own, inner* desire, without fear of impingement, intrusion, or violation" (p. 128). Freedom for inner self-recognition is basic, in this view, for recognition of the other. It is required for expression of the permeable self in which inner subjectivity and receptivity to the other are mutually enhancing. The implications of the intersubjective model for the expression of spirituality as erotic power will be developed in Chapter Two.

While Benjamin makes an important contribution in relocating the discussion of desire within the context of intersubjectivity, her refusal to look to the female body as a source of revisioning symbolic structures is a limitation of her project, from my point of view. She claims that "in a culture in which the representation of the body is organized and dominated by the phallus, woman's body is endlessly objectified in all the visual media. The element of agency will not be restored to woman by aestheticizing her body—that has already been done in spades" (1988:124). It is true that from within phallic symbolism women's bodies are represented as objects of men's desires and cannot easily be considered sources of freedom for women's expression of their own desires. It is possible to begin with the female body and attempt to construct a new symbolic order from it, one that entails a pluralistic identity and is, accordingly, compatible with Benjamin's notion of desire from within the intersubjective model. A more comprehensive expression of desire is possible through recognition of women's bodies as sources of meaning outside the phallic-driven system of meaning. The importance of the body for expression of women's spirituality will be explored in Chapter Two and the significance of the body for language will be discussed in Chapter Three.

Desire occurs almost inevitably within a context of power relations. Whether one uses an intrapsychic model or an intersubjective model to discuss desire, it is necessary to acknowledge that structural power relations shape the expression of individual desires. Hilary Lips says that power is "a process in which we all engage as long as we are part of a network of human relations" (1991:4). Power is located within the individual, among individuals as collective power, and in structurally organized systems such as universities, families, and governments. Power relations are initiated according to individual desires. Shared desires become collective goals and, if institutionalized, they are accepted as social goals to be achieved through status quo activity maintained by societal norms and enforced by laws. Institutionalized power relations impact on individuals to limit or enhance individual and collective power. If a more egalitarian distribution of power is desired, these three interacting sets of power relations must be addressed in relation to each other.

Of particular interest here is the power to satisfy one's desire to actualize one's potential for self-determination and interrelatedness. Egalitarian social structures are a prerequisite for the satisfaction of that desire by all persons. Institutionalized power relations shape individuals' interpretations of their own experiences, spiritual or otherwise. Holding one's own inner space is one prerequisite for freedom of self-expression. Another is social justice with respect to institutionalized power relations in social organization and cultural production. Although the focus of power relations here is gender relations, as I mentioned earlier they are always conjoined with other identifying qualities. I believe, however, that sex-specificity is a central part of identity. Just as one is never simply a woman or a man, without, for example, being black, white, brown, and with or without adequate living conditions, so one is never simply Native or European, poor or rich without also being a man or a woman. Despite the complexity of self-constructs, I address specifically the issue of female power.

Femaleness in most cultures, especially industrialized ones, is not closely associated with powerful concepts or images that characterize social authority. Powerful images are usually found in relation to god, physical power and sports skills, formal authority, property ownership, and expert knowledge which is beyond the reach of others. These images are more about men than about women. Dominant cultural images of women have more to do with a lack of authority than with power to define and shape social organization and cultural meanings. Women who attempt to represent themselves as powerful face an identity confusion and social criticism not common to most men because of images and attitudes that perpetuate so-called appropriate sex identification. The 'appropriate' images of power which are expressed by our cultural mythology make it difficult for images of female power to be viewed with comfort and approval. Cultural images correspond to social realities. We attribute relative status to people according to their 'fit' with the set of hierarchal power images we have in mind. Images of powerful women challenge people's mindsets about power and gender (i.e., socially ascribed characteristics relevant to the particular sex). If a person has a high achieved status, based on deserved competence, but a low ascribed status, because of her sex, then there is status incongruity.[33] That is, there is an inconsistency between the dominant set of power images and the dominant set of gender images.

A paradigm shift is occurring with respect to the relation between images of power and images of gender. The social changes that are emerging are connected to underlying narratives about the nature and purpose of women and their corresponding expressions of desire for recognition as agents. An important part of the paradigm shift is the relation between spirituality and the female body. Satisfaction of the desire for self-determination is significantly affected by cultural attitudes towards women's bodies. Spiritual experiences that include female images that do not correspond to cultural stereotypes are important sources for resisting the dominant images. Women's desires for self-expression as spiritual persons need to be reconciled with their desires to live in a healthy way in their bodies.

Notes

1 I shall use 'their' as the predicative pronoun which refers back to a singular subject. This was a common linguistic practice until the eighteenth century, when grammarians asserted that generic pronouns would be masculine because men represented humanity.

2 My own initial training in mindfulness lasted about eight months. My professor told me I needed to learn to concentrate better to translate the Buddhist text that I was working on. He agreed to help me train in mind control. At first, I sat at home for about twenty minutes each day looking at a dot in the centre of a piece of paper. The dot was about the size of a pea. The objective was to keep the dot still on the paper. That represented stillness of mind. After a month of practice I could do that. Then I began to pay attention to thoughts that would reoccur in my mind while I was sitting there. These were about beliefs that I was holding onto about myself that I needed to release. I was instructed to focus on the one that was most dominant and talk with my professor about it. Getting to the 'heart of the matter' with regard to different issues took eight months

of discussion and meditation. Finally I could do it myself. The professor agreed that I didn't need his services to instruct me further in mind control at that time. Rather, I concentrated with him on the translation. I have continued to develop deeper meditation, which eventually led into the emergence of goddess images in my consciousness and then to shamanic journeying where I became acquainted with a greater variety of natural powers, such as animals, ocean waves, and flames. I believe that mindfulness is essential to all of these ways of experiencing spirituality.

3 Anne Klein is one of the few scholars attempting to relate Buddhist epistemology, ontology, and theories of the self to women's realities. Another important scholar who is attempting this in an extended way is Rita Gross in her book on the *Sangha* in Buddhist traditions (Gross 1993). Both scholars look to discussions of the *Sangha*, a community of devotees, for insights that relate to the feminist emphasis on relationality. Rita Gross presented material from her book at the 1991 American Academy of Religion meetings in the Women in Religious Traditions section.

4 The specific text is the *Trimsika-karika (Thirty Verses)* which I translated from Tibetan (Tomm 1984). The author of the text is not known for certain; however, Vasubandhu is most widely accepted as the probable author (King 1991:6).

5 For example, Anne Klein's discussion of the self and nature of reality from the Prasangika-Madhyamika school of Mahayana provides a similar understanding. Sallie King's (1991) careful discussion of Buddha nature reveals shared views among the traditions, while pointing out the distinctions. For our purpose here, namely, to discuss the importance of connecting self-consciousness with a consciousness of the interdependency of all of reality, it is sufficient to provide the common views within the various Buddhist schools of thought.

6 *Sunyata* is usually translated as emptiness. For example, Nagao (1978) and Streng (1967). However, Guenther and Kawamura (1975), for instance, translate it as openness. The meaning remains the same. The rationale for translating it as openness is to reduce the ambiguity of the meaning, to avoid the nihilistic implications of emptiness.

7 I shall denote the *Trimsika* by *T.* and Verse by Vs.

8 See, for example, Susan Wendell (1989:104-24). She claims that her experience of becoming disabled has helped her to be more aware of the suffering of others and the knowledge that it might give them. Her own disability has freed her up to greater self-acceptance and to a more compassionate view of others. Freedom from the expectation that she should continue with the same health (body) status as she had experienced in the past allowed her to accept herself as she was. She no longer has to match an oppressive ideal. She believes, and I support her belief, that the severely disabled have much to tell others about the negative effects of ideals of perfection on self-perceptions and receptivity toward others.

9 See Guenther (1975) for a detailed analysis of the various states of consciousness in meditation. The Appendix, pp. 241-44, gives a good account of the way in which perception changes so life is experienced as a joyful rather than miserable existence.

10 See Guenther and Kawamura (1975) for an extensive analysis of the fifty-one qualities of consciousness, of which these five essential ones, the eleven positive ones, and the six basic negative ones are briefly discussed in this chapter.

11 Sheila Greeve Davaney has posed the dilemma nicely in her unpublished paper, "Radical Historicity and the Search for Sure Foundations," which she read at the 1986 meetings of the American Academy of Religion. She develops the argument further toward pragmatism and away from ontology in her chapter, 'The Limits of the Appeal to Women's Experiences," in Atkinson et al. (1987:31-50).

12 I have discussed Hume's epistemology, his view of the primacy of passion in relation to reason, desire as the motivation for morality, and his philosophy of self in Tomm (1984).

13 The injustice of the landlord's treatment of the boy is vividly portrayed in *The Brothers Karamazov*, Pt. II, bk. v, chap. 4.

14 John Hick's *Evil and the God of Love* has become a classic in theodicy studies. Still it does not touch the general outrage felt by Dostoevsky's readers. I agree with the general consensus that there is no justification for such inhumane action. This view assumes a normative measure of what it is to be human and what constitutes dehumanizing activities. Our notion of what it is to be human has both a descriptive and evaluative sense to it, as John Macquarrie points out (1983:1). If we evaluate the actions of another as not 'truly human' then we assume an 'ethical a priori' position, even though descriptively the person belongs to the human species.

15 I have discussed Spinoza's metaphysics, epistemology, and theory of self (Tomm 1984, 1987).

16 I have written more extensively about this experience (Tomm 1991).

17 This is a question that troubles Daphne Hampson (1990) in her analysis of looking at women's experiences as sources of religious knowledge. She is concerned that not just experiences are significant but rather experiences of god. Her concern is shaped by the assumption of an epistemic gap between god and the world that is partially closed through religious experience. That epistemic gap reflects a distinction between the reality of god and experiences of god. This distinction is intrinsic to theology. That is one reason why I wish to move outside a theological framework.

18 Two clearly written and highly informative books on shamanism as spiritual healing through journeying are Harner (1980) and Ingerman (1991). A book which brings the teachings of those two books directly to women in particular is Noble (1991). There are many other important resources for learning about shamanism. Mircea Eliade's *Shamanism: Archaic Techniques of Ecstasy* (1964) is a classical text which has shaped much of the research on shamanism since the 1960s. His work is important, without any doubt. It is, however, being critiqued for its blatant androcentrism (Christ 1991a).

19 The conversation can be heard on the CD, "The Glenn Gould Legacy: J.S. Bach," disc 3.

20 Andy Smith (1991) writes of the racism that she sees to characterize White feminists' uses of Native spirituality for their own self-interest at the expense of Native people. Her powerful challenge to White women trying to be Indian has appeared as a position paper for the national Women's Studies Association and is in *Woman of Power* and in *Sojourner*.

   She is correct to point out the need for political support for Native rights rather than appropriation of Native spirituality. Shamanism is closely associated with Native spirituality but is not identical with it or exclusive to it. Shamanism belongs to the histories of a multitude of cultures. My participation in shamanic practices is part of a spirituality that draws from Buddhist meditation and goddess spirituality. I anticipate exploring connections between shamanism, goddess spirituality, and celtic pre-patriarchal religions. My own roots come from England. From the time I attended Anglican services as a child in the Cypress Hills I was aware of the incongruity between the officiousness of the minister, the stuffiness of the church services, and the context of the Cypress Hills where my spirit connected with the animals and hills.

21 In his article "The Proof Is Not Always in the Pudding," Don McGillivray tells us that the saying dates "to 1623 when the pioneer British historian, William Camden, wrote that 'all the proof of a pudding is in the eating.' . . . [Th]e proverb advises people to try things out for themselves rather than to take someone else's word for it. . . . Perhaps that meaning is unchanged in 'the proof is in the pudding' but I'm not sure. Is it implied that the proof-in-the-pudding is somehow hidden? Is the new form of the saying an echo of the false assurance that 'the cheque is in the mail?'" (McGillivray 1992:A4).

22 This story was told by Ninian Smart at a plenary session at the Philosophy East and West meetings in Hawaii in 1984, which I attended.

23 Naomi Goldenberg's book, *Returning Words to Flesh* (1990), is a good example of interpreting religion exclusively in psychological terms. I have addressed Goldenberg's book in a paper entitled "Embodied Spiritual Consciousness: Beyond Psychology" (Tomm forthcoming).

24 Michel Foucault (1972) spells out clearly the relations between power and knowledge in his discussion of subjugated knowledges within hierarchal power structures. His powerful account of power and knowledge has for fifteen years dominated related discussions. His work was groundbreaking and opened up space for subjugated knowledges to be recognized as legitimate forms of discourse. At the same time his emphasis on decentring the subject in the interests of eliminating the transcendent subject has led to scepticism with respect to the category of subject. Reality is constructed, in his view, through language. The problem for us here is that the structures of language that are deemed legitimate are those that allegedly reflect reality because they have constructed it. Alternate consciousnesses are not considered real. The theory that reality is constructed through language is not any more helpful for expanding the boundaries of consciousness than a correspondence theory of truth is. Corrective measures would include ascribing a legitimate status to alternative consciousnesses and developing an expanded vocabulary for subjective states.

25 Government of Alberta, Women's Secretariat statistics for the province.

26 See, for example, Diamond and Orenstein (1990) and Spretnak (1991) for two recent important works on ecofeminism in a postmodern age.

27 Some of the most influential women writing on goddess imagery include Allen (1986, 1991); Christ (1987a, 1987b, 1989, 1991b); Condren (1989); Dexter (1990); Downing (1981); Falk and Gross (1989); Gadon (1989); Gimbutas (1982); Goldenberg (1982 and 1990); Markale (1986); Spretnak (1981); and Ywahoo (1987). The early work of Merlin Stone (1978) largely opened the dialogue on goddess spirituality as an avenue for women's escape from the restricting yoke of the patriarchal separation of women's spirituality and their sexuality. Contemporary feminist scepticism of, and sometimes hostility towards, goddess spirituality is understandable. It is based on fear of women once again being reduced to their association with reproduction.

28 Riane Eisler (1987) contrasts the dominator model with the partnership model in her inspirational account of the evolutionary drift toward egalitarianism.

29 See Kohlberg (1971), Kohlberg and Kramer (1969:93-120), and Hersh, Paolitto, and Reimer (1979) for discussions of Kohlberg's six stages of moral development. Stage six is the level of moral autonomy where there is an integration of one's ethical ideals with universal principles (this is a version of Kant's theory of moral autonomy). Kohlberg and Kramer based their model on evidence from only males and then applied it to women and found that there were significantly more women than men at level 3 which is the conventional level of moral reasoning with an emphasis on intimate personal relations. They concluded that "Stage 3 personal concordance morality is a functional morality for housewives and mothers; it is not for businessmen and professionals" (Hersh, Paolitto, and Reimer 1979:108).

30 For example, Jessica Benjamin (1988, 1986); Nancy Chodorow (1978); Dorothy Dinnerstein (1976); and Juliet Mitchell (1974).

31 For example, the emphasis on decentring the subject that characterizes the work of Derrida (1987), Foucault (1980, 1972), and Lacan (1977) has been central to postmodern feminist theory which denies a subject position which has a reality of its own apart from the construction of it through language. In this postmodern view there is no ontology, only epistemology.

32 Catherine Belsey (1991), an influential British feminist literary theorist, discussed her view (based on Jacques Lacan's) of desire as something that could never be fully satisfied or life would be nothing left to achieve. She presented her view of desire in a paper delivered at the University of Alberta in September 1991. In her view we desire someone or something because of the mystery, novelty, and interest that is provoked by the unknown. Desire is seen to disappear with the satisfaction of the desire. While this is a familiar understanding of desire, it is not the one I am developing.

33 I am indebted to Hilary Lips (1991) for her phrase 'status incongruity' in her analysis of images of power and images of feminity.

Two

Spirituality and the Body

Eros/Erotic

IN THIS CHAPTER, I explore some central issues pertaining to the satisfaction of women's desire for self-determination with regard to their spirituality and their bodies. First, I provide an interpretation of eroticism as a form of self-love (eros) that is important in the expression of spirituality energy in the body. Eroticism is contextualized within a view of consciousness as embodied consciousness. This part focusses on the influence that women's bodies have in the ways their lives get constructed. It also emphasizes the importance of images of resistance found in spiritual experiences that facilitate new ways of knowing oneself that contribute to greater self-assurance. The notion of otherness in identity is explored further with respect to gaining access to the diversity of inner subjectivity through reflecting new images, including images of the self in the mirror. The last part of the chapter develops more fully the idea of female engendering, i.e., spiritual and bodily creative activity. It is largely about rethinking the relation between nature and culture with respect to women as embodied, spiritual creators of culture as well as of physical life. This chapter is intended to take the discussion of spirituality in the last chapter into the flesh.

I take eros to be integral to self-determination. Love of oneself is a form of self-trust. Self-trust is a condition for compassion. Absence of eros, of self-love, provides the ideal condition for projection of one's own positive qualities onto another person, God, or an external object. For example, women sometimes are attracted to men who possess the qualities they do not permit themselves to have. They might marry the person they would like to be rather than trust themselves to be that person. Self-love includes love of one's body in its sex-specific form, that is in its femaleness or maleness. Eros or self-love includes feeling the power of erotic energy in one's body. Love between persons occurs within an exchange of erotic energy that empowers and energizes those who are engaged with each other. When a person is present to herself or himself, they are present to their bodies. Their bodies are the places of exchange of the immanence and transcendence of each person in the exchange. That is to say, the

---

Notes to Chapter Two are on pages 113-14.

inner subjectivity of each person reaches out to the other and in this movement toward each other each person transcends their own individual boundaries, thereby expanding their subjectivities in the intersubjective exchange of energy. This transformative process of erotic relatedness opens space for expanded consciousness of oneself and others. In this way, it is reasonable to claim that eros and benevolence are inseparable. Erotic energy is intrinsic to the desire for creative participation with others in the improvisatory process of constructing one's life through relationships. I support Audre Lorde's meaning of erotic in her claim, "When I speak of the erotic, then, I speak of it as an assertion of the life-force of women; of that creative energy empowered, the knowledge and use of which we are now reclaiming in our language, our history, our dancing, our loving, our work, our lives" (1984:55). Lorde makes a clear distinction between eroticism and pornography. While the erotic is an expression of life force, "pornography is a direct denial of the power of the erotic, for it represents the suppression of true feeling. Pornography emphasizes sensation without feeling" (p. 54). Lorde equates feelings with emotions.[1] Emotional states, or feelings, reflect the integrity of the person. That is, the integration of body and mind. Eros is about feeling the life force as well as living with it intellectually in relation to others. Personal integrity includes erotic expression of a sex-specific spiritual, intellectual, and physical individual. Self-love requires recognition of the full self. Self-knowing and self-love are closely connected, as Lorde notes in her claim that "the erotic is the nurturer or nursemaid of all our deepest knowledge" (1988:210). Responsible knowledge includes that which is propelled into consciousness by desire: desire for full recognition of our sex-specific humanity. The desire for the privacy of self-connectedness as well as for public relationality is constitutive of erotic desire. Being present to oneself and to others depends upon feeling the force of one's own energy. The erotic is often feared. It sometimes demands more than a person is willing to be responsible for. Audre Lorde says,

For once we begin to feel deeply all the aspects of our lives, we begin to demand from ourselves and from our life-pursuits that they feel in accordance with the joy which we know ourselves to be capable of. Our erotic knowledge empowers us, becomes a lens through which we scrutinize all aspects of our existence, forcing us to evaluate those aspects honestly in terms of their relative meaning within our lives. And this is a grave responsibility, projected from within each of us, not to settle for the convenient, the shoddy, the conventionally expected, nor the merely safe. (1988: 211)

Living with the responsibility of being as fully human as possible requires courage. For many, the desire to develop personal and social agency is suppressed in order to conform to conventions. This is especially relevant to women who are often socially conditioned and structurally positioned to serve the desires of others, with a corresponding self-loss.

But when we begin to live from within outward, in touch with the power of the erotic within ourselves, and allowing that power to inform and illuminate our actions upon the world around us, then we begin to be responsible to ourselves in the deepest sense. For as we begin to recognize our deepest feelings, we begin to give up, of necessity, being satisfied with suffering and self-negation, and with the numbness that so often seems like their only alternative in our society. . . . In touch with the erotic, I become less willing to accept powerlessness, or those other supplied states of being which are not native to me, such as resignation, despair, self-effacement, depression, self-denial (Lorde 1988:212).

Power-filled women live with a freedom that comes from obedience to their own self-knowledge as it arises within their sexuate body, i.e., a sex-specific body that is a unified erotic zone. Such women can be present to themselves and to each other, as well as to men, in a transformative way. Their erotic energy is expressed through their bodies, of which they are fully mindful in their manner of relating to themselves and to others. In our North American culture there is a paucity of images for women to use to imagine themselves as powerfully erotic subjects. Emily Culpepper notes how Amazon images help women develop power-filled identities. She says, in relation to Amazon identity, "my own life is immeasurably improved now that we have appeared to each other" (1986:12). Increasing numbers of women would agree with her that when women identify their own spiritual power their spirits soar, so to speak. Claudia Bepko and Jo-Ann Krestan (1993) emphasize the need for self-defined eroticism in women's love and creativity that includes 'singing at the top of our lungs.' Singing, in this perspective, is partially a metaphor for freedom of spirit. Diane Ackerman (1990) refers to an ancient Chinese adage that expresses the metaphoric consciousness of singing as a form of spiritual expression. The saying goes like this: A bird sings not because it has an answer, but because it has a song. Erotic liveliness is expressed when we sing our own songs. When we sing together we enliven each other's songs and create a powerful force for individual and social change.

John Macquarrie (1983) provides a helpful account of the continuum of eros and agapé (unconditional love or benevolence towards others). He refers back to Joseph Butler of eighteenth-century Britain with respect to the importance of recognizing our responsibility to ourselves. Butler says, "we are in a peculiar manner entrusted with ourselves" (Macquarrie 1983:177). Self-love is about respecting and making "the most of what has been entrusted" (p. 177). "It is a necessary condition of one's being able truly to help and serve others" (p. 177). Through self-love we "treat with respect and reverence the gift of one's own existence" (p. 177). Macquarrie uses the terms egoity and sociality to refer to subjectivity and intersubjectivity respectively. Egoity is differentiated from egoism in that it is the inner spiritual identity that connects one person to another across individual boundaries. It provides for the permeability of self in relation to others. Egoism, on the other hand, is the conceptualized identity constructed in an oppositional relation to others, as separate subject. In Macquarrie's view, which I support, egoity and sociality are inseparable. Egoity flourishes because of self-love, which requires sociality.

The first instance of sociality is the loving relationship with a significant other(s) at birth. This context provides the condition for self-love to emerge and for reciprocity of immanence and transcendence to occur in personal relationships as well as less intimate ones. Loving relationships, in this view, are necessary for an orientation towards social justice. The social nature of self-love connects it to benevolence, caring for another. "It is the gift of love from another that first awakens the capacity for love in any human being, and first makes anyone aware of [themselves] as a person who can be the object of love and respect" (Macquarrie 1983: 178). Self-love and benevolence between individuals is seen to correspond to peace in the larger, impersonal social context. Macquarrie gives us a view of ethics and social justice based on self-love. From his perspective, the desire for self-determination through respect for one's own subjectivity in relation to others is the intentionality which is intrinsic to human spirituality.

The usefulness of Macquarrie's view on eros here is that it provides a basic "human" framework in which to understand women's desire for self-determination. While Macquarrie ignores the different social meanings of self-love and benevolence for women and men, his account provides a useful backdrop for discussing the importance of the erotic for women. It contextualizes, for example, Lorde's claim that

The need for sharing deep feeling is a human need. . . . When we look away from the importance of the erotic in the development and sustenance of our power, or when we look away from ourselves as we satisfy our erotic needs in concert with others, we use each other as objects of satisfaction rather than share our joy in the satisfying, rather than make connections with our similarities and our differences. . . . Recognizing the power of the erotic within our lives can give us the energy to pursue genuine change within our world, rather than merely settling for a shift of characters in the same weary drama. (Lorde 1988:212-13)

Eros and agapé provide the energy which connects egoity with sociality to shape the evolution of humanity according to the partnership model described by Riane Eisler (1987). In that way power is expressed as the satisfaction of the desire for living with vitality through connectedness to oneself and to others.

Eisler's partnership evolutionary paradigm for the future, in contrast to the domination model of our past history, is a view of social and cultural evolution that is at odds with Darwinian social evolutionary theory. The main difference is that Darwin argued that evolution occurs through adaptation to the environment, while Eisler claims that there is an underlying intentionality that shapes evolution. Dominant values, attitudes, and beliefs govern our views about superiority with respect to morality, economics, politics, laws, and so forth. An infrastructure of cultural assumptions supports the evolutionary drift. Major evolutionary shifts occur when the underlying set of cultural assumptions is seriously challenged and changed. In her view, a paradigm shift from a dominator model to a partnership is occurring. Eisler argues that the social relations of the sexes is the primary thread that connects the patterns of social and cultural evolution.

In our largely biblically based Western history, there has been considerable tension between attitudes towards women's sexuality and notions about living righteously (i.e., in a right relation to God). Much of the tension has resulted from attributes ascribed to God, which have very little to do with embodiment, female or male. Another cause of tension is the close association of men with God-like attributes of omnipotence and omniscience, and women with the non-Godlike attribute of materiality. Social relations of women and men have evolved along the lines of the distinction between immateriality and materiality. Women's sexuality has been the most explicit focus of women's materiality. Women's place in the social order has been largely defined according to the way in which their sexuality has been expressed. Marriage makes a woman's sexuality acceptable, motherhood sanctifies it. Traditionally in marriages, both the woman and the children assume the man's name. Women, as sexual beings, have been evaluated primarily with reference to men as if they were part of his identity. Women and children's identities are incorporated into the corporate family name. Women's sexuality has been regarded traditionally as something that is there especially to produce corporate family identities in men's names. Women's work, whether reproductive or otherwise, has been affected by the view that women's bodies are there most importantly to fulfil societal expectations of species and cultural reproduction. In light of the fact that women's independent sexuality has rarely been described positively, it is often difficult for women to experience their sexuality as a form of personal power which they are free to share or withhold. Marriage and prostitution are both determined to a large extent by an underlying sexual contract in which men's access to women's bodies is assumed as a male right. I shall discuss the issue of the sexual contract in social contract theory in Chapter Five, especially with reference to Carole Pateman's analysis of social and political theory.

I wish to explore women's sexuality in terms of spiritual energy: energy that is freed from association with the need to control erotic desires. In this view, women's sexuality is seen as positive energy that does not require the institution of marriage to control and legitimize it. It is power we have as a birthright that gives us the ability to live fully present to each other in those rare and wonderful moments when we are fully present to ourselves. Rights and responsibilities go hand-in-hand. If we are conscious of the presence of spiritual, creative energy then we are responsible for living with it. We are entrusted with ourselves. We have the responsibility of trusting ourselves to make the most of that with which we are entrusted. Women's sexuality has been controlled largely through marriage and the morality associated with that institution with regard to the respectability of women.

Control of women's sexuality is so much a part of heterosexual relations that sometimes it is difficult to distinguish heterosexuality from sexism. Sexism is part of our belief in conjugal rights, namely, that husbands have the right to sexual privileges with wives. Of course wives have the same conjugal rights. But the fact that wives and husbands have the same conjugal rights does not translate into the same sense of entitlement for each of them. There is an asymmetrical relation between husbands' rights and wives' duties in marriages. Men's assumed rights to women's bodies and women's duty to please are repressed 'truths' of many marriages. Homosocial bonding among women in coffee groups, quilting parties, lunches, and so forth, is a means for women to 'vent' about this truth that is denied in the name of freedom of individuals to enter into marriage contractual relations. Often the freedom involved hides a covert mandate to conform to marital expectations. As we become increasingly aware of the implications of conjugal rights and duties, marital rape becomes more of a topic for analysis with respect to justice in the family. In addition to the sexism that is hidden in heterosexual marital relations, there is the heterosexism that prescribes heterosexuality as the sole legitimate expression of respectable sexual relations between persons. Since Adrienne Rich's now classic article (1980) on prescriptive heterosexuality and Marilyn Frye's (1983) challenge regarding heterosexual choice, heterosexual women have been challenged to analyze their support of patriarchy through their heterosexuality. I am not advocating lesbianism, but rather indicating the repressed truths of heterosexual relationships that mitigate women's humanity as sexuate persons.

Mary Daly points out that female potency is not easily actualized in our present social structures. She says that "quantum leaps of Fate-identified faith, hope, and Lust are in order" if women are to live with their energy (1989:197). She defines Lust as "pure Passion: unadulterated, absolute, simple, sheer striving for abundance of be-ing" (1984:3). Be-ing is intended to describe identity as a verb, "meaning participation in the Ultimate/Intimate Reality . . ." (1984:2). While I do not wish to use the notion of Ultimate Reality as something that exists apart from our ways of seeing reality, Daly's notion of be-ing is consistent with the view of identity as an interactive process of 'things out there' and individual perceptions of them. Daly's view of desire is consistent with the one discussed here. In her view, we desire to participate in be-ing. Be-longing indicates the actualization of that desire. Our happiness depends on satisfying that desire. It is only through Be-Friending that it is possible for women to actualize their potency and satisfy their desire for participating in Be-Ing. Be-Friending is "The creation of a context/atmosphere in which acts/leaps of

Metamorphosis can take place" (Daly, 1989:197). Metamorphosis refers to "changes of physical/spiritual form or substance, especially such a change brought about by Super Natural means (the metapatriarchal metamorphosis of tamed women into Wild Witches)" (1984:317). I do not agree with the claim for existence of the "Super Natural." An underlying assumption of this book is that ontology and epistemology are mutually inclusive. Apart from that difference with Daly, I agree with her view that the actualization of the desire to participate in Be-ing requires a supportive network that counteracts the anti-Be-ing forces of patriarchy, that is the control by men of women's sexuality, the economic system, and the legal system (Lerner 1986).

Daly's account of Be-Friending is not about all women being friends. It is about providing an orientation of Be-Longing for women in different contexts. She says, "Be-Friending arouses and awakens in a woman her Be-Longing, her telic focus" (1989:201). Telic focus refers to ontological passion, Lust. Her view of the individuality and relationality of women resonates with Macquarrie's view of egoity and sociality in relation to eros and agapé. Macquarrie claims that it is possible to love another only when there is love of self. Daly says, "Only confirmation of one's own Reality awakens that Reality in another" (1989:201). Macquarrie referred to the metaphorical hole in the centre of one's being as the location for spiritual energy to propel the individual into community from their own subjectivity. Just as in the Buddhist discussion of mindfulness, Daly claims that intensity of desire focusses energy and unlocks it. A woman unbinds her mind through focussed attention on her desire for Be-ing and actualizing the desire in the act of Be-Longing through the process of Be-Friending. The Lust for Be-ing is thereby awakened.

Just as the erotic is contrasted with pornography in Lorde's quotation above, so Daly contrasts Lust for Be-ing with a savaging lust that destroys Be-ing (i.e., phallic lust). "Phallic lust is seen as a fusion of obsession and aggression. As obsession it specializes in genital fixation and fetishism, causing broken consciousness, broken heartedness, broken connections among women and between women and the elements. As aggression it rapes, dismembers, and kills women and all living things within its reach" (1984:1). In contrast to the anti-life lust, Daly uses the term to refer to intense longing, enthusiasm which "launches Wild women on Journeys beyond the State of Lechery" (p. 3). She looks to the word "lustre" to develop her notion of lusty women. Just as lust has two meanings to it, so lustre can mean a glossy shine or a radiance which shines through from within. She takes the second meaning and says, "lusty women long for radiant words, to free their flow, their currents, which like our own be-ing have been blocked and severed from ancestral Memory. The Race of Lusty women, then, has deep connections with the Race of Radiant Words" (p. 4). I shall pick up this thread in the exploration of sexuality and language in Chapter Three.

While Daly assumes a female (gynocentric) essentialism, she is well aware of the ways in which sexuality is constructed socially. Her novel use of language is part of her creative attempt to subvert patriarchy's construction of female nature. Her gynocentrism is an intriguing combination of essentialism and constructivism. It could be argued that her gynocentricism is a reactionary sexual essentialism: "the idea that sex is a natural force that exists prior to social life and shapes institutions" (Rubin 1984:275). I see it as a strategy to subvert patriarchal essentialism and constructivism. I do not agree, however, with Daly's claim that woman's nature is wholly different from man's. In my view, there is no single woman's nature or man's. Each person is an interactive process of subjectivity and intersubjectivity, within a larger ecosystem. I do agree, however, that when there is little or no opportunity for describing women's own experiences of themselves within existing frameworks of meaning, something radical has to be done. We need to speak from female subject positions. This means that sexual difference needs to be constructed with two equal terms, female and male. It is not sufficient to continue to frame femaleness as the *other* term in relation to maleness as the standard one.

Female subject positions are places occupied by women as ontologically normal persons in their own right. The occupation of these positions is required for women to enter into contracts as free individuals, whether it is marriage contracts, employment or citizenship contracts. Daly's reference to Toni Morrison's *Sula* is appropriate here. Morrison writes about Sula and Nel, two Black girls in Ohio, "Because each had discovered years before that they were neither white nor male, and that all freedom and triumph was forbidden to them, they had set about creating something else to be" (1987:52). The lust for be-ing requires thinking in new ways which will create more inclusive patterns of social organization. Part of the process of constructing new pathways is to unbind our minds by removing old ways of hearing. We can then listen to new possibilities. Listening to oneself is trusting oneself. It includes listening to messages from our sexed body as the place where spiritual vitality flows. In order to live positively with our sexuality we have to experience our bodied femaleness in a strong, affirming manner. We have to reject the negativity that has been attributed to female sexuality. We have to reject our alleged sexual deviance and live with our desire for separateness and connectedness. Those are initial conditions for overcoming our lack of entitlement to our own power and for beginning to respect/love ourselves. From that standpoint we can approach ourselves, the world, and spiritual powers in our own ways.

Judith Plaskow (1988) has formulated three important ways in which attitudes within patriarchy have circumscribed women's sexuality and spirituality. Although her analysis is of Jewish attitudes, it is generalizable. The three attitudes toward women's sexuality which are in need of exploration, as cited by Plaskow are: (1) the "energy/control" paradigm of sexuality; (2) the assumption that all sexuality is marital and heterosexual; and (3) the special place of women in the economy of sexual control (1988:1). Tension between women's sexuality and disciplined control of self (both women and men) is characteristic of cultures which are heavily influenced by male-centred religions. Sexual desire is acknowledged as a basic human desire while, at the same time, women's sexuality is associated with desires that cannot be controlled and which subvert culture (Freud, 1975). Plaskow points out that the control of women's sexuality has been effected through covering women, avoiding them, and containing them in domestic environments. The control of women's sexuality through marriage and women's roles in the family, including the normativeness of heterosexual marital sex, reflects common attitudes towards the purpose of women's sexuality. Plaskow claims that marriage and divorce signify the "acquisition and relinquishment of male rights to that sexuality" (Plaskow 1988:2). The control of women's sexuality is part of a profit-oriented society's attempt to strive toward the good, which is defined "in terms of profit rather than in terms of human need" (p. 4). Women's unpaid reproductive labour (physical and cultural) and low-paid labour outside the home contribute to the efficacy of the profit motive. Because of the place of women in the economy of sexual control there is a "need to define sexuality in fundamentally different terms" (p. 3).

In the spirit of Lorde and Daly, Plaskow says that sexuality is "a continuum of bodied self-expression . . . part of a spectrum of erotic energy that ideally suffuses all activities in our lives" (1988:4). Our body space is "literally the ground of our being" (p. 4). We cannot think of ourselves without thinking about our bodies. Indeed, if we accept that all ideas are inseparable from sensations, as argued in Chapter One, then it follows that we think through our bodies. That is not merely a mode of literary discourse.[2] Metamorphosis of consciousness through shape-shifting is a possible way of expanding our thinking through different bodies. It is axiomatic to say that our encounters with others are mediated through our bodies. For women this is especially poignant. Women's bodies play a larger part in their employment, promotions, and their social authority in general than do men's bodies (e.g., Naomi Wolf 1990). That is not to say that men's bodies are irrelevant with regard to hiring and promotions, among other indicators of social value. Tall men are often preferred to short men. Men's bodies, however, generally have significantly different connotations from women's. Theirs are more connected to images of physical strength and power to dominate, while women's bodies are more associated with images of seduction that distract or inspire men. Both women's and men's bodies are seen primarily in relation to men's evaluation of their worth, which may be internalized by women.

Power has a different meaning with respect to feminine and masculine images. The representation of women's bodies is a central issue with regard to women's roles in the economy, i.e., system of ordering, of sexual control.[3] By extension, the actualization of women's participation in being, requires a new approach to the role of the body in language. Comfortable feminine images of power are non-threatening, do not directly connote power. By contrast, images of Kali, the Hindu goddess of birth and death, have generally instilled fear of female creative and destructive power. Women's power to both create and destroy was displaced into a nurturing power that supports male power of creation and destruction. Women's bodies very often symbolize that form of nurturing power, the power to empower men. Women's power, when it does not do that is viewed negatively. The witch image is the exemplary 'antitype' image of women whose power is not directed primarily at supporting men's authority. Old women are sometimes referred to as hags. This denigrating term is a form of slander which devalues the existence of women when their sexuality is perceived to be no longer of service. Mary Daly's landmark effort (1987) at rewriting the meanings of terms like crone, hag, witch, spinster, and others is an empowering strategy as women reclaim their bodies and their identities in new ways. Daly's use of 'Lust' as the passion for being is a powerful symbol of women's bodied spiritual, vital energy. As the new definition enables women to feel lusty, the old feeling of being victimized by men's lust for women loses its grip. As that happens women begin to stand up and defend themselves. They get a new sense of living in their bodies as sexually autonomous persons. They begin to resist the representations of women's bodies in terms of the pervasive beauty myth that serves to divert women's attention from actualizing their potentials as whole and healthy persons.[4]

The body is an essential aspect of self-expression, including spiritual energy. Spiritual energy is understood here as an intense dimension of human potency and can only be experienced and expressed in the *bodied* consciousness of a person. It is the energy that eroticizes the sexuate body that is invariably part of each person's consciousness. Women need new ways to express their spiritual-sexual energy which are not controlled through heterosexism or a moral code that enervates their independent power of self-determination in their natural body forms. Living with feelings includes the ecstatic ones that arise from experiencing the body as the place of exchange between one's own energy and that of another, whether it is a woman's or a man's.

Because feeling states are inseparable from bodily sensations and bodily sensations belong to a sexed body, it is reasonable to conclude that spirituality and sexuality are interwoven in bodied consciousness. Indeed, it would be unreasonable to conclude otherwise. Spiritual energy is an intense form of vitality that extends the self toward others through the body. Judith Plaskow says, "We cannot suppress sexual feelings without suppressing our capacity for feelings more generally . . . [feelings are] the basic ingredient in our relational transaction with the world" (1988:4). In her view, "When we touch that place in our lives where sexuality and spirituality come together, we touch our wholeness and fullness of our power, and at the same time our connection with a power larger than ourselves" (p. 5). This is a goal of human encounter that is impossible to achieve when women's power of being is seen to be in need of control through legal measures and institutionalized regulation of female sexuality.

This account of women as spiritual and sexual subjects has significant implications for marital relationships as well as less intimate relations. Plaskow suggests that " 'marriage' will not be about the transfer of women or the sanctification of potential disorder through the firm establishment of women in the patriarchal family, but the decision of two adults—any two adults—to make their lives together, lives which include the sharing of sexuality" (1988:7). Within such a marriage the sharing of sexuality would be through renewed consent rather than legal and institutionalized blanket consent that legitimizes widespread asymmetrical gendered relations between male conjugal rights and female duties. As Carole Pateman (1988) points out, the marriage contract has served as a model for both employment and citizenship contracts. A shift towards the independence of female sexuality in the marriage contract would likely have major consequences regarding a shift in attitudes and practices toward women as employees and citizens. The converse is also true. If, however, one agrees that the social contract is modeled after the marriage contract that conceals the sexual contract, legitimizing men's access to women's bodies, then it is reasonable to conclude that heterosexual intimate relations, such as those in marriages, are at the heart of the social relations of the sexes in the public realm. Rather than analyzing family relationships from the perspective of the market place, it might be more 'profitable' to examine gendered employment and citizenship relations from the standpoint of the marriage contract. Although I take the sexual contract to be prior to the social contract, I do not posit a simple linear relation between the two. Each person's life is a composite of influences from public and private relations. The thread that runs through the composite system of relations, however, is the sex-specificity that shapes them. Wherever women and men are, their subject position is shaped by their sex, as it is experienced subjectively as well as by responses from others. Scepticism towards female social authority can only be eliminated by reconstructing female sexuality. This needs to be done in terms of ontological and social independency. An additional requirement is a corresponding ethic of sexual difference that recognizes female sexuality as one of two equal terms of sexual difference.

Bodied Consciousness

The view of Gayle Rubin that "we never encounter the body unmediated by the meanings that cultures give to it" is an ambiguous claim (1984:276-77). I agree that we can never give meaning to body feelings, form, or structure in an unmediated way. Meaning comes through language, a cultural product. It is important, however, to differentiate between placing body experiences into an existing linguistic meaning system and discovering that the experiences do not fit into the prior conceptual framework. The claim that we can never encounter our body unmediated by cultural inscriptions disallows alternative experiential gestalts of the body such as those experienced in visions or journeys. These alternative ways of experiencing one's own body as well as the bodies of others in the forms of animals, plants, and the natural elements of earth, air, fire, and water do not easily fit into the topography of our Western cultural system of language. As indicated by those who have so-called extraordinary experiences, our ordinary consciousness exists on a continuum with other forms of consciousness that constitute other kinds of realities (Young and Goulet, 1994). These experiences cannot be conceptualized adequately when they first occur because there is no language available for them.

I assume that consciousness includes two dimensions: prereflective, felt awareness and reflective awareness. All reflective awareness (ideas) includes felt awareness (sensations, or body feelings). It is possible to experience sensations which have no particular meaning at the time. We give them meaning by filtering them through an interpretive lens. Meanings attributed to the body are invariably socially and culturally specific. The coherence of our bodies is culturally inscribed. This means that the meanings we give to our bodies comes from the cultural language system in which we are located. That claim, however, does not commit us to the view that we never encounter our bodies except through existing conceptual meanings. Indeed, the Buddhist theory of ways of knowing includes the aim of overcoming the limitations of knowledge imposed by these cultural inscriptions. It is a well-known fact that bodily experiences initiate new ways of giving meaning that only later become coherent. For example, for one pregnant woman the first movement of the baby inside her was an unexpected stimulus for the reformulation of her identity. It was the first moment when she began to have an identity. Afterwards she was able to give the experience more meaning and to develop a more satisying view of herself as a person-in-relation. Another example of consciousness without adequate expression is the situation of an unanticipated flush moving throughout one's body in the presence of another person. This occurrence sometimes dramatically alters the meaning of the relationship without either person being able to articulate it clearly. The ambiguity of lived experiences is more pervasive than their clarity. This is largely due to body agency in consciousness.

Buddhist meditation (mindfulness) is a process aimed at transforming our relationships to feelings largely through emptying our minds of concepts and images that restrict our capacity to feel the moment, that is, to be conscious of it in both a prereflective and reflective way. As the meditator lets go of categorical conceptualization, the reflective process becomes more open to the prereflective body activity. The converse is also believed to be true. Attention to body states and feelings frees one from self-imposed and externally imposed expectations about how one ought to think or feel. Wisdom and compassion, the twin goals of Buddhist spiritual development, are believed to arise from emptying the mind of prescribed meanings that shape experiences into stereotypical patterns. Through emptying the mind of cultural inscriptions a person has space to think and feel in ways that are not determined so pervasively by stereotypical thought patterns.

Because it empties the mind of restricting categorical ways of thinking, Buddhist meditation is a helpful means to enter into shamanic journeying. In shamanic shape-shifting it is unlikely that existing cultural meanings are intrinsic to the experienced "metamorphosis." Interpretations of becoming a tree, for example, come after the reality of being the tree. The radical non-ordinary quality of such an experience renders the new perceptions incoherent in light of existing perceptions. One has to create new meanings through assimilating perceptions, which alter the existing ones. Through such experiences new thought patterns develop. It is conceivable that there are many different radical encounters with the body that do not reflect cultural inscriptions. To follow the lead of Luce Irigaray and Mary Daly, it is only when we do not accept cultural inscriptions on our bodies and in our psyches that we can move out of existing cultural paradigms towards more affirming attitudes and practices.

Transformation of a person's energy toward a more power-filled existence requires extended spiritual practice. Overcoming restrictive cultural inscriptions includes accepting one's own potency. The kind of knowledge that comes from encountering oneself in a less culturally inscribed way is reflected in Lynn Andrews' reference to a medicine woman, Agnes, who says, "There are no excuses for anything. . . . You change things or you don't. Excuses rob you of power and introduce apathy" (quoted in Christ 1987a:195). Mary Daly's admonition to women to live with their potency and metamorphize into whatever is required for the actualization of the desire for be-ing is at odds with the view that we are sociologically determined. I agree with Daly's approach that we start writing ourselves into the world from the standpoint of our embodiment as women with spiritual energy manifested through our sexuality.

Affirmation of body agency is about connecting the natural body with the social one. By natural body, I mean the concrete materiality of femaleness and maleness, or the exceptional cases where the two sexes are integrated in one body. Attention to sex-specificity affirms body agency and denies body passivity. By contrast, gender neutrality affirms body passivity and emphasizes the exclusive construction of identity through socially and culturally constructed meanings in language. As argued by Nancy Jay (1991), the social body is separated from the natural one in an approach that occludes sex-specificity in the interests of gender neutrality, which privileges male masculinity over female masculinity in our patriarchal culture. The meaning of gender depends on the sex of the gendered person. Androgyny is more about male masculinity than about female masculinity or female femininity or male femininity. Sex-specific maleness is the operative term in patriarchy. Accordingly, sex-specificity is the subject to be addressed rather than gender neutrality.

Jay points out that arguments for neutralizing sexual difference in the interest of gender neutrality require two incredible assumptions: "(i) that the body is neutral and passive with regard to the formation of consciousness, consciousness is primary and determinant—implicitly a rationalist view; and (ii) the important effects of the historical and cultural specificity of one's 'lived experience' are able to be altered, definitively, by consciously changing the material practices of the culture in question" (1991:143). She is using consciousness to mean ideas separate from felt sensations. That is a different meaning than the one being used throughout this text, i.e., as the interrelatedness of sensations and ideas. Despite this difference, I agree with Jay's view of the body as an active inscriber of cultural meaning through its interaction with reflection. It is unreasonable to argue for the passivity of the body in light of bodily experiences which shape ways in which we think, such as pregnancy and involuntary body flushes. Each person lives in their body in a particular way that partially constitutes their subjectivity and affects their intersubjectivity. Every woman who gives birth to a baby has something new to say about the subject of birthing. None of them is completely determined by cultural meanings of birth, although each of the births is experienced by the individual women in a culturally specific way. In the event of emotional body flushes, the same is true. There is a shared cultural-specific understanding of the body signal, yet the individual feelings and thoughts that underlie the body expression of the flush constitute an emotionally charged consciousness that includes both the prereflective and reflective components. Denial of the prereflective aspect amounts to being out of touch with oneself, a requirement for ignoring sex-specificity.

Because our bodies are our fundamental source of connecting energy, it is important that such energy is symbolized appropriately with respect to body images. The need for goddess imagery arises in conjunction with bodied spiritual consciousness. According to Carol Christ, power symbolized by goddesses "Is not power over, but a deeply relational power, which comes from understanding the connection of my power of being to that of all other life" (1987a:105). Her own experiences of goddess power symbolized by Gaia, Demeter, Persephone, and Aphrodite have led to an increased consciousness of connectedness for her. She says,

I have felt Gaia's presence most strongly in the caves of Greece, which once were known as her womb, the place of emergence and return, the place of communion with her deepest mysteries. Demeter and Persephone . . . their ancient mysteries promising to unlock the pain of separation and joy of reunion with my mother, and to communicate the secret of life, death, and rebirth. [In] Aphrodite . . . I recognize that the transforming power of sexuality is a mystery, never to be understood or rationally controlled, only to be experienced again and again in its cycles of joyous communion and separation. I have come to understand, as Sappho also did, that the powers evoked in sexuality open the deepest source of my creativity as a writer, a poet (1987a:109).

Why do women need the goddess? Christ claims it is because goddess power is about female power. This power is about the desire to be in the world in the lusty way described by Daly, the power to define one's desire. It includes the will to be proactive rather than merely reactive, with a goal of becoming fully human in a sex-specific way. Goddess consciousness is about initiating activity that encourages interactive participation. Both goddess and shamanic consciousness are about living with spiritual power that transforms energy into healing power. Sometimes Goddess spirituality and shamanic spirituality are discussed as if they are the same. Vicki Noble says, "Shakti women are human females who are feeling the call of the Dark Goddess—the deep, serious will-to-live arousing from within the body of the planet. This demanding energy of the Death Goddess—she who would destroy the old forms in order to make way for the new—is pushing through us for healing and the realignment with nature that needs to happen at this time" (1991:7). Noble's account of the Dark Goddess is consistent with Mookerjee's (1988) description of Kali, the Hindu Dark Goddess, and his claim that this is the Kali age. It is a time in which old patterns are being destroyed to make way for new ones.

The notion of paradigm shift reflects this process of moving into new interpretations or new realities. Carol Christ's description of the paradigm shift in the academy (1987b:53ff.) underscores the belief that we are in transition with respect to new knowledges and changing social patterns. Deconstructing the ethos of objectivity and constructing the ethos of eros and empathy characterizes the paradigm shift for Christ. She says,

[Eros is] a passion to connect, the desire to understand the experience of another, the desire to deepen our understanding of ourselves and our world, the passion to transform or preserve the world as we understand it more deeply. . . . Empathy is the ability to put ourselves in the other's place, to feel, to know, to experience the world from a standpoint other than our own. Empathy is possible because we have the capacity to make connections between our own experience and the experiences of others. Empathy means not simply recognizing the connections, but also the differences between persons, texts, cultures, whatever is being studied. (1987b:58-59)

The underlying assumption that shapes this developing form of knowledge is that interrelatedness is a condition of reality. The cultural meanings attributed to various patterns of interrelatedness are constructed through social and historical contexts. Social and cultural evolution take shape according to a dominant intentionality or ideology. In Riane

Eisler's (1987) well-known theory of evolution, we are moving out of the patriarchal ideology that is characterized by the intention to dominate, and towards the partnership ideology that is shaped by an intentionality of living through connectedness. The underlying intentionality that is associated with the three forms of spirituality central to this book—Buddhism, shamanism, and goddess spirituality, is interrelatedness, directed toward social egalitarianism. This intentionality does not exclude tensions between conflicting interests. Rather it is guided by an ethos of eros and empathy and its method is negotiation rather than domination through coercion. Negotiation in the face of differences requires taking differences into account when working towards equality so equality includes equality of differences. This is relevant to race, class, sexual orientation, age, ethnicity, language, and other socially influencing factors, as well as sex-specific bodies. The sex-specific body, however, is the focus here, as it is the place where all sites of social oppression are located for each person.

If women are to be independent persons at the negotiating table where new cultural meanings are constructed, their sex-specificity must be taken as one of two normal forms of humanity. In order to move towards equality of sexual differences we need to put new symbols of femaleness into place and give them significant cultural space in the construction of new knowledge. These symbols have to reflect the developing demand by women to occupy more psychological, physical, and cultural spaces in the new partnership paradigm. Cultural symbols reflect underlying evolutionary forces that direct social patterns of interaction. Anthropologist Clifford Geertz claims that "religious symbols shape a cultural ethos, defining the deepest values of a society and the persons in it" (quoted in Christ 1987a:117). Religious symbols for women in biblical history, for the most part, have not supported women's subjectivity or the possibility for women to occupy female subject positions, that is, places where they can speak as authoritative women and be received as normal women. Without adequate symbols of the divine within us, women tend to feel that they are not legitimate in their aspirations to go beyond restrictive cultural mandates characterized by feminine dependency. Power-filled female images are necessary for women to envision something beyond current cultural images and conceptions of femininity as they are imposed on females.

Celebration of women's sexuality, of women's bodies, leads to new social meanings of femaleness. One does not have to fall into a reductionistic essentialism in order to assume that the body is a place of personal agency which can possibly alter the impact of sociological determinism. Naomi Goldenberg argues for more recognition of the "corporeal ground of our intelligence" (1990:83). An important point made by Goldenberg is that the emphasis on cognition without reference to the impact of the "flesh" is extremely problematic for women. The strangulation of the body in the symbolic ordering of meaning has had devastating implications for women. Eating disorders such as anorexia and bulimia are rampant in our society. Dieting until you die has become a reality for many young women. Self-control and anorexia are closely linked. Amenorrhea (absence of the menses) is a consequence of anorexia. Control of the body in such cases includes stopping the periodic flow of blood and mucosal tissue from the uterus, a distinctively female characteristic which is associated with female engendering power. Goldenberg is right to draw attention to the negative implications for women of the separation of mind and body in the ethos of objectivity and domination. Her analysis, however, is exclusively materialist, without reference to spirituality. It is therefore only partially useful for the discussion here about the need for goddess symbolism.

As I argue elsewhere,[5] goddess spirituality goes beyond a materialist analysis of the relation between mind and body. It includes a dimension of personal agency that gains potency through participation in a power encountered through openness and receptivity to it in one's consciousness. Perceptions of goddess power are as diverse as perceivers. For those who encounter goddess presence, it would seem that there is a belief in the existence of goddess power apart from one's perceptions. Followers of Carl Jung, however, believe that spirituality develops as the unconscious is revealed to the consciousness. In that case, there is no requirement for belief in a spiritual power that exists apart from the unconscious or consciousness of individuals and collectives. It does not matter, for our purposes here, whether goddess power has an independent ontological status or whether it is entirely a creation of human psyches. It suffices to say that consciousness of goddess power alters perceptions of the body in self-definition.

Carol Christ says, "The symbol of Goddess aids the process of naming and reclaiming the female body and its cycles and processes" (1987a: 125). Attention to the female body, however, raises fears of biological determinism. Rather than viewing menstruation, birthing, lactation, and menopause positively as reflections of regenerative, life-giving, and life-taking power, these activities do not fit into a gender neutral approach to equality and are, therefore, often labelled 'special issues.' Equality in a gender neutral approach usually means women should be equal with men, beginning with men as the standard. Women's bodies, in that approach, remain deviant. Femaleness is the *other* term in the two terms of sexual difference. Women's engendering body power is denigrated. Indeed, as Ruether argues (1983), the fear and corresponding avoidance of female body power is at the heart of dualistic epistemology, with important implications for the ecology. The emergence of ecofeminism (ecological and feminist issues) is affirmation of the female body in conjunction with the regenerative, life-giving, and life-destroying powers of the earth (e.g., Ruether 1992). Acknowledging the powers of the female body does not entail assigning women to biologically determined destinies. Rather it moves women into a rightful status which legitimates their engendering power as sexual, rational, and spiritual persons. Acknowledging body power is to return words to flesh and to ground our intelligence in our corporeality, as Naomi Goldenberg suggests. I agree with her, but wish to go further to include the body as the place where our spiritual/erotic power of transformation is located. The value of goddess symbols for that purpose is expressed by Carol Christ when she says, "The Goddess as symbol of the revaluation of the body and nature thus also undergirds the human potential and ecology movements. The 'mood' is one of affirmation, awe, and respect for the body and nature, and the 'motivation' is respect for the teachings of the body and the value of all living beings" (1987a:126).

Respect for the body develops through listening to it. Christiane Northrup says, "When I speak of the wisdom of the body, I'm referring to a belief I hold that we must learn to trust that symptoms in the body are often the only way that the soul can get our attention" (1990:16). Northrup is an American medical doctor who specializes in obstetrics and gynecology. She says, "For the practice of gynecology and obstetrics to be healing for women in the deepest sense, we must understand the experience of being female in this culture and how it affects our bodies" (p. 16). The high statistics on rape, incest, and wife battering indicate the kind of sexual terrorism pervasive in North American society.[6] Northrup's claim that the practice of medicine does not often take into consideration problematic cultural attitudes and social conditions in which women live supports Daly's (1978) ground-breaking analysis of the anti-women attitudes inherent in gynecology.[7] Daly writes large what was heretofore unnoticed with regard to clinical practices, research, and interpretations of women's gynecological concerns. Her admonition for a woman-centred epistemology derives from her consciousness of the widespread anti-woman social attitudes and practices, which are undergirded by myths about the nature and purpose of woman.

Christiane Northrup regards bodily symptoms largely as metaphors for the cultural wounding of women. She believes that the pain of individual women is part of a collective memory of pain. She says,

I believe that we carry not only our own pain, but also that of our mothers and grandmothers, however unconsciously, in our own bodies. I have twice had a very vivid experience of this phenomenon, in which I entered a place I call 'the pain of women.' During this experience, I felt as though I was experiencing the pain and wailing of every woman who ever died in childbirth or who had ever been raped or lost a loved one. This knowledge felt encoded in my very bone marrow. . . . [S]ometimes body symptoms are the doorway into not only our own individual pain but also the collective pain. (1990:18)

Knowledge that is encoded in one's cellular system is like a collective unconscious that is passed down through the generations. We feel some of the things that our ancestors felt. It is shared knowledge that allows us to feel the joys and pains of others, being part of our individual conscience as well as a collective social consciousness.

Northrup's account of collective pain is consistent with the experiences of thousands of women in 1989 when fourteen women engineering students were singled out and killed at the Université de Montréal, Québec. They were killed, and many others were wounded, because they were women in an engineering class. The murderer wrote before he died that he hated feminists. His definition of feminist included any woman who was in a male-dominated area of work or study, regardless of her relation to feminism. The shop clerk from whom he bought the gun said the man appeared to be in a calm state of mind when he bought it. He apparently planned the mass murder for days in advance. He entered the classroom and ordered the men outside. They went. He then proceeded to shoot the women. Many say that it was the action of a madman, not to be associated with cultural attitudes and practices toward women. But as Australian singer Judy Small points out in a song, women go crazy too. She asks, "Have you ever heard of a woman killing fourteen men?" The pain of thousands of women was shared collectively around that fateful day, December 6, 1989. The day is now marked in Canada as a National Day of Remembrance. The massacre of the fourteen women has awakened the consciousness of many more individuals to the anti-women attitudes and practices which run as undercurrents and visible torrents in our society. People who go crazy usually act on the existing undercurrents of prejudice rather than inventing new ones. They write large what was there in small print.

Memory of the killing of the fourteen women in Montreal continues to be part of the pain of many women associated with sexual terrorism. It is part of their energy as they develop their own healing rituals. In Northrup's words, "it is indeed an act of political warfare to take care of our bodies" (1990:18-19). Healing our bodies is closely connected with overcoming painful social attitudes and activities concerning women's bodies, psyches, and citizenship participation. Spirituality is an important means through which the connection between our bodies and the world-as-body is made. Spirit-at-the-centre-of-the-world lies at the heart of honouring our bodies.

The value of goddess spirituality in positively connoting women's bodies is clearly argued by Charlene Spretnak (1991) who associates positive attitudes to women's bodies with the contemporary cultural shift toward living with the "Earthbody." Drawing from Peggy Reeves Sanday's anthropological work (1981), Spretnak says that in ancient cultures where food came from the earth or water there were positive attitudes to women's elemental power. By contrast, in cultures characterized by migration and the pursuit of large animals, the orientation was towards violence and domination. In those cultures nature was not considered sacred, something in which one shared in the mysteries of creativity. Ultimate power was not associated with the "Earthbody" but rather with a distant, transcendent male-imaged sky-god. From about five thousand years B.C.E. onwards, the importance of the sky-god escalated. In biblical history, for example (beginning around eighteen hundred B.C.E.), the earliest sky-god was Yahweh, the god of Abraham and his descendants. The exemplary sign of allegiance to Yahweh was, and continues to be, male circumcision, clearly excluding women.

Women's allegiance to Yahweh comes primarily through their relations to men. It is a second-order allegiance to a male-imaged god. Women's allegiance to god in such a structure is shown most appropriately through their roles as wives and mothers. Their sexuality is morally evaluated according to its service in those two roles. The good woman's sexuality, as well as her authority, is contained within the home. Women who challenge the confining of women's authority to the home are labelled Jezebels. The original Jezebel in biblical history was the wife of a ninth-century B.C.E. Israelite king, Ahab. She worshipped Baal, a Canaanite god who was the consort of Astarte. She refused to worship Yahweh and was therefore considered unrighteous. She was murdered (1 Kings).

Men claimed certain cultural spaces for themselves and excluded women from them, such as "the priesthood, higher education, law, medicine, business, government, the art world" (Spretnak 1991:116). Elemental powers of women were feared, denigrated, and controlled. Woman's "capability to grow people of either sex from her flesh, to bleed in rhythm with the moon, to transform food into milk for infants" (p. 116) was superseded by culturally constructed forms of power. Contemporary postmodernists' claims (e.g., Derrida) that the body can be known only through conceptualizations which are culturally constructed is antithetical to women's interests. Patriarchal symbolic constructions of meaning with respect to sexual difference, with maleness as the operative term and femaleness as the *other* term, is precisely the locus of the binary dualisms that shape social organization. To decentre subjectivity by nullifying the agency of the body is to continue to bury women under the layers of patriarchal cultural constructions.

The cultural construction of women's bodies that we have inherited from patriarchy is built on the premise that women are dependent because of their bodies. "Patriarchy" means "rule by the father." In patriarchy "men and women are socialized to understand that males should legitimately act as controlling cultural fathers, while females should appropriately act as dependent, obedient minors" (Spretnak 1991:116). To deny the value of sex as a category for analyzing power is to give the power to patriarchal cultural constructionists. It is to agree that culture determines nature without any impact of nature on the evolution of culture. I agree with Spretnak's view that one cannot claim to be outside patriarchal constructions while denying the elemental power of women's bodies and the "Earthbody." It was that denial which contributed towards social and cultural evolution characterized by domination and violence. I support the claim of Riane Eisler, Humberto Maturana,[8] Peggy Reeves Sanday, and Charlene Spretnak, to mention a few, that social and cultural evolution continues to be shaped by a dominant intentionality. The cultural shift to patriarchy included an intentional move away from female power associated with life-giving and life-taking activities. A cultural shift away from patriarchy requires an intentionality directed at integrating nature and culture in self-definitions as well as between human beings and the environment.

The notion of desire is often associated with a deviant drive that opposes rational will power. Women have been closely associated with such deviance and, therefore, have often been regarded with suspicion in so far as their will power is concerned. The separation of the powers of desire and will is part of patriarchal consciousness. The attempt to suppress desires connected to body consciousness became characteristic of anorexic views of the will as disembodied. The separation between desire and will is challenged in views of bodied consciousness, especially within feminist spirituality. Spretnak describes desire as a motivator that became "mutated into the desire for violence against desire" (1991:120). Men's will was to be governed by rational principles based in a transcendent, disembodied sky-god. Women were seen to suffer from lack of will because of their day-to-day activities, supportive of others who were allegedly more self-determining. Ironically, women's alleged weakness of will was defined as a feminine strength, adding to their vulnerability which was supposed to be attractive to men. The view of women as vulnerable by nature underscores the belief, a cornerstone of chivalry, that women need men to protect them. Women's alleged vulnerability is closely connected with the 'proper' expression of their sexuality. Patriarchal morality with regard to women's sexuality separates women's spirituality from their sexuality and subsumes both under male authority.

An outstanding example of the separation of spiritual consciousness from body consciousness in the interests of men's authority is found in the morality of Immanuel Kant, an eighteenth-century philosopher at the height of the Enlightenment. His construction of sexual difference and the associated ethics of sexual difference that he develops continue to impact negatively on the ontological, social, and ethical status of women. Kant was "awakened from his slumbers" by David Hume's claim that morality is motivated by desire and determined by historical phenomena. Hume denied there is a transcendent foundation for morality. Kant's *Grounding for the Metaphysics of Morals* (1981) is largely a response to Hume's claim that morality is motivated by human desire and social conventions. Kant argued that moral principles are the basis for free action and that they had to be located outside the world of historically changing conditions. He believed that moral responsibility required the grounding of morality in principles that could be established with certainty. In that way moral principles would take precedence over conventional whims. A person could then be justly held accountable for violation of the rights of others rather than excused because of socially determining conditions such as poor parenting or bad schooling.[9]

Freedom and responsibility, for Kant, were to be grounded in principles that could be ascertained through reason and applied universally. In his view, the experience of obligation implies the freedom to choose to do something or to not do it. When we feel obliged we experience the freedom to follow our conscience or to succumb to a desire that leads us away from it. If there is free choice there must be freedom. He believed that the freedom to act morally is inconsistent with historical determinism. According to Kant, expression of free will is the spontaneous expression of conscience, the will of god that is understood through reason. Reason, morality, and religion, for Kant, are pieced together into a single collage. Immortality is the reward for spontaneously loving one's neighbour as oneself and, thereby, expressing simultaneously one's own free agency and the will of god. Kant believed that free will, expressed through moral conduct, is necessary for human dignity. Human dignity is a dimension of self-determination. If one didn't know better, one would assume that Kant was referring to women and men in his discussion of human dignity. In his *Observations on the Feeling of the Beautiful and Sublime*, however, he has a different account of woman's nature. Indeed his autonomous person can only be a man. Kant says,

[Women know] nothing of duty, nothing of compulsion, nothing of obligation. . . . I hardly believe that the fair sex is capable of principles, and I hope by that not to offend, for these are also extremely rare in the male. But in place of it Providence has put in their breast kind and benevolent sensations, a fine feeling for propriety, and a complaisant soul. (Mahowald 1983:196, quoting Kant)

There are major problems with Kant's account of sexual difference and his ethics of sexual difference that is played out in the dictum "different but equal." One is that it is straightforwardly insulting to women. It is an egregiously unethical position that is embedded in one of the most influential ethical theories in Western philosophy. The ethics of sexual difference amounts to an ethics based on being reasonable for men and being devious for women. Second, the views of man and woman are explicitly unequal in social and cultural evaluation of human dignity. Women's power through sly glances rather than rational persuasion is a part of patriarchal culture in which sexual difference is constructed oppositionally. Devious power has been a means by which patriarchal women have exerted power. It is a method of resistance used by disempowered individuals in all social situations. It may have a short-term usefulness, however, in the long run it is counterproductive for those who engage in it. Women are often considered untrustworthy because of their deviousness. The cause of their deviance has been inappropriately attributed to their nature rather than to cultural and social circumstances that encourage it.

A third problem with Kant's account of the natures of woman and man is the one that has been critiqued most widely by feminists and other deconstructive postmodernists, namely, his idea of the autonomous person. The autonomous person as an end in themselves (i.e., subject) rather than an object to serve the interests of another is, I believe, a view of the self which is valuable for women in patriarchy. The problem is not with the notion of "end in oneself" but rather with the view of the autonomous self as a separate self modeled after the view of an omniscient and omnipotent transcendent god who is the supreme moral authority. This separate self model has fuelled patriarchal accounts of sexual difference and is foundational to the existing patriarchal ethics of sexual difference. The attempt by postmodernists to define reality exclusively in terms of text[10] is another patriarchal message to separate culture from nature and, thereby, to control nature through cultural constructions. Postmodernists, such as Jacques Derrida and Michel Foucault, aim to deconstruct this view of the transcendent subject. This postmodern interest in destabilizing the subject includes advocating multiple gender subject positions and doing away with the notion of subject or subjectivity. Such an exercise is problematic for anyone who has never been constructed as a subject and has never experienced speaking from their own subjectivity. In order to provide cultural space for women to speak as subjects in their own right rather than as women-for-men, it is necessary to retain the categories of 'subject' and 'woman.' Otherwise, men can continue to speak like women without listening to what women have to say and women will likely continue to speak from the position of responding to the desires of men. The issue here is to construct sexual difference differently so there are two normal terms in the discussion of sexual difference, with an ethics that underscores the human dignity of both women and men as ends in themselves, in relation to each other. This is a feminist project that goes beyond the postmodern one of shaking the foundations of the notion of subject, woman, or any other universal category of identity. It includes an attempt to construct a new cultural house of language in which the partnership of nature and culture is recognized. The shift towards a partnership model of evolution is supported by attention to sex-specificity in cultural constructions as well as to listening to the spirit-at-the-centre-of-the-world that is part of consciousness of self-and-world-as-body.

A view of self and the world that includes spirit emphasizes the importance of will as power. Power, i.e., the ability to use energy and to transform it from a negative to a positive form of expression,[11] is a manifestation of faith in life. This is in contrast to the notion of will to power in the sense of survival of the fittest. The will to live as an expression of personal power, in this view, is about living with the spirit-at-the-centre-of-the-world. It is an integrating power that facilitates openness towards others as well as an inward attention to one's own desires and intentions. Self-determination requires a will to carry out one's desires and intentions. In Carol Christ's view, many women have the "sense that their lives are defined not by their own will, but by waiting for others to take the initiative" (1987a:127).

Although women are taking more initiative, their efforts often mimic men's forms of initiative from within the dominator model of social relations, rather than from a more egalitarian perspective. An example of this is found in a local newspaper. It is about fourteen-year-old girls taking the initiative sexually with boys because the boys are "too dumb" to take the initiative. Instead of finding their own initiatives, they model them on the existing patriarchal initiatives. One result of this type of "initiative" is a continuing rise in teenage pregnancies. This example of women taking initiative does not illustrate self-determination in the sense of coming from a grounded sense of self in connection with spirit-at-the-centre-of-the-world. Rather it reflects a lack of self-determination. It is an example of girls taking initiative within a culture that says their power as girls depend on sexual relations with boys, regardless of the consequences to themselves. This example reflects a break in the connection between spirituality and sexuality in girls' subjectivity as well a a lack of female models of initiative.

Sometimes when young mothers act on their will with respect to self-determination our laws obstruct them. On the CBC news on February 12, 1992, we heard about an eighteen-year-old woman from Barrie, Ontario who decided to go through with an unwanted pregnancy because of religious beliefs. She planned ahead to allow the baby to be adopted so he/she would have a loving home. She and the nineteen-year-old father discussed and agreed on the plan. After the baby was adopted, the father decided he wanted to raise the baby. His father and he took the case to court. The court decision was to take the seven-week-old baby away from the adoptive parents for return to the mother. On the news broadcast we heard the mother crying and saying that she wanted the baby in a home with a mother and a father. She did not want to raise the baby as she wanted to develop a life for herself, knowing that the baby was well taken care of. She didn't want the baby to be raised by the father who lived either with his parents or alone.

Increased attention to fathers' rights is a double-edged sword. The woman bears and gives birth to the baby; there is a bonding process that often occurs. Her body and often her life is altered drastically during the process. At the same time, the father has some parental rights. Should they be equal parental rights? That is a good question. In my view, this is a situation where so-called equal rights privileges men in our patriarchal culture. This is an issue of sexual difference. The symbiotic relation between the body of the pregnant mother and the child growing inside her is an experience that only a woman can have. There is no comparable one for men. Experiences of pregnancy cannot be adequately discussed within a gender neutral framework of rights. Parental rights are legal issues which don't always deal with the sex-specific, even though pregnancy, birth, and lactation are exclusively sex-specific human experiences. I agree that rights of fathers must be taken seriously. These rights, however, make sense from the perspective of an ethic of sexual difference only when they are placed in a dialogical relation with the experiences of the people involved. In the case of pregnancy, women's body experiences are central. Human rights and human experiences need to be integrated so that the legal issues of parental rights deal adequately with women's bodied consciousness. If women's body experiences were taken as normal rather than as *other*, and if they were then adequately framed within cultural discourse as normal, then women's right to life and security of the person would logically include their body rights regarding pregnancy and childbirth. In keeping with the principle of sex-specific human dignity and treating each person as an end in themselves, fathers' rights also ought to be respected as fully as possible. In the end, though, the father's body is not as integral to pregnancy and childbirth as the mother's body. Accordingly, fathers' rights, if logical consistency prevails, will be decided with reference to the centrality of the mother's subjectivity in pregnancy. This is not to deny fathers' rights; it is merely to put them in perspective in an ethics of sexual difference, with a focus on personal integrity rather than ownership of property.

If women's bodies were taken as normal and women were considered one of the two equal ontological categories of human beings, then the term "special privileges" for women would be recognized as inappropriate.[12] It requires the prior assumption of male normativeness. Similarly, the notion of "illegitimate child" presupposes father rights over mother rights. If the mother was seen as a person in her own right, her child would invariably be born free of the social stigma of illegitimacy, which depends on the patriarchal construction of children belonging primarily to fathers. Women's legal rights over their bodies and the children they have from their bodies continue to be restricted by this underlying patriarchal orientation toward male ownership of females and their children as property. Paternal rights are formulated and interpreted largely from this perspective.

In order for women to live out their subjectivity as spiritually integrated sex-specific persons, a new ethics of sexual difference needs to be legally and socially implemented to facilitate the realization of women's full citizenship. The Legal Education and Action Fund (LEAF) and the Canadian Abortion Rights Action League (CARAL) are two Canadian organizations that aim to bring about changes in the legal system with respect to women's personal and property rights. CARAL is largely funded through private contributions, while LEAF is supported by the federal government as well as private donations. The government funding for LEAF's Charter Challenges Program was cut and then restored, following protests from women across the country when the cut was announced.

The Charter Challenges Program is designed to protect women who LEAF members believe have been violated according to the Charter of Rights. Financial and legal resources are basic requirements for women to actualize their wills. A disposition toward self-determination is coextensive with the material conditions that enable it. The two dimensions are integral to each other. Christ states that in a goddess-centred context "a woman is encouraged to know her will, to believe that her will is valid, and to believe that her will can be achieved in the world" (1987a:128). The idea of will here is not an independent will, but one that is energized and known largely through connectedness with the wills of others. One's will is affirmed in community. Such a "mood" of affirmation is seen to provide "motivation" to work with other women in life-affirming ways. It is part of "Be-Friending" (e.g., Daly 1989) women in general. Be-Friending is about providing the context of affirmation of women's wills so they can be exercised in their own ways. The existence of LEAF and CARAL, among other important feminist organizations, illustrates material realities that co-exist with women-centred empowering contexts which set the mood and activate motivations for facilitating the actualization of women's wills.

Social activism on behalf of women requires political solidarity among women. One aspect of cohesiveness for group identity is the existence of a shared heritage. Rituals help to remind us of shared participation of women in life events that many women experience. Spretnak's (1991) example of a prenuptial ritual is relevant here to illustrate the celebration of a woman's erotic power that she takes into her loving relationship with another. It is a power that not only belongs to her but is part of her ontology as a woman and which she participates in with other women. The ritual focusses on the wonder of the woman's erotic power and the beauty of the power that she takes into the forthcoming marriage. It is a ritual about women-for-women who bring their strong subjectivity into relationships.

As Spretnak describes it, the ritual begins with the women forming a circle and invoking the presence of the four directions. The table in the centre of the circle is covered with flowers, candles, figurines, shells and other objects which had significance to the women. They bless the water, symbolizing the flow of love. They bless the fire so that passion would burn. The air is blessed for purification of the new beginning. They bless the earth so the relationship would remain grounded. They invoke the presence of several goddesses: Isis, Astarte, Diana, Hecate, Demeter, Kali, Inanna, Hera, and Aphrodite. Blessings are offered by each woman. A journey of transformation is embarked upon, sloughing off and renewing her identity. She eventually is led into the "grotto" along a path of rose petals. The women chant. The grotto is "filled with a profusion of flowers, numerous candles, and fragrant incense. Her warm bath of water and scented oils is sprinkled with petals, and she is left alone to immerse as gently lilting music plays" (1991:148). When she returns to the group they rub her body with oils while reading "poems of eros" near her ear. Near the end of the ritual they dress her in "an extravagantly beautiful sleeping gown" and then bless her further. Finally they break the circle and "eat voluptuous fruits and cakes" (p. 148).

This was a ritual of bonding and connecting with women's heritage of women coming together before the marriage of one of them. It bears little resemblance, however, to the patriarchal "showers" that emphasize showering the bride-to-be with household implements that will facilitate her domestic role. The celebration of the bride-to-be as a person with her own special powers to take into the relationship differs significantly from the focus on her role as a wife or household manager. The ritual described by Spretnak enables women to "come to their senses" in a fully conscious way. Such a consciousness is referred to by Spretnak as a state of grace: a bodied and deeply connected way of knowing. It is "a consciousness of awe from which negative mind states are absent, from which healing and groundedness result. For these reasons grace has long been deemed 'amazing'" (1991:26). This ritual and others like it provides a means whereby women can experience themselves as power-filled with the awe-fullness of a graced consciousness that connects women with women, as well as with men, in a self-directed and connected way as permeable selves. In a patriarchal culture it is a major challenge for a woman to experience herself with a sense of awe.

Reflections in the Mirror: From Artifact to Artist

Activities of Be-Friending, such as the ritual described above, provide a context in which women can "speak into the silence so that our many voices might begin to be heard" (Brock 1989:237). Another form of Be-Friending is described by Rita Nakashima Brock in her discussion of Asian American women and the use of the mirror as a means of reflecting women's subjectivities. She writes of the importance of women mirroring back the suffering of the speaker who speaks into the silence. She tells us about the caves of silence that Asian American women are pushed into through such structures as language, racism, sexism, and religion (1989:236). If we are to heal ourselves we must first embrace our own suffering. Sharing our suffering enables others to mirror it back for us to see it. Brock uses the metaphor of the mirror in her discussion of women speaking to each other from their caves of silence because "the mirror is one of the most sacred symbols in Shinto" (p. 235). Special mirrors are passed down from mothers to daughters. "A good mirror tells us the truth about ourselves and through its illuminating power gives us wisdom, the wisdom that comes with self-awareness and knowledge. Without a true mirror, we cannot know ourselves. And without mirrors we remain in caves of silence" (1989:235-36).

The Japanese myth of the Sun Goddess, Amaterasu, is described by Brock as a source for revisioning the use of the mirror as a reflector of inner demons as well as positive powers. In the myth, Amaterasu retreated into a cave, full of anger and hurt because her younger brother had desecrated her sacred places. After a long period of no sun, the community of gods hung a mirror at the front of her cave. Another goddess, Amenouzume, does a shamanic dance which brings Amaterasu to the mouth of the cave. She is fascinated by her image in the mirror. She sees her suffering and her power and is drawn into herself. While she is reflecting on her reflection the gods block her passage back and she is forced to remain out of the cave. Her relationship to her emotions of anger and sadness is transformed and she is once again the compassionate Sun Goddess. The sun returns to the community. The mirror is associated with the reflection of inner pain which must be embraced in order for healing to occur and compassion to be expressed. Shamanic trances are used in Asian religions to "reveal the spirit through the integration of feeling, thinking, and sensuality" (Brock 1989:241). Brock points out that shamanic trances (alternative forms of consciousness) were participated in equally by women and men earlier in Japanese history. The emergence of male dominated shamanism is believed to mark the rise of patriarchy in Japan (1989:241).

The relation between the sex of spiritual leaders and the gendered power relations in society is closely correlated in studies which trace the rise of patriarchy.[13] As Miriam Robbins Dexter points out, with the rise of patriarchy the three-tiered caste system evolved: priests and scholars, warriors, and nurturers. Social leadership is supported by the nurturers and protected by the warriors. Spiritual healing was a form of social leadership in prepatriarchal societies. With the emergence of patriarchy, those social spaces were prohibited to women. Spirituality became increasingly marginalized and separated from socially respected methods of healing. The rise of the medical profession in industrialized countries sealed the fate of women's spiritual healing. During the last twenty years in Canada there has been a renaissance of spiritual healing, with women leading the way through goddess-oriented spiritual healing. The use of the mirror as a reflector of hidden emotions such as fear, anger, sorrow, joy, and compassion is part of goddess and shamanic traditions. It is a tool which is useful both metaphorically and concretely in the process of constructing self-identity. In patriarchal cultures, such as in North America, the mirror has been associated largely with women's vanity. Vanity, along with many other feminine ascriptions, is being deconstructed. Women's lack of confidence rather than an overwhelming self-appreciation is seen as their motivation for the extensive use of mirrors. The mirror, in patriarchal cultures, is more often a reflector of discrepancies between culturally defined standards of feminine beauty and a woman's physical appearance. Recent attempts to re-image the mirror as a positive tool for the construction of identity through reflection of inner subjectivity is one path toward more positive bodied consciousness for women. Mirroring each other in rituals or in ordinary relations is part of Be-Longing. It is a way of participating energetically in each other's Be-ing, a way of living with one's energy. The fact that we can never see our own faces means that we are dependent on some kind of reflecting process for self-identity throughout our lives. Most often the reflecting process is interpersonal. Sometimes, however, it is between oneself and the mirror as reflector of personal energy, i.e., erotic power.

The use of the mirror is often written about differently by men than by women. Jenijoy La Belle says that "It is no accident that male poets, such as John Updike, Jonathan Swift, and Lord Byron, rhyme 'mirror' with 'error,' since for them the glass does not directly reveal the self." By contrast, La Belle points out that for female poets, such as Sylvia Plath, 'mirror' corresponds with 'terror' (1988:23). Compare John Updike's and Sylvia Plath's poems, both called *Mirror*. John Updike's reads like this with the words in the left column mirrored in the right one:

When you look	kool uoy nehW	
into a mirror	rorrim a otni	
it is not	ton si ti	
yourself you see,	,ees uoy flesruoy	
but a kind	dnik a tub	
of apish error	rorre hsipa fo	
posed in fearful	lufraef ni desop	
symmetry.	.yrtemmys	(1988:22)

Sylvia Plath's reads:

Now I am a lake. A woman bends over me,
Searching my reaches for what she really is.
then she turns to those liars, the candles or the moon.
I see her back, and reflect it faithfully.
she rewards me with tears and an agitation of hands.
I am important to her. She comes and goes.
Each morning it is her face that replaces the darkness.
In me she has drowned a young girl, and in me an old woman
rises toward her day after day, like a terrible fish. (La Belle 1988:1)

The identification of self with the reflection in Plath's *Mirror* contrasts sharply with the distance of self from reflection in Updike's. In Plath's poem the mirror is used to construct the self as well as to reveal it. In Updike's poem there is an 'apish error' which reflects slippage between the perception and perceiver. The perceiver is the object of the perceiver's perception. The separateness of the identity of the self from the reflected image is assumed in Updike's account of the mirror image. This lack of identification with the reflection in the mirror is illustrated further in the writing of Christopher Isherwood, *A Single Man* (1964). After getting out of bed and shuffling around doing morning bathroom activities, the man stands in front of the mirror. "What he sees there isn't so much a face as the expression of a predicament" (1988:22, quoting from Isherwood 1964:7-8). The reflection is of the man's present situation, the consequence of a personal history. The reflection is something to look at. It is not a thing with which to identify. The perception of the reflection does not affect the self-consciousness of the "shambling" man any more than Updike's man is affected by the reversed image that he depicts in the aesthetics of his poem.

La Belle notes the limitations of a mirror for both women and men and then she points to a significant difference between the ways in which women and men relate to the mirror. She says, "The external presence registered by the glass can never be more than a sign of a reality which is within, but different in kind from, that sign. What is remarkable . . . about so many women in front of mirrors is that the image in the glass *is* the character, the personality, the soul" (1988:22). The difference is between the impersonal attitude that most men have toward the image and the deeply charged personal one of many women. The mirror is not such an important tool in the construction of male identity as it is in female identity. That may be one reason why it has not been a subject of study with respect to women's bodies and knowledge. The mirroring stage, as discussed by Lacan and others, is an infantile stage. Mirroring as a metaphor (e.g., Rorty 1979) has been used effectively in constructionist accounts of the self. The mirror as a concrete tool in the construction of self throughout a lifetime has not been much of a subject in research. It is only recently that it has become a topic of exploration in theories of self-knowledge, especially with regard to women.

When the mirror is used as a reflector of the look of men that women often internalize, it serves as a form of personal disqualification for women. It instills anxiety. When that happens, a woman often forgets to look *into* herself. She is busy looking *at* herself through the eyes of a special man or perhaps representations of women's beauty, as expressed in the public culture of media, films, magazines, and fairy tales.

When women have men on their eyeballs, so to speak, it is very difficult to see through their own female lenses. Women might very well see themselves as deficient because it is a rare occurrence for a woman's actual physical presence to correspond with patriarchal culture beauty ideals. Women often attempt to bridge the gap between ideal perfection and their own images by spending more time in front of the mirror. According to Naomi Wolf (1990), pressure on women is increasing to meet impossible standards of culturally determined feminine beauty in order to qualify for jobs. The male look of approval or disapproval can make or destroy a woman's career plans.

The activity of men looking at women is not symmetrical with that of women looking at men, in situations where men dominate over women's sexuality, economics, and the legislation, interpretation, and enforcement of citizenship rights. A consequence of the imbalances in power relations between women and men is that the look between men and women often instills uneasiness and sometimes terror in women, while those are appreciably less prevalent experiences for men. Men sometimes say that they wish they would be treated as sexual objects. I have only heard that from men who are in relatively powerful positions. I have not heard that wish expressed by any young men who were treated as sexual objects by women in more powerful positions. The young men generally worry about the negative consequences if they do not comply with the uninvited advances from the women whose power over them can have serious consequences. These men, like women in similar positions, experience this uninvited attention as a limitation on their freedom, i.e., they experience being harassed. While some men are unjustly subjected to harassment, the normalization of the male sex-right in patriarchal culture continues to result in greater harassment of women by men. The male sex-right is about men's access to women's space, whether by actual physical intrusion of her, through the gaze that takes in a woman's body at a glance and encloses her within the frame of the gazer's interests, or by pushing into conversation and manipulating it with little or no regard for her desire to be part of it. The assumption of male sex-right co-exists with the belief that normal women want men's attention above all else. Patriarchal culture reinforces this belief in the minds of both women and men. Asymmetrical power relations between women and men are hidden in the male gaze, which is an expression of patriarchal male sex-right.

Julien Murphy (1989) contrasts the analyses of "the look" of Jean-Paul Sartre (*Being and Nothingness*) and of Adrienne Rich (*The Dream of a Common Language*, *A Wild Patience Has Taken Me This Far*, and *Your Native Land, Your Life*). Both Sartre and Rich claim that movement from oppression requires seeing with new eyes. The problem is, as Murphy states, "What fresh views of ourselves can we develop—without illusion—while existing within societies which assert emphatically that we are less than men?" (1989:102). Murphy's question presents a justified scepticism with respect to women using the mirror to reflect their own self-worth in light of the male gaze. Sartre's analysis of 'the look' did not include a gendered power analysis. He takes the individual to be an abstract reality and assumes a symmetry in 'the look' between them. Sartre believed that each person objectifies the other through 'the look.' The assertion of self as subject, for Sartre, reduces the other subject to the "other," that is less than oneself as subject. Intersubjectivity, in this view, is a form of competition to retain the self as subject, moving out of immanence toward transcendence. Preservation of self meant, for Sartre, keeping the other at a distance, in order to avoid self-loss. In his view, self-loss inevitably occurs through intimate encounters. Reaffirming one's subjectivity includes looking back at the other as separate from oneself. This is a separate-soluble self model. It does not allow for expansion through relation as entailed in the permeable self model. For Sartre, two subjects looking at each other are assumed to be in an equal stand-off.

He never considered the difference between men looking at women and women looking at men within a social system structured by asymmetrical power relations. He did not include an analysis of males gazing at women's bodies on streets, in classrooms, in boardrooms, in examinations, on assembly lines, in the stacks of libraries. Rich says, "How many men have touched me with their eyes more hotly than they later touched me with their lips" (Murphy 1989:102, quoting from Rich 1975). Sartre's analysis of 'the look' has nothing to say about a woman walking down the street in a business suit, carrying a briefcase and not paying attention to the men working in a "manhole" on the sidewalk when suddenly she is whistled at, looked at from the perspective of the hole in the street, and hearing her body commented on by the three men in the hole. These experiences are often reflected back into a woman's consciousness as she sees herself in the looking glass through the eyes of men, through "the look." While for Sartre there is a mutually oppressive look of the other in intersubjectivity, for Rich the oppressiveness of the male look for the female often means she cannot look back.

A theory of self that ignores differences between women selves and men selves is a deficient theory as well as a damaging one. It is damaging because it renders important life experiences invisible in the analysis. When experiences of a group of individuals, such as women, are made invisible through so-called gender neutral theories, those experiences are not counted as subjects for investigation. Knowledge of such experiences is not included in the theorizing, which is in fact male subjectivity written into so-called neutral theorizing that is supposed to have universal value. Women often find that their experiences do not fit with theories about how they are supposed to think, feel, and act. It is unethical to deduce from this that women have the problem. In the interests of a social ethics that recognizes women's subjectivity as one of two forms of human subjectivity, it is necessary to pay attention to the spiritual, physical, and intellectual self-determination of women as well as men when theorizing about 'human nature' and human activities.

The diminishment of women's power through the male gaze is responded to variously by women in different cultures. For example, Muslim women who cover themselves more or less thoroughly so as not to be seen by men sometimes associate their dress with their own power to see without being seen. They interpret their culturally prescribed mandate to cover themselves as an opportunity to express their power over men by remaining illusive and less subject to scrutiny. One could say they are resisting the male gaze or are turning it to their advantage. This interpretation might be viewed as a form of resistance rather than submission. Covering the female body, however, so it cannot be seen by the male gaze does not challenge the right to the male gaze as an objectifier of women. Women covering their heads and limbs as well as the rest of their bodies might be seen more in terms of accepting the objectifying look and implicitly legitimizing it.

Women in North American culture perform acts of resistance to men devouring them with uninvited lustful looks. For example, in the film *Frankie and Johnny* two waitresses conspire to 'accidentally' spill a jug full of cold water into the crotch of an annoying male professor customer who was hitting on one of them. Devious forms of resistance are common among oppressed groups. Dealing directly with the problem often compounds it rather than stopping it. Perhaps it is more appropriate to see it as a survival technique for oppressed persons who do not have sufficient power to confront more socially powerful persons with the injustices they are perpetrating. Using the male gaze to their own advantage is a strategy for survival among women in limiting conditions. For example, in the film *Alice Doesn't Live Here Anymore*, the long-time waitress tells Alice who has just arrived to work in the diner, that she will get better tips if she undoes another button on her blouse so more of her cleavage shows. Economics and sex are probably the two most important forms of oppression for women in patriarchy. It is not surprising that sex is used to improve a woman's economic position, whether it is in heterosexual marriages, prostitution, in the mainstream paid labour force, or in eateries. Men seem surprisingly willing to pay for sex or some facsimile of it. The domination of women's sexuality by men means that there is widespread victimization of women by men with respect to sexual relations. This does not mean, however, that there is necessarily a predominance of a victim's mentality among women. Structural victimization and individual psychological victimization can be differentiated, although they often occur together.

I have been describing structural victimization of women's sexuality. Women who have some self-esteem and who defend themselves against the sexual aggressions of men are often not applauded. Two movies in which women resist the male right of access to female bodies are *Nuts* and *Thelma and Louise*. The protagonist in *Nuts* is encouraged by her lawyer, family, and friends to plead insanity for accidentally killing the man who was attempting to rape her. She refuses to plead insanity and insists on justice. She claims it was a matter of self-defence and is prepared to take the consequences. She rejects the view that women must be crazy to defend themselves. She fights her way through the court proceedings and wins her case. Most of her family and friends have abandoned her by the end of the proceedings.

Rather than taking an isolated incident, like the rape and murder case pertaining to one woman's life, to make a point about women legitimately defending themselves against violence, the film *Thelma and Louise* is about the pervasiveness of male aggression in the everyday lives of women. It portrays the subjection of women who work in the home, work as waitresses, and women who are raped because they are attractive and friendly. The two women, Thelma and Louise, were going on a short weekend trip to get away from the unhealthy conditions in which they were living and working, most of which had to do with their relationships to their male partners. On the road trip, Thelma is raped outside a diner where they stopped for a break. The man who rapes her is a local sexual nuisance. Both he and Thelma drink too much, dance together, and arouse his lust. She wants to call it quits but he persists. She resists his unwanted advances and he begins to rape her on top of the hood of a car in the parking lot, where they had gone to get some air. Louise shows up in the middle of the rape scenario. She puts a gun to his head (one that Thelma had brought for protection at the isolated cottage they were supposed to stay at). He releases Thelma at gunpoint, but uses macho language that obscenely reflect his claim to the male sex-right. His attitude and behaviour triggers bad memories in Louise. She loses control and shoots him, killing him immediately. She is sick afterwards. Her rage is against men's sexual aggression towards women, stemming from her own rape as well as from the general pervasiveness of male abuse of women. As the film progresses, bad events accumulate and they drive intentionally into death over the edge of the Grand Canyon to get away from the guns of the state troopers.

The movie is sometimes referred to as a feminist manifesto about hating men. Women who defend themselves against male violence are often accused of hating men. It takes a great deal of courage to resist cultural pressures to remain a victim. It is difficult to take responsibility for one's well-being in the face of disapproval from men and women who share the view that women's sexual, economic, and social dependence on men is a good thing. Independent women who defend their rights as self-determining persons are often targets for slander and exclusion.

The expectation that women ought to satisfy male desire when it is expressed either forcefully or peacefully is integral to the asymmetrical look from men to women. The reward and punishment system is organized to a certain extent around 'the look.' Women's bodies play an important role in their self-construction; consequently women's self-identification is often shaped significantly by the male gaze. Sometimes women equate desiring looks from men with their self-worth. If a woman depends on men's approving gazes for her own self-approval, it is difficult for her to see what is problematic about those gazes. The possibility that her self-determination might be undermined by her dependency on such an external approval, indeed a culturally pervasive kind of approval that mandates her dependency, is foreign to her mind set. Without an analysis of gendered power relations it is difficult for women to see that their own powerlessness is likely to be reinforced rather than enhanced through the asymmetrical look from men to women. Sartre also missed the point. His main concern was the polarization of Subject and Other in the preservation of Self as Subject. Postmodern attempts (e.g., Foucault) to decentre the Subject are largely responses to a view of the self such as the one described by Sartre. It assumes a separate self that is invariably in tension with other separate selves. Feminists generally assume a connected self, in some form. Accordingly, the project of decentring the self is not embraced by all feminists, including myself. The preferred project is constructing a centred self.

In light of Simone de Beauvoir's (1953) ground-breaking analysis of the construction of woman as Other in patriarchy and the consequent feminist analysis which has been built on that insight, the issue of the internalization by women of the male look is central to the construction of self-identity for women. Not all women are affected the same way by the male gaze. Some internalize it, others react against it, some ignore it as much as possible, and others deny its relevance to their lives. Its pervasiveness in patriarchal culture, however, cannot be ignored. In Murphy's words, "The destructive nature of the look lies in its capacity to annihilate the freedom of the individual who is looked at" (1989:104). The mirror often serves as a signifier of the look which negates the independent subjectivity of women. Women glancing into mirrors can be understood as reflecting their insecurities more than their vanities. La Belle sees the internalizing of the male gaze as having the effect of turning women into artifacts rather than artists (1988:170). They look at their reflections/themselves as constructions through the eyes of others. Their own agency is hidden from them. Indeed, as artifacts, the existence of their agency is in question. It is unlikely that anyone would experience themselves totally devoid of artistry, i.e., creativity, but women's widespread low self-esteem is conducive to self-objectification as artifact. In order for the mirror to reflect one's agency it is necessary to include the notion of artistry in self-identity.

As I have argued elsewhere,[14] the usefulness of the mirror is that it can give us a vision of the groundedness of our consciousness in our body. La Belle discusses the character Connie in D.H. Lawrence's *Lady Chatterley's Lover* (1928) with respect to the freedom that the mirror can provide for women in their own self-discovery and construction. "When Connie went up to her bedroom she did what she had not done for a long time: took off all her clothes, and looked at herself naked in the huge mirror. She did not know what she was looking for, or at, very definitely, yet she moved the lamp till it shone full on her" (La Belle 1988:174-75, quoting from Lawrence 1928:72). La Belle interprets this gesture as an act of Connie exploring herself "in terms given by her own body—rather than in terms established by the mirror as a representative of societal values" (p. 175). She is looking at her body as something which presents itself as it is to the world, to her own consciousness. She can take that identification of self with her reflection as new, bodied knowledge that informs her participation in the social world. The constructive use of the mirror in this way is continuous with affirmative mirroring from others. Lovers, for example, love themselves more through loving each other. Experiencing love of one's own body through another's love of it is similar to affirming oneself through identification with the reflected image from the looking glass. It is not a matter of evaluating one's image in terms of its proximity to an ideal but rather of an expression of one's immanent and erotic power, power to transform oneself into artist from artifact. Included in self-transformation is the transformation of others with whom one interacts as agent. The mirror can be an important part of the transformative process from artifact to artist. It is not necessarily a tool to be used in solitude. Some women's groups use mirrors as ways of facilitating discussion of self-reflections. Through shared self-reflections our perceptions are altered with respect to ourselves and each other.

The identity of oneself with the image in the mirror is an illustration of the interrelatedness of a person's way of being (ontology) and perceiving (epistemology). The relation between the image and the corporeal consciousness is mutually informing. One's otherwise hidden subjectivity is reflected back, informing it. The process of reflection affects the content of the image and the corporeal consciousness. In other words, the mirror is a means for seeing the inseparability of the way things are (i.e., the real) and how they are perceived. This is consistent with a central insight of Buddhism, namely, that the objects perceived, the sense perceptions which convey the presence of the objects to a person's consciousness, and the interpretive process simultaneously constitute reality for any person. The mirror can be used as a reflector of social values in which the self is experienced as artifact or as a tool for construction of the self as artist, depending on the consciousness of the woman looking into the mirror. In our society, special effort is required for women to be free of the male gaze and to create space for positive consciousness which is not merely a reaction to limiting identity narratives.

A spiritual consciousness in which one's creative energy is grounded in an infinite referent such as goddess energy, nature power, spirit-at-the-centre-of-the-world, etc., provides a mindfulness towards self as a process of creativity. From a spiritual perspective, the awe and respect that is part of "amazing grace" might be reflected in the image of the mirror. An attitude of wonder characterizes this kind of spiritual awareness of self and is commensurate with a sense of gratitude. The Buddhists have a story that expresses this awe-filled view of the self. It is about the staggering odds against any one person actually coming into existence and the appropriateness of feeling grateful for being born. The story is about a turtle swimming under water in a vast ocean. An inner tube is floating aimlessly on the ocean. The turtle and the inner tube are entirely independent of each other. At a particular moment, the turtle is required to come up for air. Coincidentally, just as the turtle surfaces for air the inner tube floats by and the turtle's head emerges from the water through the centre of it. The miraculousness of this moment in the turtle and inner tube metaphor is intended to parallel the unlikeliness of a particular person's birth. Gratitude is regarded as an appropriate response to the fact of one's existence. This is characteristic of "graced consciousness" where one sees oneself as a gift to be entrusted to oneself. The mirror can be a tool to reflect self-trust, especially with regard to women's bodies. Tools help to develop skills. The mirror can facilitate the re-membering of corporeality in consciousness from the perspective of the insider, that is, the bodied consciousness reflected in the mirror that is irreducible to an external gaze.

Bringing our flesh into consciousness has extraordinary implications for women. To ground our consciousness in our bodies is to deny the power of patriarchal culture in which women must deny their bodies to participate in social authority. Bodied consciousness is not about restricting women's activities to domesticity and nurturing men as warriors and social leaders. It is about knowing ourselves as women, as one of two normative forms of humanity. It is not about being a woman in a restricted sense of biological determinism. It is about receiving an infinite variety of otherness in one's identity as one exists as a permeable self. The construction of oneself as a woman occurs within a bodied consciousness. As Terence Penelhum has clearly pointed out, it would seem that most of us believe in bodied knowledge and can make very little sense of disembodiment at all (1970). Although he was exploring the notion of disembodiment in the context of discussing life after death, his point is relevant to life before death. Penelhum's argument against the coherence of disembodiment can be extended to the notion of disembodied knowledge. The development and sharing of knowledge occurs among bodied folk. Self-knowledge is the pre-eminent form of bodied knowledge. One is self-conscious before knowing that one knows about anything else. Accordingly, all knowledge is bodied knowledge. I assume that knowledge implies a knower. That assumption excludes the possibility of pieces of knowledge existing like birds in a cage to be plucked out when needed for an argument (as, for example, in Plato's *Theatetus*). Self-knowledge is required for self-construction. If all knowledge is bodied knowledge, then self-consciousness is bodied consciousness.

Postmodern attempts to deny bodily agency in the pursuit of gender neutrality is a contemporary twist to 'modern' dualism. It supports the patriarchal flight from women's bodies in the search for transcendent, immaterial knowledge. To claim there is nothing apart from the text, that the body can never be experienced apart from the cultural meanings attributed to it is to affirm the separation of culture and nature through an implicit assumption of disembodied knowledge. In contrast, returning flesh to consciousness brings women as full-bodied knowers into the symbol-making process. The mirror as a subordinate instrument in the larger process of social mirroring is one way of learning about ourselves as bodied agents who project transformative energy through our physicality. As the learning process evolves in each person's bodied consciousness, the image in the mirror transforms from artifact to artist.

Female Potency and Engendering Activities

Creativity that arises out of the positive potency which is inherent in women's sexuality, rationality, and spirituality is 'Lusty' power. It is erotic power that mobilizes engendering activities through love. 'Lust' is the love of life and the disposition to actualize lively potentials. Actualization of individual potency is an engendering process that includes epistemological and ethical responsibilities. Experiencing one's own sexuality, rationality, and spirituality as interdependent is a form of personal integrity. Knowing that one's integrity is part of the improvisatory process of interpersonal relatedness is basic knowledge out of which arises basic respect for the integrity of others. Expressions of personal integrity are engendering activities in which others participate and gain greater balance, thereby providing support for one's own centredness. Centredness of self requires community connectedness. A person's community may be relatively fixed in identity or it may be constituted by relations that are varied and intermittent. I am using the notion of community in the sense of friends of mind, soul, and body. Engendering power is most importantly about persons creating community. Leadership is an expression of the power to do this.

Occasionally women's engendering power in its totality is recognized in the form of social leadership. Karen McCarthy Brown describes her research on women's leadership in Haitian Vodou in Haiti and in Brooklyn (1989, 1991). She found that there were two main characteristics of the women who were supported by the communities as their leaders: freedom and responsibility. These women emerged as leaders in communities where the "social control of the patriarchal extended family" (1989:226) had broken down. Brown points out that following Haiti's slave revolution (1791-1804) patriarchal culture prevailed in most of the communities, with men as spiritual leaders. Recently, especially in the more urban areas, with the breakup of patriarchal families women are the authorities and often the major breadwinners. The correlation between spiritual leadership and freedom from sexual and economic domination is obvious in her research, especially with reference to Mama Lola. According to Brown, Vodou priestesses have heavy social responsibilities. Their main function is to restore balance to the community when tensions become disruptive.

Brown's research shows that Haitians accept conflict as a basic fact of life. There is no attempt to deny it; rather, the point of rituals is to reduce tensions between differences. From Brown's perspective, Vodou is about healing relations between people and between people and the spirits. She believes the focus on relationships that characterizes female spiritual leadership is grounded in women's daily relationship experiences. The connection between the style of leadership and the daily ways of living with others is supported by Brown's observations since she began her research in Haiti in 1973. Leadership is a matter of facilitating the health of members of the community through active participation in spiritual rituals. Rituals organized to call in spiritual powers are integral to the morality and health of the community. She says, "moral discernment is focussed on the health and liveliness of fluid relationships, not on the essence of persons or their acts" (1989:226). In Haitan Vodou rituals, a particular person or act has no significance outside the context. Brown draws an analogy between the way the Vodou leader participates in the community rituals and African drumming.

In African drumming "the content of the music is the community that performs it" (Brown 1989:228). Brown says that often Westerners listening to African drumming wonder where the main beat is. They are passively listening for it, as is the custom in Western cultures. The beat in African drumming comes from the dancing of the people, not the drummers. The stamping of feet and clapping of hands provides the beat. The music is polyrhythmic. "The various rhythms . . . interweave in complex ways" (p. 228). Each drummer plays a different rhythm. The lead drummer provides the "metronome sense" which allows the interweaving of the various rhythms, the clapping, and stamping of feet to form a connected tapestry of sounds. It is participatory music. The individual, repetitive rhythms are not heard as simple repetitions of the same rhythm but rather as changing rhythms. The reason for this is that "the listener's focus shifts from one rhythmic line to another" creating the impression that the 'one' they are listening to is changing. The 'one' is really 'the many.'

Just as African drumming is a participatory process with a centred "metronome sense," so Vodou ritual is organized around the "metronome sense" of the priestess. The metronome provides the beat which centres one in the midst of rhythmic variations. "Hearing another rhythm to fit alongside the rhythms of an ensemble is . . . a way of being steady within a context of multiple rhythms" (Brown 1989:229). The metronome rhythm, however, doesn't make any sense by itself any more than any of the other rhythms. Mutual responsibility creates the meaning. Responsibility in Vodou ritual, according to Brown, includes bringing one's own life into the ritual. The priestess is like the lead drummer. She uses her beat to call the others into dialogue. She does not emphasize her own beat. Her power lies in her ability to transmit messages from the spirits to each of the participants. Each one uses the messages in relation to their own life rhythms. They do not attempt to readjust their own rhythm to that of the leader but to the synchronicity of the group. The priestess is responsible for realigning the rhythms (conversations, ways of expressions) so that tensions are reduced and peace is possible.

The test of her power and the success of the ritual is whether the participants in the ritual are realigned in ways that allow for integrated par-

ticipation by members of the community. Calling on the spirits is an attempt to bring greater understanding and balance. The leader's "metronome sense" facilitates the process and is strengthened through it. Just as
Bateson pointed out in her analogy between the development of self and
jazz improvisation, individual rhythms only make sense in relationship.
Brown says about the moral wisdom of the priestess that "it is precisely in
responsive and responsible relation to others that one has the clearest and
most steady sense of self" (1989:233). Laughter is perceived as an important aspect of integrating differences. "To laugh is to balance, and like all
balancing within Vodou, is achieved not through resolving or denying
conflict, but by finding a way of staying steady in the midst of it" (p. 233).
The organization of life energy is the accomplishment of the priestess, as
described by Brown. Her power is the power to empower, to engender
new patterns of thinking and acting.

     The same kind of power as that of a Vodou priestess is reflected by
Audre Lorde when she says, "This is why the work [her writing] is important. Its power doesn't lie in the me that lives in the words as much as in
the heart's blood pumping behind the eye that is reading, the muscle behind the desire that is sparked by the work—hope as a living state that
propels us, open-eyed and fearful, into all the battles of our lives. And
some of those battles we do not win. But some of them we do" (1988,
back cover). Lorde wrote *A Burst of Light* while she was living with cancer which pervaded her body and took her life in 1993. Her work is a testimony to embracing pain and fear without being conquered by them. Her
vision of hope is empowered by the erotic power of her being, her engendering, transformative power. She expresses gratitude in the midst of her
suffering. She says, "each of us is blessed in some particular way, whether
we recognize our blessings or not" (1988:130). In her view, responsibility
for using the powers one has is a consequence of having them. To live
fully is be engaged in resisting oppressive forces that restrict freedom of
self-determination within a context of community balance. She says,

For me, living fully means to live with maximum access to my experience and
power, loving, and doing work in which I believe. It means writing my poems,
telling my stories, and speaking out of my most urgent concerns and against the
many forms of anti-life surrounding us. . . . If one Black woman I do not know
gains hope and strength from my story, then it has been worth the difficulty of
telling. (1988:130)

Lorde's inspiration and hope has affected people around the world and
her death is mourned by everyone who was touched by her. Her spirit
lives with us as we strive to live out our female potency in engendering
activities.

     The spiritual strength of Lorde, of the Vodou priestess, of Aboriginal
women spiritual leaders, and many others, provide inspiration and hope
to members of communities where oppression is severe because of race,

nationality, colour, class, and so forth. It is not a pie-in-the-sky hope that is intended as an opiate for the oppressed. It is hope fuelled by a life force that is directed at resisting oppression. In these views there is no inconsistency between love for community and anger at social injustice. Both provide the motivation for removing "the big black boot of freedom" that "is smashing down your doorstep" (Lorde 1988:133). Lorde says, "I train myself for triumph by knowing it is mine, no matter what" (p. 133). The power of the erotic is the power of engendering effective action. The path of action differs according to each person's particular circumstances. Knowledge of the different forms of oppression is powerfully revealed through autobiographies or other forms of personalized knowledge. The accumulation of personalized knowledge builds a broad evidential basis for theorizing about human creativity in ways that contribute to activism directed toward social justice. Each person's rhythm is different and to some extent at odds with the rhythms of others. Healthy tensions are maintained through an intention towards balanced relationality. Audre Lorde's erotic power and her mindfulness of balance provides the confidence for her to assert that "triumph is mine, no matter what." The triumph is in the passionate participation which contributes toward social justice.

Laughter is powerful. It may be laughter of the spirits, as in Vodou rituals, which awakens the ability to laugh at oneself and to laugh at the attribution of power to one's oppressors. As we learn from Brown and Lorde, balancing one's power and the power of communities depends on our ability to see the ways in which we have attributed disproportionate power to ourselves or to others. This recognition of our puniness, as well as our connectedness to awesome power, is also one of the fundamental insights of Buddhism. It is at the heart of the doctrine of no-self, which teaches there is no basis for imaging a separate self and then becoming attached to it. The mistaken notion of a separate self is considered to be the cause of misery because of erroneous expectations that develop around the belief in a separate self. This belief is the foundation for egocentric activities that are unethical and self-defeating. They are self-defeating because they place too much emphasis on the individual as either blameworthy or praiseworthy and cause unrealistic expectations with regard to the subject as well as the responses of others to the subject. Frustrated expectations produce negative energy which overpowers the person's creative energy as well as causing negativity in others. The possibility for laughter in such a situation is minimized or eliminated, causing further blockage in the web of connectedness.

A similar view of the interdependency of any particular person's power in the network of community relatedness is central to shamanism. Community in this perspective, as in the other spiritual orientations discussed in this book, extends to the wider natural life system in which humans are only one aspect. In shamanism one's power comes from recog-

nizing the many kinds of spirit powers active in one's life. Spiritual healing is possible in this way of living only through the connectedness of
one's power to other natural powers such as spirit guides, animal powers,
or any of the elementary powers such as fire, earth, air, and water.

Sometimes knowledge gained through insights from journeying with
the help of these natural powers makes one laugh at how they are living
out an irony in their own lives because of ignorance. An example of this
is an experience I had of spontaneously bursting out in laughter after another person had journeyed for me and was relating the images to me
that he had encountered on his journey. He had found an adolescent girl
who had made "a bad judgment call" and had lost a great deal of self-
trust because of it. Among other things, he also found my solar plexus
area was full of fear and was blocking the flow of energy in my body.
During our conversation about the journey, the connection was made
between the earlier event of loss of self-trust and the current situation of
being restricted by fear. Prior to the journey made by this man on my behalf, I was waking up almost every night with a dreadful feeling in my
solar plexus area and feeling shaky all over. The stress in my life provided
sufficient explanation for the dreadful feelings; however, I could not think
my way out of the limiting fears that had got a grip on me. When the connection was made between my adolescent experience of loss of self-trust
and my current fears, I burst out laughing before I understood what I was
laughing about. The man who had journeyed laughed as well because he
could see that I had just had an "aha" experience. I experienced the irony
of trying to hang onto the image of myself as a confident person while
shaking with fear. There was a misalignment of body and mind. Facing
the contradiction made me laugh. My body had been telling me one thing,
namely, that I was suffering from a loss of self-trust and was shaking because of it. My head was telling me something else: that I was supposed
to be able to think through the fear. If I couldn't, then I was deficient and
rightfully fearful.

The knowledge of the early experience of loss of self-trust and the
connection of that to my fears was secured by the man who journeyed
through the help of the animal powers that he called on to help him
find what was necessary to know. This soul retrieval journey included not
merely finding what was lost but also bringing it back home, so to
speak. There were other important facts that were discovered and aspects
of myself that were returned to me during this experience. The predominant result was an increased sense of well-being, decreased presence of
fear, and greater confidence to act effectively in the context of stress. I
think I laughed at myself the moment that I realized that I had been trusting others' opinions of me more than I had been trusting myself. The
ironical part is that I spend a great deal of time on both intellectual and
interpersonal work having to do with engendering trust in oneself. Since
that moment when I burst out laughing at myself, I continue to smile

when I think of it. Laughing at oneself is a very good experience of self-acceptance.

Feminist spirituality shares the Buddhist and shamanic emphasis on knowing oneself as an aspect of a larger system of natural powers. This is the condition for not exaggerating the significance of oneself while, at the same time, it is a way of experiencing the awesomeness of being a participant in the system of natural forces that allows one to go beyond the hidebound separate self. Recognition of one's own power within this network of interrelatedness frees one to stand tall and laugh at the exaggerated power one has attributed to others and has given away from oneself. As mentioned earlier, Carol Christ's *Laughter of Aphrodite* provides an account of women's integrated engendering power that integrates spiritual, intellectual, and sexual potency. Her discussion of the power of Aphrodite in women is consistent with descriptions of symbols and myths of women's power from various cultures. These include Paula Gunn Allen and Dhyani Ywahoo (American Native); Mary Condren (Ireland); Miriam Robbins Dexter (twelve Pre-Indo-European cultures); Nancy Falk and Rita Gross, eds. (cross-cultural anthropological studies); Judith Plaskow and Carol Christ, eds. (American); and Charlene Spretnak (religious pluralism). These authors provide models for thinking and feeling outside of patriarchal constructions of female power. Their use of symbols of female sacred power that is intrinsic to women's social power is a useful strategy for developing positive social constructions of legitimate female autonomy.

Feminist spirituality is an important dimension of the evolution toward new meanings and alternative ways of experiencing ourselves as women. Carol Christ's personalized account of Aphrodite power in her own life contributes importantly towards the restructuring of women's ontological, social, and ethical status. In Christ's account, the internalized laughter of Aphrodite symbolizes the transforming power required for both subjective and intersubjective connectedness. That power is expressed well in the image that Christ describes of herself where she stands tall with her legs wide apart, her hands on her hips, and her head thrown back—laughing aloud from deep inside. Christ's laughter, i.e., the laughter of Aphrodite, is the laughter of a whole and healthy woman.

With that laughter, she joins the sentiment expressed in The Uppity Blues Women compact disc recording of "(No Need) Pissin' on a Skunk" (1991). The woman who sings this song says, "I'm a whole and healthy woman. I'm not crazy, I'm not drunk. Just no need for me to be pissin' on a skunk." The Uppity Blues woman sings this in reference to a man whom she recently met on a street. When she initially encountered him she became angry because of the pain he had caused her. Then she realized that there was no need to reduce her own potency by creating bad energy with regard to him. The song is her response to her positively constructed view of herself as a woman who could choose to respond as she wished. Her choice was to be positive about herself and disregard him as former bad news. Positive energy, i.e., joy and compassion, spills out of the person and is directed toward creative activity rather than being blocked in negative reaction to abusive conditions. That is not to say that the transformation to positive energy excludes fear, anger, or sadness. Rather, it signifies a transformed relation to them which facilitates effective action.

The more usual association of Aphrodite with a teasing sexuality directed at men is not the meaning of the power of Aphrodite in Christ's account. Rather, Aphrodite symbolizes the integration of adventure, courage, and strategy with tenderness and caring. She reflects the coexistence of boldness and vulnerability that is part of self-determination and interdependency. Christ's interpretation of Aphrodite power is commensurate with Jean Shinoda Bolen's (1984) view of Aphrodite as the alchemical goddess. Alchemy is about transforming something of little value into something of considerable, sometimes inestimable, worth. The metaphor of the alchemical goddess is aptly applied to a creative power that transforms women as sexual beings into intrinsically positive, valued persons. Aphrodite symbolizes female spiritual power expressed in women whose natural and social bodies are connected in the construction of their identities as ontological, social, and ethical subjects. When women look in their mirrors and see this integrity reflected back to them, they can laugh at the attempts in patriarchal culture to diminish women's engendering activities.

As we break free of the predominant view of women as sexual beings who serve the interests of an evolutionary intentionality characterized by male dominance and female subordination, women are awakening to themselves as agents of erotic energy which propels them into work where their sexuality, rationality, and spirituality are integrated. It is triumphant energy which empowers a positive consciousness to resist oppression. Goddess consciousness is experienced variously. There is no single example that can serve all women. There are only personal experiences that have been articulated in ways that others can learn from and then go on to trust their own experiences.

Inés Talamantez, as mentioned in the Introduction, provides another glimpse into goddess consciousness that opens space for women to think in different ways about goddess symbolism. She describes what it means to live with goddess presence by relating a dream where she met the goddess Isanaklesh (1989), the Apache goddess Mother Earth, the life sustainer. Talamantez dreamt that the goddess came to her in a female form, spreading pollen on the path by a river that she was walking along. Further into the forest, she sees the woman again walking towards her. The woman has on a deerskin dress with fringes and other decorations. As she walks away, pollen flows from the fringes of her dress. She tells Inés Talamantez that she has come to do a ceremony for her. Isanaklesh is integral to the initiation ceremonies of Apache girls into womanhood.

Talamantez had been attending the preparation rituals for the initiation ceremony of a daughter of one of her friends who lived on the Mescalaro Apache reservation in New Mexico. In the dream she realized that Isanaklesh was now ritually bound to her, in a similar way as her mythology is integral to the girls' initiation into womanhood. From the women elders she learned that the pollen symbolized the earth's life-giving powers. To be bound to Isanaklesh or live with her presence means for Talamantez "to live in balance and harmony, like the balance and harmony that we see in nature" (1989:249). For Talamantez, living with goddess presence is about living as fully integrated as possible. From the point of view of this book, living in a right relation to goddess presence is an intentional motivation which shapes the evolutionary drift toward partnership. Such a relation includes accepting one's connection to spiritual power and the authority it grants one to participate as one of many significant rhythms in the creation of music, of community. If this kind of consciousness is developed, it might be possible for increasing numbers of women to look in the mirror and laugh the laughter of Aphrodite, meet Isanaklesh with the pollen flowing from her, and say with Mama Lola, "plenty confidence in myself."

Feminist spirituality supports the activity of constructing positive meanings regarding women's sex-specificity. For example, in *The Laugh of the Medusa*, Hélène Cixous says, "It is time to liberate the New Woman from the Old by coming to know her—by loving her for getting by, for getting beyond the Old without delay, by going out ahead of what the New Woman will be, as an arrow quits the bow with a movement that gathers and separates the vibrations musically, in order to be more than her self" (1991:224). Coming to know the New Woman requires accepting the reality of her womanness, her sexuality. Feminists generally agree that knowledge cannot be entirely separated from the knower. A consequence of that claim is that the task of knowing a woman is inseparable from the question posed by Lorraine Code, "What can she know?"[15] A reasonable response is that she can know, among other things, herself as a whole and healthy woman. A consequence of that knowledge is that she can have confidence in herself as an epistemological subject who deserves to occupy cultural spaces of authority that shape the evolutionary drift.

Lorraine Code (1991) makes it clear that in arguing for knowing as women, that she is not arguing for an essentialist way of women knowing. Her notion of essentialism is the traditional one which claims a fixed essence for woman's nature. She says "By 'essentialism' I mean a belief in an essence, an inherent, natural, eternal female nature that manifests itself in such characteristics as gentleness, goodness, nurturance, and sensitivity" (Code 1991:17). I agree with her rejection of essentialism from the perspective of the classical meaning of essentialism she uses. If, however, essentialism is not used in that restricted sense, but rather to refer to the essential process of changing and interacting historical conditions, including spiritual power, then there is no need to reject the term. If the body is taken as an active part of one's perceptions, namely, the felt sensations part, then to overlook the significance of women's bodies in women's ways of knowing is unreasonable. Ignoring women's bodies or sex-specific knowledge as a way of avoiding classical essentialism gives too much away. It gives away the basis for celebrating women's bodies and continues to fuel the denigration of them. In addition, it supports patriarchal dualisms, especially those which separate nature from culture and mind from body, assuming the neutrality of the male body while incorporating it into language.

By contrast, bringing women's bodies into discussions of knowing with integrity grounds women's knowledge in an integrated consciousness. This is not to restrict women's knowledge to knowledge that only women can have. Rather it is to include knowledge that only women can have into the larger corpus of knowledge that also includes exclusively male knowledge as well as shared 'human' knowledge. The diversity of the large corpus of knowledge is enhanced through the inclusion of sex-specific kinds of knowledge or ways of knowing. Including sex-specific knowledge in the larger body of knowledge doesn't reduce it to sex-specific knowledge. Neither does it reduce a particular person's knowledge to sex-specific knowledge. All consciousness is bodied. Bodied consciousness is not restricted to sex-specific knowledge. It is, however, constituted in part by it.

Because women's bodies have been represented problematically in Western culture, women have often experienced their own bodies as obstacles to their cognitive activities. For example, one woman told me that earlier in her life she could never concentrate on what someone else was saying, whether it was in a university lecture or in a causal conversation. The reason she stated for her lack of concentration was self-consciousness. She was ashamed of her thighs, which she thought were much too big. She thought everyone was looking at them and judging her unfavourably. She entered into a downhill spiral with respect to her learning difficulties. As a result of her preoccupation with her body image, her university grades were as low as her self-esteem. They contributed to her feeling increasingly worse about herself. Her self-esteem continued to plummet until she was relatively immobilized. She chose to confront the problem of her body and eventually began to experience herself positively. It took several months of hard work to reach a level of self-acceptance that would propel her forward. She was successful in learning to express positive energy through her body and to let go of self-defeating attitudes towards it. Although her body shape did not alter very noticeably, the energy that she began to express was very attractive. She became the lovable person she aspired to be. Her grades soared along with her self-esteem.

This particular woman's experience is unique to her. The problem of the body getting in the way of a woman's creative expression, however, is common to many women. The strong affirmation of women's bodies in feminist spirituality makes spirituality a valuable resource in the development and expression of women's knowledge. While feminist spirituality focusses on female images, it is compatible with other spiritual traditions and practices, such as Buddhism and cross-cultural shamanism. The use of new and revisioned spiritual images, concepts, and symbols that affirm women's ontological, social, and ethical status is part of a larger feminist endeavour directed toward the same end. The structuring of language and methods of logical thinking are particularly important areas that are being deconstructed and reconstructed by feminists who wish to affirm women's status through constructing sexual difference differently. This can be done in part by creating a new cultural matrix with regard to the meaning of women's bodies. If women's potency is to be expressed, then the language we use to express it must include appropriate spiritual symbolism.

Notes

1 In contrast with Lorde, I believe that feelings are more appropriately equated with felt sensations rather than with emotions (as in Hume's theory of perceptions). Lorde's use of feeling is more akin to the meaning of emotion in my own way of conceptualizing.

2 I discuss Jane Gallop's *Thinking Through the Body* (1988) in Chapter Three.

3 I am not discussing the important literature on the issue of slimness and women's bodies, as that will take me away from the central issue of spirituality and the body. That is not to say that thinness is not relevant to the discussion, but rather that it is a large topic which cannot be addressed adequately in the space here. For a helpful analysis of the issue of thinness and representation of women's bodies, see, for example, Susan Bordo (1990).

4 The Uppity Blues Women song, "(No need) Pissin' on a Skunk," is about a woman who accepts herself as her own authority. The song, as the rest of their songs, is a good example of lusty, middle-aged women who are creating a new atmosphere for women.

5 In my chapter "Embodied Spiritual Consciousness: Beyond Psychology" (Tomm forthcoming).

6 An important article on the extent of negativity toward women expressed directly at women's bodies is Carole Sheffield, "Sexual Terrorism" (1992).

7 Daly (1978) argues forcefully that the abuse of women's bodies by gynecologists is part of the more general gynocidal practices within patriarchy that are similar to the genocidal practices of the Nazis and to Christian persecutions of women as witches. Gynecology as a medical discipline, in contrast to the spiritual healing by shamans and other spiritual healers, is depicted as an anti-woman discipline which reflects the denigration of women's bodies.

8 Humberto Maturana (Maturana and Varela 1987) describes social evolution in terms of "drift" that is given direction through intentionality. While the use of the term "drift" is problematic alongside "intentionality," his meaning is consistent with the view that I am developing. The view of evolution as a process that is shaped primarily by ideology rather than adaptation to the environment is the main point. As Maturana points out, the "adaptation to the environment" explanation of social Darwinism is a backward glance explanation. It tries to look back and explain why some things survived and others did not. It does not explain why social organizations developed as they did in conjunction with environmental conditions. Maturana's theory of evolution includes the basic claim of this book that ontology and epistemology are mutually informing. The reality that one adapts to depends in part on the way one perceives the reality. Looking at it the

other way around, one's perceptions of reality depend on what there is to perceive. The ontology and epistemology are in an endless dance with each other. That improvisatory dance constitutes the evolutionary process for Maturana, myself, and the others cited.

9 The debate between freedom and determinism continues today as an issue in punishment/treatment orientation to criminal and juvenile offenders. It is not merely an academic issue. It also applies directly to spousal murders. Men kill their wives and lovers more often out of rage against their insubordination, while women kill their husbands and lovers more often out of self-defence. If one were to obey the command "Thou shalt not kill" without reference to the conditions in which the murder occurred, it would be difficult to argue for different forms of punishment in the different cases. At the same time the command not to kill another person is basic to each individual's rights to protection from interference from others. A problem with a self-defence killing by a wife or woman lover is to decide how much prior interference by the man constitutes sufficient grounds to kill in self-defence, while maintaining the right to life of each person.

10 Derrida's claim, for example, that "there is nothing outside the text" (Spretnak 1991:125) disallows the impact of felt sensations on cognition. Gayle Rubin's claim that "we never encounter the body unmediated by the meanings that cultures give to it" (1984:276-77) is an example of a postmodern account of sexuality which contributes significantly to our understanding of the politics of sexuality within a cultural framework. It does not allow, however, for transformation of cultural meanings through sensations which radically challenge existing cultural meanings and, thereby, impact on them to create new meanings. The denial of the agency of the body is a position which extends patriarchal dualisms, privileging male-centred cultural constructions.

11 Sandra Ingerman (1993) uses this view of power in her discussion of healing power that can be developed through rituals that focus one's intentions to bring about healing effects for oneself, others, and the ecology.

12 For a good discussion of rights for women in a legal system organized within a patriarchal culture, see Lynn Smith's article, "What Is Feminist Legal Research?" (Smith 1989).

13 Examples of important work which correlate spiritual leadership and gendered power relations are Gerda Lerner (1986), Riane Eisler (1987), Allen (1986), Ruether (1983, 1974), Stone (1978), Gimbutas (1982), Gadon (1989), Dexter (1990), Condren (1989), Christ and Plaskow (1992), Plaskow and Christ (1989), Christ (1987a), Spretnak (1991), Daly (1984, 1978), and Goldenberg (1979).

14 See my article "Otherness in Self-Disclosure: A Woman's Perspective" (Tomm 1993).

15 In her book *What Can She Know?: Feminist Theory and the Construction of Knowledge* (1991), Lorraine Code argues that a relativistic approach to knowledge is useful because it brings into focus the conditions of the knower. At the same time there needs to be a basis for choosing among alternatives. Such a basis is seen to come from "second person" knowledge, which is shared, intersubjective knowledge. Her investigation of responsible knowledge in an earlier book, *Epistemic Responsibility* (1987), points out that a "mitigated relativism" or "mitigated realism" is part of knowing responsibly. While knowledge is invariably shaped by social and historical interests and desires of the knower, responsible knowledge is participatory. One's self-interests and desires are interwoven with those of the community in which one is situated.

Three

Sexuality and Language

Logic

LOGIC IS ABOUT discerning truth. Language expresses particular logical methods used throughout history to secure stable judgments about changing circumstances. Logic is generally believed to be necessary for getting beyond material transience in the search for continuing truth. Language, as the vehicle of logical thought, is often considered to be independent of the particular conditions of the thinker. It is the main form of discursive symbolizing. By this I mean language is a system of concepts and relations of concepts which give conceptual meaning to our experiences. Language is a major medium by which cultural values, attitudes, and beliefs are shared. For this reason it is important to connect language to its users, namely, bodied persons, in order to gain greater understanding of the connectedness of language to lived experiences.

In this chapter I shall explore the assumption that physicality and language are mutually influential in attempts to negotiate coherence of meaning in the midst of lived ambiguities. This is especially important with respect to women because language in North American society, the context from which I speak, is shaped more by men's ideas and activities than women's. Because neither men's nor women's ideas can be separated from their subjectivity and socially constructed subject positions, it is important to ask, 'How is language connected to biology?' In other words, 'How does nature influence culture?' A significant reason for asking this question is to attempt to redefine the relation between nature and culture as a mutually exclusive one. It is also a way of employing feminist analysis to transform humanism. Prior to feminist analysis, humanist ideas were shaped by a view of sexual difference in which one term of sexual difference was constructed as 'subject' and the other term was constructed as 'other.' The goal here is to think through sexual difference differently so that the two terms of sexual difference (female and male) are equally symbolized as subject terms. Language plays a major role in this resymbolizing process in which logic is connected to living subjects in the construction of meaningful claims about diverse realities in the pursuit of reliable knowledge.

Notes to Chapter Three are on pages 164-66.

The history of language in Western culture is inseparable from the history of logic (Nye 1990). Different cultures are shaped by their particular dominant logics, just as different disciplines in universities have their own differentiated methods of reasoning. A common feature, though, of the history of dominant logics and of different academic disciplines in Western culture is the assumption that thought is separated from materiality. That assumption is integral to the variations in particular forms of logic and disciplined-based methods of obtaining knowledge. Training in academic disciplines is largely about acquiring the correct kind of knowledge in prescribed ways. That is referred to as disciplined learning. One learns to think and act like one's colleagues, guided by the experts who are granted their authority by the community of scholars in the discipline.[1] Senior scholars train junior scholars to think as they do. Junior scholars desire approval by their authority figures. Senior scholars often achieve their desired immortality through the adoption of their ideas by students. In this process knowledge is canonized and tradition is established and passed on as received knowledge. Received knowledge is often equated with responsible knowledge that takes on a reality of its own. Responsible knowledge is understood to embody truths which can be learned by anyone who is adequately trained in the prescribed methods of acquiring knowledge in a particular discipline. New insights are accepted as creative innovations so long as they comply with the rules of logic that are intrinsic to the prescribed method of inquiry used in the pursuit of knowledge.

In her examination of the history of Western logic, Andrea Nye points out how logic (in the discipline of philosophy) is seen by logicians as the activity that reveals the structure of truth. She says ironically, "The logician does not speak; he does not tell the truth; he exhibits it" (1990:4). According to Nye, logic in Greek philosophy can be traced back to Parmenides, sixth century B.C.E. He was directed by the goddess beyond herself toward disembodied truth. The object of Parmenides' search was "a well-rounded sphere, uniform and not admitting of degrees, homogeneous and not subject to any death or destruction" (p. 12). That is the nature of Being, for Parmenides. It is the perfected object of desire that is not contaminated by the confusions, changes, and ambiguities of physical objects of desire. The contrast between the eternal perfection of transcendent Being with the uncertainties of nature characterized the flight away from the immanence of nature toward the transcendence of Being in the beginning of Western logic. Truth was initially to be found in transcendent Being. Transcendent thought was a correlative of transcendent Being. By the nineteenth century C.E., transcendent Being was rejected by logicians; however, transcendent thought was retained. The cultural shift from embodied knowing to disembodied knowing in Western philosophy can be traced to this period, the beginning of the history of logic.

The trivialization of materiality in the search for transcendent, disembodied truth included a rejection by logicians of their own bodies. The negation of their own bodies was projected onto women's bodies. Women's bodies were associated with the chaos of nature that the logicians wished to avoid. They symbolized the physical objects of desire that the logicians were fleeing from as they aspired toward transcendence. Fear of women's bodies became a feature of patriarchal consciousness in the attempt to transcend the immanence and materiality of nature. Nye says, "in logic there is no intercourse of being with non-being, and therefore no disappointment of ambiguity, only the perfect fidelity of the unmoveable, unchangeable, perfect 'well-roundedness' of truth" (1990:16). In logic there is no untidy birthing process, no fearful dying, no intercourse between physical bodies in the creative process. The birth of pure thought is uncontaminated in the logician's method of reasoning. That which is born from the climax of reasoning or intuitive apprehension is believed to remain in the same form eternally.

The notion of essence changed from plurality of identity through connected, embodied knowing to singularity of identity through separate, disembodied knowing. The ambiguity of connected, embodied knowing was to be disambiguated through structures of logic which exhibited eternal truths. The necessity of truth would be made clear to those who learned the method of logical reasoning, i.e., organization of terms (or marks) in propositions such that the truth or falsity of the proposition could be determined by rules that were known to those who could apply the rules and avoid the fallacies which were specified in the logic game. The ambiguities of natural language would be avoided by logicians who could exchange mathematical numbers and equations for words and establish with certainty the soundness and completeness of any thought. Any thought which could not be restated in a mathematical formula was no thought but merely opinion. Logical reasoning, according to the methods specified by the logicians, has structured the language of the universities, the courts, the legislators, the health care systems, and the economic institutions so that the ignoring of human needs which cannot be expressed in a language which is organized according to the rules of logic is legitimated. Social policies and practices are derived from interests which can be expressed in such language.

Nye claims that logic is politically motivated and is not a disinterested pursuit of truth. Logics have been as diverse as the social matrices in which they were constructed and the men who constructed them. She argues that the dominant form of logical reasoning in different historical periods and geographical locations reflected the social and political desires of the civic leaders at that time and place. She argues that the particular forms of logic developed in the various schools reflected the desires of kings, prelates, magistrates, and landlords to control the citizens, usually in the courts. Ownership of property, religious, and political power shaped the development of logical reasoning so that those in power could not only persuade others of their interests but exhibit the necessary truth of them. She says,

Parmenides, searching for an eternal *what is* in a Greece only just emerged from the dark ages that followed the destruction of Mediterranean culture by migrating Greeks; Plato, insisting on absolute Goodness in the midst of the disintegration of the traditional order of the city-state as foreigners, speculators, and moneylenders crowded into Athens; Aristotle, promoting a science based on necessary truth as he watches the collapse of Athenian hegemony in the Aegean; Zeno the Stoic, constructing a grammar of the cosmos as he and others try to come to terms with life in the new Hellenistic empire of Alexander the Great. Could they all have been thinking the same thing? The things as Abelard and Ockham thought, centuries later, when God, the divine Logos, was thought to have spoken and all relations between God and man were being renegotiated; or as Frege thought, the logicians' logician, working out the elegant details of his new logical notation in Bismarck's Germany, surrounded by economic crisis and infected by the ethnic and racial hatreds that would eventually support Fascism? (1990:4)

In light of an analysis of the social history in which logical methods of reasoning are constructed, it is reasonable to relate social motives and purposes with logical methods of reasoning. It is important to determine the relation between the interests of dominant groups and the so-called "truths" revealed by logic. Descartes' method of reasoning in the seventeenth century, for example, is largely an attempt to reconcile the tensions between religious and scientific authority. He grounded the uncertainties of knowledge gained through the senses in the reality of God as the creator of ideas such as certainty, adequacy, and completeness of thought. According to Descartes, the scientific method of reasoning has its foundations in the mind of God (Descartes' *Meditations*). Only those who were skilled in the proper methods of reasoning could know what God knows about the laws of nature: the principal object of scientific study in his view. Descartes' method of reasoning supported Francis Bacon's representative claim of the sixteenth and seventeenth centuries that the goal of science was to make nature reveal her secrets. The orientation of science changed in the sixteenth and seventeenth centuries from that of describing nature to explaining her. The explanation of women, as correlatives of nature, by scientists was institutionalized especially in the emergence of the medical profession. The same kind of male authority has characterized much of Western rational thought. The frequent scepticism toward women who claim their own knowledge is one of the consequences of projecting embodiedness onto women, separating thought from sensuality, and systematizing authoritative methods of reasoning which allegedly exhibit eternal truths about what is. The authority of philosophers, religious leaders, and scientists throughout the history of Western culture has been closely associated with the desire to control women's bodies as part of the more general desire to control nature. It is debatable which desire is the more deeply embedded in patriarchal consciousness.

The search for certainty in the pursuit of power over social, political, and economic conditions involved the separation of self from context to the point where the objectification of one's own subjectivity (as in Frege's nineteenth-century logic) became the basis for a presumed objectivity. Removal of the personal (the 'I') from the motivation behind any claim of truth meant that the claim could be made by anyone. The objectification of the person who was making personal claims would eliminate the emotive sense of the claim and allow its essential meaning to be understood by anyone. Essence, here, means the impersonal truth which is separate from the knower of the truth. In some logic frameworks, such as Aristotle's, essence is a substance that can be known independent of the personal input of any knower. In twentieth-century logic, essence is the truth reflected in a proposition, an assertion, which states something about reality. Its truth is determined by the relation of concepts or mathematical notations within the proposition. An intention of scientists is to supply the empirical evidence which ties the truth of propositions to the facts of reality.

The control of knowledge depends on asking the right questions in order to elicit the correct evidence. If one is to be in control of the answers one can only ask questions to which one knows the answers. The so-called pursuit of truth is sometimes primarily a process of confirming first assumptions. One of the earliest assumptions that shaped the history of Western logic and the pursuit of truth is the need to transcend the so-called disappointments of the body. Disappointments of the body refer to changes in the body. Bodies obviously grow, they are impaired in various ways. The fact that they are subject to constant change belies belief in eternal sameness. Truth, on the other hand, in dominant Western logic, is about eternal sameness.[2] It is about fixed natures. The ambiguity of body sensations interrupts the alleged certainty of transcendent ideas. The confusion of changing materiality was associated with immanence, the immediate world around us. Women's bodies became symbolic of immanence. The assumption of woman as essentially material, without the proper form to actualize reason to its fulfilment, is a pillar of Western logic.

The beginning of Greek logic with Parmenides is the juncture of poetic language and logical method of reasoning. It was motivated by the desire to find fulfilment through identification with the object of thought. Since the object of thought was thought itself, one could be fulfilled through knowledge of one's self-sufficiency. The patriarchal coup in Parmenides' poem is that it is the goddess who directs Parmenides to the truth beyond herself. The male author uses the muse to direct attention away from her own powers over men's creativity and towards the intrinsic creativity of their own ideas. She represents the old world view in which fulfilment is found in love between lovers. Her role as the inspiration of men is now overshadowed by men's own power to know themselves as purveyors of "truth." Nye says, "Sexuality is central in the older view. The Spirit-at-the-centre-of-the-world creates Eros first . . ." (1990:18). In logic, however, "Nothing is needed for this love affair except one's own thought" (p. 18). The idea of man's essential nature shifts from one of connectedness through love to separateness through knowledge. Women's sexuality henceforth is scorned, avoided, feared. Parmenides uses goddesses to serve men's love of themselves. Ananke, the ruling goddess of the cosmos who guides the social order, now guides Parmenides beyond herself to search for essential disembodied thoughts. Dike, the goddess of Justice who reflected a natural order of integration, now is the gatekeeper, the jailer who holds the keys for Zeus. She prescribes necessary paths to truth and proscribes others, she keeps out the common people who are ineligible for the path to ultimate fulfilment. After Dike lets Parmenides through the double doors (the two lips) into the cave (womb) where the erotic Ananke greets him, she closes the door to the enclosure. Inside the reception cave, however, there is not the usual erotic union in which generation through sexual intercourse occurs. "The goddess points Parmenides not to the final embrace with herself but beyond herself so he can have a love affair with his own thoughts" (Nye 1990:18). Fulfilment is found "In the blissful union with this imaginary object, the Spirit's eternal generative process will be arrested. Self-identity replaces birth, equivalence, intercourse" (p. 19). Parmenides goes forth, helped by the hostess/goddess, to develop a logic of oneness, of Being.

Being, for Parmenides, is 'what is.' Non-Being is 'what is not.' Identity is either in terms of being or non-being. The logical bases for exclusive categories were established with Parmenidean logic. Most fundamentally the distinction between disembodied, eternal Being and the politics of daily life were separated. His logic paved the way for the hierarchical relation between transcendent thought and immanent flesh that has shaped cultural constructions of male rationality and female sexuality. Spirituality and active female sexuality especially were separated in the development of Western logic. Male identification with thought and the further association of thought with Being led to the identity of maleness with Being. Everything outside of Being was non-Being. The chasm between the two kinds of realities was unbridgeable. The categories of Being and non-Being were considered exclusive of each other. The assumption of exclusive categories underscored all the major schools of Western logic. In each school, logic allegedly establishes the certainty of truth that stands above social chaos and individual desires.

Plato (427-347 B.C.E.) separated essential, transcendent Forms from inessential, immanent matter. Plato asserted that Transcendent Reality is eternally the same. Absolute truth is discerned through apprehension of the Real. Such apprehension depends upon the development of the rational part of the soul. Unity with the Real is possible only after the so-called baggage of the body is discarded at death. Aristotle (384-322 B.C.E.)

rejected his teacher's transcendent idealism but retained a metaphysical dualism between mind and body in his doctrine of Substance. While he declared that all substance consists in both form and matter, he proclaimed that form is the active principle of substance. With respect to human nature, form was identified with the rational principle. Skills in logic were associated with the ability to reason. Skilful logicians, then, could consider themselves superior human beings because of their methods of reasoning and their corresponding ability to establish truth with certainty. The truth of the conclusions was tied to the assumptions which initiated the search for truth. The assumptions were often unexamined. The method of reasoning toward the conclusion was considered the main target of analysis. It was possible, therefore, to argue from the assumption that women were less rational than men to the conclusion that women's happiness was less than men's. The middle premise ties happiness to rationality. If the conclusion follows from the premise set, it is valid. The truth of it, however, depends upon the truth of the premises. The first premise, in this case, is the unfounded assumption of the inferiority of women. Assumptions, by definition, are unexamined 'truths.' So much for the certainty of logical truths. Certainty in logical reasoning is about method. It is not about content.

The next major Greek school of logic was founded by Zeno of Citium (Stoic, 340-265 B.C.E). He claimed that reality is created through the Word of God. According to Zeno, the Word of God can be known as complete thoughts expressed through the rules of logic. Those who learn the skills of logical reasoning are, then, in the position to describe reality to those without the skills. Logical skills and absolute knowledge were considered to be coextensive with each other. This close association of knowing with certainty, having prescribed methods to arrive at such knowledge, and having God's word as the divine sanction for the content and process, gave an authority to men's knowledge to which women generally did not have access. When they do, women sometimes wonder, as did Andrea Nye, what led to this kind of knowledge and unusual ways of knowing. Her response was to study the history of logic to understand how it arrived at the position it holds today.

Similar to the logic of Zeno, Abelard's logic of the Middle Ages (1079-1142) equated god's word as logos (reason) with the logical reasoning of logicians. Ockham (1285-1349) separated revealed knowledge and empirical knowledge, arguing that logic enabled one to apprehend eternal truths and clarify the changing, empirical world. The progression toward transcendent logos culminated in the nineteenth century with the logic of Gottlob Frege (1848-1925). He attempted to marry mathematics and language so that truth and falsity of propositions could be entirely free of natural language, the language of non-logicians. In Frege's view, according to Nye, "Natural language is ambiguous, unsystematic, and uneconomical" (1990:129). For Frege, communication depends on the ability to share transcendent thought reflected through sentences in which the concepts are properly arranged to reflect the structures of transcendent thoughts. Transcendent thoughts require removal of the person so they can become 'hardened.' In this view, one becomes an "independent owner of ideas" (Nye 1990:157). Communication is possible among those who can formulate their transcendent thoughts in propositions which reflect no sense of personal interference. One's subjectivity is to harden into an objectivity. Frege's idea is illustrated, for example, by doctors and scientists who put on a white lab coat as a way of separating themselves as persons with unique perspectives from their personae as experts with impersonal and objective knowledge.[3]

Nye effectively shows how logic, as developed by logicians throughout the history of Western philosophy, turned language into a hammer-like tool which can be used effectively to shape the cultural construction of truth according to the interests of a few. Nelle Morton (1985) notes that logical forms of linguistic constructions are like jars[4] which hold the content of meaning and from which authority is extracted. Access to those enclosures of truth, today, is guarded by the gatekeepers: not Dikes, as in Parmenides' poem, but scientists. The enclosures are not conceived as womb-like caves into which one walks, but rather erect structures that one confronts. Twentieth-century philosophers such as those from the Vienna Circle (1922 to the late 1930s)[5] strove to establish the authority of science. They believed that physics is the exemplary model of the automatism of science in which reference to the personal can be eliminated. Carnap, a student of Frege, was interested in true theory which is exclusive, in his view, from personal expressions. True theory is scientific and is expressed in logical syntax. Science was to replace metaphysics as the source of authority in the search for absolute knowledge.

Social and political motives are generally denied in the pursuit of logical or scientific truth. The logicians' denial of their own desires led to the stipulation of such common fallacies as the genetic fallacy and ad hominem fallacy. One is said to commit a genetic fallacy when one thinks that the genesis of an idea is relevant to its truth or falsity. It is a mistake, in that view, to connect the source of a claim with the truth or falsity of it. An example of this is when a claim is believed to be true because a social or cultural authority made it. A scholar's claims to truth often affect students and other scholars in this way, inhibiting their own investigations. One such claim is that spiritual experiences are not to be counted as scholarly material. Similarly, one is guilty of an ad hominem fallacy if one looks for congruity between a statement and the person making it. It should not be surprising, therefore, to hear a philosopher of ethics speak disparagingly about his daughter when he cites her as an example of a point he is trying to make in a philosophy seminar. It is, however, disconcerting. The fact that it is disturbing is an indication that the ad hominem fallacy is inappropriate. Frege, and others, believed that rules of logic are independent of social attitudes such as racism, homophobia, or sexism. Ironically, Frege's diary of himself as a racist is the context in which he wrote about transcendental thoughts.

Attempts by postmodernists, phenomenologists, feminists, and others to contextualize knowledge in relation to the knower's values and desires have significantly undermined the hammer-like use of logic to establish irrefutable claims that have been used to support the social and political interests of a few. The use of exclusive categories and the practice of isolating essential features that distinguish each category has been seriously called into question. The Russian political term 'Glasnost' characterizes the many contemporary approaches to methods of discourse. The desire is to open space for more interactive dialogue. The tendency is toward eliminating the reductionistic notion of essence in discussions of identity. Pluralistic identity defies a fixed essential, defining characteristic. Identity is constructed within language. The logic of language is, therefore, important in the construction of identity. Exclusive categories such as thought and sensations, mind and body, form and matter, spirituality and sexuality, culture and nature, male and female are rejected.

Spiritual consciousness, as I have discussed it with regard to Buddhism, shamanism, and goddess spirituality, aims to overcome categorical thinking. Spiritual consciousness is about getting a whole picture of interactive causal relations. That is the intention behind the Buddhist doctrine of *pratityasamutpada*, interdependent origination. At the same time the need for linear expression remains. This means that language is categorical and can organize meaningful expressions of experiences only through the relations of categorical ideas. This process flattens out the multidimensionality of lived experiences. Language cannot convey holistic impressions. From the point of view of a spiritual consciousness of reality, language is always trying to perform the impossible. With language we attempt to convey in a flat way a reality which is round and spiralling, without boundaries around the circulating energy forms. Language comes from experiences. It is not an abstract symbolic structure that is constructed independently from the process of causal interrelatedness in which each of us lives as a person with sensual knowledge as well as intellectual reflectiveness. Language is always the product of embodied consciousness. Consciousness is invariably emotively toned, as I discussed in regard to Buddhist mindfulness in Chapter One. It is never without emotionality because it is partially constituted by sensations. The other part is ideas. Sensations and ideas in consciousness are inclusive. They are not independent of each other. Emotions are the consequence of the interaction between sensations and ideas. The formulation of ideas in language occurs within the context of interacting sensations and ideas, the emotional climate of the subject. Language, therefore, is emotionally laden.

It is a truism to say that we attempt to express ourselves through language. What are we expressing when we express ourselves? At least we are expressing our ideas. We are also expressing our emotions. If ideas are inseparable from sensations in consciousness, as I am suggesting (along with David Hume and others), and emotions are the product of ideas and sensations, then we express body consciousness when we express ourselves in language. If we agree that no person's consciousness can be said to be entirely disembodied, then it follows that every person's consciousness includes body consciousness. It is reasonable to conclude that language includes the expression of body consciousness.

I reject the logic of essentialism, as referred to above, which separates categories according to reductionistic single essences. At the same time, however, I believe that language is grounded in the body. Bodies are identifiable by their sex, by their anatomical specificities. In some cases there is a blurring of anatomical differences. With regard to the vast majority of people, however, women and men are clearly anatomically distinguishable. That is not to say that the anatomy of a person is the sole determining characteristic of character or purpose in life. Neither women nor men can adequately be defined in terms of a fixed essential quality. Persons are processes of becoming fuller human beings through participation in their communities as well as through incorporation of otherness within their own subjectivities. Pluralistic identity is intrinsic to consciousness in the view developed here. Language is the medium through which we attempt to convey pluralistic consciousness. Language requires categorical thinking. It is impossible to eliminate categories from language. Language is by definition categorical. To say that language is categorical does not commit one to reductionistic essentialism. It merely commits one to retaining categories that distinguish one thing from another. My aim here is to retain the category of body in the construction of language. More specifically, I wish to emphasize the importance of focussing on women's bodies in relation to the construction of languages that could more adequately express women's experiences. The history of logic is founded on the flight from bodies toward transcendent thoughts. If the logic of our language is to be reconstructed more favourably for women (and for men), it is important to take bodies seriously as agents in consciousness. Just as it is important to reclaim women's bodies in positive images and concepts, it is also consequential to make explicit the ways in which men's bodies have actually influenced men's ideas. Denial by men of the effect of their maleness in their thinking has been possible largely because they projected body business onto women. Their dissociation from their own bodies is tied to that projection and the corresponding emulation and/or repulsion of women's bodies. Language as we have it today is not healthy for women. It is mandatory for women's health to develop linguistic expressions which facilitate women's health. Self-determination requires a healthy mind and a healthy body, both of which are largely constructed through language. Because language gives meaning to what each person experience, it is central to a person's self-consciousness. Cultural meanings and self-knowing are inseparable from each other. Both are tied to the language system of meaning specific to the local conditions of each person. This is not to say, however, that language completely constructs the meaning of any person's self-knowledge. There is the factor of body experiences that can provide an impetus to reshape language meanings.

To emphasize women's bodies in language is not to fall back into a depressing biological determinism. Rather it is to celebrate the reality of women as embodied knowers. It is to integrate intellectuality with passionate sensations. It is to acknowledge desire in will. Acknowledging sex-specificity is to accept female and male bodies as sources of knowing. It is not to treat sex-specific ways of knowing as exclusive ways of knowing. By contrast it is to open up the interactive process of dialogue by introducing strong subjectivity. Each person's expression contributes to the whole picture. The whole picture is more adequately expressed through the participation of strong agents who can celebrate their "immanent flourishing of the divine in the flesh" (Irigaray 1992:73). The aim here is to use language to express our perpetual increase in ourselves as we grow in relation to others.

I agree with Luce Irigaray that philosophy is the search for love. Eros is a seeker after wisdom. Love is a kind of divination which yields generative action. Language should be able to express self-love (eros) and compassion in its wisdom. It should be able to do that from a woman's perspective. Women have a right to speak as women. That includes, among other things, that their ways of speaking reflect their embodied consciousness. The same is true for men. That does not automatically lead to exclusive ways of speaking. Rather it could lead to more dynamic ways of speaking with each other so that possibilities are opened up for infusion between speaking subjects. Fluidity rather than fixity characterizes personal, group, national, or global identity. Linguistic categories need to be developed to reflect that fluidity. Identity is constituted by diversity in the view developed here. Part of a person's diverse identity is sexual. By using sex-specificity as an identifier, I am not claiming exclusivity of identity by sex. I do wish, however, to bring into focus the importance of sex-specificity in the construction of language. It is through language that social meanings of sexuality are constructed. If we accept that language is part of consciousness and consciousness includes body consciousness, it follows that sex-specificity is a factor in both the construction of language and the social construction of sexuality through language. Several feminists, among others, are contributing to the 'Glasnost' process occurring in the reconconstruction of language and the social meanings constructed through it. The aim is to make both forms of construction more user friendly for women by bringing into focus the participation of women's bodies as active agents in thoughtful expressions.

Diana Fuss makes an important point with respect to the creation of essentialist texts: one needs to ask what motivates the search for essences. She claims it is not always a reactionary motivation. In the climate of postmodernism in which essentialism is largely a proscribed topic, there is for some "the call to risk essentialism" (1989:xi). It can be used as a discourse of resistance as well as a legitimization strategy. Using it as a discourse of resistance is a way of thinking that resists the erasure of bodily experiences which are not entirely sociologically determined. My definition of consciousness as a process of perceptions which include felt awareness and reflection requires the presence of body in the construction of language (expressions of reflections). It is important to clarify how I am using essentialism. I would prefer not to use the term because of its historical baggage. I use it because the charge of essentialism (in the reactionary sense) is brought against an author when she regards sexuality or the body as anything more than a cultural construction. I reject the view of the body as exclusively a cultural construction as a reductionist form of sociological determinism. It is a further example of the logic of Western philosophy which constructs language and meaning out of dualistic categories. Prescribing the meaning of sexuality exclusively through language and proscribing the body in its fleshiness continues the Parmenidean flight from women's sexuality.

The way in which I am using essentialism is as outlined in Chapter One and developed further in Chapter Two. It is a view of reality in which identity includes difference, including various forms of consciousness. It is a view of reality in which the presence of differences constitutes the essence of reality. This is not the view of essentialism that "seeks to deny or to annul the very radicality of difference" (Fuss 1989:xii). In my view, arguments for gender neutrality that exclude sex differences are a form of postmodern essentialism: women are essentially the same as men in that neither has a subject position as "I." The irony is that this doctrine of postmodern essentialism was initiated by men who had a strong sense of "I" which was in jeopardy of being dislocated by the presence of women claiming their own subjectivity. The obvious move was to dislocate them first. As Bernice Reagon pointed out so effectively, "At a certain stage, nationalism is crucial to a people if you are ever going to impact as a group in your own interest" (Hartsock 1990:163, quoting Reagon).

To claim that women's sexuality is essential to women's identity is not to claim that all women experience their sexuality in the same way, even remotely in the same way. There are women who cannot bring themselves to look at their bodies. There are others who express themselves most effectively by dancing naked in front of audiences. And there are others who experience their bodies as comfortable media of erotic expression in a variety of intersubjective encounters. Sexuality is experienced positively by some women in sado-masochistic relations with other women or with men. Some women experience their sexuality as a way of attracting men, some as a way of attracting women. Some think of it essentially as a means of having babies. Others, as a form of social energy which enlivens all social participants. There are as many ways of thinking about one's sexuality as there are about one's spirituality, or one's rationality. Each woman probably thinks of her personal sexuality in more ways than another woman could imagine. The point of focussing on women's sexuality as a category of analysis is not to claim a singular essence but to recognize the existence of women's sexuality as a concrete reality and to show that it has important implications for developing new structures of thought which reflect women's subjectivity rather than a flight from it.

I do not see any necessary opposition between essentialism and difference. Essentialisms are constructed according to differences. An important thing to remember is that essentialisms can also include differences. Fuss says that essentialism and constructionism are "co-implicated with each other. . . . Constructionism is fundamentally dependent upon essentialism to do its work" (1989:xii). Constructionism and essentialism are polarized around culture and nature in the usual debate. This debate depends on a separation of ontology and epistemology. It relies on the exclusivity of historical consciousness, on the one hand, and a consciousness of a non-historical reality, on the other hand. In other words, anti-essentialism or constructionism depends on the categorization established in Greek logic and the cultural constructions developed from categorical reasoning. If we accept that patriarchal culture developed out of a flight from women's sexuality, then there is little future in defining women's sexuality exclusively in terms of cultural constructions. The task, rather, is to return to women's sexuality, for however long it takes, to restore women's subjectivity as a basis for the structuring of language. That is, not to develop a feminist logic to attack masculinist logic; rather, it is to develop a strategy which will overcome the negation of women's sexuality and work toward developing a language that will acknowledge the body as an infrastructure of the symbolic order and to recognize the sex differences of bodies and the implications of those differences. The ontological essentialism which I adopt is inseparable from epistemological variations. There is no exclusive separation between ontological and linguistic orders of essentialism in the view developed throughout this book. That is, there are no real categories as opposed to nominal categories. All categories are nominal and yet they are connected to an ontology that is a process of changing conditions, including changing perceptions and epistemologies. Within the process are actual things like bodies.

Luce Irigaray claims that male logic came out of male morphology: the form and structure of men's bodies. It is largely a logic of separation, based on the independence of individual units from each other. The penis is considered the central signifier of men's place in the world, which is developed in both the imaginary and the symbolic. It largely signifies self-sufficiency and the centrality of mens' logic of individuation in the cultural specific language system. In her analysis, she starts from the psychoanalyst's interest in the unconscious. Femininity is seen as a construct from male language. She says 'In a woman's language, the concept as such would have no place" (Irigaray 1985a:123). Language is only part of the 'symbolic' for Irigaray. There are three components to it: body, psyche, and language (Whitford 1991a:37). The symbolic interacts with the 'imaginary': unconscious fantasy (p. 65). The point of psychoanalysis, for Irigaray, is to change the imaginary and, thereby, create new possibilities for language. She does not agree with her teacher, Jacques Lacan, that there are immutable structures in the unconscious which cannot be altered. She sees the imaginary in women and men to be dominated by fantasies which do not facilitate wellness for women. The imaginary has to be reconstructed in relation to language for women to be able to experience and express themselves positively as women. The construction of identity requires mirroring within one's own private subjectivity between the imaginary and the symbolic. It also requires social mirroring that reflects positive social attitudes towards women. Irigaray correctly assumes that change in social attitudes requires change in the imaginary, the underpinning of individual and social consciousness.

Like Jenijoy La Belle, Luce Irigaray believes that mirroring is a continuous process rather than a stage in early childhood of ego formation.[6] Ego formation is described as a life-long process which is shaped by the forces of the imaginary in conjunction with those of the symbolic. In order to change the symbolic structures of consciousness, she sees the task of psychoanalysis to be that of mirroring, through speaking new words, alternative ways for the unconscious to fantasize. The body is integral to fantasies and, through fantasies, it is intrinsic to symbolic constructions. Just as the male body is integral to male consciousness and the formation of linguistic structures, so the female body is the foundation from which women's consciousness is constructed. This seems to be axiomatic unless one accepts the existence of disembodied consciousness. Although it is axiomatic that consciousness occurs in bodies, there is resistance to the claim that a consciousness that is associated with a woman's body is different in some ways from that which is male-body identified. From Irigaray's perspective, psychoanalysis for women is centrally about creating the imaginary (unconscious phantasy) which will enable symbolic structured meaning to reflect the reality of the prereflective aspect of consciousness. The unconscious is something equated with the prereflective aspect of consciousness in my model of consciousness.

There is some ambiguity in specifying the unconscious in relation to prereflective, felt awareness of consciousness. If one posits the existence of an unconscious, then if one were interested in expanding one's consciousness one might well dig into the unconscious. In this way of speaking it sounds as though the unconscious is a real thing, like a cauldron (e.g., Dourley, 1990). In my view of consciousness there is a continuum between reflection and prereflective sensations. Reflective consciousness, in my account, is about conceptualization and theorization. Increased consciousness involves becoming more conscious of one's sensations and ideas. To be conscious is to be awake to them: one may be dreaming, on a shamanic journey, in a meditative state, doing chores around the house, or any kind of activity. The idea is to develop power of attention.[7] Increasing one's consciousness includes bringing into consciousness what wasn't there. To say that it was in one's unconscious leaves considerable room for speculation of its status: lost memory, collective memory to which one did not previously pay attention. This question of the status of the unconscious is relevant to my discussions of spiritual consciousness, as mentioned earlier. I am ambivalent about the meaning of the unconscious and therefore am not entirely comfortable with the psychoanalytic project of revealing it. At the same time, I am disposed toward increasing consciousness in all possible ways, therefore psychoanalytic approaches hold a certain fascination.

Rationality for Irigaray is inseparable from the imaginary. A fertile rationality requires the imaginary. Otherwise, the sterility of Parmenides' logic of unitary Being and the anorexia of Frege's transcendent Thoughts characterize rationality. Whitford says,

> For Irigaray, the conceptualization of rationality is inseparable from the conceptualization of sexual difference; thus the imbalance in the symbolization of sexual difference is a clue to other forms of imbalance that have far-reaching consequences: sexual difference is a "problematic which might enable us to put in check the manifold forms of destruction of the world. . . . [S]exual difference could constitute the horizon of worlds of a fertility which we have not yet experienced." (1991a:58)

Western logic, from Irigaray's point of view, is about individuating and reducing ambiguity. Her view is consistent with Andrea Nye's study of the history of logic. While the logicians exhibit relations between concepts, pure thoughts, and mathematical notations with the purpose of establishing truths, Irigaray depicts equations between "the (symbolic) phallus, stable form, identity, and individuation" (Whitford 1991a:59). The logic of identity is seen by Irigaray to parallel the singularity of the male sex organ (Irigaray, 1985a:26). By contrast, she notes that the two lips of the female genitalia constitute no single form, but rather a presence or nearness to each other. The two lips "keep woman in touch with herself, but without any possibility of distinguishing what is touching from what is touched" (p. 26). Her appetite is for touch not for separation. Parmenides flight from the embrace of the goddess, his reduction of her presence to hostess, within the cave, after entering the two lips, is the point at which logic becomes the extension of man's love affair with himself as an engenderer of truth apart from women's sexuality. Irigaray's focus on women's desire for embrace brings us back to an orientation toward the truth of connectedness through a rationality that is shaped by its connection to the imaginary in which presence and contiguity of difference is central to identity rather than separation and singularity.

To focus on women's sexuality is not to argue for biological determinism or any form of determinism. Multiple determinacy is a central issue. Women's sexuality is experienced in as many ways as there are women. I am not referring to an idealized form of sexuality which is expressed in an ideal femininity. I am alluding to the sexuality of women that is part of the disappointments and enjoyments of the flesh in which women's consciousnesses, just as men's, are grounded. Women's sexuality, in Irigaray's terms, is fertile with creative potential. It is part of the imaginary that interacts with language. Revisioning our sexuality is integral to developing new symbolic structures which reflect the fertility of the imaginary and creative potency of our speech. Our bodies are sexual bodies which enter our speech in indeterminate ways. Our power is in our attention to our creative potency. Our bodies reflect our power. The ambiguity of women's relations to their bodies, owing to explicit and implicit cultural messages, often causes discomfort for women as speakers as well as for women and men as observers.

Hélène Cixous says,

Listen to a woman speak at a public gathering (if she hasn't painfully lost her wind). She doesn't 'speak,' she throws her trembling body forward; she lets go of herself, she flies; all of her passes into her voice, and it's with her body that she vitally supports the 'logic' of her speech. Her flesh speaks true. She lays herself bare. In fact, she physically materializes what she's thinking; she signifies it with her body. In a certain way she *inscribes* what she's saying, because she doesn't deny her drives the intractable and impassioned part they have in speaking. (1991:226)

Women sometimes feel like spectacles when they speak. That is due in part to the way their bodies inscribe their speech. A male friend told me that he notices when women speak they often reflect a nervousness which manifests itself in red blotches on the neck. He said he has never seen the same thing happen with men, at least not in such a marked way. The amount of courage if often takes for a woman to speak with authority in public is considerable. Women are generally acutely aware of themselves as possible spectacles in those situations. Cultural prescriptions to keep quiet or speak tentatively are enormous. Perhaps that accounts in part for the exaggerated body expression in women's speech. There is also, however, a real sense in which women's consciousnesses are permeated by body consciousness that makes it virtually impossible for them to speak as if their bodies were invisible. One cannot menstruate every month, for example, without a certain amount of body consciousness. If a woman has had a baby there is almost certainly an extended period of heightened body consciousness. The combination of these experiences and cultural images of women's bodies, makes body consciousness an important issue in a discussion of women's consciousness.

Women's bodies, of course, are not always as obvious in their speech as Cixous makes out or as indicated in my friend's observations. It can be argued, however, that women's bodies are a significant part of their consciousness when they speak. While men have attempted to ignore their bodies in the development of rules of logic, their logic reflects their imaginary, grounded in their bodies. Their imaginary has developed within the context of separation from women's bodies and the association of their bodies with the power of refutation and the erection of their independent supremacy. The reality of women's bodies as bodies that engender has been repressed and distorted. A consequence is that women have been buried in the construction of cultural inscriptions which write the body but which are not written on by the body. Irigaray points out that if women are not going to be buried alive, as was the fate of Antigone,[8] they have to remain attached to their bodies as sites of their own becoming. Cultural inscriptions have to reflect the engendering activities of women's bodies.[9]

Irigaray's notion of the sensible transcendental is an attempt to rethink the cultural division between the body and intellect. She defines the sensible transcendental as "the material texture of beauty" (Irigaray 1992:75). Beauty is embodied beauty. Irigaray equates love with beauty. Both have regenerative power that evokes receptiveness and responsiveness in one's own being as well as in others. Ugliness, by contrast, is that which cannot be loved. It has no engendering power. Rationality without love/beauty has no power to facilitate growth. Rationality is to include the body component. Conceptualization is not free-floating, transcendental but is sensible transcendental. As Whitford notes, the transcendental field for Irigaray corresponds to the symbolic order (Whitford 1991a: 154). It is our cultural dwelling place. If women are to dwell in culture they cannot be relegated exclusively to the sensible, as they are in men's logic which is founded on a flight from women's bodies into transcendent thought. For women to create their own subjectivity in terms of the sensible transcendental it is necessary for men to open space by reclaiming their grounding in women's bodies (i.e., their mothers') and then to locate their subjectivity in their own bodies in relation to women's bodies.

I agree with Irigaray's view that the sensible transcendental is knowledge of the power of the "immanent flourishing of the divine in the flesh." It is that kind of knowledge that is aimed at through spiritual practices which are directed toward the integration of wisdom and compassion in consciousness and corresponding ethical action. Knowledge of the sensible transcendental, of beauty in the engendering power of women's bodies, supports the power of ethical action. Expression of such knowledge through language requires attention to women's bodies as places where spiritual power dwells. The same argument applies to the body of the earth, as I shall discuss in the last chapter.

If men were to accept their dependence (as in birth dependence) on the engendering of women's bodies there might be less inclination for them to deny the influence of their own bodies on the reflective component of their consciousness. This is to say that if men were more connected to the maternal ground of their being, they might be more aware of their own bodies as part of their consciousness. Their ideas, then, would be more contextualized by the sensible transcendental. The transcendent might be experienced as spirit within each person's materiality. Accordingly, there would likely be less inclination to search for the alleged transcendent power of thought. Jane Gallop (1988) points out that Jacques Lacan's theory of the distinction between the symbolic phallus and the biological penis is "a division which exemplifies the mind/body split, disembodying the phallus and rendering it transcendental. The disembodied phallus is the linchpin of the move that raises maleness, a bodily attribute, to the realm of the spirit, leaving femaleness mired in inert flesh" (Gallop 1988:8). The denigration of the sensible, and the corresponding rejection by men of their connection to the maternal body, propelled men in the search for transcendence and immortality through the logical relations of disembodied thoughts.

A return by men to their birth place (i.e., the maternal body) would allow for positive connotations of embodiment in their imaginary. Unconscious or non-conscious positive attitudes towards their connection to their mothers' bodies might facilitate greater positive consciousness of their own embodiment in the construction of their identity. Their imaginary would then be developed from an orientation of connectedness rather than separateness. The connectedness would be twofold: to themselves and to women. The prescription to ignore one's dependency on the maternal and to deny the influence of one's bodily impressions on one's ideas would be undermined in the process of connecting to body as the infrastructure for thought. The possibility of a new male symbolic structuring of men's subjectivity could occur along the lines of the sensible transcendental. The inseparability of ideas and bodily awareness in men's consciousness would be grounded in their acknowledgment of women's bodily engendering. The body would be included in rationality.

If that were to happen (which is likely), women would be freer to define their own subjectivity as sensible transcendental. They could conceptualize from their bodies without apology or fear of making spectacles of themselves. Their imaginary would develop in relation to their dwelling place in the symbolic order, the transcendental field. The transcendental field would develop in relation to the indwelling of the sensible. The interaction of the sex-specific transcendental fields would contribute to new developments in the imaginary of women and men in continuously different ways. This is not a form of essentialism which maintains the division between the rationality of men and the biology of women. Rather, it is a strategy to develop a more comprehensive, integrated view of the essence of rationality in which consciousness is understood as an interactive process of felt sensations, conceptualizations, and theorizing.

Jane Gallop's rejection of the criticism that Irigaray's attention to sex-specificity reinforces biological determinism sums up the approach which I am attempting to articulate. Gallop says with reference to Irigaray, "I find she is not trapped in the body but uses anatomical figures to renew thought, to move it out of its ideological ruts. The tendency to dismiss Irigaray as trapped in biologism bespeaks the split which makes us suspect that any sustained attention to the body must fall outside the bounds of serious thought" (1988:8). Irigaray's notion of the sensible transcendental is inconsistent with biological determinism. It is also inconsistent with social constructionism, a form of sociological essentialism.

Inscribing Meaning

Elizabeth Grosz argues that the body is "the central object over and through which relations of power and resistance are played out" (1990a: 81). Her claim reflects the views of Luce Irigaray, J.F. Lyotard, G. Deleuze, J. Derrida, and M. Foucault, among others. She says of these authors that "each is committed to a non-reductive materialism, a materialism which, rather than mere brute physicality, also includes the materiality of discourses, as well as psychical desires and unconscious presences" (p. 81). The body is seen as a site of enfolded interior and exterior inscriptions which cannot be independently identified. Subjectivity is constructed through social and psychical inscriptions, in conjunction with bodily materiality. In Grosz's writing, it is not clear to me whether she is willing to grant an actual reality to the materiality of the body, whether the body is wholly a function of cultural inscriptions, or whether she is not quite certain how to describe relations between body and language. I take her to have more affinity with the second position than the other two. She makes it clear that she rejects social constructionism which ignores the place of the body in analysis of socio-economic power relations. In particular, she rejects the sociological essentialism of Marxist approaches. I support her in that rejection. For Marxist feminists and those who claim that subjectivity is the product of social construction[10] the body is "an object whose functioning is political and which socially marks male and female as distinct, and separate from mind" (1990b:3). Gender rather than sex is seen as the proper focus of attention in Marxist feminist analysis. Proper resocialization is believed to yield gender neutrality from that perspective. Attention to sex-specificity is seen by social constructionists as irredeemably biologistic. I agree with Grosz that the view of self as sociologically determined relies on the old split between biology and cognition. Analysis of bodily production and reproduction occurs in terms of social and economic material production that determines the prevailing ideology. The economy of sexuality is explained by reference to the economy of material production. Marxist feminists' and other social constructionists' focus on the material conditions of production while ignoring the materiality of the body is an egregious embarrassment in their account of production/reproduction. This is an illustration of how deeply engrained the logic of Western thought runs. It is also an example of how new thought, such as feminist theory, grows out of old patterns and is not discontinuous with them.

By contrast, Grosz says that "feminists can meaningfully talk about women as an oppressed group, or a site of possible resistance, only by means of the specificity of the female body, and its place in locating women's lived experiences and social positions" (1989:2). Subjects, in her view, are produced through the process of inscribing meaning on the body. The traditions of psychoanalysis and phenomenology emphasize the lived experience of the body.[11] Psychoanalysis studies the psychic map that is inscribed on the body, whereas phenomenology has more to do with social mapping. The two are not necessarily exclusive approaches, but they have different focusses which can lead them in different directions. I am concerned here with psychoanalysis rather than phenomenology, as that is the tradition out of which Luce Irigaray writes. Psychoanalysts describe the mapping process in somewhat different ways. Freud, for example, talked about 'primary narcissism' as the period of child development when a unifying image emerged in a child's consciousness. That is the formation of the ego. The underlying fragmentation and swirling desires of the pre-oedipal phase are contained within the structure of identity a boy child forms in relation to his father, who represents rational control of unconscious desires. Freud's developmental theory is in line with the logic of Parmenides and the flight from womanhood. A girl child's identity remains associated with chaotic bodily urges which are never disciplined in the way a boy's must be for the development of his ego.

Jacques Lacan's moment of identification or ego formation is at the mirror-stage (about six months). His mirror-stage corresponds to Freud's primary narcissism in that the significance of the body is reflected in the ego image in the mirror. The psychic map of subjectivity is reflected back in a unified, specular image. The specular image is the body outline of the psychic and social inscriptions. The fantasy of the body is internalized in the specular image. That fantasy, for Lacan, is the 'imaginary anatomy' and is sometimes experienced, for example, in hypochondria or phantom limbs. The map and the body are not always in accord with each other, especially in extreme situations like phantom limbs. Those extreme situations indicate possibilities about the lack of identity between the body and psychic maps of it in more normal conditions. The point is that body consciousness is inseparable from psychic consciousness, which is embedded in social consciousness. In the psychoanalytic tradition social consciousness is not always accounted for. For example, neither Freud nor Lacan challenged the sex-specificity (i.e., the maleness) of psychoanalytic theory of ego formation. The separation from chaos and identification with order was a condition of adequate subjectivity of men in the accounts of Freud and Lacan. Women were feared and/or extolled for their position outside the symbolic order of alleged rational discourses. Freud and Lacan claimed that rationality develops as the ego cuts loose from its maternal moorings. In their theories, the bodily engendering of women is forgotten or denigrated.

Feminist psychoanalysts have emphasized the significance of maternal connectedness in both their theories of personality development and their theories of moral development, to develop an alternative understanding of the self-determining individual. Of the feminist psychoanalysts (including the mothers of psychoanalysis: Melanie Klein, Helene Deutsch, Anna Freud, and Karen Horney),[12] Luce Irigaray is probably the one who has focussed most intensely on the significance of the body as a site of psychical, social, and cultural inscriptions. Her focus, according to Grosz, is on the importance of morphology rather than anatomy. I am uncertain what that distinction means for Grosz. Morphology is defined by Grosz as "the shape or meaning of the body. . . . [which] as a social, cultural and discursive object is produced yet may form a site of resistance to its social inscriptions" (1990b:6). Grosz wants to avoid identification of women with the body, per se. And for good reasons. Men have assigned women to the place of the body in their conceptualization of themselves as mind in their quests for God-like immortality, absolutely free of the disappointments of the body. The maternal infrastructure has been taken for granted and denied at the same time. Women were assigned to the roles of bodily engendering by men who tried to forget their indebtedness to women for their engendering. Such indebtedness cannot be acknowledged without also recognizing the power of bodily engendering. Refusal to acknowledge their debt allowed men to develop a logic of reasoning that they could view as the ultimate mode of engendering: creation by words of power. Categorical reasoning inscribed women's bodies according to the interests of the inscribers. As Grosz points out in her agreement with Irigaray, it is only when men "return the masculine to its own language" (1990b:7) that they won't be everything (humanity) and there will be space for women to include femininity in language.

The current 'isomorphism' between discourse and male sexuality as described by Grosz, largely based on Irigaray's analysis, consists in the following five areas of 'morpho-logic.' They are the privileging of unity, the form of the self, the visibility of the body-shape, the specularizability of the body parts, and the importance of the erection. We remember from Parmenides' unity of Being that differences are occluded in identity in order to postulate an essential sameness. Sameness or unity was located in transcendent thoughts beyond the reach of desiring, perspiring, menstruating, or pregnant bodies. Men's bodies were inscribed with the power of reason. The phallus was designated to signify that power. For Freud, the visibility of the male body shape is reflected back in a primary narcissism, a moment of identification through unification. For Lacan, the specularization of the body in the mirror-image reflects the psychic inscription of self-identification with bodily representation. It is the body as fantasized in the psyche, not just a blank-slate representation. The power of the psychically inscribed and specularized body revolves around the symbolic phallus which is the discursive analogue for the specularized erect penis. By the time the baby identifies himself as a unified body-form with psychic representation, parents have inscribed their attitudes towards the body of the baby. Differently sexed bodies are inscribed with different meanings from the time the parents are aware of the sex of the fetus or baby. When ego formation occurs in early childhood the body is already inscribed. The child is 'always already' listening as self-identity develops. The process of identification occurs within a set of power dynamics between the body and inscriptions onto it. The parallelism between specularized male morphology and words of power is not paralleled by the relation between female morphology and women's words of power. There is no parallelism between women's bodies and the controlling power of reason as it is expressed in patriarchal language.

Irigaray claims in *This Sex which Is Not One* that in order to subvert the isomorphism between male morphology and language it is necessary to determine *"the conditions under which systematicity itself is possible"* (1985a:74). Irigaray does not believe in unmediated speaking of the body for women any more than she accepts the male subject as disembodied word. For her, body and language are necessarily mutually influential. She says,

The reciprocal integration of language and the body, in which the imaginary originates, decentres man in relation to himself and marks the beginning of his wandering [errancy]. The impossible return to the body as the secure locus of his self-identity is its ineluctable corollary. From now on, he is mediated by language and one will only find trace of him in the word of the other. (Whitford 1991a:41, quoting from Irigaray)

In *Speculum of the Other Woman* (1985b), Irigaray analyzes Plato's myth of the cave from Book VI of *The Republic*. This is an example of spelling out the ways in which sexuality is encoded in an influential epistemology. It uses psychoanalytic attention to mirroring as a necessary condition for self-identification and its parallelism with the power of knowledge. In the myth of the cave there are three kinds of knowing which are identified with three kinds of realities. The realities are the transcendental realm of the Forms (Reality), the world of sun and trees and other natural existents (reflections of Reality), and the cave (shadows). The corresponding ways of knowing are Truth, beliefs, and opinions. Margaret Whitford (1991a:105-18) points out that in patriarchal history men are the Real (the Same), patriarchal women are the reflectors of the Real (the other of the Same), and independent women are shadowy figures which exist outside the realm of knowledge or representational beliefs (the other of the Other). Independent women's 'truths' are rejected in the name of Truth. Creation starts from the realm of the Real. The world is real insofar as it participates in the Truth of the transcendental Real. The inhabitants of the cave live in an unreal realm where the light of reason doesn't shine. The natural objects of the world bend in the direction of the Sun. In the myth of the cave, the idea of natural derives from its ability to reflect the causal power of transcendent creativity. The cave (symbolizing the womb) is excluded from the process of representation of the Real. Male identification with the Real and their engendering power through the Word (logic) reflects the systematizing of isomorphism between male morphology and knowledge as represented in language.

Whitford says, "The effect is that the male function takes over and incorporates all the female functions, leaving women outside the scene, but supporting it, a condition of representation" (1991a:106). The engendering power of women through the womb (the cave) is associated with mere opinion. The reality of men's dependence on women's bodies for their existence is denied or forgotten in the establishment of men's creative authority through impregnable, transcendent Ideas. According to Frege, communication depends on the transmission of Transcendent Thoughts between disembodied minds. Frege cleaned the flesh off the bones of logic. His goal was to set out the anorexic truths of Transcendent Thoughts. Fleshiness or messiness was repulsive.

Women who aspire to learn these Truths often have a difficult time with their menstruating bodies. Monthly bleeding is probably the most poignant reminder to a woman that she is a woman who is grounded in her immanence, regardless of her aspirations to be transcendent in her ideas. The cost of sharing in these Truths is high, namely, distancing herself from her own bodied knowledge. But the alternative has a high cost as well. Women who express their 'truths' from the cave are denied credibility. Their 'truths' are defined by lack. They lack participation in the Real. They do not reflect the Real, they are without insight. They, therefore, can be forgotten. At that point, Irigaray says *no* to forgetting women's bodies in the economy of knowledges. She says, "Let's not immobilize ourselves in these borrowed notions" (1985a:217). The task is to bring women's bodies into a new paradigm of knowledges. She says, "Let our imperatives be only appeals to move, to be moved, together" (p. 217). Irigaray's strategy includes women talking together so that we are not buried alive in male language. Separation of women from each other by attributing credibility to women only when they reflect the realities of men is a technique for continuing to bury women alive in cultural spaces dominated by men.

The myth of Antigone is used by Irigaray as a representation of women's place when they identify with their mothers. Antigone is the daughter of Jocasta who was the mother of Oedipus. After the social catastrophe between Oedipus and his mother, Antigone affirms her blood ties with her mother at the expense of her identification with the nation state's admonition for severance of that identification. Identification with the edicts of the state overruled one's association with a family member. Whitford points out that "Identification with the *mother* in this kind of situation means obliteration of the *woman*, or her 'death.' She is punished by being walled up alive to be a guardian of the dead. Whitford claims that "Antigone in the tomb, walled up alive, is an image of woman in patriarchy, walled up, unable to be heard, but also a guilt-producing fantasy. The threat represented by women's refusal to be 'unconscious earth, nurturing nature' . . . is the threat of the fantasy/phantasm returning and the guilt it brings with it for what has been done to Antigone/the woman" (1991a:118).

Men's fear of women resisting their places and their positions as reflectors of men's realities is built into the systematizing of the power of knowledges through linguistic structuring. The logic of men's reasoning is designed to exhibit the truth of their concepts. It is a matter of arranging the concepts correctly so the truth of the propositions cannot be rejected. The structures of language require certain conditions of ordering of concepts in order to be communicated. Learning the rules of logic is a condition of communicating the Truth.

Irigaray claims that within this system of language there is no possibility for women who identify themselves as other of the Other (in contrast to other of the Same) to express their truths in existing linguistic structures. Her task is to subvert existing structures and to develop alternative modes of communication which reflect the presence of women's engendering agency. This can only be done, from her point of view, if we bring women's morphology into discursive forms of communication. In my interpretation of Irigaray there is not a clear distinction between morphology and anatomy. I agree with Vicki Kirby that "Morphology . . . is not anatomy, or indeed biology, although it must nevertheless include them" (1991:16). Just as it is problematic to make much sense of the phallus as a symbolic signifier of power as though it were not grounded in the anatomical penis, so it is difficult to separate the signification of the two lips from the anatomy of the two lips. This does not mean that any sense can be made of the two lips (or the penis) without reference to their inscribed social and cultural meanings. It does mean, however, that the body as an agent in relation to inscriptions must be acknowledged.

Irigaray says about the body as an infrastructure for language that it is the material on which language depends.

Language [*langage*], however formal it may be, is sustained by blood, by flesh, by material elements. Who and what has sustained it: how to pay that debt? . . . [How] to bring the maternal-feminine into language [*langage*]: from the point of view of theme, motif, subject, articulation, syntax, etc. (Whitford 1991:45, quoting from Irigaray)

With reference to the two lips as a material infrastructure for women's language Irigaray claims that the syntax would be different from that of men's language as we have it today. It would not be constructed according to a unified subject and a predicate which reflected static attributes. Rather the syntax "would involve nearness, proximity, but in such an extreme form that it would preclude any distinction of identities, any establishment of ownership, thus any form of appropriation (Irigaray 1985a:134). Whitford points out that for Irigaray there is an isomorphism between language and culture. In her view the two lips can be interpreted in terms of a feminist politics which initiates a new way of speaking that entails dialogue of mutuality. She says, "two lips stand for what has been left out of the social contract: namely the maternal genealogy, and women's relations between and among themselves" (Whitford 1991a:101).

Diana Fuss (1992) claims that Irigaray establishes a metonymic relation between body and language in her use of the two lips. Metonomy is the use of one element of a thing to signify the whole, such as a 'sceptre' for 'sovereignty' (Random House dictionary example). The two lips stands for contiguity. Fuss holds that contiguity is the distinguishing feature of *parler femme*, speaking as women. The two lips represent touching or nearness. They are neither double nor single but are in relation. Their reality is constituted by contiguity, proximity. Elizabeth Grosz takes the notion of contiguity further and suggests that the two lips act in a deconstructive way which initiates undecideability into the structuring of language. Rather than an either/or structuring with an abyss between the categories, the two lips provide a metaphor of continuity. They are neither inside (vagina) nor outside (clitoris), neither invisible nor visible, neither subject nor other.

Irigaray's use of the image of mucous pushes the metaphor of continuity further than the two lips. She goes beyond nearness, which includes the existence of boundaries, to a blurring of boundaries and the fluidity of physical space. The mucous image also stretches the notion of acceptability with respect to difference. Whitford says mucous represents the most 'abject'[13] about the body, the unspeakable and unthinkable. Mucous exists on the boundary between the inside and outside, like the scum on milk after it is boiled. It challenges the dichotomy between transcendent and immanent, which has been maintained in part through the projection of body disintegration onto women. Immanence is about changing conditions, decomposition, and regeneration.

De Beauvoir drew our attention to the problem of women's immersion in the immanent and the need to dissociate ourselves from our bodies in order to move into the transcendent. In this view she was consistent with Sartre's view of the subject/other as *being for the self* and *being in the self*. The former constitutes transcendence while the latter reflects immanence. In Sartre's view the struggle of becoming is the struggle between the transcendent self and the immanent self. Encounters between subject and other, in his view, invariably include self-loss because the transcendence of a subject is displaced by immanence when one is present to the other as subject. Although De Beauvoir provided the world with the important insight into the construction of woman as Other by male Subjects, she did not challenge cultural symbolic structuring which is based on binary oppositions. In particular she did not question the separation of transcendent and immanent into exclusive categories. In her view it was necessary for women to overcome their connection to their bodies in order to strive for transcendence and, thereby, gain freedom of being. She admonished women to become transcendent like men in their rationality. Her *Second Sex* remains a monumental contribution to feminism because of the analysis of woman as Other. It is a very supportive text for women in that it justifies women as subjects. It does not, however, help women to live in their bodies and celebrate them.

By contrast, Irigaray sees her task as working toward the construction of new symbolic structuring based on a logic of continuity rather than of exclusion. I support her claim that new images are required in the imaginary for the possibility of thinking new thoughts which reflect images of women-for-women. The symbolization of mucous as a reality that is partly open, is neither fluid nor solid, suggests continuity. It reflects the ontology of interrelatedness that underscores the spirituality, epistemology, ethics, and social theory explored throughout this book. The image of mucous is a radical signifier of body messiness. Because of its radicalness it is a useful image with which to break through the barriers surrounding the constitution of bodies and their functions. The placenta is another image that might be useful for that purpose. There is only a short step from images of messiness to images associated with the female body, such as menstrual blood. A breakthrough in representations of the abject would possibly open space for positive images of women's bodily functions and fluids, as well as those of men. The point of developing a woman's language is to reflect women as subjects within the larger system of language. Whitford brings our attention to an important distinction in Irigaray's use of language. The distinction is between language as *langue* and language as *langage*. *Langue* is "the corpus of language available to the speaker" while *langage* is "the corpus as used by a particular person or group, e.g., the language of the mentally ill, or the language of lovers" (Whitford 1991a:42). Irigaray, from Whitford's perspective, is not intending to set up a competing language system but rather to work toward articulating a "communication system" among an identifiable group.

Just as Mary Daly writes of the importance of Be-Friending, Luce Irigaray claims that a matrix of supporting conditions is required to generate change. Be-Friending is about creating contexts in which women, from whatever class, race, ethnic group, sexual orientation, etc., may communicate with each other as friends and/or lovers. While the philosophy of language that Irigaray is developing is global in its intentions, it can only be experienced by each woman in the place where she dwells. Accordingly, there can be no single language for women, but rather different forms of discourse which express localized knowledges. Irigaray's global approach is an umbrella approach which can be interpreted and used variously. It is part of the process of Be-Friending. Be-Friending is about making it possible for women, wherever they dwell, to participate in the community with which they identify and share their knowledges. Out of their collective strength the possibility might emerge to move beyond their own group and communicate their interests to members of other groups.

In this way political solidarity across group boundaries is possible. That is the political import of Irigaray's admonition to women to develop languages that express their subjectivities. Daly's idea of Be-Friending is a global idea which is to be applied in particular cultural conditions. In a similar way, Irigaray claims that women need a language in which they can speak from their own positions, rather than as cultural Others or as predicates in sentences. The context required for the development of a women's *langage* are those of loving relations among women as they relate between themselves as subjects. Whitford says,

The conditions of emergence of female subjectivity are simultaneously, then, love between women (a female homosexual economy) which is the matrix which can generate change, and language or discourse as a process of enunciation, a dynamic exchange between interlocutors which can transfigure flesh and blood. This is also the prerequisite for dialogue between the sexes, so that each can offer a house or home to the other. (1991a:48-49)

Homosexual, for Irigaray, is the equivalent of monosexual. An alternative word is provided by Ann Ferguson (1991): homosocial. It refers to groups which consist of one sex. In my view, homosocial captures the intention of Irigaray's admonition for women to establish relations among themselves for the purpose of freeing themselves for full expression of themselves as women, without being subjugated to male prescriptions of femininity. In Irigaray's view, the symbolic order is structured from a male monosexual or homosexual (i.e., homosocial) economy. It is based on the exchange of goods and women among men. Cultural practices are supported by men's words of power to define the objects of relations and the power dynamics of the relations themselves. Relations between men are relations between subject and other, with an exchange of subject positions according to the rules of fair play. There is very little opportunity in that economy for women to speak as subjects apart from reflecting the truths of men. Women's construction as objects, both in language and culture because of their sexual difference leaves them almost no possibility for congruency between their subjectivity and their female identity as it is culturally constructed. They cannot enunciate their subjectivity. That is, women cannot be speaking subjects as other of the Other, they can only be other of the Same. Their female identity in the male economy depends on their ability to reflect back the male ego without being seen.

Irigaray's psychoanalytic approach to studying the systematization of the male homosexual (homosocial) economy includes two focusses: she looks for how philosophers project their own egos onto the world and how they ignore their ties to their mothers. Whitford describes these two focusses respectively as the analysis of the "structure of specularization" and the "infrastructure." The structure of specularization refers back to Lacan's mirroring stage in which the ego is formed. From then on the male projects his own ego onto the world, the world becomes the mirror, he sees himself everywhere, and women are the material out of which the mirror is made but which does not reflect itself, like the tinfoil behind the mirror. The infrastructure refers to the mother holding the child before the mirror in the specularization process, the mother is eclipsed and forgotten in the manner of matricide, men conceal their occlusion of the mother. The mother holding the mirror is analogous to the maternal-feminine in the flesh and blood. The infrastructure which supports the reflection of the ego is excluded from the realm of discourse. She is one of the women in the cave who is other of the Other.

If women are to become the enunciators of their own lived experiences, they need to reflect each other in loving contexts. Through dialogue with each other they might develop their own language and bring it into the larger system of language to change the logical structures. The bodies, psyches, and language of women co-construct each other through the emerging subjectivities of women as they speak from love within their own selves and with their own communities. Speaking truths within the context of love, women will build their own houses in which they can welcome visitors from elsewhere. The status of women with an independent ontology, a corresponding ethics of intersubjectivity and social realities characterized by greater egalitarianism through negotiation of differences is the kind of vision that guides my enthusiasm for pursuing new forms of enunciation for women, as well as for men. Men need to reclaim their imaginary as the rightful infrastructure of their symbolic structuring. Then they could connect to the underlying non-rational factors which are currently denied in the name of rationality.

Hermeneutics of Scepticism

In this section I shall explore the logic which leads to the either/or distinction between essentialism and constructionism and the either/or distinction between gender neutrality and sex-specificity. The two distinctions are contiguous with each other and yet are sufficiently different to warrant separate discussions about them.

Andrea Nye's study of the history of logic clearly shows the construction of exclusive categories in conceptualizing and theorizing social organization. She says with respect to the logician, "all of his natural life is only dead skin that falls away to reveal the hard bone of thought itself" (1990:3). For Nye there is no single theory about logic and language, it is a matter of different logics by different men with particular interests motivating them. In her view, logic is what men do and say. "The relations between speakers that logic structures are alien to feminist aims" (1990:177). They are relations based on the purposes and desires of men, while denying the intervention of the personal in the structures of logic. The formulation, by logicians, of the two logical fallacies described earlier (genetic fallacy and ad hominem fallacy) indicates the attitude of excluding the personal from alleged truth claims. While she advocates feminist challenge to the structuring of language through existing logical rituals, Nye rejects the notion of women's logic or women's language. She suggests a reading response rather than a logical response. A reading response, she believes, would allow for diverse interpretations and would stimulate thought rather than deny challenges, which is what current logical structuring does in the name of certainty.

Nye does not refer to any particular author in her rejection of the development of a woman's language. It would seem, however, that Irigaray would be a likely target. Irigaray's attempt to develop ways of speaking that reflect women's subjectivity is the purpose of her focus on women-centred language. Despite Nye's disclaimer, there is considerable similarity between her tentative suggestions, on the one hand, for women to develop ways of speaking where their interests are not lost in the rules of logic and Irigaray's attempt, on the other, to develop a strategy for women to speak as women. Nye's suggestion that women respond in ways that prick (!) the inflated male vanity rather than refute their logic could be interpreted in much the same way as Irigaray's call to women to listen with new ears, see with new eyes. Irigaray's metonymical use of the two lips and of mucous to break into new ways of thinking through the use of new images is a positive, reconstructive move that is contiguous with Nye's suggestion to expose the denials and non-thought in logic through challenging male vanity with respect to transcendent ideas.

Margaret Whitford claims that Irigaray's use of images that are not symbolized discursively such as the two lips and mucous opens up possibilities for many interpretations and new discoveries. In her view Irigaray unleased images that she cannot control. They are "impregnated with layers of symbolic meaning" (1991b:101). Because of the undecideability of interpretations of the images, they serve to break through a static orientation to definitions. They reflect the undefineability of femininity and are not to be taken literally, just as 'feminine,' as used by Irigaray, cannot be understood within the categories of men's logic. Irigaray's strategy is to develop alternate ways of speaking, based on a new imaginary. The imaginary, for her, refers to unconscious fantasies, which includes images and related desires. Prereflective feelings (sensations) which are felt in relation to images shape our ways of speaking. If we are to speak differently we must have different feelings about images that are inseparable from self-consciousness. Healthy speech requires healthy feelings. Both depend upon receptivity of oneself. Repression of images and feelings leads to distorted speech. Irigaray does not use the term 'alternate consciousnesses'; however, it is what she aims to bring about. She believes that a new imaginary is necessary in order to bring about a new symbolic order, in which language is situated.

Alternate consciousness is a breakthrough into a new kind of consciousness, compared to normative consciousness, as I discussed earlier. Alternate consciousnesses are sometimes equated with craziness. For example, from the point of view of normative consciousness, spiritual consciousness is often difficult to distinguish from craziness. It seems discontinuous with normal perceptions. The same can be said about some mental breakdowns. It is possible that some 'breakdowns' could be understood as 'breakthroughs,' as in spiritual breakthroughs to alternative consciousness. A major difference between a breakthrough and a breakdown is that the former has positive connotations while the latter has negative ones. Perhaps a breakdown is a condition for a breakthrough to alternative consciousness. It is likely that there is a need to let go of old patterns of thought and action before there is space for a new form of consciousness to develop. Indeed, that process characterizes the deconstruction and reconstruction in philosophical, psychological, literary, or socio-political analysis. There are different ways of letting go of old thought patterns and actions. One way is to abandon problematic concepts and images as much as possible in an attempt to formulate new symbolic systems of meaning. Another way is to use problematic concepts and images in subversive ways. Gender neutral approaches in feminism tend to make more use of the first method, while sex-specific approaches more characteristically employ the second (two of the most notable examples are those of Mary Daly and Luce Irigaray). I believe that both approaches are necessary at different times and in different contexts. They can be understood as contiguous rather than contradictory to each other. The important thing to remember is that in both approaches there is a breakdown with respect to old usage and a breakthrough into new ways of listening, seeing, feeling (touching!), tasting, and speaking.

The distinctions between new feminist essentialisms and social constructionists are not clear. Essentialism, as it is understood in this book, is about interacting processes of changing conditions. Social constructionism is about constructing reality through ways of seeing, feeling, listening, hearing, and so forth. The material conditions of each person's existence largely determine the kind of existence that is referred to as that person's reality and which forms the basis for describing reality in general. An important part of these conditions is the body of each person. It is through the body that a person interacts with all the other conditions. Accordingly, it is reasonable to pay attention to the body as a significant site of personal power and social power relations. Gender neutralists aim to undermine differential power relations between the sexes by locating body politics outside the body exclusively in the social realm of meaning. Language is the main medium of meaning, therefore, language is seen as the channel through which new meanings of the body are to be constructed. The body is seen to be written on by cultural meanings in language, without itself having a power to impact on the construction of meaning.

A sex-specific approach, by contrast, affirms body agency in the social construction of meaning. It is necessary, therefore, to use body images in the development of new meanings. A major challenge is to use images of bodies or body parts in ways that do not reinforce what is being deconstructed. Reconstruction requires alternate consciousness. This means, with regard to sex-specific approaches, that old images, such as the two lips, need to be imaged with new eyes and spoken about with a new language. The new language must convey new social meanings. The aim is not to develop a new language that can be understood only by a few. Rather the aim is to bring about new social meanings that can be understood by the majority and which will bring about new cultural thought patterns and social organization. The sex-specific approach of Luce Irigaray, for example, is not a reactionary essentialism. On the contrary, it is explicitly subversive in its use of female genital images to break down patriarchal meanings and break through into a celebration of women's sexuality. Luce Irigaray is wide awake. She can see that power is in attention. Women's power is most importantly in attention to their bodies as expressions of their legitimacy as females, apart from their relationships to men. The power that comes from experiencing one's legitimacy as a woman and the legitimacy of other women is not restricted to personal power. It is power that shapes the desire for social equality, including fair p(l)ay, healthy working conditions, and just treatment in the courts. In order for social justice to develop, it is necessary that women's power is adequately expressed in a shared language. An initial condition for that is a breakdown of oppressive social meanings with respect to women's bodies and a breakthrough into new ones. New meanings depend on new forms of consciousnesses that can be expressed through new languages. There is no single approach to the development of new social meanings, only the interaction of various voices.

A major difference between the orientations of Irigaray and Nye is the attention to the body. Irigaray's analysis of power and knowledge is situated in the body. Nye's is not. Situating the source of power struggles in the body is regarded with scepticism by those who are primarily interested in gender neutrality. Attention to the agency of the body is usually regarded as reactionary. Resocialization is considered the solution to the problem of the social construction of gender roles. Gender neutralists have a social constructionist view of the self which excludes body agency. I shall refer to this view of social constructionism as restricted social constructionism. It is restricted in that it excludes body agency. Sex-specificists, such as Luce Irigaray, also have a social constructionist view of the self, but they include body agency. A gender neutralist is sceptical of attempts to bring women's genitals into discursiveness because of the "traditional equation of women with their genital organs" (Whitford 1991b:97). There is a wariness of "producing images which are not immediately recaptured, or recapturable, by the dominant imaginary and symbolic economy in which woman figures for man" (p. 97).

The scepticism of gender neutralists with regard to images which have been widely denigrated is understandable. It is risky to take an image like the two lips and use it as an icon for women's liberation from sexual oppression. Images of women's genitals are easily recaptured by dominant negative cultural meanings that reduce women to body parts and support a functional view of woman's nature. In my view, Irigaray's 'philosophy in the feminine' is powerfully subversive precisely because it focusses on the labia, which is more or less an unspeakable body part in respected discourses. It does not automatically evoke positive thoughts, feelings or images about women's independent power. While the penis has long been associated with social power and privilege, the labia has not. The association of women's genitals with 'lack' is entrenched in the imaginary of patriarchal consciousnesses of women and men. Irigaray addresses the asymmetry between male anatomy and female anatomy in relation to social power. She shows very explicitly how the personal is political in her focus on the labia as an important image for the construction of a new imaginary that will reshape the symbolic order.

In Irigaray's view, a necessary condition for placing positive images of women in the symbol system is the existence of an imaginary in which women are imaged in their sex-specificity. There are no such images secured there now. Elizabeth Grosz points out that "it is not possible to position female-oriented images in place of male ones, where the underlying structure accords no specificity to the female" (Whitford 1991b:98, quoting Grosz). Sex-specific approaches aim to establish specificity to the female in the paradigm shift from patriarchal consciousness to one in which women's bodies are taken to be one of two normal kinds of bodies which can be experienced from within a web of social meanings that constitute social-sexual democracy. The road to constructing social-sexual democracy is, however, a risky one. One is in constant danger of falling into 'manholes' and becoming immured in dark places.

It is axiomatic to say that female specificity requires reference to women's embodiment. There is, however, no normative form of women's embodiment. Each woman is uniquely embodied. Women's embodiments are lived in accordance with the conditions of their class, race, ethnicity, sexual orientation, ableness, and a multitude of other determinants which inscribe their bodies. Differences among women's ways of living as women are as varied as women. Exploration into the vast differences makes one wonder what women have in common. There is no doubt that attention to particularities is necessary (might I say essential) in order to understand any one person or social and cultural patterns in different periods of history and geographical locations. At the same time, social change for women requires political solidarity among women. Political solidarity depends on some kind of shared identity as a group or set of groups that can relate on the basis of shared goals. A shared goal of feminists is that of social justice for women. That goal is embedded in the larger aim of social justice for all unjustly marginalized women and men.

Feminism focusses explicitly on justice for women, while recognizing the need to work for social justice for women and men. The focus on women depends on retaining the category of women as a unit of analysis. The single common feature about all women is their anatomy. It is given different meanings according to different social contexts. There is no single meaning that can be attributed to women's bodies. It cannot be denied, however, that the widespread oppression of women in our society today and in previous periods in history and places on the globe has to do with women's bodies. Yet, as Elspeth Probyn says, "one of the major problems . . . is that mere mention of the body is taken as shorthand for the reinscription of a realist epistemology" (1991:112). That is, it is assumed that the body is taken as raw material from which truth can be ascertained. Privileging the body in a realist epistemology means regarding the body as untainted and natural, independent of psychic and social inscriptions. It is this realist epistemology which informs arguments that derive destiny from biology.

For obvious reasons feminists recoil from the view of women's bodies as raw material in which the truth of their nature can be found. An alternative is to think of the body "as an image, a concept, within theory, and the strategic possibilities of pulling the image of the body into discourse" (Probyn 1991:115). The purpose is political: to create an enunciative space where the body is the conjuncture of feeling and structure (inscribed meaning). The two dimensions of consciousness (felt awareness and reflection through symbolization) would then be present in the enunciation of one's subjectivity. While Probyn is helpful in trying to bridge the split between a view of the body as the source of natural truth and the body as disembodied in postmodernism, it is unclear whether she is willing to admit to the concreteness of the body and the associated agency of it. She says, "it is not the 'fact' of the body that concerns me here . . ." (1991:117). Scepticism or hesitation with respect to acknowledging the agency of the physical presence of the body is widespread in feminist theory. Elizabeth Grosz says, "Few concepts have been as maligned or condemned within feminist theory, and with the by now monotonous charges of biologism, essentialism, ahistoricism, and naturalism continuing to haunt those feminists theorising the body" (1989:2).

Vicki Kirby points out that "Emerging discussions of essentialism are attempting to confront feminism's anxieties in order to exorcise the somatophobia that underpins the legacy of phallocentrism's mind/body split" (1991:10). Even when the body is accepted as the site of political struggle, there are differences with respect to the importance of anatomy as a referent. Luce Irigaray's work serves as a focal point for discussions about the relation between anatomy and "the play of textual intervention" (Kirby 1991:11). In Jane Gallop's view, Irigaray's use of the two lips depends on anatomical referentiality. She is not opposed to such referentiality because in the logic of exclusive categories the body got strangled. The emphasis on thinness of women's bodies in our culture to the extent that women die of starvation from anorexia illustrates the crisis of strangulation of women's bodies. Gallop points out that strangling "stops the life-giving flow between [the head and the body]" and that it can be used as a "figure for the 'cruel disorganization' that prevents us from thinking through the body" (1988:5). There is a sense of urgency here about bringing the body into discourse so that women do not enter into the disembodied logic which has denied them space.

The dilemma is that because the history of logic includes the projection of body (materiality) onto women's bodies in the flight from the sensible, an emphasis on women's bodies could support men's logic and perpetuate the marginalization of women. That logic, however, depends on the reductionistic view of woman as body, with its traditional essentialist implications. Gender neutralists, as anti-essentialists, aim to avoid that 'reductionist reality.' They speak of gender rather than sex. The claim is that gender is historically constructed and can be historically reconstructed into a form of gender neutrality which would eliminate the relevance of sex-specific differences within the context of other social differences. Gender neutralists, or anti-essentialists, usually are identified as constructionists. As mentioned earlier, I refer to a social constructionist view that excludes body agency as restricted social constructionism. It is to this restricted view that Diana Fuss alludes when she says, "constructionists are concerned above all with the *production* and *organization* of differences, and they therefore reject the idea that any essential or natural givens precede the processes of social determination" (1989:2). An important contribution of such a constructionist approach, according to Fuss, is that "it reminds us that a complex system of cultural, social, psychical, and historical differences, and not a set of pre-existent human essences, position and constitute the subject" (p. xii). For some theorists these differences are so profound that the category of gender is called into question.

Elizabeth Spelman suggests there are many genders, dependent upon the social differences which predicate one's identity and shape one's subjectivity. The category of 'woman' often obscures the heterogeneity of women's realities. She is, however, aware of the problem of 'problematizing' the category of woman as a gender category. She says, "Isn't our shared gender identity precisely where we'd hope to find the foundation for [a unified voice as women]?" (1988:175). A main concern of Spelman's, and other constructionists, is that feminist theory which uses generalizing categories uncritically helps "to disguise the conflation of the situation of one group of women with the situation of all women" (p. 177). While the category can be used to exclude differences and silence those who are not represented in theoretical representations of gender, it is a category, according to Spelman, that ought to be extended into all conceptualizing, theorizing, and social organizing. "The idea that gender is constructed and defined in conjunction with elements of identity such as race, class, ethnicity, and nationality rather than separable from them helps explain why gender ought to be studied in connection with every academic discipline and not only in women's studies departments" (pp. 175-76). The claim that gender is inseparable from the social determinants in which gender is constructed leads Spelman to conclude that we ought to "Take the full implication of what gender is and be prepared to talk about women's different genders" (p. 177).

Spelman's attention to the diversity of socially constructed identities of women is necessary in the interests of creating enunciative space for women who dwell in different places. As feminist criticism has made clear, it is no more justifiable for one woman to speak for another than it is for men to speak for women. For a single woman or a group of women to adopt the position of speaking subject on behalf of all others is antithetical to the feminist endeavour of Be-Friending, that is of creating contexts in which different communities of women facilitate communication among each other. An interesting inconsistency in Spelman's focus on inclusion rather than exclusion, is her exclusion of sex-specificity from her constructionist view of identity. The construction of identity is based on sociopolitical difference in Spelman's otherwise insightful account of the plurality of identity. The body is mapped by social and cultural inscriptions. There is no folding of interiority and exteriority in Spelman's account of inessential woman. The body has a reality only insofar at it represents sociological determinants.

Moira Gatens rightly points out that a sociological deterministic account of consciousness disallows input from the psyche or from the body. They both have to be seen as "passive *tabula rasa*" (1991:140). She says,

for theorists of gender, the mind, of either sex, is a neutral, passive entity, a blank slate, on which is inscribed various social 'lessons.' The body, on their account, is the passive mediator of these inscriptions. The result of their analyses is the simplistic solution to female oppression: a programme of re-education, the unlearning of patriarchy's arbitrary and oppressive codes, and the relearning of politically correct and equitable behaviours and traits, leading to the whole person: the androgyne. (1991:140)

Attention to gender exclusively is to accept the principles of logic which placed women outside the set of definable categories of the logic of identity. The difference between female masculinity and male masculinity is overlooked in the interests of male masculinity (Gatens' distinction, 1991:145). Androgyny takes on the form of masculinity. The distinction between male femininity and female femininity is even more striking than between female and male masculinity. This is a consequence of the more attractive images available for masculinity than for femininity, which was constructed as the negation of the masculine.

Nancy Jay's outline of the three principles of logic which underlie the construction of identity is helpful here. They are the principle of identity (if anything is A, it is A); the principle of contradiction (nothing can be both A and –A); and the principle of the excluded middle (anything, and everything, must be either A or –A) (Jay 1991:92-93). Privileging the A category is entailed in the logic which defines identity in this framework. If gender is to be 'neutral' within this systematization, there is little doubt about which way the 'neutrality' will bend. It will bend toward the Reality of the Subject in the A category. Remembering Irigaray's critique of Plato's myth of the cave, the –A category is constituted by women as other of the Same (the world) and women as other of the Other. Both are excluded from the A category, with the chasm of the excluded middle separating them. The immanence of women is excluded from the transcendence of male subjectivity reflected in the logic of identity of sameness. In this view equality is coextensive with sameness. Gender equality is equality within a category of sameness. The A category takes precedence over the –A category. The logic of identity dictates that gender equality is the same as gender sameness within the A category. Androgyny is equated with male masculinity. Female masculinity is different and therefore does not belong to the same category in this manner of categorizing.

A possibility for undermining the exclusive A/–A categorization is to assert sex-specificity. That is not to claim a fixed essence of sexual identity, but rather to affirm the normativeness of femaleness, which is located in women's bodies in their various social locations. Exclusive categorical constructions are embedded in our ways of thinking about every aspect of identity. Judith Butler points out how Monique Wittig depends on exclusive or essentialist categories in her critique of *The Straight Mind*. Butler says,

Wittig's radical disjunction between straight and gay replicates the kind of disjunctive binarism that she herself characterizes as the divisive philosophical gesture of the straight mind.

My own conviction is that the radical disjunction posited by Wittig between heterosexuality and homosexuality is simply not true, that there are structures of psychic homosexuality within heterosexual relations, and structures of psychic heterosexuality within gay and lesbian sexuality and relationships. (1990:121)

The view of identity as pluralistic and uncontainable has the consequence of undermining discontinuities between categories and affirming contiguities.[14] One's sexual orientation is one dimension of one's sexual identity, just as one's class, race, or height might be. Irigaray claims that women's identities are inseparable from their bodies as sites of political struggle. Her view of the body is not, however, compatible with Foucault's claim that "the body is the inscribed surface of events" (Butler 1990:129, quoting Foucault), which Butler supports. Butler claims that gender is not merely a cultural construction corresponding to a sexed subject, rather "gender must also designate the very apparatus of production whereby the sexes themselves are established" (p. 7). I take Butler to mean that the total meaning of a body is what is written onto it from social and psychic forces, without any agency on the part of the body. She allows for an active consciousness which is not wholly sociologically determined, but not felt sensations which might impinge upon the reflective component of consciousness. Sex-specificity for Butler is gender produced.

There is a conundrum embedded in the claim that biological sexual realities are exclusively sociologically determined. The conundrum is this: A goal of feminist endeavour is to create enunciative space for women from different places; however, the condition for change is not available within the system of production that exists. The necessary condition for collective action is the sexual identity of women as a group. If it is accepted that women's bodies (and hence their sexualities) are exclusively the products of cultural inscriptions, there is no logical possibility for women as a group to unite for the purpose of subverting existing symbolic structures of inscription. The inscriptions would normally be male-centred or, at best, gender neutral. The basis of women-for-women does not exist without a sex-specific basis of identity. By now it should be clear that identity is understood here more in terms of uncontainable and permeable rather than as sameness and exclusivity. The construction of women's identities as women-for-women requires new imagery which reflects the strength of women's felt bodily experiences as well as the psychic and social inscriptions onto the body surface. The conjuncture of felt sensations and symbolization through images and concepts constitutes consciousness of one's subjectivity and one's relationality. The expansion of consciousness through new positive female images is a subversive strategy which has the effect of destabilizing exclusive categories of sameness and the construction of identity through interrelated forms of otherness. The effectiveness of that strategy depends upon assuming bodily agency in conjunction with the psyche and social determination. If consciousness is constituted by felt sensations (bodily agency) and cognitive reflection, then it can be reasonably concluded that the development of new images and concepts includes body consciousness.

Hermeneutics of Affirmation: Constructing Alternatives

Charlene Spretnak claims that men have been authorized to be cultural fathers largely from fear of women's elemental power. Elemental power is "the capability to grow people of either sex from [their] flesh, to bleed in rhythm with the moon, to transform food into milk for infants . . ." (Spretnak 1991:116). Socialization within patriarchy has included learning about which cultural spaces are to be occupied according to sex. Miriam Robbins Dexter (1990) notes that the development of Indo-European cultures (from the fifth millennium B.C.E. onwards) led to the three-tiered structuring of patriarchal cultures: priestly caste, warrior caste, and nurturing caste. In Indo-European cultures, women's spaces were largely defined by the boundaries of the nurturing caste. Dexter points out that prior to that time, women and men shared the same cultural spaces to a greater degree. The three-tiered religio-socio hierarchy is not evident in pre-Indo-European cultures, according to scholars such as Dexter, Gimbutas, Gadon, Condren, Stone, Eisler, Lerner, and Spretnak. As Spretnak points out, the findings of these authors support those of anthropologist Peggy Reeves Sanday who claims that cultures which depend on living with the produce of the earth reflect more egalitarian attitudes. By contrast, those cultures which are more oriented toward claiming possession over the earth exhibit greater tendencies toward violence and domination. The assigning of women to the nurturing caste placed women in cultural spaces which were devalued in a cultural orientation toward domination. It is a chicken-and-egg question about whether fear of women's elemental power contributed initially to domination of nature by men or whether domination of nature was the condition for the attribution of women to the nurturing (nature) caste. It is reasonable to infer that the two conditions are very closely related to each other.

Indo-European cultures are patriarchal with an orientation toward domination. Women's bodies and the earthbody are evaluated largely in utilitarian terms. There is a widespread attitude toward acquiring and using up. The intentionality is "to have" rather than "to live with." Within the patriarchal construction of meaning, women's bodies have been impediments to women's participation in the meaning-giving process of what is called the symbolic. Not surprisingly, many women opt for gender neutrality rather than sex-specificity in their attempts to enter into cultural spaces previously occupied exclusively by men (e.g., priesthood, medicine, law, professorships, business, and military). Boys' sports train men for positions in men's occupations (see Helgesen 1990). Girls' sports are on the increase. A possibility is that if girls are trained in sports as boys are they will aspire to the same kind of work organization as men. Another possibility is that feminists, and others who are feminist-minded, in sports are altering the ways in which sports are organized, which could lead to differently organized workplaces. Both women and men have been socialized within patriarchy to denigrate the elemental powers of women and associated activities.

There are, however, women-centred women and women-centred men. These people acknowledge women's elemental powers and esteem the work they do as mothers. On the other hand, there are male-centred women and male-centred men who do not share such a positive view of women. For these, the denigration of women is as natural as the air we breathe. The ideal situation would be to not have to choose, but to affirm both sexes. In a male-centred culture, women-centred persons are the minority. An example of male-centredness which undermines identification of women with women is a remark I overheard by a woman about another woman who had stayed home to care for her young children, had gone through an extensive education process, and then re-entered the professional world. She was referred to as a "recycled housewife." The phrase might be funny if it came from a woman who had gone through the process and was free to laugh at herself. It is painful, however, when it comes from a woman who did not have children and who believes that professional work is superior to child care work. Her identity as a woman includes negating her identification with women who actualize their elemental powers. Her comment could be interpreted as a reflection of her acculturation into patriarchy, which separates 'biological agents' from "cultural agents" (Spretnak 1991:128-36). It is a reminder of the fact that one woman does not speak for all women. It also reminds us how important it is to extend the practice of Be-Friending so the climate is healthier for women as women. A sex-specific approach to women is concerned to integrate nature and culture in the representation of women as whole and healthy self-determining subjects.

Postmodern attempts to decentre the subject were initiated by men such as Derrida, Lacan, and Foucault. Postmodernism might be seen as the ultimate flight from women's bodies. Everything is a narrative, nothing remains outside the text. A narrative identity is one which is exclusively culturally constructed, without reference to an actual body or body parts. They are products of cultural inscriptions or are surfaces on which to inscribe meaning, without reciprocity. Spretnak says, "because 'the body' is so strongly associated with woman in patriarchal cultures . . ., the deconstructive-postmodern 'erasure of the body' is foremost the erasure of the female body" (1991:122). The useful project of historicizing the subject has evolved into further escape from the female body. Spretnak points out how Foucault's subject position in his attempt to decentre the subject perpetuates the logic of patriarchy. She says he fulfils the

core desires of patriarchy, such as the negation of the female body: Foucault proposed that rape be reclassified as simple assault since, after all, our notions of sexuality are merely an arbitrary social construction. . . . This is an example of the 'desexualization' he recommended to the feminist movement as a comprehensive goal. . . . The patriarchal desire to disempower the body is served by the deconstructive-postmodern assertion that abstraction, or conceptualization, is all. (1991:124)

Restricted social constructionism proclaims that there is nothing but the historization of identity through socially constructed meanings, independent of sensate data. Consciousness is unidimensional: it is wholly that which comes from the reflective component. Felt sensations are not counted as determining factors of consciousness. In a restricted social constructionist view, their reality is circumscribed by their interpretive value according to their social meaning. There is no possibility, in this view, of felt sensations altering the reflective component of consciousness. The reduction of consciousness to the reflective component, at the expense of felt sensations, is required for a gender neutral account of identity. Restricted social constructionism relies on a view of consciousness as unidimensional: reflection only, without sensation.

Language is treated independently of body. Identity is narrative identity. That is characteristic of a postmodern view of identity. It reflects a postmodern interpretation of reality, namely, that reality is exclusively a matter of interpretation. It is epistemology without ontology. The story is the reality. Re-storying brings about new realities. This view of identity and, more generally, of reality is useful in that it allows for subjects to speak from their own perspectives rather than being coerced into adopting the perspective of another in the name of Truth (the truth of the Subject). Reality is, to a large extent, mind over matter. We often make things happen because we believe we can and that we deserve to do so. There is little doubt in the efficacy of positive thinking. Interpretation is a large part of the nature of reality and allows individuals to have some control over their realities. One who defines her own reality has more control over it than having it defined by another. The subject of hermeneutics (interpretation and justification of that interpretation) has opened up spaces for diverse interpretations in the pursuit of wisdom. Largely because of the work done in hermeneutics and with related epistemologies, identity is now more readily understood in terms of plurality. Reality is experienced more in terms of changing conditions. Essences can be, and are, interpreted in terms of process rather than fixed substance.

A problem with postmodernism, however, is that the anti-modernists are opposed to essences as if they had to be understood as fixed substances. Spretnak says, "the deconstructionists have once again opted for the assumptions of patriarchal Western philosophy: the focus on substance rather than process. Hence they arrive at a dualistic conceptualization: *either* fixed essence *or* social construction" (1991:126). The three previously mentioned underlying principles of logic (in reference to Nancy Jay's work) are intrinsic to the view that essentialism is about fixed substances, ideal forms, or god-given innate ideas. None of the three principles allows for contiguity. The principle of identity is about sameness; the principle of contradiction indicates only exclusive, irreconcilable categories of difference; and the principle of the excluded middle affirms disjunction between fixed essences. The exclusiveness of mind and body is essential to the restricted constructionist's rejection of biological agency in favour of cultural construction exclusively. Restricted social construction-ism depends upon sociological essentialism: reality is essentially sociologi-cally determined. As Diana Fuss points out, constructionism depends on essentialism.

In contrast to sociological essentialism, the sex-specific approach to improving social conditions for women by changing social inscriptions with respect to women's bodies assumes a reciprocal relation between body and language. Reality is essentially an interactive process. Personal identity is part of that changing, multifaceted reality. Reality is con-structed through the interaction of epistemology and ontology. Concrete bodies are interpreted. Sensations from bodies affect interpretations. Re-flections affect sensations from the bodies. Cultural symbols are meaning-ful because they express shared knowledge about reality. Their power to move people to work for common goals depends on their capacity to unite people in a shared social consciousness. Cultural symbols bring people to-gether. They have a unifying effect.

Expressive symbols reflect both cultural meanings in a public sense and privately felt sensations, i.e., feelings. Emotional attachments depend on both beliefs and feelings. If there is little coherence between felt expe-riences and cultural symbols, the symbols lose their meaning or the users lose touch with their felt sensations. They may interpret their feelings to match the cultural meanings or they may experience alienation and with-draw from cultural participation. Women in our society often withdraw because the expressions of meaning do not reflect their experiences. That is characteristic of patriarchal culture. Women are perceived as having less to say because the form of discourse or symbolic expression has little to do with their lived experiences. Alternatives of accommodation or with-drawal are often chosen. Another alternative, that of resistance, is pos-sible. Luce Irigaray's attention to women's bodies as sources of knowledge in the imaginary and symbolic structures of consciousness is an act of re-sistance to what we are 'already always' listening to in patriarchal culture. She rejects gender neutral proposals as a way of moving out of patriarchal symbolization. That line of argument is seen to contribute to the existing erasure of women's felt experiences in the construction of cultural mean-ings. Gender neutral arguments are entailed in restricted social and cul-tural constructionist perspectives. I have discussed above how they con-tribute to the continuation of categorical exclusivity by assuming the sepa-rateness of biological and cultural agency. The separation of men's thought from women's sexuality is a basic assumption in patriarchal cul-ture. The thinking woman, as woman, is a challenge to this assumption. Gender neutral advocacy, on the other hand, neither helps to expose the assumption nor does it serve to remind men of what they forgot, namely, their connection to the maternal bodies and, by extension, to their own bodies.

The separation of biological and cultural agency is not restricted to gender neutral arguments. It is also found in arguments supporting sex-specificity. The hesitancy on the part of, for example, Elizabeth Grosz to affirm Luce Irigaray's reference to concrete body parts, and her rejection of anatomy in favour of morphology, could be interpreted as a variation on postmodern efforts to separate narrative from the physical. That is not to say that bodily sensations exist outside culture or that Irigaray ever indicates such a possibility. Rather it is to point to the fluidity between sensations and ideas rather than their exclusiveness. Irigaray is concerned, above all, with how language can be altered to reflect the subjectivities of women. Her act of resistance is to start from the place that stands outside patriarchal culture, namely, women's bodies. To claim that she is not actually talking about anatomy is difficult to maintain in light of her critique of the construction of patriarchal symbolism in the imaginary and the symbolic. In her view, patriarchal symbolism was constructed apart from women's bodies. Andrea Nye substantiates this claim in her insightful history of Western logic. Parmenides' flight from the goddess to embrace his own thoughts in the ultimate act of love and wisdom represented a turning point in the development of patriarchal consciousness. Postmodernism is a reaction to modernity's (seventeenth to the twentieth centuries) affirmation of classical essentialism in terms of fixed essences. It retains, however, the basic Parmenidean move beyond women's sexuality and their elemental creative powers.

The postmodern love affair is with the text, that is the narrative of the historically determined subject. There is no truth apart from the text. Bodies, in particular women's bodies, are known only through social and culturally determined scripts which are internalized in one's psyche and externalized through representation of the self. There remains in these interpretations a separation of biological agent from cultural agent, and a privileging of cultural agency in an attempt to avoid biological reductionism in the sense of fixed biological essentialism. While attempting to escape from Scylla these interpretations play into the hands of Charybdis. In the attempt to avoid classical biological essentialism they fall into the trap of supporting the flight from the sensible, in particular, the flight from women's sexuality.

An alternative is to follow Irigaray in her admonition to bring women's bodies into focus in the imaginary and symbolic as agents which interact with cultural and psychic inscriptions in narrative identities. Carol Christ's classic article, "Why Women Need the Goddess: Phenomenological, Psychological, and Political Reflections" (1991b), is useful to place alongside Irigaray's attempts to develop new avenues for women to speak as subjects. Christ says, "The simplest and most basic meaning of the symbol of Goddess is the acknowledgement of the legitimacy of female power as a beneficent and independent power" (1991b:277). Goddess symbolism affirms a separate ontological status for women that is not provided for in the religious symbolism of patriarchal religions. Christ points to the importance of symbolism in the unconscious as sources of psychological dispositions (moods) as well as social and political action (motivations). Christ sees ontology, epistemology, and ethics to be inseparable in ways that resemble Irigaray's philosophy. Symbols which influence the imaginary (unconscious) shape underlying intentionalities with respect to the way we experience ourselves as subjects, the ways in which we know and construct reality, and our ethical and political activities. Goddess images, like female body parts, provide women with a source of legitimacy as female subjects.

Attempts to create new ways of imaging and conceptualizing through goddess imagery or the metonymical use of the two lips to connote connectedness and nearness often raise questions about the sexual exclusivity of the aims of the project. I believe that goddess imagery as female imagery is important, like that of the two lips, as a strategy to break through the existing pervasively male-dominated interpretive framework. Until the female body has adequate positive and powerful representation in the imaginary or in the symbolic ordering of meaning, such strategies are helpful. I do not see them as ends in themselves, but rather as ways of moving in the direction of normalizing the female body as one of two normative human forms. They are not only relevant for ontological purposes but also for epistemological and ethical purposes. An ontology of connectedness and nearness is coextensive with an epistemology which assumes the inclusiveness of sensuality and intellect. The corresponding ethics is one of affiliation, based on respect for feelings as well as rights. Mutual respect of persons entails self-esteem.

Self-esteem requires an underlying legitimacy. The search for new forms of linguistic expressions of women's subjectivities is supported by goddess symbolism which affirms women's independent ontological status. As Christ points out, the social and political struggles for better conditions for women are strengthened through recourse to an underlying empowering structure of female imagery. In times of increased stress we draw motivational energy from the infrastructure. If it is constituted by male images of power, as is the case in patriarchy, it is more disempowering than empowering. Margaret Whitford claims that the imaginary, as discussed by Irigaray, can be interpreted in at least two ways. It may be understood as "the unconscious of western thought—the unsymbolized, repressed underside of western philosophy" (1991a:89). In this reading, the imaginary is equated with women's unarticulated and chaotic ways of expressing themselves, as in 'women's intuition.' This derogatory sense of the imaginary contributes toward a willful separation of the symbolic from the imaginary by those who aim to articulate distinct and adequate ideas. An alternative reading of Irigaray's imaginary leads to the claim that it "does not exist" and "still has to be created" (Whitford 1991a:89). It is the latter interpretation which I am following up on here.

Within patriarchy it is difficult to imagine the necessary conditions for a female imaginary to exist. Accordingly, there is a need for remythologizing. That is to say, it is necessary for women to develop new symbols which would infuse the imaginary and, correspondingly, create a different symbolic system in which the myths or stories are expressed. Mythology, ontology, epistemology, ethics, and social theory and practice are inextricably intertwined. Language is their primary connecting thread. Goddess images provide strong symbols for women to redescribe themselves as embodied females.

Sharon Golub discusses the negative language used to describe menstruation in countries as diverse as Egypt, India, Britain, Yugoslavia (prior to the political changes in 1992), Philippines, Jamaica, and the United States. She says, "The myths and taboos associated with menstruation can readily be seen in the words we use to describe it" (1992:5). Menstruation is not generally associated with creative images but rather with inhibiting ones. Women tend to use different terms than men. Women's terms are often associated with secrecy and embarrassment while men's reflect the idea of unavailability. One of the expressions used by men is "too wet to plough," which reflects the view of women as fields to be cultivated by men's planting activities. Another expression used by men is "flying baker": a navy phrase meaning "keep off" (Golub 1992:7). Women's expressions have changed significantly over the past twenty years. Earlier ones represented an attitude toward menstruation as a sickness, while current terms have more to do with menstruation as a nuisance ("wrong time of the month"), relief that one isn't pregnant ("the red flag is up"), cyclicity ("period"), visitor ("I've got my friend"), or with menstrual accoutrements ("on the rag"). Women's language also includes a few positive terms ("mother nature's gift") as well as those which indicate sexual unavailability ("red light"). Golub cites several terms in each category and concludes by saying that "it is easy to see that most of the terms are negative" (1992:7). In her view, menstruation is the most obvious difference between women and men and has been used to keep women in subordinate cultural spaces. Menstruation remains a taboo topic in most places. This central difference between women and men is inherent in dominant/subordinate mythology which underlies the logic of ontology, epistemology, ethics, social theory, and practice.

The other two "blood topics," pregnancy and menopause, are part of the construction of women's difference from men in terms of deviance and deficiency. Patriarchal language reflects the negative imagery associated with women's sexuality. An article in the magazine *Vanity Fair* by Gail Sheehy (1991) reveals the politics of menopause in the United States. Sheehy's article, "The Silent Passage: Menopause," indicates what is well known: that menopausal women are considered powerless and on the way out. That means they can easily be disregarded and psychologically abused. Women don't have to read studies to know that. In light of that 'wisdom,' issues such as body representation and aging are of vital concern for most women in industrial societies which have separated productivity from connections to the reproductive cycles of the body of the earth. Patriarchal language denigrates women's menstrual blood, associates pregnancy with illness,[15] and equates menopause with being 'over the hill.' Within the patriarchal symbolic system women's identification with themselves is inevitably problematic. It is necessary, therefore, to construct an alternative symbolic system through the creation of new symbols.

In order for women to identify with themselves, they require images which affirm menstruation, pregnancy, and menopause. Such images are found in goddess spirituality. Historically goddess spirituality and shamanism were part of the same orientation toward living with the body of the earth. Within patriarchy shamanism became associated more with men, while goddess spirituality was related to women's witchcraft. Both were marginalized. Shamanism, however, was not persecuted as violently as witchcraft. This is consistent with the comfort of the presence of powerful men and discomfort with powerful women in patriarchal consciousness.[16] The denigrated female body is central to patriarchal constructions of masculinity and femininity. Patriarchal language pervasively moralizes against independent female sexuality.

The control of women's fertility continues to be a legal and moral issue in our society. Female ontological dependency is intrinsic to patriarchal language. Carol Christ's call to develop a new set of female symbols which empower women's identification with their bodies is reiterated in Luce Irigaray's call to women to listen to themselves rather than to the 'already always' heard within patriarchy. As Christ suggests, affirmation of female power is associated with the body, the will, and women's bonds and heritage (1991b:276). To listen to our bodies in the construction of new symbols is not to separate the body from the mind and reduce women's ontology to reproductive vessels. Listening to our bodies does not reduce knowledge to information circumscribed by the private sphere. Acting in relation to our bodies does not limit ethical conduct to uncritical caring. Honouring our bodies does not mean developing social policies and practices which allocate child care exclusively to women as nurturers. It does not mean that women who choose not to have children should be considered abnormal. Paying attention to our bodies does not need to lead to reductionistic accounts of women either as nurturers, as sex objects, or as symbols of extraordinary ability to stay youthful through exercise, cosmetic surgery, and diets in order to stall the disappointments of the female body which are aroused by patriarchal prescriptions of femininity. This is not to say that aging is not also a problem for men in cultures which extol the virtues of youth. Rather, the point is to emphasize the particular problematic of women's bodies in the construction of patriarchal symbolization.

Goddess consciousness, like shamanic consciousness, is intrinsically materialist. Contrary to Naomi Goldenberg's claim (1990) that spiritual archetypes are to be avoided because they contribute to the split between mind and body, the claim here is that spiritual consciousness is inseparable from historical consciousness. Historical consciousness locates knowledge within the material conditions of the knower. From the point of view of historical consciousness, knowledge is invariably shaped by the interests and assumptions of the knower. Hermeneutics is a method of revealing the perspectives that are implicit in knowledge claims and justifying claims from a particular perspective. Deconstructive endeavours have aimed to undermine truth claims which deny their particular local perspective. Language is the dominant medium for communicating knowledge. Despite the important contributions of hermeneutics and deconstructionism, historical consciousness is often reduced to textual meaning, excluding the existence of any form of reality apart from linguistic interpretation. The exclusion of body agency is largely because of the separation of epistemology from ontology. In addition to the exclusion of the body as agent, spiritual consciousness is usually rejected as ahistorical and, therefore, is considered irrelevant. The topic of women's bodies as well as spirituality within this restricted view of knowledge becomes a non-topic. Accordingly, possibilities for the celebration of women's bodies as expressions of spiritual energy are severely restricted.

The remythologizing which is necessary for women to feel, think, and speak differently requires that we honour our bodies, not merely as passive receptors of cultural inscriptions but as active agents which have power to effect change. Goddess symbols are important forms of new knowledge in the development of a female imaginary. The metaphor of goddess refers to diversity within unity. The power of identification with goddess imagery comes from the realization of one's participation in the ontological process of interrelatedness. Spiritual experiences are integrative. They are also expansive. They defy categorical language. The linearity of language cannot represent the fluidity of interrelatedness. Spiritual experiences can inform our epistemologies and help to put into perspective the limitations of language as well as the possibilities for communicating new ideas through language. Truths, from the point of view of a spiritual consciousness, are not arrived at through mathematical equations or the correct relation of premises in a logic. They are found in experience. The most profound experiences are thought to be those in which consciousness is emptied of ego boundaries. In *The Color Purple*, Alice Walker aptly points out that all truth comes from silence. Through language we can only point to the activity in process which constitutes reality. The body is part of the activity. Experiences such as shape-shifting increase one's awareness of the fluidity of the body. Childbirth experiences are other ways of knowing about radical changeability of the body. Menarche and menopause are two other experiences of changing identity through bodily awareness. For women to be whole and healthy it is necessary that their identities can be represented with as much diversity in their unity as possible. Attention to sex-specificity is necessary for women-friendly cultural symbols to emerge. Symbols that honour women's bodies almost certainly affect women's construction of their sexuality. Language evolves in relation to experience. Experiences are shaped by language. Women's experiences of their bodies as expressions of their humanity in terms of changing forms, expanding boundaries, caressing lips, fluidity of solids and solidification of fluids (as in mucous), call out for symbols which can inform linguistic expressions in our consciousnesses.

A women-friendly language would be more oriented toward permeability of selves than a language shaped by the desire for domination by separate selves. It would consist more in concepts and images that reflect the reality of continuity between birth, life, and death. Goddess symbolism is an important resource for the development of a language which emphasizes inclusiveness rather than exclusiveness. It is most importantly about continuity. The concept of death, for example, would be differently understood. Rather than promoting fear it would connote transformation. Death in goddess consciousness or shamanic consciousness means letting go of disruptive thought patterns and habits. In Buddhist theory it is about emptying one's consciousness of egotistical ideas of the self as a static something to be preserved from ego-deflation. Death in these views is about shedding old skins which are no longer relevant and about giving birth to new realities.

If these forms of spiritual consciousness were to inform cultural symbolic meanings, the image of Kali, for example, would be interpreted not as fearful but rather as symbolizing death to destructive or 'dead' patterns of thought, actions, or ways of being. She would be invoked when there is a desire or need for new growth. Death would not be feared or shunned, but rather accepted as intrinsic to creative new birth. If, as Mookerjee (1988) claims, we are now in the time of Kali, it may mean the death of patriarchal culture and the birth a new cultural order. The new order is based on interrelatedness of birth and death through continual regeneration. The snake shedding its skin is associated with death in the regenerative cycle. The snake goddess is one of the oldest symbols of women's regenerative power. The bird goddess is the other of the oldest symbols of women's power. The bird-headed goddess represents the power to see from a distant perspective. It is the wisdom of the heavens which complements the wisdom of the earth, symbolized by the snake.

Women's spiritual and intellectual wisdom is coextensive with body consciousness. Remythologizing with goddess imagery is an important means by which the search for a new language to express women's subjectivity can be facilitated. Symbolization of women's erotic energy through images and conceptualizations which reflect the powerful spiritual, intellectual, and physical creative activities of women will alter cultural and psychic constructions of women's sexuality in the imaginary and symbolic structures of consciousness. Such a process of symbolization can emerge only in conjunction with expanded consciousness through altered perceptions. Spiritual consciousness and culturally determined consciousness are coextensive.

In contrast to the logician's interest in the correct arrangement of words in the formulation of truth claims, the intention here is to use language in ways that express experiences. Rather than attempt to shape experiences to fit acceptable forms of linguistic expressions which can be tested according to truth tables for truth or falsity, the purpose of a search for new forms of symbolization is to more accurately reflect diversity of experiences. Janisse Browning says, "as women from diverse experiences we have different relationships with words and different ways of working" (Browning 1992:18, quoting Lizbeth Goodman). The search for new symbols which might constitute a female imaginary and, correspondingly, restructure the symbolic ordering of meaning is not about a singular form of expression. Just as identity in this view is pluralistic, so the construction of meaning through language must reflect that pluralism. Differences within each of us as well as among us require adequate expression for subject positions to be enunciated. Daly's notion of Be-Friending is about creating cultural spaces in which women can express their differences and similarities within the spaces where they choose to speak.

The different relationships to words is reflected not only in the forms of linguistic discourse we use to enunciate our subjectivities, but also the various kinds of mediums which communicate meaning apart from speech. Art, drama, and music, for example, are ways of bringing to our attention ideas which lie dormant within us. The images in Vicki Noble's tarot cards, the music of Saffire: The Uppity Blues Women, and the drama of Catalyst Theatre of Edmonton are ways of raising awareness of the connection between personal lived experiences and social and political realities. They are Be-Friending activities which enlarge the cultural spaces in which women can express their diverse identities. Increasingly women's relationships to words are developed through creative imaging in the arts. The interdisciplinarity of the project of developing new languages, which are not constricted by the desire to claim totalizing truth but rather by the activity of Be-Friending, characterizes the relationship between sexuality and language discussed here. Insights from spiritual experiences are continuous with those, for instance, from music, art, drama, literature, philosophy, and psychoanalysis. The underlying intentionality is a process of interrelatedness. The ethic is one of responsibility toward the creation of cultural spaces for different relationships to words and to patterns of lived realities.

In this view, ethics is coextensive with ontology and epistemology. The independent ontological status of women is required for an ethics of responsibility toward each other as subjects. Social justice depends on listening to the expressed needs and desires of those from marginalized social categories and acting responsibly in relation to them. Responsible action is inseparable from responsible knowledge. A condition for knowing responsibly is listening to the different ways in which others' needs and desires are expressed. It is remembering that there are infinite ways of arranging the relationships of words, based on the different relationships with words that individuals have. For women in patriarchy it is particularly important that their identities are symbolized through words that strengthen their will to effect social justice as women. The differences among women which arise out of social factors (e.g., race, class, sexual orientation, age, religion, or language) need to be expressed in languages which adequately express the subjectivities of women with pluralistic social and psychic identities. Sexual identity is intrinsic to those forms of identity. Accordingly, the relationship between sexuality and language is part of the relationship of women to words in all social and psychological constructions of meaning.

The independent ontological status of women reflected in goddess symbols contributes to the development of an empowering female imaginary which acts as the infrastructure for language. Goddess consciousness and shamanic consciousness are ways of moving out of normative patriarchal consciousness. New symbols are incorporated into one's consciousness, thereby creating new forms of knowledge. The new knowledge needs to be shared among those who experience it in order for a language to develop which reflects shared meanings and lifts individual experiences into the larger social domain. In this way spiritual consciousness and historical consciousness are continuous with each other. Ontological awareness of self as radically changeable (as in shape-shifting experiences) and as intrinsically intertwined with the conditions of existence grounds one in knowledge of self as permeable. Boundaries are there but they change shape. Identity is located within the experience of radical otherness. Nearness and presence of otherness is characteristic of spiritual experiences.

Responsible knowledge, in this view, includes knowing how to incorporate radically new perceptions into the pattern of sensations and ideas which already exist. The attempts of Luce Irigaray to radicalize language by incorporating images of the labia and mucous as well as other parts of the body that are rarely spoken of positively, if at all, is part of the larger paradigm shift away from a dominant relationship to words toward acknowledgment of many relationships to words. Focusing on images of women's bodies is one way of affirming women's independent power as beneficent rather than morally corrupt, of integrating physical presence with psychic and social presence, and of connecting women through history and in various cultural spaces today. Irigaray's linguistic project is supported by goddess or shamanic consciousness which is constituted by knowledge of the independent ontological status of women and which motivates social and political action directed toward social justice. For Irigaray and for those whose knowledge includes awareness of goddess presence and shamanic consciousness, symbols function to alter perceptions. Lived experiences are invariably body experiences. Reflections or cognition are embodied. It is, therefore, reasonable to claim that positive symbols of women's various forms of embodiment or body parts would affect women's will to self-determination within a context of interrelatedness.

The will to self-determination, while acting responsibly towards others, is central to ethical relations and social justice. The enactment of social justice requires adequate enunciation of individual subjectivity through language. Just as sexuality and language are mutually influential, so sexuality and ethics are inseparable. Social justice for women depends on acceptance of their independent ontological status and on their various relationships to words. Social consciousness is continuous with individual consciousness. An individual consciousness grounded in perceptions of identity constituted by plurality, if consistent, would be motivated to work toward a similar social consciousness. Ethics is understood here to be part of the discussion of ontology, epistemology, and social theory.

Notes

1 As I mentioned in the Introduction, the contributors to Young and Goulet (1994) use the 'experiential method' in their anthropological research. It is described as a 'radically empirical method' that they consider to be characteristic of phenomenology. In their view it goes beyond ethnographic methodology, which is about description of the activities of others. This kind of phenomenological method, namely, experiential method, includes the anthropologists' personal experiences. Young and Goulet claim that their phenomenological approach is properly phenomenological in that the interpretation of the experiences of others is from the perspective of a person who actually has something to say about it from first-hand experience. It is not merely descriptive in the ethnographical sense of interpreting another's experiences from a participant-observer's perspective. In anthropology, the participant-observer method has been cautiously used because of the possibility of 'going native.' In such instances the researcher is initiated into another cultural's rituals and ways of thinking. There has been considerable scepticism toward this method, especially in light of the work of Castenada. His accounts of his shamanic experiences have been doubted by several scholars. Partially because of Castenada's accounts, anthropologists have not readily supported personal accounts of 'extraordinary' experiences. In contrast to this scepticism, Young and Goulet's anthology of personal experiences of anthropologists explicitly avows the relevance of the anthropologist's experiences of the phenomena that she/he wishes to describe.

2 I qualify this account of Western logic with the use of 'dominant' because there are Western logics which do not entail the belief in eternal sameness. Spinoza, Hegel, and Marx are three examples. Their forms of reasoning are not, however, usually taught in 'History of Logic' courses in Philosophy. They are resources for the reconstruction of logical reasoning in the epistemological orientation of this book.

3 See, for example, Ruth Bleier (1986).

4 Nelle Morton (1985:23) refers to "The Jar of Male Structures" which prevent new images and words from entering the content of the jar. She points out that it is only when

something from outside enters mainstream (gets into the jar) that the content changes. The other alternative is to destroy the jar and let the contents inside mix with the images and words outside to give new structural contours to our forms of communication and ways of living. In other words the logic of language systems would be more personal and reflect communal rather than hierarchical ways of living.

5 The Vienna Circle included Mach, Schlick, Neurath, Carnap, Quine, Nagel, Ryle, Ayer, and Russell.

6 Margaret Whitford points out that Jacques Lacan spelled out his theory of ego formation through the use of the term 'imaginary' in his article, "The Mirror Stage as Formative of the Function of the I as Revealed in Psychoanalytic Experience" (Whitford 1991a:63; Lacan 1977:1-7). Ego formation amounted to what Freud called "a coherent organization of mental processes" (Whitford 1991a:63; Freud 1973-74, Vol. 19:17).

7 A very interesting account of the development of power through focussed attention is found in Kay Cordell Whitaker's autobiography (1991) where she describes her training with two shamans from the Amazon. The purpose of the training is to achieve balance. That means living with centred power. It includes death to habitual patterns that obstruct one's alertness to changing conditions. Centred power is transformative power. It allows one to live through various forms of death with regard to negative thought patterns and disabling emotions. Balance, in Whitaker's account, is developed through clarity of thought that is grounded in body consciousness. Power is located in attention to the interacting energies which connect the circumstances in one's consciousness. Increased consciousness of the interacting energies is necessary for the shamanic activity of healing.

8 Whitford (1991a:149) refers to Irigaray's discussion of the myth of Antigone from Irigaray's *Ethique de la différence sexuelle* (1984).

9 Irigaray's use of the two lips as a positive image significantly subverts the meaning of the labia in, for example, the Dutch language. In Dutch, the labia is called *labia-schaam lippen*, shame lips. I appreciate Jeanette Schouls for bringing the Dutch meaning of the two lips to my attention.

10 Examples of feminists in this category, as cited by Grosz, are Juliet Mitchell, Julia Kristeva, Michele Barrett, and Nancy Chodorow. Others are Dorothy Smith, Heather Jon Moroney, Gayle Rubin, Elizabeth Spelman, and Ann Ferguson. As Grosz points out, most feminists are in this category.

11 Examples of feminists in this category, as cited by Grosz, are Hélène Cixous, Mary O'Brien, Adrienne Rich, Gayatri Spivak, and Moira Gatens. Others are Luce Irigaray, Jane Gallop, Diana Fuss, Margaret Whitford, Jenijoy La Belle, and the spiritual feminists such as Charlene Spretnak, Carol Christ, Paula Gunn Allen, Naomi Goldenberg, Judith Plaskow, and Karen McCarthy Brown.

12 Janet Sayers' book, *Mothers of Psychoanalysis* (1991), illustrates the difficulty these women had with their own self-images and personal relations as they challenged assumptions about penis envy, women's narcissism, sexual intercourse, identification with their mothers or fathers, the effect of mothers' responses to external events (such as wartime bombing) rather than the events themselves.

13 The 'abject' is Julia Kristeva's term for what is repulsive about the body, including body fluids, emissions from the body, and the decaying nature of materiality. See Fletcher and Benjamin (1990) for an extensive discussion of Kristeva's work in this regard.

14 An example of a person grouping diverse identities together without considering their distinctions was unintentionally provided by a doctor who was practising in the 1950s in southern Alberta. The doctor attended to a member of the family of a church minister. The minister offered to pay the doctor for his medical services before he left the house (at that time doctors customarily made house calls). The doctor replied, "I don't charge Indians or preachers." Perhaps the reason for him identifying church ministers and Natives was their mutual lack of substantial income. At any rate, this identification across boundaries had the effect of the doctor not receiving any remuneration from either group.

15 Associating pregnancy with illness in patriarchy has more benefits than describing it in healthy terms. For example, in an article entitled "Ruling a Benefit to Moms" in the *Calgary Herald* (June 20, 1992:B4), maternity leave was legally included in 'health-related' time off from workplaces with sizeable benefit plans in place. The term 'health-related' minimizes the connotation of sick leave. The subtitle of the article, however, is "Employers Grapple with Ramifications of Rulings on Maternity, Sick Leave Benefits." It is reported in the article that a Calgary female doctor refused to sign a slip entitling her client to sick leave because the doctor "argues that pregnancy isn't sickness." That is a progressive attitude but it doesn't benefit the client. Pregnancy has to be valued positively in order for a woman to get leave from work. In a social context where productivity is measured exclusively in terms of profit and ignores the well-being of the workers or quality of life, pregnancy is regarded as a sickness. Having children is put into the same category as having a heart attack. It is not counted as productive labour.

16 See H. Lips (1991) for a good analysis of the incongruity of images of power and images of femininity. The lack of congruity between the two leads to confusion when women of power are present. Their presence sometimes leads to violence against them, as was the case during the "Burning Times" (from the fourteenth to the seventeenth centuries) when women in Europe were burned as witches.

Four

Ethics of Connectedness and Resistance

Ontology and Epistemology in Ethics

IN THIS SECTION I wish to show that ontology, epistemology, and ethics are inextricably intertwined. I discuss the three interrelated topics in terms of two different, but contiguous orientations to ethics: justice and caring. An ethic of justice is seen to be more closely connected historically to an ontology (more accurately a metaphysics) that assumes a separation between transcendence and immanence. A consequence of that assumption is the attempt to separate rational principles from feelings. The term 'morality' suggests that separation, although it doesn't entail it. It does not matter to me whether one uses morality or ethics in a discussion of rights and caring in the pursuit of justice and compassion. The pursuit is more relevant than the terminology. The association of the term 'morality' with a dualistic metaphysics, however, makes one cautious when using it.

Just as a metaphysics of separation is historically linked to a morality constituted largely by rational principles, without due attention to feelings, so it is integral to an epistemology that separates intellectual knowledge from feelings. The separation of reason from emotion in so-called truth is part of the package of a dualistic metaphysics, a search for transcendent thoughts, and a morality of rights which is organized around the right of each person to non-interference from others. I do not wish to undermine the value of the right to non-interference. Nor do I wish to ignore the importance of strong principles of conduct which respect and ensure that right. I acknowledge the significance of an ethics of justice. I wish, however, to move it out of a dualistic metaphysics and epistemology and integrate it into an ontology of interrelatedness. The corresponding inclusive epistemology assumes the interaction of sensations and ideas in consciousness. Feelings and ideas in this epistemology constitute consciousness. It is part of this claim that consciousness is regarded as body consciousness. Emotions reflect states of consciousness. They are, therefore, part of decision-making and ethical conduct. An ontology of interrelatedness is basic to an epistemology in which reality is known more or less differently by each person.

As discussed in Chapter One, there is no clear distinction between the nature of reality and the ways of perceiving it. In my view, a major goal of human endeavour is to become increasingly conscious of ways of balancing tensions and letting go of emotions that do not contribute toward balance. Emotions are the reflectors of sensations (body feelings) and ideas. Balanced emotions indicate balanced ideas. That is not to say that justified fear, anger, or sadness, for example, indicate imbalance. They are as appropriate as joy and compassion in certain circumstances. Balance, in this view, has to do with ways of interpreting reality and corresponding action. For example, identifying derogatory material in university curricula as a form of institutionalized discrimination towards women is seen as justified cause for anger. I do not believe that ethical principles and conduct can be separated from issues of justice. Both justice and caring are facilitated by an ontology of interrelatedness which assumes a disposition toward balance in human consciousness.

The ontology outlined in Chapter One provides the basis for the discussion of ethics in this chapter. An ontology of interrelatedness is the context in which the self is situated. Interrelatedness with respect to reality and epistemology, reason and emotion, mind and body, public and private, personal and social, is part of the ontological essentialism which informs this exploration. The organization of social relations around assumptions intrinsic to ontological interrelatedness would, if they were consistent, be shaped by an ethics of caring and connectedness. Ethical theories and actions would derive from an epistemology that assumed the inclusiveness of ideas and feelings. The desire for making connections would shape the pursuit of wisdom within a consciousness of interrelatedness. An ethic of affiliation is a logical extension of an ontology of interrelatedness and an epistemology shaped by the assumption of inclusiveness of ideas and sensations. Affiliation here is not restricted to 'feeling close' but rather it refers to the commitment to create social and cultural spaces in which individuals and groups can be connected according to their similarities. Group affiliation provides unified strength among an identified group so there is a basis for outreach to other groups and a formation of coalitions among different groups. An orientation toward Be-Friending from different social and cultural spaces is central to the ontology of interrelatedness which underpins this discussion of ethics.

I believe that affiliation and caring are not only consistent with rights but benefit from the legal enforcement of them. An ethic of rights focusses on the right of non-interference, while an ethic of affiliation concentrates on connectedness. Both are important for the purpose of balancing tensions between competing interests. An ethic of connectedness does not exclude resistance within social and cultural contexts of structural inequalities. Social relations are political relations. Each individual's sex, social class, colour, country of origin, citizenship status, age, religion, or any other predication situates them in a particular relation to another person. Groups, like individuals, invariably relate according to relations of power determined by their social predication. This issue will be discussed more extensively in Chapter Five.

Nona Plessner Lyons (1988) notes that there are two major orientations to morality: choice-making around particular issues and a type of consciousness. The view which I am developing encompasses both orientations; however, a morality of consciousness is regarded as the more basic. Moral sensitivity that characterizes moral consciousness is inimical to violence (Mary Pellauer, 1985). Morality as rational choosing is compatible with violence. Justification for violence is possible, for example, through adopting an oppressor's perspective and blaming victims of oppression for their own oppression. Internalization of the oppressor's blame by the victim is manifest in self-blame. Victims then perpetuate their own victimization through self-blame. Conscious awareness of individual rights and compassion for oneself and others, by contrast, makes it likelier that blame and responsibility will be distributed more appropriately. A morality of consciousness is a logical extension of an ontology of interrelatedness. While a morality of consciousness is necessary for humane interaction, it is not adequate within a social order that is shaped by an underlying ideology of competition that entails domination by certain groups over others. Systematic injustices occur with regard to individuals who are identified with subordinate groups. Collective rights, therefore, need to be considered along with individual rights.

As noted in Chapter Three, social and cultural evolution since about the fifth millennium B.C.E. has been shaped by an underlying intention to dominate through acquisition. Acquisition entails control over something. The underlying intentionality of the dominator model of evolution is 'to have' rather than 'to live with.' Progress and growth are measured largely in relation to acquisition and ownership. A morality of rights was constructed in the evolution of the dominator model. It is most importantly a morality of protection against violation of property. An ethic of respect for ownership of property is intrinsic to respect for an individual as an end in 'himself.' A morality of rights aims to prevent interference of one person's or group's privileges with respect to property. Property may include bodies of people as well as real estate, intellectual property, and other forms of proprietorship. The close identification of one's identity as a person with one's property supports a morality of protection.[1]

A major problem with this moral orientation is that there is an underlying evaluation of the worth of individuals in terms of property ownership. The rights of non-propertied or less propertied persons are often not so well protected. In the case of women whose bodies are closely associated with the property of related men, their rights do not appear as distinct as those who are the owners of most of the property. For example, the rights of women who are raped have to be fought for. They are not readily acknowledged. Also, the rights of women to choose to have an abortion have to be fought for. Both examples illustrate a reluctance to recognize the rights of women to protection against interference with their own bodies. Women's relative lack of ownership of property that is external to their bodies is connected to their lack of ownership of their own bodies.

The tradition of individual rights, in which justice is implemented through constraints against interference, assumes an equality among individuals. It often does not pay adequate attention to social factors which favour some individuals and groups of individuals over others. Structural discrimination against less propertied individuals and groups becomes institutionalized in the system of so-called 'equality.' Claims of structural discrimination are often regarded as pleading of special privilege. It is always possible that particular claims are unjustified. That does not, however, negate the reality of systemic discrimination. It merely means that some sorting of responsibility is always necessary to distinguish as clearly as possible between personal and structural responsibility. A traditional Western liberal moral assumption is that everyone is free to achieve the same goals of property acquisition if they work hard and observe the rules of 'fair play.' The possibility that the rules may have been designed by an exclusive group to suit their interests is generally not considered. The rules of the game of acquisition of property do not benefit the majority of people who are pawns in the game rather than players. For those who qualify to be protected by the rules, the rule of non-interference is the first rule of fair play which protects their interests. One can expect moral and/or legal consequences from a violation of individual rights of property (i.e., rights of freedom). Rights are most importantly tied to property rights and they, therefore, benefit the more propertied to a greater extent than the less propertied.

Despite the injustice which is intrinsic to rights associated with property, a morality of rights is beneficial to everyone. Indeed, oppressed individuals and groups need those kinds of rights precisely because of their lack of social power to influence decisions in their favour. A minimal morality of rights is necessary in any model of society. Treating others fairly need not have anything to do with feeling compassionate toward them. Many would be happy if that minimal requirement of decent human interaction prevailed. A Black man wanting service in a southern United States restaurant, a Canadian mountie with a turban commanding respect in central Alberta, a single woman working outside the home and depending on child care facilities are examples of those who deserve justice regardless of whether the others involved care for them. Moral and legal rights are required for the protection of everyone in any society. Legal rights are inseparable from moral rights. The legal right to abort, for example, depends upon the moral rights which women can claim with regard to their independent personhood. It would seem that the right to non-interference with one's body is a minimum right.

The rights of individuals developed within the framework of brotherhood societies circulate around property rights, with the body being the first property. Civil society was organized around rules of ownership of property, including nature. The split between social and natural was included in the notion of civil society. The claims of women to independent personhood are only partially supported by Western liberal rights. Women were considered closer to nature than men because of their close association with their bodies. Like nature, women were controlled by the ethics of the brotherhood. Justice, the 'first virtue' (Rawls 1971)[2] was understood as fair play according to the rules of social organization developed by the brotherhood which protected each man from violation of private ownership. Protection of one's family came to be a sign of a man's self-respect and honour. Indeed, he would willingly give himself for his family, in the name of his honour. Protection of women's bodies from rape by other men was (is) part of the honour code among men. Rape of a man's wife or his daughter constituted violation of his property in this view of ownership, and was subject to severe punishment. By contrast, rape of a single woman without strong ties to a father or husband caused no great concern. The right of a woman not to be raped by her husband has only recently been defined by the law. Previously, as the owner of her body, he was privileged to access it when and how he wished. She exchanged her independence for his protection of her from other men. She was not, however, protected from him.

There is little doubt that moral and legal rights are important for women of all races, classes, ages, and sexual orientations. Without rights, there is no assurance of protection against violence. While the existence of moral and legal rights does not ensure protection against child abuse, wife battering, and homophobic activities, among other forms of violence, it is surely a basic condition of social relations. More is needed, however, if social relations and organizations are to include compassion, a form of protection against alienation and a friend of wisdom. The claim I wish to pursue here is that compassion is a form of self-love and benevolence which requires consciousness of the moral significance of each individual. The moral significance of one's own status, as well as that of others, is closely associated with recognition of the independent ontological status of each person within a context of interdependency.

Eros (love of oneself) and agapé (love for others) are continuous in a consciousness of reality in which creative power is interactional—in which there is no distinction between a higher order of unchanging transcendence and a lower order of changing immanence. Spirituality is about healthy relatedness in the social order, based on participation in a more universal process of connectedness. The separation between a divine order and an historical one served the purpose of those who identified with

God and used that identification as an argument for the divine sanctioning of the male-dominated social order. Within that social order the Christian ethic of caring became the ethic for the oppressed. They were encouraged and coerced into supporting the socially powerful who identified with the features attributed to god (e.g., self-sufficient, all-powerful and all-knowing). The Christian ethic of caring belonged more to the disempowered than to those with social power. As discussed in Chapter One, the ethic is inconsistent with a metaphysics of dualism. This is because of the domination-subordination model used to describe god and humanity. The attributes of god (such as all-knowing, all-powerful, and omnipresent) do not constitute a good model for human ethical development. They contribute more toward a model of social domination and subordination. To become like god within an epistemology of metaphysical dualism is to have power over. By contrast, an ethic of caring, grounded in interrelatedness, is about helping others to develop their integrity as fully as possible.

The command to love one's neighbour as oneself (the basic Christian ethical command) is to be carried out through the help of god. Without his help, it is said, humans cannot love as they should. A right relation with god the father is a condition, in Christianity, for a right relation with one's neighbours. It is also a condition for a right relation to oneself, which is integral to a right relation to one's neighbour. Central to the mandate to love one's neighbour as oneself is the belief in the relationality of self. But that is not central to the notion of god, indeed it is the opposite. God is singular and above the phenomenological world (the world of historical consciousness). The ambiguities of the world are not characteristic of god. In contrast to the completeness of god, historical consciousness is invariably characterized by change, uncertainty, and confusion. Spiritual consciousness as god consciousness, in monotheism, is about transcending historical consciousness. It includes perceiving the power of god outside of history to predetermine events in history, or to interact from time to time, or to participate all the time in changing history. Regardless of how god's participation in the world is perceived, god is believed to be the singular source of spiritual power. The power of god is invariably something that exists as a power over the events of the world. God is perceived basically as power over even when He works through nature. Human beings are perceived as being dependent upon a higher power for their agency. The distinction in monotheism between human and divine depends on that perception of god.

Ludwig Feuerbach's reaction to god (1967) is intrinsic to Marxist, socialist, and other humanist rejections of religion as a mere projection of our own agency onto god. Feuerbach claimed that in Christianity we are told to attribute all our good qualities to god and think of ourselves as worthless. Our self-worth then is seen to depend on our capacity for seeing ourselves as without worth. The idea is to be humble. Father knows best, so to speak. Feuerbach, Marx, Freud, and others rejected the authority of God the Father in favour of Man's (i.e., men's) authority. The sons overthrew the father in the development of humanism in order to restore self-determining power to man. Neither monotheism nor humanism, however, grants women self-determining rights as persons. Both traditions are shaped by the drive to overcome immanence in the thrust toward transcendence. Humanists decided they would assume the position that was previously occupied by god. This led J.P. Sartre into the depths of despair because he recognized that men's attempts to be god-like were futile. He could see that the move toward transcendence is invariably confounded by one's location in immanence. One could try to be 'for oneself' as a transcendent self but one always remained partially 'in oneself,' that is, stuck in immanence. De Beauvoir rightly pointed out that men's attempts to transcend their immanence as Subjects and to be like god included the relegation of women to the role of Other who represented immanence. Women were to absorb immanence if men were to become transcendent. This scenario is analogous to the development of transcendent thoughts through logical construction of the relation of words to each other, without interference from the sensations and emotions associated with the flesh. In some respects, anorexia today can be seen as a concrete manifestation of the flight from immanence to transcendence, with fleshiness representing weakness of spirit/mind.

De Beauvoir's contribution in revealing the construction of woman as Other in patriarchy is complicated by her acceptance of discontinuity between transcendence and immanence. As a humanist she gave a privileged status to transcendence. Genevieve Lloyd (1984) notes that extolling the immanence (flesh) of women within a symbolic system of meaning that denigrates immanence is of no help to women. It is necessary to change the symbolic system of meaning so that flesh can be understood as embodied spirit. The integration of flesh and spirit requires a breakdown of the exclusive categories of transcendence and immanence. Unfortunately, liberal humanism inherited the disparaging attitude towards immanence that is intrinsic to the notion of a transcendent god.

The association of transcendence with disembodied reason and the alignment of reason with maleness facilitated the association of moral superiority with men. God the spiritual father was eliminated in favour of men, the rational sons. The notion of the singular, the transcendent subject, is central to both narratives of agency: monotheistic and humanistic. Neither is compatible with an ethics that reflects person-in-relation, an ethics which is mandated in the command to love one's neighbour as oneself. The ideal of loving one's neighbour as oneself is part of the larger notion of moving toward the city of god where communality rather than individuality characterizes social relations. The difficulty in thinking about moving toward union with a singular, transcendent, all knowing, all powerful god is that it is incompatible with egalitarianism. Thus, moving toward a self-sufficient god cannot, logically, mean moving toward equal

relations with others. Rather it necessarily retains a hierarchical orientation. Within a monotheistic model, one has to overlook the logical inconsistency between the notion of god and the mandate to grow out of selfishness
and into unselfishness through god's power. In fact, most institutionalized
religious structures are consistent with the belief in hierarchical power
rather than egalitarian power. As Rosemary Radford Ruether (1983),
among others, has pointed out, the ecclesiastical magisterium is the dominant form of Christian church practice, while the spirit-filled practices,
which enact egalitarian principles, are marginalized within Christendom.
The rejection of religion-based ethics by Western humanistic liberalism was
largely a rejection of the father in favour of the son, just as the establishment of the social contract was a rejection of the father in favour of the sons
(the brotherhood). I shall discuss social contract theory in Chapter Five,
with respect to the centrality of the brotherhood and the institutionalization
of dominant/subordinate sexual relations in social organization.

Ethics or morality developed into a discussion of decision-making
theories associated with respecting the property of individuals. Moral development theories were largely designed to measure the degrees to
which individuals are capable of making independent, rational decisions
in the face of hypothetical dilemmas concerned with conflicting rights
claims. They reflect a close association between dispassionate reasoning
and moral decision-making. A consequence is that one could never assume anything about the presence of compassion or the lack of it in a person who rates high on moral development scales. The split between compassion and morality in Western liberalism is an untoward consequence of
Kant's close association of morality with reason. That split, though, is entirely consistent with the belief that it is a mistake to connect a knowledge
claim with the source of the claim (the genetic fallacy). In the Western liberal view there is no proper connection between the knower and the
knowledge. A moral philosopher may well be one of the most obnoxious,
least compassionate person one encounters. But that person will respect
the rights of others. Treating one's neighbour fairly will be part of such a
person's lifestyle of activities. Treating others fairly need not have anything to do with feeling compassion toward them. That is fair enough. For
example, on one occasion when I was living in an apartment building I
banged on the neighbour's door to ask him to turn his stereo down. I
didn't care if he was pleasant so long as he turned it down. The rules of
the lease agreement assured me of my rights. He slammed the door in my
face but turned down the sound. It is evident that a morality of rights,
with legal enforcement, is important, independent of compassion. A
morality that includes compassion as well as ensuring basic human
rights, however, goes beyond 'professionalism' and actively promotes self-
determination through relatedness. My preference is that we take morality further in this direction.

The inconsistency, as described above, between the metaphysics of Christianity (or any monotheistic religion) and the Christian ethics of love is a reason to reject Christian metaphysics. It is not, however, a reason to reject Christian ethics as it is found in the command to love your neighbour as yourself. Christian ethics is an ethics of compassion even though it is part of a metaphysics that supports domination. The ethic of compassion (agapé) is not restricted to Christianity. It can be described more generally as an ethics of spirituality. The contribution of spirituality to ethics, in the view that I develop in this book, is the understanding of self as embedded in an ontology of interrelatedness. The self is partially constituted, in this view, by a desire toward connectedness, as discussed in Chapter One. Personal drives toward connectedness are believed to be individualized expressions of an ongoing reality of interrelatedness. This view of the self in which nature and culture intersect in the construction of self is expressed similarly, for example, by Jessica Benjamin (psychoanalyst), John Macquarrie (theologian), and David Hume (philosopher).

Jessica Benjamin theorizes about the self as being driven by the desires for both privacy and connectedness. John Macquarrie suggests that the dual drives toward egoity (individual centredness) and sociality characterize self-determination. David Hume assumes a tension within the self between selfishness and benevolence, which is resolved by mediating selfish desires with the interests of others. In all three approaches, desire motivates moral or ethical action. Self-determination is a process of balancing self-regard with regard for others. Eros and agapé are understood as part of the same phenomenon rather than polarities to be reconciled. The inclusiveness of eros and agapé is integral to an ethic of affiliation. Self-love and love of others is grounded in a consciousness of ontological interrelatedness. An affiliative ethic is a logical consequence of an ontology of connectedness in which one becomes conscious of spiritual experiences, which are interpreted as integrative experiences. They dispose one to be more attentive to connecting events, people, and things in one's life.

Affirmation of connectedness does not entail denial of strife. It might, however, transform one's relation to strife. Spiritual consciousness of ontological interrelatedness supports or, in some instances, creates a disposition toward receptivity and responsiveness. The disposition toward relatedness is a motivation for responsible action that addresses tensions constructively through receptive listening and effective negotiating. Spiritual leadership is represented, for example, in Karen Brown's account of a Vodou priestess who reduces conflicts in a Haitian community by leading rituals in which the people of the community express their points of view and listen to others. The metronome beat of the priestess is not a dominating force. It is the beat which provides the context for the rhythms of others. It is a connecting beat. The metaphor of the metronome in Haitian rituals designed to realign community members and the metaphor of jazz improvisation for the construction of self are apt images for the picture of

ontological connectedness and ethical social relations which I am exploring here.

Spiritual leadership by women is supported by an ontology which
does not separate immanence from transcendence. Apart from leadership,
a view of women as persons with independent rights is supported by a
view of reality that does not separate nature from culture. An ontology of
interrelatedness does not allow, logically, for such a separation. Where
bodies are not denigrated in the interests of spiritual and social leadership, there is more likelihood of women's rights being acknowledged
automatically. That includes rights over their bodies. An ontology of interrelatedness allows for ontological independence for women in ways that
are virtually impossible in a metaphysics which privileges disembodied
transcendence over embodied spirituality. An ontology of interrelatedness
supports an ethics of rights as well as of affiliation. The self is understood
as permeable, neither entirely separate nor entirely soluble. Grounding in
interrelatedness provides a centredness from which to balance one's disposition to act. Self-determination, from a spiritual perspective, is the life-
long process of developing balanced action: wisdom and compassion. Wisdom is not to be equated with rationality.

We are not as rational as we often think we are. Sometimes, for
example, the most intransigent sexism is found in those who present
themselves as so rational that they drive another person crazy with their
apparent rationality. Such a person may seem so rational that another
person feels mildly hysterical in his or her presence. The possibility of defending oneself against what feels like dominating, sexist behaviour fades
in the presence of manipulative logic. Both persons often believe that one
of them is superbly rational while the other has 'a problem.' Usually the
one who allegedly has the problem knows there is something wrong
somewhere but is not quite sure where. In my view, the problem can be
located in the unacknowledged influence of non-rational factors in reasoning. Non-rational factors, in this epistemology, are part of all thinking.
They are constitutive of consciousness in the form of sensations (feelings).
I assume (with Hume and Spinoza, for example) that feelings and ideas
are mutually influential. In this view, all thoughts are more or less emotively toned. There are plenty of non-rational reasons why we do not act
according to what we say we believe. We pass along mixed messages
when we don't recognize the emotional component of our carefully articulated reasons. Fear, anger, sadness, desires, and hopes often get in the
way of doing what we actually think or intuit to be the correct thing to do.

I do not wish to distinguish between rational and non-rational reasons for acting. There is no basis for such a distinction in an ontology of
interrelatedness and an epistemology that assumes an inclusive relation
between sensations and ideas in consciousness. The distinction depends
on a dualistic metaphysics: separation of mind and body, which corresponds to the metaphysics of transcendent-immanent. I do not accept the

distinction between rational and non-rational because of my assumption of the inseparability of reason and emotion in consciousness. In this view, all ideas are emotively toned just as all sensations are put into an interpretive framework. It happens sometimes that we have sensations that we are unable to articulate. We have gut feelings, for example, which may motivate us to act in another's interest. Are we to say that the actions are non-rational? Normally that is what would be said. Such actions are referred to as non-rational because reasons cannot be given for them. That is, they have no apparent justification.

While I do not distinguish between rational and non-rational beliefs, I do differentiate between non-rational and irrational. Irrational beliefs are those which are inconsistent with other beliefs held by a person. They are incoherent with respect to the rest of what the person claims to believe. Irrational actions are erratic, just as irrational beliefs are. It might be useful to jettison the notion of rationality because it connotes the separation of reason from emotion. It implies that a person is either rational or irrational. Perhaps coherent, integrated, or balanced could be used in place of rational.[3] Coherent reasons would be those which can be integrated into the existing set of perceptions in a person's consciousness. Incoherent ones are those which cannot be integrated due to their discontinuity with existing perceptions. Radically different experiences such as spiritual experiences fit into the category of incoherent reasons for belief. They might eventually be made coherent or they may remain unexplainable but still inform the person's way of knowing and living.

The articulation of reasons depends on diverse conditions such as the skills of the individual to articulate at all, or to articulate in a way that is considered by others to be appropriate, or to articulate new experiences or perceptions which we have no acceptable way of symbolizing in our linguistic system. Due to socialization patterns and the history of logic, women often suffer from a lack of articulation, which is associated with lack of self-esteem. For some, articulation develops before self-esteem, while for others self-esteem emerges silently. Mostly, however, self-esteem and articulation are closely interrelated. This is why the relation between sexuality and language is so important. Enunciation of subjectivity requires a language that is appropriate to the speaker and which communicates her meaning to others. Equality between subjects is not possible without languages that reflect various ways of knowing. It is necessary to bring forth new images from the female body into symbolization in order that women can speak as women. Justice requires that women have adequate symbolism to represent themselves as ontologically independent subjects. Speaking with authority depends on having authoritative language to use. The ideas of women must reflect their felt sensations. They know themselves with their own eyes, ears, touch, and so forth, in order to articulate themselves. Using a borrowed language makes articulation difficult for many women. The development of a language through which one can speak coherently is a condition for social justice. Goddess symbolism is a possible source for the development of new ways of knowing ourselves as ontologically independent women embedded in a process of interrelatedness.

The notions of self-love and benevolence, for example, can be grounded in experiences of goddess presence. Goddess consciousness can be described in terms of 'virgin' power. It is the power of independence, of woman-unto-herself. It is the power of generativity. Knowing that such power is available in her gives her moral status as a unique human being. Self-loving is facilitated through goddess consciousness. It facilitates her will to act creatively in relation to others. When she experiences a deep coherency within herself, between herself and other persons, and between herself and the rest of nature, her consciousness of ontological connectedness is enhanced. Her way of knowing grounds her actions towards affiliation and social justice. Her theorizing and conduct arise from her knowledge of herself as both powerful and interdependent. When many individuals have similar experiences and share them through a language that adequately conveys the meanings of their experiences, it might be possible for a different social and cultural mythology to emerge. For example, within the past twenty-five years of feminism, more women are included in the decision-making process in their homes as well as where they work for a salary. Attitudes and practices are changing with regard to women in their various places. This is not to say that we have an egalitarian social order, but rather that partners and employers are listening more to women's desires and reasoned points of view. Such a shift, even if it is slow, contains the conditions for a new underlying evolutionary intentionality to emerge, such as that suggested by Riane Eisler (1987) in her partnership model of social and cultural evolution. In the process of remythologizing, a new ethic of affiliation is developing in conjunction with the morality of rights. Self-love and benevolence constitute the flesh on the anorexic bones of justice. Calm passion motivates moral conduct.

An ethic of self-love and benevolence is consistent with a view of the self as unique and relational in an ontology of interrelatedness. It is contiguous with moral theory which asserts justice as the first virtue. Legal and moral rights are necessary, although insufficient, measures for maintaining stable social relations and protecting justified self-interests in the event of conflicting interests. For women to enjoy more than precarious rights, a cultural remythologization needs to occur. Symbols and images of women's bodies and creative agency are needed in the new cultural mythology. Symbols which indicate connectednesses, which reflect power to empower are needed in the development of an intentionality which will redirect social and cultural evolution towards the partnership model. An ethic of care is needed in addition to justice when individuals are understood to be persons-in-relationship. Ontology in which the self is essentially both a self-determining subject and a relational subject requires more than a justice which protects against non-interference, even though that is a minimal moral requirement in social relations. It requires an ethic of compassion. In addition, it is supported by an epistemology which reflects knowledge of the process of interrelatedness. An ethic of compassion and wisdom such as that found in Buddhism and shamanic and goddess spirituality, for instance, augments moral theories of justice. A new cultural mythology is required that embraces women's ontological status as interdependent creative individuals, each with a moral significance that demands both justice and compassion.

Power and Trust

An ethic of care, of compassion, of self-love and benevolence, of affiliation, and so forth, entails trust. I wish to explore the role of trust in coercive power relations. What does it mean to trust others in social organizations that are characterized by hierarchical power relations? What is the relation between self-trust and trust of others in situations where trusting others is not practical? The ethic of self-love (eros) and benevolence (agapé) includes self-trust and trust of others. Spiritual ethics is about mutual love and trust. Are spiritual ethics relevant only to personal friendships and utopian social visions? I shall explore these questions in light of my continuing argument that an ethics of care is contiguous with an ethic of justice. They reinforce each other. Justice is necessary because the utopian ideals of spiritual ethics are not practical in competitive and aggressive social organization. Apart from utopias, social order is maintained through social justice as it is legislated by government, enforced in the courts, and protected by police forces.

Those structures are necessary when differential power relations obtain, as they do in anything but a utopia. They are depicted at their worst in dystopias. One of the functions of dystopias (e.g., Margaret Atwood's *The Handmaid's Tale* [1985]) is to awaken readers to possibilities for the future if present conditions continue unchecked. In dystopias, justice is depicted as dehumanizing in the extreme. Dystopias serve as warnings about uncritical acceptance of current patterns of social relations and rules of fair play. When justice serves the purposes of the powerful few who control social organization through the legal system, then it becomes institutionalized injustice. Dystopias write large the injustice inherent in current social and cultural patterns of justice. Feminist dystopias reveal the future consequences of contemporary unjust policies and practices with respect to women. They are alarms for those who are still sleeping and are confirmations of the worst fears of those whose social consciousness has awakened.

Utopias, on the other hand (e.g., Charlotte Perkins Gilman's *Herland* [1979]), depict visions of what life could be like if an ethics of compassion and wisdom prevailed. In utopias, justice is exercised because of the associated ethics of self-love and benevolence. The two forms of ethical

orientations are intertwined. The distinguishing feature of feminist utopias like *Herland* is the absence of hierarchal power relations. Such
utopias have been tried among religious communities. Barbara Taylor's
Eve and the New Jerusalem (1983), for example, describes Owenite socialism in early nineteenth-century England. It was a feminist socialism.
Women's rights were taken seriously just as men's rights were. Children
were an important part of the community. The people lived respectfully
with the earth. Robert Owen had a vision of communal living. It survived
until Marxist socialism and the industrial revolution emerged as social
forces. Women's work, thought, and existence were quickly subordinated
to the cause of Marxist socialism in the face of the social injustices of the
industrial revolution. Since the industrial revolution, progress has been
measured by quantitative productivity. Morality is closely connected to social goals. Those goals changed remarkably during the industrial revolution from a more community based consensus of goals to the interests of
those who controlled the means of production. Those without the means
of ownership might internalize the goals of their bosses, or they might
disassociate themselves from their work and find their significance outside their work. They might develop patterns of resistance to their oppressive work conditions, or escape into television or videos, for example,
where one can shut down and simply watch the activities of others. The
hero of *Being There* comes to mind. He spends most of his time watching
television. When he goes out of the house he takes his remote control
channel changer with him and attempts to change the scene when he sees
something in which he is not interested or which gets in his way. He is
characterized by alienation from himself as well as others.

Alienation from oneself includes lack of trust in oneself. Authority is
projected onto others. The projection of authority onto others and defer-
ential behaviour toward them is sanctioned by monotheistic metaphysics.
The separation of the 'expert knower' from the 'less-than-competent' lay
person is supported by monotheistic metaphysics. The not unusual projection of authority outside the self onto another is satirized in the Monty
Python film, *The Life of Brian*. The hero, Brian, is an ordinary man. Inadvertently, however, a large group of people believe he is Jesus Christ.
Brian cannot do anything to convince the believers that he is not the Son
of God and has nothing of importance to say to anyone. They take his dis-
claimers as further proof of his humble nature as the Son of God. His incoherent speeches are taken as talking in tongues. The satire illustrates,
among other things, the strong desire of people to look to an external authority for guidance. The projection of their own beliefs onto Brian as the
Son of God increased their own foolish behaviour.

Ludwig Feuerbach's (1967) influential critique of the projection of all
the positive human qualities onto God and the alleged worthlessness of
oneself is writ large in *The Life of Brian*. Feuerbach's attacks on Christian
beliefs as pernicious forms of human alienation by which human beings

project their power onto a transcendent God were influential in Marxist ideology as well as Freudian psychology. The humanism of the Western liberal tradition, which replaced faith in God with faith in men's reason, joined forces with the humanism of Marxist materialism and the humanism of Freud's psychoanalysis. In all cases reason is believed to be shaped without reference to metaphysics. One of the purposes of Freudian psychoanalysis was to exorcise the residual cultural effects of Christianity and explain the stages of human development exclusively from within the individual's psyche. Psychological and social analysis since Marx and Freud has been largely without reference to spirituality.

The work of Carl Jung is an exception in that it connects psychology to spirituality. Jung is a resource for feminists who reject an exclusively humanistic psychological social analysis of power relations. While I am hesitant to give Jung much credit in advancing the cause of women's rights, his work is being used effectively to understand connections between spiritual consciousness and historical consciousness, which is a basis for moral consciousness. For example, Jung's notion of synchronicity is described by Jean Shinoda Bolen (1979) as the central concept in his view of reality as interrelated. Synchronicity means meaningful coincidence. Bolen says, "synchronicity is a descriptive term for the link between two events that are connected through their meaning, a link that cannot be explained by cause and effect" (1979:14). She claims that cause and effect relations are always understood linearly, while synchronicity is inexplicable. I take her to mean that synchronicity, as meaningful coincidence, is experienced in non-rational ways which support beliefs in ontological interrelatedness. Synchronicity is taken as evidence of spiritual connectedness. It is a spiritual experience that is given meaning as it is integrated with other experiences. Through synchronicity, spiritual consciousness is integrated into historical consciousness. Spiritual consciousness is a resource for social change in that it brings to historical consciousness a dimension that is not contained in typical social or psychological perceptions. Spiritual consciousness allows for new ways of seeing, listening, and feeling that are not represented in cultural or psychic inscriptions from which spiritual knowledge is excluded.

Visions of egalitarian morality are inspired by spiritual experiences of interrelatedness. The ideals of religious ethics are ideals of communal ethics of caring. The inconsistency between patriarchal religious ethical ideals and patriarchal dualistic metaphysics understandably led to the rejection of religion by many. Regrettably the baby gets thrown out with the bath water. Religious ethical ideals are consistent with feminist social ideals. I prefer to use the phrase 'spiritual ethical ideals' rather than 'religious ethical ideals' because I wish to disassociate spirituality from patriarchal religion. Spirituality is about interactive power, without subordination to a controlling power. Patriarchal religious traditions generally reflect belief in a dominant power which one obeys, adores, and subordinates oneself to. The dominant power is associated with male social power so that male authority seems natural. By contrast, spirituality is about living with one's power through the power of spirits in the form of other persons, the earth, animals, birds, and the rest of nature. Generativity is both female and male. The spirits of the body ground one's airborne spirits. The spirits of the air (intellect) keep a person from getting stuck in one place (materiality). The passionate spirits of fire (the will) interact with the spirits of fluids (love). The interaction of the intellect, concrete practicality, determinated, principled action, and compassion is constitutive of spiritually directed self-determination. This is not to say that any particular person integrates all four powers completely, but rather that the goal of self-determination is to work towards such balance.

Trust is seen to be a motivator, a sustainer, and a goal of such human endeavour. A spiritual point of view of ethical conduct, would be that trust is the first cause, the efficient cause, and the final cause of a person's activities. New ways of knowing include death to old ways of listening, thinking, and speaking. This transformative process is about developing balance. Balance of intellect, practicality, will, and love is experienced as power. Power in this perspective is strength. Consistent with Buddhist mindfulness, strength in goddess and shamanic consciousness is about "mind-force" (Noble 1983:90). Mindfulness or mind-strength is not about intellectual control over one's emotions, control over others, or control over nature. Rather, it is about being grounded in one's energy and knowledge. Mindfulness is coextensive, in this view, with moral strength. Compassion and wisdom are moral strengths. Moral strength is constitutive of centred power.

Buddhist mindfulness brings the emotional and mental parts of consciousness together in a balance of compassion and wisdom. Buddhist theory and practice, however, is not friendly to the body. The body is considered largely as an illustration of decaying material. In Buddhism it usually serves as a reminder not to get too attached to things because they never remain the same. The exception is Tantric Buddhism in which bodily ecstasy and sexual union are included in the process of transformation through death and rebirth. Tantric Buddhism is especially compatible with goddess and shamanic spirituality. All three approaches include body images in their theories and practices.[4] They are helpful in grounding morality in body desires, which create dispositions toward connectedness.

Social orders in which justice is possible need not be utopias, but they require an infrastructure of appropriate attitudes and beliefs, i.e., an underlying intentionality, that is motivated by connectedness. Self-love and benevolence are closely connected to simultaneous psychological desires for one's own space and for relationships with others. Self-love is necessary to overcome or to reject a lifestyle of alienation. Caring for others is intrinsic to egalitarian social policies and practices. The separation of a religious ethic of caring from a liberal ethic of rights has resulted in the denigration of religious ethics as hopelessly romantic or utopian. The rejection of anything more than a humanistic understanding of the self and social relations, including relations to the earth, has led to a reductionistic and somewhat barren landscape from which to search for new possibilities with respect to ethical theorizing and practices. Changes in the social order require, as Irigaray so forcefully claims, a new imaginary. Spirituality has much to contribute to such a new imaginary.

New images provide sources for alternate metaphors and alternative forms of consciousness whereby individuals can describe their experiences. Images of connectedness support attitudes of trust. For example, the image of a woman, as illustrated by Spretnak (1991), who has been raped and who is now sitting in a pool of water surrounded by flowers, a healing circle of women, and special artifacts which convey safety and beauty, is a powerful image. Rituals serve to heal through trust. They are not intended to pacify but to strengthen through connection with the transforming powers of the elements and friends. The elemental power of nature, including human nature, is imaged in this picture as a way in which pain is turned into strength and motivates social action to reduce instances of pain. An ontology of interrelatedness is the grounding of an ethics of justice which includes compassion. It is constitutive of an underlying intentionality which might shift social and cultural evolution toward an integration of culture and nature. Such an intentionality is necessary to undermine the contemporary industrial-militaristic social order in which justice is largely about protection against claims which restrict one's privileges with respect to one's property.

Differential power relations require that principles of justice be in place and that the rules be enforced. In contemporary industrial societies which are organized in militaristic style, the issue of trust is problematic because within hierarchical structures each of us is in bondage to the power structure. We merely occupy different positions, with some standing over others and some bending in deference to them. Regardless of which position anyone occupies, all the occupants of the positions experience restrictions to their freedom. Trust between individuals in such situations is problematic.

It could be argued that mistrust is more appropriate than trust in such a hierarchical organization. Terence Penelhum notes that "mistrusting people consists in looking behind their statements and deeds to unacknowledged motives and purposes."[5] In a system of punishments and rewards organized around adherence to dominant-subordinate relations, fear tends to dominate people's consciousnesses. In such cases, hidden motives and purposes can reasonably be assumed. Mistrust, therefore, would be more appropriate than trust. At the same time, loyalty to the system is drilled into the consciousness of occupants of all positions. Initiative that does not go through the designated appropriate channels of authority is regarded as an 'end run.' Football language is adopted by both women and men in entrenched cultural institutions such as universities, professional corporations, and factories. The majority of workers in all these places, as well as in others, pick up the dominant cultural language. Justice is seen to require a 'level playing field.' The ethics of hierarchical institutions are concomitant with the underlying ethos of dominance/subordination. The rules of the game dictate the nature of justice. Trust between occupants of positions in hierarchical structures amounts to loyalty to the officers of the institution. If an occupant of a middle position is caught between conflicting interests of those below her and those above her and cannot act effectively for either one she is the target of accusations of betrayal from both. She is seen as untrustworthy from both points of view. Her continued occupancy of the position generally depends on her loyalty to her 'superior.' 'Licking up' and 'spitting down' pretty well depicts her position. For many occupants of positions within hierarchies there is no practical choice regarding loyalty, if retaining the job is important. Decisions of loyalty in stratified workplaces depend to a large extent on the seriousness of the issue, from the point of view of the decision-maker. While trust is a key issue among friends, it is not a straightforward measure of moral integrity within a hierarchical social order. The concept of trust is easier to apply in more egalitarian contexts where compassion is part of moral integrity and power is expressed constructively through love rather than destructively through fear.

Annette Baier (1985) suggests that 'appropriate trust' might be used as a central notion in moral theory, i.e., an understanding of what morality is. In her view, 'appropriate trust' brings together obligation and love. Obligation (ought) is the loveless organizing notion in the contemporary moral theory of the neo-Kantian tradition (e.g., Piaget, Erickson, Kohlberg), while caring was the moral concern found by Gilligan (1982) among the women and girls that she studied. The ethics of care has been a contentious subject within feminist theory since the publication of Gilligan's ground-breaking book, *In a Different Voice*. Gilligan's work challenged John Rawls' claim that justice exclusively is the first virtue. In accordance with Gilligan, Baier (1985) claimed that the first virtue is better described as conditional trust. In Baier's view, it might be any one of the following: appropriate trustworthiness, appropriate trustingness, appropriate encouragement to trust, or conversely it might be judicious untrustworthiness, selective refusal to trust, or discriminating discouragement of trust (1985:61). The subordination of women to male authority in patriarchy makes the last three virtues necessary for a liberation ethic. Caring for one's oppressor often reinforces one's victimization. That is true in the home as much as in the workplace. An ethic of care is problematic if it merely supports an existing unethical system of dominant-subordinate relations. Baier says, "However keen women now are to end the lovelessness of modern moral philosophy, they are unlikely to lose sight of the cautious virtue of appropriate distrust, or of the tough virtue of principled betrayal of the exploiters' trust" (1985:62).

An example of moral justification of 'principled betrayal' is found in Anne Wheeler's film, *Loyalties*. The doctor's wife continued to be loyal to her husband even though he was forced to leave his homeland (England) because he had raped a young woman. In addition, he was unloving toward his wife. As a well-educated English women she had internalized the identification of wifely loyalty with herself as a good woman. A growing friendship with her housekeeper, a Métis woman, began to lead her more into a woman-centred way of life than she had previously experienced. She continued to support her husband, however, even though she found him exasperating much of the time. Near the end, her loyalty to him was seriously challenged when he raped her friend's daughter (the second rape) who was babysitting their children while the two women were out for the evening. They came home to the teenager's screams. The English woman physically prevented the other one from shooting the man. It appeared as though she was going to continue her loyalty to her husband. In the end she reported her husband to the police. Her loyalties had changed. The film depicts principled betrayal of a husband, by a wife.

Resistance to sexual violence requires that principled betrayal becomes a virtue. The betrayal by slaves or those working in slave-like conditions is another obvious example of the virtue of principled betrayal. Wife abuse, incest, paedophilia in boarding schools, and domestic servant exploitation are examples of legitimate reasons for principled betrayal of trust. All forms of abusive relations are contexts for principled betrayal of trust. Mandated loyalties are often maintained through systems of rewards and punishments. Courage is required to break out of such situations of bondage, especially if they are institutionalized and, thereby, normalized. In all these kinds of situations, and many more, it is necessary that virtue includes the possibility for the victimized to end an abusive situation. Principled betrayal, judicious untrustworthiness, selective refusal to trust, and discriminating discouragement of trust are important virtues alongside those of trust. The orientation to mistrust is sometimes as necessary for survival as trust.

Trusting is an attitude which reflects positive beliefs, feelings, and emotions towards others, while distrusting is the opposite, in the view of Trudy Govier (1990:1). Govier claims that we selectively interpret others' actions according to whether we trust or distrust them. Sometimes there is insufficient reason to know whether to trust or distrust another. Perhaps there have been mixed experiences or no experiences. We learn to trust or distrust others according to our experiences with them. In situations where people are governed by fear, and hidden motives and purposes lie behind their actions, trust amounts to guessing the motive or purpose. Correctly guessing the hidden agenda allows for accurately predicting the person's actions. This is a different version of trust than that based on positive feelings towards another. Positive feelings towards another are part of believing that the other person has good will toward you. Trust and good will are constitutive of freely chosen loyalties. Where loyalties are not freely chosen, trust is irrelevant. Knowing the motives of the other is more relevant. That characterizes mistrust.

A 'coercive justice of morality' (Baier 1985:60) which functions with bribes and threats is common in dominant/subordinate relations in the workplace and in the home. The politics of morality in a militaristic-industrial society dictates obligations independent of love. An ethics of love in such a social order will almost inevitably be mandated to care-givers and denigrated as a low level of morality. For example, L. Kohlberg and R. Kramer placed such an ethic at level three of a six-stage moral de-velopment scale. In their view, "stage 3 personal concordance morality is a functional morality for housewives and mothers; it is not for business-men and professionals" (Hersh, Paolitto, and Reimer 1979:108). Gilligan challenged her former colleague, Kohlberg, about his schema. She held that his six-stage development scale was biased in its methodology as well as in its account of the nature of morality. Since her landmark book, *In a Different Voice* (1982), there have been continuing debates about the use-fulness of an ethics of care for women in a society where they constitute the majority of caregivers, often to their own detriment. At the same time, an ethics of care is necessary to put a heart into morality. The dilemma is that those who are most concerned about mixing love with justice are those who are most victimized because they live according to the principle of caring.

An ethic of care fits into our society as women fit into the workplace and wives and mothers fit into the home. They are most often the source of comfort in a combative social structure. An ethic of care is not institu-tionalized explicitly into social organizations. Professors in universities, for example, are sometimes told that the university is a place of learning and not a social work agency. That admonition is intended to guard against listening too seriously to students' explanations of problematic life circumstances which affect their academic achievement. Such an orienta-tion indicates an either/or approach to intellectual pursuits and emotion-al involvements. It reflects an attitude of separation between the public and private aspects of people's lives. A female professor who listens sym-pathetically to students is sometimes referred to in a derogatory way as a 'mother confessor.' Her image is closely associated with that of the 'recy-cled housewife.' She is told that her skin isn't tough enough. Perhaps this is valid in particular instances. The problem is that an uncaring attitude is often seen to be more acceptable than a caring one. Professionalism is characterized more by non-interference than by caring. Most people would likely agree that caring is undeniably important in our workplaces. Progress is being made in the direction of changing chilly work climates into friendly ones. As long as the cultural paradigm is one of domi-nance/subordination, however, power relations in both the public and private spheres will be guided predominantly by an ethics of right to non-interference rather than of connectedness. The rights of the dominant are protected by interlocking social systems of domination such as the education system, the legal system, the political system, the health care system, the family, religion, and so forth. The relatively disempowered are asked to be the caregivers to those who dominate them.

The term 'caretaker' is interesting in this context. It usually refers to someone who performs janitorial services or housekeeping duties. Caretakers take care of another person's property. One could interpret caretaker, however, to be the opposite of caregiver, meaning the person who takes care *from* the caregiver. Hierarchical relations are generally constructed on an asymmetry between caregivers and caretakers. The privileged caretakers provide protection for the caregivers. Egalitarian relations, by contrast, are characterized by symmetrical relations of caring. Trust is developed through such relations. Trust relies on mutual caring about the interests of the other. In relations of trust, self-interest is contiguous with the interests of the other. In other words, self-love and benevolence are constitutive of trust. Whereas justice is the first virtue in a context of mistrust, care is more appropriate in situations of trust.

Self-Interest

Caring includes self-love and benevolence. Compassion and wisdom require responsible love toward oneself as well as toward others. Responsible love includes responsible knowing. Knowledge of hierarchical power relations and resistance to them is important if caring on the part of the subordinates is not to reinforce oppressive conditions between caregivers and caretakers. A spiritual understanding of persons and nature includes an ethics of affiliation. It is about 'living with' rather than 'having.'

An important issue for many of us as women is living with our bodies in a spiritually powerful way. This means taking our bodies as sources of knowledge and as influences in our attitudes of self-regard. Body consciousness is intrinsic to self-regard as well as to the ways in which we connect to others. In a culture which has a history of denying the body in the interests of rationality, there has been little support for attention to body consciousness. This is especially true with regard to menstruation, pregnancy, lactation, and menopause. Women's health with respect to gynecological issues has not been served well in cultures where the elemental powers of women's bodies has been both feared and, accordingly, denied, since fear and trust are incompatible with each other. Women's bodies have been feared in patriarchal consciousness. Both women and men have internalized that fear. Women have suffered because of the denigration of their bodies. They have been subjugated partly out of fear of them. It is not in the interests of women to continue to deny their bodies. From the point of view of a spiritual understanding of the self, it is important for women to experience their bodies as a locus of spiritual energy. Drumming circles, healing circles, dance, discussions of pregnancy, lactation, menstruation, and menopause are possible ways of increasing bodied spiritual consciousness.

In 1991, I participated in a workshop which was about raising spiritual energy in the body through drumming and dancing. The intent was to open the energy centres and allow the energy to flow freely through the body. Through those activities the body is enlivened and one becomes more fully awake. This happened in my case and seemed to have the same effect on others. Following the day-long workshops which were attended by both women and men, the women met in a circle to discuss menstrual and lunar cycles. After the day of drumming, dancing, and experiencing high level energy soaring through our bodies and out the top of our heads, we were very conscious of the agency of our bodies. We gathered in a circle to listen to each other's experiences and theories about going into body consciousness each month when we menstruate. Some women told of what it is for them to have ceased menstruating and to have passed into a new phase of living with their bodies in menopause. Others talked of the meaning of menstruation to them and its relation to premenstrual stress. The relation of the body to dominant cultural attitudes towards it were discussed. It was generally agreed that the negative attitudes towards menstruation contribute to the stress associated with menstrual periods. The discussion was a time of affiliation among women speaking from a heightened body consciousness and reinforcing it through openness and responsiveness to each other. Participation in the circle was health enhancing.

The leader of the group opened up connections between subjective consciousness and social consciousness. She owns a business in the United States where she employs several women. The employees each have two days a month off from work in addition to the normal time off. The two days include the day before they begin menstruating and the first day of bleeding. The women are given those days to look after themselves, to go inward and pay attention to the changes that are taking place in their bodies. The owner of the business claims that it is cost effective to give the women time to take care of themselves. The employees' level of production increased, the morale in the workplace improved, and there was less time taken for sick days.[6] Treating menstruation as a normal reality of women's lives rather than as a problem depends upon assuming that women constitute one of two normative forms of humanity. It includes a positive view of women's bodies and menstruation. Men's bodies are not taken as the standard for everyone. They are only one of two forms. In order to take women's bodies as a normative form of human bodies, women's ontological independence must be acknowledged. If that is recognized, then the issue of women having control over their own bodies should not be a problem.

Menstruation is at the womb of self-love for women. If menstruation is to be regarded positively, women's bodies must be seen as one of two standard measures of normal human bodies. It is in women's self-interest to experience menstruation positively. It is difficult to imagine a balanced consciousness that is upset regularly each month for thirty-five to forty years. In the interests of women's well-being it is important to jettison the patriarchal idea that menstruation is problematic because it gets in the way of a woman working, playing, thinking, or feeling like a man. Living with menstruation in a good way requires having a woman-identified consciousness. It is to assume personal power and not to give one's power as a woman over to men. It is unlikely, if not impossible, for male-identified women to experience menstruation positively. The power of defining menstruation was taken over by men in patriarchal culture and internalized by both men and women. The power of defining the meaning of menstruation is symbolic of the power to define women's bodies. Women in patriarchal cultures generally find it difficult to have good body experiences because their bodies are defined as problematic in their differences from men's bodies. Experiencing menstruation positively is symbolic of experiencing one's body more generally in a positive way. It is to take it as normative rather than deviant. If women's bodies are taken to be normative, then, if we are to be logically consistent, we must dispose of the idea that women's bodies ought to be controlled by the legal system, by husbands, by fathers, or by anyone other than the embodied woman. Women's rights with regard to their bodies would, in this case, be respected. Further, their menstrual cycles would be taken into account as a matter of fact in the workplace, the home, and among friends. Justice and compassion are served when women's self-interest is taken into account, especially as they concern the realities of women's bodies.

Women often align their menstrual times with moon times, full moon or new moon. The symbolism of full moon is the power of the moon over fluids: fluids as different as those of the body and the ocean tides. When the power of the moon to pull the tides is symbolized in women's menstruation power, it is no wonder that men fear women's elemental power. Negative attitudes in industrialized-militaristic societies toward menstruation can reasonably be attributed in part to fear of an uncontrollable power. Living with nature rather than controlling it is a frightening prospect for those who pride themselves on control and prediction. Men's religious rituals in which bleeding is facilitated through cutting various body parts, such as the penis, to make it look like a bleeding vagina (Gross, 1989), can be interpreted as men's attempts to emulate the blood power of women. While the full moon symbolizes the outward expression of elemental power, the new moon indicates an inward-looking time of consolidating one's power. Going deep into body consciousness during menstruation is a time of renewing elemental power and experiencing growth through change. The sloughing off of the lining of the uterus is a condition for new growth and new possibilities. The body process is a metaphor for shedding old ideas and old patterns of behaviour to make space for new developments, just as the snake shedding its skin is a goddess symbol of the transformation through death to new birth. The regenerative process (letting go and coming into a new being) is initiated at puberty and is re-enacted each month until menopause, when a major letting go occurs and a new birth emerges, the birth of a new body consciousness. Life is a cyclical process of new ways of knowing oneself. It is a cyclical process each month that spirals toward a new phase. Self-love includes letting go of worn out habits and accepting initiation into new ways, feelings, ideas, and activities. Each menstrual cycle is a small death, a mini transformative process which moves toward the moment of menopause. This view of reality as a process of transformation through birth, life, death, and re-birth that is symbolized by menstruation provides a context for understanding the self as a process of coming into being and letting go again. Such an ontology of self, through body consciousness, supports the view of self as constructed through change. It disposes one to live with one's body rather than take flight from it. This acceptance of the embodied self is conducive to an ethics of affiliation: with respect to oneself, other persons, and the earth.

In this view, self-interest is a requirement for ethical responsibility rather than an obstacle to it. Body consciousness is necessary for self-love, especially for women. The epidemic proportions of eating disorders among women reflects a hatred of the body. Or, at best, a profound dis-ease with it. Naomi Wolf (*The Beauty Myth* [1990]) claims that four-year-old girls no longer pretend to be grown up by standing in front of the mirror in their mothers' high-heeled shoes. Instead, contemporary four-year-olds stand on the bathroom scales watching their weight. Prescriptions for women to stay young, be slim, have big breasts with the help of silicon implants are inimical to women's love for themselves or other women. The late Barbara Frum, as host of *The Journal* (a Canadian television news interview program) asked: Aren't women complicit in these prescriptions? Don't women choose to buy the expensive cosmetics which promise to keep them young? Don't they willingly go for cosmetic surgery? Don't they continue to go from one diet to another? Why blame culture for what women willing choose to do? Naomi Wolf points out that women often do what is not in their own interests in order to get jobs or social approval with respect to their appearance. A women's appearance is often a criterion for getting a job in ways that a man's is not. In order to be heard at all, never mind hired, a woman often has to comply with cultural representations of femininity which may not be conducive to her own health.

The importance of informed choice is obvious if individuals are going to take self-interest into account as much as possible when making their choices. Informed choice, however, is never entirely free of the interests of those who provide the information. There is always reason for caution with respect to knowing what one's self-interests are. Some women in our society believe that the amenorrhea (absence of menstruation) that can result from the self-starvation of anorexia is a bonus. Women in sports sometimes experience amenorrhea because their body fat is diminished. As I write this early draft (June 1992) women coaches across Canada are meeting in Ontario to discuss the issue of women's appearance in sports. The coaches realized they have to be more accepting of their own bodies before they can teach self-acceptance to their female students in sports. They claim that women, more than men, are judged by their body image. Women divers, for example, will be told they looked good rather than that they dived well. Thinness is an obsession among athletes in general. It is exaggerated among female athletes. In a culture where slimness is idealized and menstruation is seen as a problem, the absence of healthy body fat and of menstruation is experienced positively. Women's alleged self-interest is often aligned with prevailing cultural attitudes that negate women's bodies.

When a feminine ethic of care is introjected into a cultural milieu in which women's bodies are denigrated and women loathe their bodies, the effect is virtually assured to be an unhealthy one. Within a climate that is not healthy for themselves, women are mandated to care for others. An ethic of care obscures an ambiguous concern for women in our society. One's body is integral to one's identity. Consequently it is part of one's self-interest. If morality is minimally concerned with protecting the rights of individuals for self-determination, it is also importantly about Be-Friending, creating contexts for diverse self-interests to be enunciated. In order for the self-interests of women to correspond to affiliation rather than dis-ease with their bodies, responsible moral theory and action needs to be directed toward changing the cultural context in which self-interests, in the case of women, get defined. This is not to say that the self-interests of all women are the same. Self-interests of women from different social and cultural spaces require relevant contexts of Be-Friending for their particular interests to be taken into account. Contexts that are friendly to women's bodies are a condition for the widespread construction of self-interests which are conducive to women's well-being regardless of where they are located.

Including self-interest in moral decision-making raises the problem of conflicting self-interests, those which are intensely personal as well as those which border on the impersonal. Decisions have to be made in the face of oppositional interests. Negotiating those differences is a dimension of moral or ethical activity. Without a 'normative' morality from which to draw shared moral principles, what might constitute a basis for negotiating differences? If self-interest is the guiding principle, then it seems unlikely that there would be an acceptable starting place for the negotiations. Or, does it? If self-love and benevolence are two dimensions of the same phenomenon, then self-interest would be part of benevolence, just as self-determination is inseparable from relationality in this account of identity and morality.

The notion of bodied mindfulness in Buddhism, which was discussed in Chapter One, is central to this view of the self and the corresponding theory of rights and responsibilities developed here. Embodied mindfulness is about focussed attention on interrelated causality. A Buddhist claim is that increased consciousness of relationality leads to compassion and wisdom. Letting go of linguistic definitions of the self as a separate reality is considered the first condition for experiencing causal interdependency. This 'letting go' is made possible through meditation. It is believed that altered consciousness through meditation allows one to experience one's interdependency and to overcome egocentricity. Egocentricity is defined as inappropriate attachment to oneself, with the attendant disturbing emotions. Negative consciousness is associated with egocentricity. One hangs on to one's attachments and is blind to the multiple causes involved in the situation of disturbance, least of all to one's own attachment to an inflated view of one's own importance. Consciousness of oneself as a part of a larger synchronistic process, without disproportionate significance, is constitutive of compassion and wisdom that ensues from embodied mindfulness of interacting conditions of existence, in a Buddhist view of self. Whereas the self-interest of a person without a developed consciousness of interrelatedness is associated with egocentricity, the self-interest of one who has a developed consciousness of causal interrelatedness is constituted by awareness of 'no-self.' The notion of no-self, here, does not mean that the person doesn't exist as an individual but rather there is no separate self which exists as an island or an atom. The self is a process of transformation. The interests of one person are connected to those of others. Accordingly, if one were to live on the basis of self-interest one would, if consistent, take into consideration the interests of others. It is in this manner that self-interest and benevolence are continuous. Self-interest that is based on the wisdom of non-attachment is the same as compassion and is the opposite of selfishness.

The compassion and wisdom of Buddhist ethics are analogous to eros and agapé in Christian ethics as discussed, for example, by John Macquarrie (1983). An ethic of love is at the heart of the religious ethics of all world religious traditions, despite their politics to the contrary. The usefulness of the Buddhist view of compassion and wisdom for our purposes here is the way in which it depicts enlightened self-interest as the motivation for moral action. The Buddhist view of the mutually influential relation between ontology and epistemology provides a compelling argument in support of the claim that self-interest is a condition for moral action. It is understood that self-interest is best served when there is consciousness of self as a permeable self with changing perceptions and soft boundaries.

The idea that self-interest need not be equated with egocentricity may be somewhat of a revolutionary idea in Western moral theory that emphasizes guarding against self-interest. It is compatible with a dispassionate morality of rights, however, so long as self-interest is understood to be shaped by the wisdom and compassion of connectedness. Compassion, in the Buddhist view, is not about caring for others at the expense of oneself. It is believed that compassion arises from the experience of mutual self-interests. The problem with this account of compassion is that it doesn't take into consideration the conditions in which self-interests are lived out in personal relationships and social organizations. Buddhist ethics do not critique systems of power relations in which separate selves (caretakers) dominate soluble selves (caregivers). A dispassionate morality of rights is a minimal condition for the protection of self-interests in an oppositional system of social relations. It does not assume an epistemology or an ontology of interdependency. A morality of rights assumes the reality of separate selves who struggle with each other for advantage or supremacy and who need protection from each other in order to carry out their agendas within community parameters of decency. Buddhist ethical theory, by contrast, assumes the possibility of permeable selves and points to that view of the self as the goal of meditative practices.

An ethic of compassion, such as that in Buddhism, cannot be effectively implemented in a social order in which the self is understood as separate and knowledge is about control, prediction, and domination. Such an ontology and epistemology demand an ethics of rights. In order for an ethic of care to be effectively implemented, the underpinnings of our social structures have to be re-imagined. Spiritual experiences of ontological interrelatedness help to shift the imagination in the direction of mutually shared interests.

The confusion around self-interest and morality derives from the different views of self. In one view the self is separate and is in competition with other selves for autonomous supremacy. Such a view of self requires the existence of a soluble self to support the interests of the separate self. Indeed, many soluble selves are needed to keep a singular hero focussed on a mighty quest, unencumbered by the time-consuming and energy-draining tasks of daily maintenance. The heroes of the privileged brotherhood were right to devise rules of morality which would allow them to romp freely so long as they didn't interfere with each other's quests. The welfare of their soluble womenfolk, slaves, and other nurturers was part of their responsibility in exchange for the services they provided. The morality of the patriarchy included a circumscribed ethics of care within its system of individual rights. Fortunately this offered a wedge through which increased space for women could be achieved. For example, the 'moral superiority of women' was used as a reason why women should get the vote or go into politics or into the public realm at all. Co-education was introduced initially so that girls in schools would mitigate the unhealthy activities that the boys were engaged in with each other. The girls were to act as prophylactics.[7] Within patriarchy there has been an ambivalence toward the role of caring in social relations and institutions. It was relegated largely to the disempowered who were extolled for their role as keepers of a superior morality, albeit impractical in matters of ultimate significance like wars.

Reframing the self in terms of connectedness, as permeable rather than as separate, allows for a different starting point for moral theory and social organization. It is part of the development of a new underlying intentionality that can shape social and cultural evolution. An important consideration in Buddhist theory of motivation for ethical conduct is the relation between reason and emotion in self-determination. Buddhist theory is shaped by an ethics of affiliation. Accordingly there is a strong emphasis on letting go of negative aspects of consciousness and developing a positive orientation toward non-judgmental acceptance of differences. That does not mean apathy. Non-attachment, in Buddhist theory, is non-attachment to the self. Non-attachment to other things is seen to follow from non-attachment to oneself. It is believed that a heightened consciousness does not attribute excessive causal power to oneself or to anyone or anything. Awareness of the many causes in each situation allegedly frees one from getting stuck on any particular thing or person as *the* cause of one's happiness or distress. Thus, Buddhist theory foreshadows postmodernism. Both struggle with reducing egocentricity or cognicentricity. Postmodernism extends the analysis to ethnocentricity, gendercentricity, or any category. A major difference between Buddhism and postmodernism is that postmodernism denies the reality that Buddhism assumes, an ontology of interrelatedness. Postmodernism reduces reality to epistemology exclusively.

Buddhist meditation is about the development of positive, non-attached consciousness. It is about accepting continuous transformation. Interacting, changing conditions constitute the nature of reality. Different realities exist according to different causal conditions. Emotions, like ideas, are part of the conditions of reality. Chairs and tables are part of reality. Our bodies are part of reality. The concreteness of things such as bodies is not denied. Their meaning is a product of the interacting conditions of (1) perceptions, (2) the skin, mucous, fluids, bones, muscles of the body, and (3) the interaction of (1) and (2). Consciousness of our bodies, for example, is a function of those three interacting sets of conditions. That is the reality of our bodies. The same holds for anything. Everything is a function of these three interacting conditions. It is in one's self-interest, in Buddhist theory, to focus one's attention sufficiently to experience this interactive process in a way that liberates one from hanging onto notions of the self as anything more than such a process. Effective *action* is believed to arise from understanding causal conditions. Lack of such understanding is seen to yield merely a *reaction*. A negative mind set is believed to reflect a *reactive* consciousness rather than an *active* one.

There is reason to believe that a paradigm shift is occurring in social and cultural evolution. As Riane Eisler and Carol Christ, among others, point out, we are moving out of the patriarchal cultural paradigm toward one that is more egalitarian and caring. A major thrust within this shift is the increase of spiritual consciousness of connectedness. An ethic of affiliation is part of a consciousness in which positive action is possible through release from the negative effects of egocentric attachments.

Although spirituality emphasizes freedom from disruptive emotions, it is not about transcending the emotions. Rather, the development of a positive consciousness is about transforming one's relationship to the emotions. Anger, for example, is an important motivator with regard to resisting injustice. From a Christian perspective, Beverly Wildung Harrison says,

That the locus of divine revelation is in the concrete struggles of groups and communities to lay hold of the gift of life and to unloose what denies life has astonishing implications for ethics. It means, among other things, that we must learn what we are to know of love from immersion in the struggle for justice. (1989:214)

An ethic of love includes the attempt to facilitate increased possibilities for self-determination. In a social order in which systemic oppression is widespread, struggle against oppression is central to both a morality of rational choice-making and a morality of consciousness. Sensitivity to injustice is inseparable from anger, an important motivating force for social change.

Resisting Oppression

Interlocking systems of domination create patterns of resistance. Domination exists on a continuum from slavery to 'good-natured bullying.' Resistance to oppression, for example, by Africans in colonial countries (such as the United States and Canada) is shaped by their heritage of slavery. Katie Cannon describes 'slavocracy' as "the rude transformation of African people into marketable objects" (1988:36). African slaves were imported into Nova Scotia in 1686. According to Patricia Hill Collins (1991:6-7), there are three dimensions to the structuring of African American Black women's oppression: the exploitation of Black women's labour (economics); exclusion from politics; and ideological domination. The exploitation of Black women's labour is symbolized by 'iron pots and kettles,' referring to the ghettoization of their service occupations. The denial of the vote, withholding of judicial equality, and lack of educational opportunities were compounding forms of disenfranchisement. The relative absence of Black women in political leadership positions, lack of justice with respect to legal protection against sexual violence, and underfunded inner city schools are examples of continuing historical political oppression of Africans in North America. Black women contend with racism in regard to the dominant culture and sexism with regard to both the dominant culture

and their own Black culture. In the ideological dimension where controlling images are projected by the dominant culture, "certain assumed qualities are attached to Black women and then used to justify oppression"
(Collins 1991:7). Images such as mammies, Jezebels, breeder women,
smiling Aunt Jemimas, Black prostitutes, and welfare mothers are all negative images which Black women have resisted. Collins says, "For Black
women, constructed knowledge of self emerges from the struggle to reject
controlling images and integrate knowledge deemed personally important, usually knowledge essential to Black women's survival" (1991:95).
Their legacy of struggle against oppression has included a strong determination for self-definition which belies social definition by the dominant
ideology that constructs them as Other and renders individual uniqueness
invisible.

Black women, like many oppressed people, developed safe places in
which to articulate their silences. These silences were necessary to protect
themselves in the larger society. It is an act of courage to move from silence to enunciation. Visibility is fraught with danger for those who are
targeted for abuse by the more powerful. According to Collins, Black
women developed public masks of conformity to the dominant White culture and defined their inner selves to each other through their relationships to other women, blues music, and writing. Through talking with
each other and expressing themselves in music and writing, some were
able to journey from internalized oppression to the 'free mind' (Collins
1991:104). The strong emphasis on the development of individuality
through the community with which they identified, primarily through relations with other women, often included the conjunction of bitterness
and anger toward Whites, on the one hand, and affiliation and accountability to the Black community, on the other. Being accountable to one's
neighbours or sister-friends is part of creating safe places where Black
women can live without their masks. Respect and connectedness characterize Black women's relations, according to Collins. It is recognized that
respect for each other is coextensive with respect for oneself.

The ethic of love isn't sufficient in situations of oppression. Social
justice is required to protect the rights of those who are 'under the
thumbs' of the more powerful. In the process of self-determination, "Black
women journey toward an understanding of how our personal lives have
been fundamentally shaped by interlocking systems of race, gender, and
class oppression" (Collins 1991:106). If self-respect is to include accountability to those in one's marginalized community, then it must include
knowledge of the tension between oppression and activism. Consciousness of that tension is expressed by the claim, "I'm awfully bitter these
days because my parents were slaves" (Collins 1991:105). Self-respect
that includes a consciousness of a heritage of oppression also includes a
righteous anger (not to be confused with self-righteous). As June Jordan,
a Black feminist says, "I cannot be expected to respect what somebody

else calls self-love if that concept of self-love requires my suicide to any degree" (Collins 1991:108).

Just as an ethic of caring is not sufficient for self-determination within structural oppression, so an ethic of justice is inadequate to ensure equal opportunity. Both are required for self-determination. Justice assumes a laissez-faire attitude toward competition among free individuals. Katie Cannon claims that "dominant ethics makes a virtue of qualities that lead to economic success—self-reliance, frugality and industry" (1988:2). The idea behind that view of ethics is that each person is equally free to pursue the acquisition of wealth and thereby extend their domain of freedom. The suffering of others, in the pursuit of individual wealth, is taken as normal in a free market economy. Charity is an institutionalized mechanism for looking after those who can't compete successfully. Cannon says, "In the Black community, the aggregate of the qualities which determine desirable ethical values regarding the uprightness of character and soundness of moral conduct must always take into account the circumstances, the paradoxes and the dilemmas that constrict Blacks to the lowest range of self-determination" (1988:3). The journey toward self-determination for Blacks often includes purging themselves of the self-hate that gets turned in on themselves from the negative inscriptions of the White culture. Cannon contributes to the purge of self-hate and the development of Black women's dignity, grace, and courage by uncovering some of Black women's history with which they can identify.

Mary Daly's notion of Be-Friending, as mentioned earlier, is relevant here. It refers to creating contexts which allow people to enunciate from their own subject positions. Narrative identity is necessary for self-love as well as benevolence. As individuals tell their own stories they construct their self-identities. Knowing who you are, so to speak, is a source of power. In an article entitled "Black Women in Nova Scotia: From a Site of Resistance" in a Canadian feminist newspaper, *Kinesis*, Andrea Fatona says that "Traditional histography has been a process of collecting the stories of the 'victors' and distorting the history of the 'other'" (1992:7). Fatona refers to the work of Sylvia Hamilton, a Nova Scotian filmmaker (*Black Mother, Black Daughter*, NFB film), who is uncovering Black women's thoughts and deeds in Nova Scotia. Contemporary Black women are supported in the construction of their own identities through knowledge of and identification with their foremothers. The re-articulation of history through narrative is an avenue for the construction of identity in the face of cultural insensitivity and hostility. As Fatona points out, "history is based on *where* the narrative begins and *whose* story is told." The following quotation illustrates the importance of constructing the self and reality through narrative. David Shannon says,

According to current folklore, a young boy was once told about the many conquests of hunters over the lion. This story intrigued the little boy; he was puzzled and inquired: "If the lion is supposed to be the king of the jungle, why is it that the hunter always wins?" The father responded: "The hunter will always win until the lion writes his own story!" The same may be said about African Americans, who have also been victimized by having their story told by others. As long as this tendency persists the real story of African Americans will not have been told. Fortunately, this is now changing. (1991:98)

Part of writing or speaking one's own narrative is having the freedom to interpret thoughts and events in ways that positively construct one's identity. Renita Weems says of any Black woman, "of all the interpretative communities to which she belongs [American/Western, African American, female, and Christian], the African American female interpretative community (whether in the church, the academy, or the civic club) is the only one that has consistently allowed her to hold in tandem all the components of her identity" (Weems 1991:70). According to Weems, who refers to Mary Helen Washington's work on the lives of Black women in America, the distinguishing feature of the literature of Black women is their recording of "the thoughts, words, feelings, and deeds of Black women . . . [which] make the realities of being Black in America look very different from what men have written" (Weems 1991:note 25).

The discrepancy between the negative social definitions of Black women and their own self-definitions within their own culture means that in narrative identity Black women must resist internalizing the oppressors' standpoint and establish their own, 'right' stance which comes from their lived experiences. That 'right' stance often includes 'righteous' anger toward the oppressors' standpoint. Self-respect or self-love includes 'righteous' anger at structural oppression. I have referred to Black women's oppression to illustrate the point that an ethics of affiliation could lead to a kind of suicide by those who are victimized. In such instances, caring is immoral. Acting as a caregiver for an oppressor (caretaker) is immoral in this view. It undermines the self-love of the caregiver and the benevolence of the caretaker. Because it is assumed here that self-love and benevolence are inseparable from each other, an oppressive situation negatively affects self-love and benevolence of both the caretaker and caregiver. The relationship includes coercive trust and loyalty. Self-love and benevolence cannot be actualized in a context of oppression. It is unlikely that any society would be completely free of oppressive relations; accordingly, care needs to be qualified with other ethical approaches such as justice that includes an ethic of resistance, or principled disloyalty.

Instances of the need for principled disloyalty are widespread. For example, In in 1992, the Constitutional talks dominated the media in Canada. Native groups were rightly demanding more participation in the talks. Native rights to self-government were (and still are) at stake. No one is entirely sure what 'self-government' by Native communities would mean. Would they be subject to the Canadian Charter of Rights or not? As reported in the *Calgary Herald*, March 21, 1992, the National Native Women's Association of Canada (NWAC) was challenging the right of the

Assembly of First Nations (AFN) to speak for all Natives in the Constitutional talks. The AFN is dominated by men. The leaders of the AFN do not want the Canadian Charter of Rights to override their self-government. The NWAC wants the protection of the Charter of Rights. It protects the rights of women. NWAC is concerned that women's rights will not be protected under AFN self-rule. The history of Canadian Native women's struggles with their male band leaders is sufficient cause for concern (Janet Silman, 1987). Non-supporters of NWAC wanted the issue of women's rights dealt with after the AFN negotiated its position for self-government in the Constitutional talks. They claimed that advocacy for women within the negotiations for Native self-rule would detract from discussions about self-rule. As it turned out, Canadians voted against Native self-rule, among other things such as greater power to the provinces over social services.

The struggle between the ruling men of AFN and the women of NWAC over control of their own interests is a good example of the pervasive belief that women's interests ought to be those of their menfolk. Such identification glosses over important differences. For example, Native women are subjected to greater violence from their menfolk than any other group of women in Canada. In a fifteen-month study, funded by the Ontario Women's Directorate and Community Services Ministry, it was revealed that Native women were at least six times as likely as non-Native women to be killed by an intimate male partner.[8] Native women's concerns about their rights are moral concerns. Their anger about their victimization is righteous anger. Their self-interests are not identical with the interests of the men in their communities. That does not mean that their interests are entirely different. Native women are pulled between their loyalties to their communities, led predominantly by men, and their loyalties to themselves and to each other as a sub-culture within their communities. There is a justified concern on the part of all Natives, where it exists, that the government will take advantage of this internal disagreement to divide and conquer.

The conflict between the aims of AFN and NWAC reflects the dilemma of the multiple oppression of Native women. Like Black women, they are not adequately represented in White patriarchal culture because of its racism and class privileging. They are subject to sexism within both the White culture and their own Native communities. In addition, they have not been visible in feminist theory because it has been predominantly White and middle class. Native women's anger in Canada is very important if their rights are going to be protected at all.

Another cause for righteous anger is the treatment of women in the health care system. For example, in the *Calgary Herald* (March 21, 1992) there is an article entitled "Women Misdiagnosed." It reports that "Jasenka Demirovic of the University of Miami found in his study that 27 per cent of men admitted to hospital with a heart attack undergo a standard diagnostic test called angiography, while only 15 per cent of women get it. More reports are coming out that women are under-diagnosed rather than under-treated" ("Women Misdiagnosed," p. 3). The mistreatment of women in health care has been abundantly documented.[9] The lack of respect for women in the larger culture is reflected in this lack of initiative to diagnose accurately the medical concerns of women.

The problem is magnified if the women are immigrants. When immigrant women are given the opportunity to speak about their experiences in the health care system, they describe their humiliation and isolation. In a *Kinesis* article, "Sexual Misconduct: Immigrant Women and the MDs," the authors ask, "when an immigrant woman who speaks no English is abused by her doctor, to whom can she go for help? The consequences of telling her partner or family may result in victim-blaming, a perceived loss of the woman's honour within her community, and possible divorce" (Walsh, Loughe, and Assanand 1992:4). Immigrant women suggest that doctors receive cross-cultural training in medical school. They claim that there should be greater access by visible minorities and immigrant students to the medical schools. The use of foreign-trained doctors who can speak the language of the health care recipients would reflect some degree of respect for immigrants. Before they are granted immigrant status a medical examination is required. Women report rough treatment and sexual improprieties during the examinations. This kind of physical and mental abuse of immigrant women in the health care system indicates a double standard in the way in which an ethics of rights is practised in our society. When it is not integrated with an ethics of care, there is little reason to suppose that the rights of marginalized persons would be protected unless they happen to be lucky. Relying on the good will of those in authority is very risky in a culture in which the underlying intentionality is one of dominance and control. An ethics of rights is fundamental to humanitarian social relations. Its dependency on the assumption that persons are equally free to be self-directed, however, is a mistake. Systematic oppression of marginalized groups is often normalized within the context of individual rights, despite the best intentions behind a morality of rights.

Victimization of individuals, such as Native children in Catholic residential schools in Canada, needs to be challenged through both an ethics of rights and an ethics of caring. Anger is an effective motivator that can move a victim out of the position of being a "good little victim," who has internalized the victim's mentality, to an "angry victim" who claims her rights because she cares about herself. Her loyalties and responsibilities are toward herself and others like her, rather than toward the oppressor. Caring about the oppressor takes a back seat to self-interest as righteous anger motivates action. Self-love is connected to taking responsibility for one's self-determination in the face of oppression. Taking responsibility is often motivated by the awakening of anger and the refusal to internalize the self-loathing that characterizes the victim's mentality.

Susan Wendell (1990) provides a helpful analysis of taking responsibility and making choices within oppressive social structures. She posits four perspectives: the oppressor's, the victim's, the responsible actor's, and the observer/philosopher's. The oppressor's perspective is one of blaming the victim exclusively. The victim's perspective is that of blaming the oppressor exclusively. The responsible actor seeks to make responsible choices about blaming and to find empowering ways to act responsibly. The perspective of the observer/philosopher allows for sorting out where responsibility lies and it provides an understanding of the conditions in which responsible action can occur.

Responsible action is supported by awareness of causal interrelatedness. Personal responsibility and structural oppression have to be put into perspective for responsible action to occur. Responsible knowledge is the handmaiden of systematic, responsible action. It is possible, of course, for responsible action to happen without knowing about relational causality. It is unlikely, however, for a pattern of effective and continuous responsible action to develop without the accompanying responsible knowledge of the observer/philosopher's perspective. Such knowledge of the interactive relations of cause and effect is not the privileged knowledge of a trained philosopher. Rather it is knowledge that is available to anyone who pays attention to the complexities of any situation, including hidden cultural assumptions about whose knowledge is assumed to be authoritative and whose is discounted. The power of knowledge is a source for overcoming an oppressor's and a victim's mentality. The knowledge of responsibility includes knowing about where to place the blame and how to act according to that knowledge to resist external oppression and the internalization of unwarranted blame by others. It also allows a person to accept responsibility for their part in their subjugation, if that is appropriate. Slavery is the extreme situation of systemic oppression in which it is irresponsible to attribute responsibility to the slaves. With other forms of social oppression such as class, race, sex, ethnicity, disability, and age, the balance of responsibility between external sources and personal responsibility varies. In all cases of structural oppression, however, personal responsibility is less dominant than social responsibility. This claim underscores the slogan 'the personal is political.' The reverse is also true. The political is personal. Systemic oppression of particular groups requires organized resistance to imposed limitations on the members of those groups.

Recognizing systemic oppression is a condition for freeing victims from self-blame for their suffering and bad choices. If restrictive conditions are imposed by another person, another group, or are institutionalized according to another group's interests, then the victim need not feel responsible for her or his dehumanizing circumstances. The oppressor's perspective of blaming victims for their oppressed conditions is supported by holding up exceptional people from underprivileged groups as examples of what one can do if one really tries. Exceptions do not contradict the situation, they only prove the rule. Pointing to one Native woman, for example, who has succeeded in becoming a doctor as an example of the opportunities available for Native women in general to become doctor, is to use that woman to keep others invisible. It is to say that there is no problem for Native women to do anything they want to do. It is to ignore the Statistics Canada reports which show that Native or Aboriginal women occupy the lowest position in Canada with respect to income. They are followed by visible minority women, disabled women, and then the category of all women. While the different social categories reflect systemic inequalities, the biggest difference is between women and men in each category and between all women and men in any particular category. The average 'all women's' income is lower than any men's incomes in the four designated categories of all women, Native women, visible minority women, disabled women and the corresponding categories for men.[10] Recognizing these categorical differences is an important condition of acknowledging differential power relations among various social groups and their corresponding unequal opportunities for self-determination.

Gloria Steinem's book, *Revolution from Within: A Book of Self-Esteem* (1992), is about the importance of women rejecting the oppressor's perspective and its associated self-blame. From Steinem's perspective, social revolution requires personal revolution. Members of disempowered groups suffer from poor self-esteem because of the tendency to internalize the perspective of the oppressor. There are other reasons due to individual differences; however, the general tendency to internalize and become self-oppressive is widespread among individuals within marginalized groups. In addition to self-blame, internalization of the oppressor's perspective leads to scapegoating those who have only minimal power. Those who have the greatest power in shaping the structure of interpersonal relationships are generally the ones who receive smiles from their less powerful associates.

In contrast to the oppressor's perspective, the victim's perspective is about uncritically blaming the oppressor, without attending to the possibility of any personal agency. It is a hopeless mentality which leads to the image of the 'good girl victim.' She places herself at the mercy of those who work on behalf of victims and does not see any possibilities for her own initiative to find a way out. Coping with victimization rather than overcoming it, takes over in a victim's perspective. In extreme situations such as Black slavery, child sexual abuse, prostitute slavery, and other conditions of almost complete dehumanization, a victim's perspective of uncritically blaming the oppressor might be the only possible response. Blaming the victim, then, would be irresponsible. In many cases of victimization, victims need to adopt the victim's mentality so they can reject the oppressor's perspective and the disposition toward self-blame. A victim's mentality includes anger toward the oppressor and anger is usually required to move out of self-blame and into self-esteem.

Self-esteem requires a sense of achievement. Patrice L. Dickerson tells Patricia Hill Collins that "a person comes into being and knows herself by her achievements, and through her efforts to become and know herself she achieves" (Collins 1991:35). One can achieve, however, only with the help of others. The activity of Be-Friending is necessary for movement out of the victim's perspective and into that of the responsible actor. Conditions of oppression often limit one's imagination with respect to self-worth. Women students in university, for example, who are single parents without adequate financial resources but who strive to improve their conditions through higher education, are faced with a university curriculum which emphasizes men's thoughts and activities. They learn about the history of wars and political parties led by men, of social history in which the great thoughts and actions of women are not included; philosophies which are based on a flight from women's bodies; theories of moral development which denigrate connectedness and extol separateness; and a sociology of work which excludes reproduction in its analysis of productive labour. They learn that having babies and raising children is not a basis for knowing anything important. They learn that 'organic' knowledge which is taken for granted in common sense living is subjugated to academic knowledge which permits experts to tell them about their alleged unimportant lives as mothers.[11]

Because of these conditions, women need a context of Be-Friending. Women's Studies is a forum in which many women develop self-esteem through the process of reconstituting knowledge in a way that they can begin to rearticulate their identities and the conditions in which they live. A transformation often occurs with women in Women's Studies as they move from the oppressor's perspective and/or the victim's perspective toward one of responsible actor. The reconstitution of knowledge in which they participate in the construction of new identities and social orientations helps them also to adopt the perspective of the observer/philosopher. As Wendell points out, "People with this perspective seek understanding; the understanding they seek includes a causal picture of some portion or aspect of the universe" (1990:33). Such a perspective characterizes most feminist theorizing. It includes a critical analysis of causal interrelatedness and provides an interpretive framework for social action directed toward greater justice. The integration of academic knowledge and common sense knowledge in the reconstitution of knowledge means that everyday experiences should be included in theory construction. Theory construction is an important way of reconstructing narrative identities.

Susan Wendell's philosophical argument that responsible action requires rejecting the oppressor's perspective as immoral, moving out of the victim's mentality of feeling hopeless in the face of oppression, and going on toward self-determination through responsible action based on an understanding of the conditions of oppression can be described as elitist.

Patricia Hill Collins defends the positive value of so-called elitist positions which aim to bring about positive social change for victims. She says that feminist theory allows us to see the oppressive conditions with fresh eyes and to develop a coherent voice with which to articulate the problems. A necessary condition for the effectiveness of feminist theory, Collins claims, is that it is constructed from concrete experiences and expressed in ways that common sense intellectuals can use. The charge that the language of elites merely reinforces existing systems of oppression is a particularly poignant criticism for feminist theorists. The disconnection of theory from experience and common sense language is another area of ethical concern for most of us engaged in trying to integrate experience with theory in an academic context. Teaching feminist theory in university to women who are working in battered women's shelters or substance abuse centres, or women who were clients in these centres, is challenging with respect to making the theory relevant to the lived experiences of the students. The challenge is to lift individual experiences into a larger theoretical perspective that will allow for new insights for changing existing problematic conditions. When that happens the students experience the process of moving ahead in both their theoretical understanding as well as in their practical work skills. Their experiences help to ground the development of theory. Their participation in the process of theorizing, as well as their increased confidence at work, usually increases their self-esteem.

The development of self-esteem through taking responsibility for oneself generally includes passing through a period of intense anger toward the oppressor(s). Awareness of external causal conditions for one's suffering might lead to hopelessness and depression, a kind of suicide of the self. Or it might lead to anger and activism and possibly to self-esteem. A victim's perspective is the moment for change. If anger is combined with accountability, both with respect to the oppressor and to oneself, then there is hope for resistance to oppression and effective action toward constructing better external conditions and internal identity. A community in which caring supports a network of connectedness is necessary for disempowered persons to move into power.

While an ethic of care is grounded in experiences of connectedness, these experiences are shaped by implicit ontological assumptions of interrelatedness. Caroline Whitbeck (1989) makes an explicit connection between an ontology which assumes a relational view of self and practices which reflect a morality of responsibility that is supported by a morality of rights. In her view, the fundamental moral notion is responsibility. A consciousness of responsibility arises through relationships. In light of the assumption that a person is essentially relational, moral practice facilitates individual creativity within community. Whitbeck's non-oppositional view of the self is expressed similarly by Patricia Hill Collins' account of the development of self and practice among Black women. She claims that because of the restricted mobility of most Black women, they develop a community sense of self as Black women rather than focussing on an individual self in opposition to others. She says that "By being accountable to others, African-American women develop more fully human, less objectified selves" (Collins 1991:105). Women's practices often are circumscribed by their local communities. An interdependency characterizes their daily life. That is not to say that all women of any colour live with a restricted mobility or that it is merely because of restricted mobility that a sense of self as relational is basic to their practices. Nor is it to say that men do not live in similar conditions. Rather it is to say that it is an empirical reality that more women than men experience interdependency rather than individualism in their daily activities because of the nature of the tasks they are performing, such as child care, laundry, sewing, and so forth. It is not surprising that those with less property develop a different sense of self than those who dominate through ownership, whether it is of ideas, of real estate, or of family members. The current ideology of domination/subordination contributes to the sense of self as separate, supported by a soluble self whose interests are those of the separate self. Women's homosocial groups, such as neighbourhood women doing their washing at a local washing place or women sharing in child care activities, can serve as models for the construction of a permeable self. Interdependency characterizes the permeable self and usually includes an ethic of care. A consciousness of interdependency is facilitated by communities that are characterized by mutual respect and responsibility. A permeable self is constructed in such communities.

This view of the self and the corresponding ethical practices which facilitate mutual self-determination are believed to be supported by spiritual practices grounded in an ontology of interrelatedness. Realization of a relational self is expanded and strengthened through a spiritual consciousness of self in relation to a more universal pattern of connectedness. Spiritual experiences in which one's identity is open to other forms of identity through shape-shifting into animal forms, trees, and so forth, serve as powerful resources for expanding a pluralistic notion of identity. The context is one of interdependent relatedness, not just to other human beings but to other living beings. The fluidity of boundaries and substance displaces the stasis of fixed identity. There is greater permeability between the hide-boundness of oneself and others as a result of spiritual experiences which include diverse images of creative power with which one identifies. Luce Irigaray's image of mucous helps to shift away from exclusive categorical distinctions between fixed identity of one sort and another. The boundaries of mucous respond to external pressure but are not readily distorted by it. It is an image that helps us to think of identity as changing. Spiritual experiences such as those of shape-shifting help to loosen the grip of exclusivistic conceptualization in theorizing about the self. Participation in spiritual experiences expands self-identity. Because of this it disposes one toward reaching out. Action is experienced as interaction.

The interactive process is not without tensions between differences. The struggles for self-expression, however, do not arise from a view of oneself as the metronome beat in the organization of social relations, but rather as being guided by a more universal or community-oriented beat which allows for the various individual rhythms to emerge and be expressed in symphonic harmony. Listening to each other's rhythm and living with it helps to alleviate tension without obliterating real differences. Making the connections between an ontology of interrelatedness and an ethics of affiliation, supported by a morality of rights, has important implications for economic, social, and political realities. Those implications are explored further in the next chapter.

Notes

1 See Judith Jarvis Thomson (1990) for a clearly articulated description and defense of rights. She uncritically adopts the view that the body is owned by the self and uses that view to argue for the right of women to protect claims against their bodies by men or embryo. She points out that when a mother murders her children the claim against her rightfully comes because of a violation to the individual murdered, not a violation of another person, such as the father of the individual murdered. Further, she says, an embryo is a piece of a human being which needs further development to be one. In her view, to claim that an egg is a human being is an irrational claim and cannot be disputed rationally. Central to Thomson's argument against antiabortionists is the view that a woman who is pregnant owns her body and has privileges over claims against that which she owns, just as an owner of a piece of real estate has privileges which prohibit others from staking claims on that property.

2 For a sympathetic but critical account of moral theories which affirm justice as the first virtue, see Annette C. Baier (1987). As she points out, justice suits the view of society as a composite of separate individuals but does not fit well with a communal view of society.

3 Hume's theory of the calm passions is a good source for re-interpreting rationality in terms of integration of ideas and sensations.

4 I find that meditation on Vicki Noble's *Motherpeace* (1983) tarot card images is helpful in listening, thinking, seeing, and writing differently. Asking an important question, meditating on it, and then drawing a card on which to reflect further can be a useful practice for increased mindfulness.

5 Terence Penelhum's definition of mistrust is taken from personal correspondence, June 1992.

6 I didn't ask whether there were any men in this group. It seemed as though this kind of question was out of order at the time. It would be interesting to know, however, whether there were only women in this particular workplace where women had time off for their 'moon time' or what compensation, if any, was given to men.

7 I am indebted to Patricia Rooke for the reference to the prophylactic function of girls in the establishment of co-educational schools in the nineteenth century.

8 The study is called "Woman Killing: Intimate Femicide in Ontario, 1974-1990." The study shows that of the 969 homicides in Ontario during that period, only 2 percent were committed by women.

9 Apart from landmark books like Ehrenreich and English's *For Her Own Good* and Mary Daly's *Gyn/ecology*, wide-ranging studies have been conducted during the past decade that document the mistreatment of women with regard to their health. A useful reference book is Nancy Worcester and Mariamne H. Whatley, *Women's Health: Readings on Social, Economic, and Political Issues* (1988). Women's health collectives have been developed across North America in response to increased awareness of the need for

women to take more responsibility for their own health care. That does not eliminate the need for health experts. Health collectives are designed to improve client knowledge and personal responsibility. Sophisticated medical expertise is sometimes required, but not always.

10 In the 1987 Statistics Canada report of "Salary Distribution of the Designated Groups" [i.e., Aboriginal people, disabled, visible minority, and all workers] who work full time in places governed by the Federal Employment Equity Act, the average salary of those in the workforce full time was $31,047. The salary range in the report was from under $10,000 to $70,000 and over. At the bottom of the chart, under each of the four designated categories is listed the percentage of each category earning $27,500 or more. Aboriginal women constituted the lowest percentage at 23 percent. Visible minority men constituted the highest percentage at 78 percent. All the female categories were clustered around the Aboriginal women (all women category at 30 percent, disabled and visible minority women at 24 percent) while the male categories were clustered around the visible minority men at the other end (all men at 77 percent, disabled men at 77 percent, Aboriginal men at 68 percent). The high achievement orientation of visible minority men is reflected in the statistics. These statistics are supported by Statistics Canada figures for 1991, published in 1993. An added negative feature of these figures in the 1991 statistics is that the ratio of female to male earnings between 1987 and 1991 has declined from 76.8 percent to 70.9 percent. The ratio of earnings of women and men full-time workers, however, increased from 67.6 percent in 1990 to 69.6 percent in 1991. A significant reason for this increase is that there has been a continuing rise in the average salary of women's full-time work while the average salary of men for full-time work has remained the same. The inconsistency in ratios (i.e., between the ratio of earnings of women and men's salaries in general and the ratio between male and female full-time workers) is accounted for largely by the fact that the average salary for part-time women workers has decreased disproportionately to men's part-time salaries (6.0 percent for women compared to 5.1 for men). Because women work more in part-time jobs than full-time ones and their salaries are dropping faster than men's in this category, the overall ratio between women's and men's salaries is decreasing.

11 I wish to acknowledge Patricia Hill Collins' discussion of deconstructing 'intellectual' into academic and 'organic' (1991:13-16).

Five

Exclusionary Politics at Work

Insider/Outsider Identities

SO FAR I HAVE been discussing mindfulness with regard to spirituality and bodied knowledge, and living ethically in relation to oneself and to others. Now I shall focus primarily on social places that have defined many women's identities. A large part of each person's identity is constituted by characteristics projected by others in the communities of which they are a part. These aspects of a person's identity may be experienced as 'other-identified' or they may be internalized to become 'self-identified' qualities of a person's way of knowing themselves. Another dimension of identity is the private knowledge each person has of themselves that allows for resistance to possibly debilitating 'other-identified' images that are externally imposed on them. All three dimensions of identity (external, other-identified; internalized, other-identified; and private, self-identified) influence patterns of exclusion of persons from social places. Private self-identity can contribute to exclusion through rejecting the insider group's projections of identity onto outsiders. Outsiders' private knowledge of their own identities serves as a buffer against the oppressive negative identities of the dominant cultural inscriptions onto them. Exclusion is invariably a consequence of identification by others, with little or no input from the subject who is assigned to a particular social place. It is something that is done to another person or group. Subjects do not choose to be excluded, although they may choose not to be identified with a group or with another person. This chapter is largely about the labelling of women from outsiders' perspectives and the resulting places in the social order to which they are assigned. Their own private perspectives are often not part of the process that determines their destinies. The absence of a subject's own voice in the determination of their place in society often leads to the experience of self-loss. It is an inevitable consequence of treating another as an object of one's own projections and neglecting to listen to their particular expressions of self-identity.

Notes to Chapter Five are on pages 262-65.

Self-loss occurs when there is confusion or absence of self-identification. In radical experiences of self-loss there is no presence of self as a particular character. I had such an experience recently following an operation for lung cancer. After surgery to remove the lower two lobes of my right lung because of the cancer, complications arose with a postoperative pneumonia and empyema (infection of fluid in the pleural space). I was asked to agree to a further surgical procedure to drain the infected pleural fluid and was told that I might remain in the recovery room a couple of extra hours on a respirator to help expand the remaining upper lobe before returning to my hospital room. Instead, I woke up in the intensive care unit on a forced air respirator where I remained for approximately twenty-four hours. My arms were tied to the sides of the bed and I had tubes going down my throat as well as out my back and other places. I was unable to speak or move and was monitored by machines, with almost no personal contact from the health care workers. No one close to me was allowed to stay overnight. Throughout the night I gagged, watched the clock on the wall in front of me, and cried periodically, without being able to wipe my face. I concentrated on watching the minute hand and believed that if I closed my eyes I would disappear. It was a terrifying experience of complete aloneness on the edge of life. Finally morning arrived and my husband was allowed back in the unit. A repeat portable x-ray showed that the attempt to expand the lung was not working, presumably because of the pneumonia. Within a couple of hours the tubes were pulled out of my throat and I was released to another unit ('step-down') for further careful monitoring before being moved to a regular unit. After about two weeks I was released from the hospital with only one tube draining fluid from the chest cavity. That was removed within three weeks, but it took a few months to feel any degree of body integrity and personal security.

Less than six months later I suddenly passed out one night and was subsequently found to have a brain tumour metastasis which required further surgery. After the brain tumour was successfully removed, I was advised to follow through with whole brain radiation therapy. An oncology team at the cancer clinic decided what dosage I was to be subjected to and the oncologist told me the nature of the treatment. When I asked about the possible long-term side effects of the radiation which are reported in the literature, he told me he "wasn't talking long term." The plan was to give me a dosage that would minimize short-term risks of recurrence of brain metastases, without regard for the long term. I had no opportunity for participating in the decision about dosage. As I read more of the literature and heard from other radiation specialists, it became apparent to me that the possible benefits did not outweigh the possible risks such as memory loss, loss of balance, loss of bladder control, or dementia. When I spoke to the local oncologist about using a therapy plan that was proposed by a large cancer research centre where my chart had been privately sent for consultation, his response was to ignore that opinion and remain fixed in his position. A major reason for him to limit the choice to the protocol outlined by his clinic was that there are not sufficient radiation therapy machines to conduct radiation, as proposed by the research centre, over a longer period of time with lower doses. The only option I had was to say yes or no to his proposed treatment plan. I decided not to accept radiation but rather to focus on getting healthy through working with complimentary health care workers like a naturopath, acupuncturist, Tai Chi teacher, macrobiotic cook, and others. As this is written in January 1994, sometimes I am overwhelmed with despair and other times I am excited about the possibilities of interacting in healing ways with these healers and with friends who are healthy to be with. The medical system has served me well with the surgery that was necessary. Now it is time to focus on strengthening the immune system and to draw as much as possible on resources outside the medical model oriented towards hope, rather than depressing statistics that guide many medical doctors in their treatment plans. I am now connected to several health care workers, including my family medical doctor, who work in an interactive way with those they are helping. Rather than being assigned to a particular place in the spectrum of cancer patients and treated according to a generic plan that fits with the government's health care resources more than with a particular person, I am treated as a person in a way that is congruent with my own self-identification. It feels healthy to be included as a participating subject in the treatment process. Not too far in the future one hopes the medical model will shift away from such exclusion and become more inclusive in its orientation towards the people it is designed to help.

Exclusionary politics, however, has a very long history that shapes the organization of social places according to the power relations of insiders and outsiders. The social construction of people according to labels and role prescriptions is a major power in the assignment of people to exclusionary categories where social authority is withheld from them and self-identification plays little part in determining the places to which they are assigned. The remainder of this chapter is taken up primarily with ways in which the social construction of women's identities and places are largely responsible for the life-negating activities to which many women have been subjected.

Bad Girl/Good Girl Sexual Power

The most notable instances of the designation of women's power as profane occurred during the fifteenth to the eighteenth centuries in Europe,[1] when thousands of women were tortured and killed because they were accused of being witches in league with the devil. Witches can be either women or men. Records indicate, however, that 80 percent of those who were accused of being witches were women and 85 percent of those prosecuted were women.[2] Many of the men who were persecuted were

associated with the women who were accused. They were often condemned by association. As I shall discuss, the success of the witch persecutions in Europe established a secure context for the development of
social contract theory which would legalize the subordination of women
in Western nations. The witch craze was a culmination of longstanding
distrust of women. Pope Innocent proclaimed a bull in 1484, "expressing
the intention to persecute witches" (Christ 1978:268). Under the Pope's
orders, two Dominican priests, Heinrich Kremer and James Sprenger,
wrote *The Malleus Maleficarum* (*Hammer of the Witches*), which was made
public in 1486. It was the handbook used to justify this particularly viru-
lent form of violence toward women. The misogynism of the text is outrageous. I am not willing to reproduce any of its contents here. It is available in translation (1971). *The Malleus Maleficarum* was the authoritative
text of the Christian church used to torture and murder thousands of
women accused of many different offences to the church during "the
burning times."[3]

The precise dates of the so-called burning times are impossible to
specify. Historian Anne Llewellyn Barstow (1986, 1988, 1994) discusses
fourteenth-century witch burnings in France. Barstow claims that witch
persecution in France was occurring in both the secular and church courts
by the fourteenth century. The Christian church, however, was the most
fervent persecutor of witches. Those who were labelled as witches were
associated with diabolical spirits. Ordinary magic practised by village
healers was interpreted as devil worship by the church authorities. The
magical powers of country women, in addition to their sexuality, instilled
fear in those who wished to have control over the conscience and practices of the people.

According to Barstow (1986), magic is part of Christian, as well as
folk, practices. In this view, magic is about the performance of miracles,
occurrences which can not be understood according to usual principles of
reason. In the twelfth century, the doctrine of transubstantiation became
official. The eucharistic miracle is about the identification of Christ's body
and blood with wafers and wine. Barstow notes that the administration of
the eucharist is an institutionized role of priest as miracle worker (1986:
41). In her view, the struggle over magic characterized the struggle between the official Christian church and the many different folk religions
of the rural population. By the fifteenth century, there was a transition
from hunting Jews and Muslims, as well as heterodox Christian 'sects' to
witch-hunting. The bubonic plague of the fourteenth century led to a drop
in income for the church because large numbers of landlords had died in
the 'Black Death.' Faith in the Christian sacraments as protection against
the plague flagged. Internal politics created a schism between France and
Rome in the fourteenth century. Two popes were simultaneously elected
in 1378, one in Avignon and the other in Rome. The church feared loss of
control of the population, 70 percent of which were rural and had their

own religions. Christianity was the official religion of noblemen and university-trained theologians. Local priests were often more loyal to their parishioners in the country than to the distant pope. The church of Rome was concerned to establish spiritual authority throughout Europe. In the fifteenth century the issue was "*who* could declare *what* spiritual experience to be authentic" (Barstow 1986:19).

Gifted lay spiritual women were not uncommon during the Middle Ages in Europe. During the thirteenth and fourteenth centuries, the Beguines flourished. They were communities of spiritual laywomen whose mystical experiences were common occurrences. Persecution of their leaders are recorded from the fourteenth century. A notable Beguine leader is Marguerite Porete. She wrote *A Mirror for Simple Souls*, which was about the voice of God speaking directly to her and other women and men like her. She claimed that a state of grace is when the soul is in union with God. In her view, the church was irrelevant to spiritual connectedness to God. Her book was burned in her presence by the church. She was burned later, in 1310. The heresy trials and condemnations of the fourteenth century foreshadowed the fury of the witch persecutions that developed in the fifteenth century. The uncontrolled spirituality of women was the target of the church's fear and hostility.

As Barstow notes, the prime image of disorder is woman-out-of-order. Woman-on-top is woman-out-of-order. A woman who claimed her own spiritual autonomy in the fifteenth century was like a red flag waved in the eyes of the papal inquisitors. Joan of Arc (ca. 1412-31) is an example of a woman-out-of-order. She was burned as a heretic and witch at the age of nineteen. Her condemnation was that "She does not submit herself to the judgement of the Church Militant, or to that of living men, but to God alone" (Barstow 1986:83). Because of her insubordination, she was accused of being in league with demonic forces (her Voices). She refused to have her truth corrupted by the authority of the church. This woman-out-of-order was burned alive like many other unknown women and some men who held fast to their spiritual truths.

Such autonomous spirituality, when combined with female sexuality, created fear and hostility. Barstow describes autonomous spiritual women as 'bad girl' mystics, such as Mechtilde of Magdebury, Prous Boneta, Marguerite Porete, and Anne Hutchinson. 'Good girl' mystics, by contrast, did not challenge the authority of the church. They include Catherine of Siena, Teresa of Avila, Therese of Lisieux, and Julian of Norwich (Barstow 1986:xviii). Joan of Arc was made a saint five hundred years after her death. In Barstow's view, with which I agree, that was possible only after a long period of reinterpreting what she represented.[4] She was reinterpreted as a martyr for the church rather than as a heroine, a 'bad girl' who stood up to the church and was murdered because she did so. Barstow claims that Joan of Arc does not fit the model of 'good girl' mystic that can be accommodated by church doctrine and practices. Rather, she portrays Joan as a model of female self-direction. Joan, in this view, represents autonomous female spirituality, the defining characteristic of the 'bad girl' mystic, the witch.

The witch image is a classical antitype: the Other.[5] Antitypes are categories onto which individuals and groups project qualities that they do not accept in themselves. Those qualities are 'exteriorized' onto the Other, developing a we-they dichotomy, with differences defined as deviances. Extreme outsiders are the antitypes of stereotypes from the insider's perspective. The female witch is the antitype of dependent femininity. She is the archetype of independent female power. The refusal by the church (supported by the state) to allow women to practise healing and midwifery (their main activities) was fuelled by several factors.

Barstow points out that the sixteenth century was a time of change with respect to the roles of women. Prior to the sixteenth century, women were accepted in their local communities as healers, midwives, and counsellors. They used their common sense wisdom and magic. Common sense wisdom included the use of natural herbs for healing practices which were passed down by women from one generation to the next because they were successful. Unsuccessful practices or witches who were ineffective did not attract clients. Those who were respected demonstrated their power to heal or to assist birthing mothers. In empiricist language, there was an observable correlation between their intentions and the expectations of others, on the one hand, and the consequences of their actions on the other. The motto of healing witches is "if you harm no one, do as you will" (Eilberg-Schwartz 1989:77). Black magic is not a practice of healing witches. There is a valid distinction between black magic and white magic. That distinction, however, was not made by the accusers of witches during the witch craze. All alleged witches were accused of black magic.

During the sixteenth century there was an increasing gap between the poor and the rich (Barstow 1988:7). As the gap widened, basic options for women narrowed with corresponding legal changes. Barstow claims that with the witch allegations, women as a group were identified as legally responsible citizens. Before that women were considered minors. As legally responsible adults they could now be charged with acting irresponsibly. Barstow says, "Women thus entered European legal history by being accused of witchcraft" (1988:8). The increasing gap between the rich and the poor played a major role in the persecution of witches. The widening gap included greater intolerance toward folk healers. University trained doctors and priests replaced local healers and midwives. The enlarged gap between the rich and the poor had the effect of devaluing folk spiritual and healing practices of women. At the heart of that devaluation was the connection of women's sexuality and spiritual power.

Part of many witch practices is the sacred energy dance. This is true of shamanism, goddess spirituality, and other "folk" spiritual orientations. These forms of spirituality were deemed "primitive" and less civilized than the official religion of the nobility and educated. They do not separate immanence from transcendence. In earth-based spirituality, bodiness is inseparable from spirit. Body energy is a manifestation of spiritual energy. Spirituality is largely about energy. The sacred dance raises energy for the purposes of healing. Body energy is transmuted into healing energy. It is enhanced through group participation in activities like drumming circles, dancing circles, and chanting circles. Development of personal energy, in this view, depends in part on social interaction as well as receiving spiritual power from the spirits, such as animals, trees, birds, ancestors, and so forth. The healer channels this energy to the the person requesting healing. The heat that one feels when doing healing work is healing energy. Altered consciousness in shamanic healing invariably is accompanied by a 'heating up' of the body. Healing through touch was a common practice among witches. The power to heal is not thought to be contained entirely within the healers. They are considered channels for spiritual powers. The body is the grounding of spiritual, healing energy.[6] The integration of mind and body is intrinsic to any holistic spirituality, which is about many spiritual powers interacting with one's own energy field. The interrelatedness that characterizes earth-based spirituality is antithetical to religions that assume the existence of a transcendent God who exists as the One above the many.

Throughout biblical history there was a conscious attempt to overthrow polytheism with monotheism. This development corresponds with the change from many tribal clans that included elders and kinship structures to more centralized cities with kings and separate families. There was a shift from living with nature and each other to conquering nature and each other. This shift corresponded with the demise of women's authority as healers and teachers. Mary Condren says that in Ireland witches' success depended on "how closely they could be in tune with natural processes and listen to their wisdom" (1989:80). A witch was generally a charismatic personality with skills effective to guide others to health. As Condren says, "her success was judged directly by the people whom she was serving. Should she continue to give wrong judgments or fail in her arts, such as those of healing and midwifery, people would just refuse her services" (Condren 1989:80). As the church's power in Ireland increased, there was a steady regression in the evaluation of the folk healing of the "wise women." In Condren's view, there were three steps of regression with respect to the invalidation of women's roles as community leaders. First, Christianity merely asserted its superiority over existing spiritual and healing practices. Then it claimed that women's healing powers were associated with evil. Finally, the church denied that the women ever had any sacred powers in the first place. Their sacredness was transmuted into profanity in light of the self-designated sacredness of the church's power. The gods and goddesses of the "bushes, holy well, and sacred groves" were trampled upon and slandered and often destroyed.

Logically speaking, prostitution was impossible prior to patriarchal culture which includes the control of women's sexuality. In pre-patriarchal history, temple priestesses who performed sexual rituals as channels of goddess power, where goddess power represented virginal power, could not be appropriately described as prostitutes. Rather, virginal power meant power unto oneself as a woman. It is the positive expression of independent power. Prostitution means "base or unworthy use, as of talent or ability" (*Random House Dictionary* 1968:1063). Not everyone would agree with this definition of prostitution. Sex workers sometimes argue that they are the most liberated women of all. Many claim they use the rules of patriarchy against the rulers of patriarchy. They make more money as prostitutes than they would as secretaries, nurses, or clerks. They are not restricted to serving the sexual interests of one man, as married women are supposed to be. They are free to use their sexuality to make their own money and live independently. Their freedom is generally not unconditional, however, because of men who control their activities and their earnings. Despite the fact that many prostitutes become entangled in a network of johns and drugs, with little opportunity for their own choice making, they are not mandated to filial obligation. It is a moot point which kind of woman has more freedom to use her sexuality as an expression of her own desires.

How does women's use of their sexuality in prostitution differ from witches' use of their sexuality as "virginal" power? Both uses are seen as immoral by those who think women's sexuality can only be expressed morally within societally sanctioned heterosexual relations such as marriage. What is wrong with prostitution from the point of view of a witch? Prostitution, from this perspective, is seen to be wrong because it includes the exchange of services of parts of the body for money. Parts of the body are seen as integral to the person. They cannot be separated from the integrity of the person. It is believed that fragmentation of the person is required for an exchange of fee for service. This critique of prostitution applies equally to the practice of surrogate motherhood. In surrogacy, however, the woman exchanges the use of her womb, rather than her genitals and breasts, for money. Fee for service is part of social contract theory in which it is assumed that free individuals enter into exchange relations for their own benefit. Social contract theory is the cornerstone of the legal system in industrialized nations. A basic idea of it is that there is an exchange of one thing for another. It usually is about working for money or providing a service for protection. Renting out parts of one's body, whether for sexual services or for gestation, is legitimate within social contract theory; however, the legalization of either of them necessarily entails a view of the person as fragmented. Both practices are part of a social order in which prostitutes and surrogate mothers are used to make money for entrepreneurs, who are usually men. It is not only the parts of a woman but the woman herself who is regarded as a means towards the satisfaction of another's goal. The goal of both the woman and the entrepreneur is profit. That goal is shared by the majority of the population in industrial societies. It is inconsistent, however, with a holistic perspective of personhood that has the goal of personal well-being.

A spiritual perspective of personhood, as I understand it, is holistic. Prostitution and surrogate motherhood are seen as functions of patriarchy where those with money (mostly men) can buy the services of women's (girls') bodies (as well as those of men and boys). While the fragmentation of men's (or boys') identities is an important subject, just as the abuse of their bodies is, I shall continue to focus on female bodies because the vast majority of sexual violence among adults is perpetrated against women.[7] To ignore the fact that it was mostly women who were persecuted as witches is like referring to the fourteen women murdered in the 1989 Montréal massacre simply as students, without noting that they were all women who were purposefully separated from the men in the class before they were shot down. They were women who were in Engineering, a male-dominated faculty. They were exercising their rights as individuals to pursue their interests. They were killed for it. Whether any of them were feminists or not is beside the point. They were likened to feminists by the killer because they were occupying spaces that were previously occupied exclusively by men. Barstow says, "the dread of a woman taking the place reserved in the cultural pattern for men is a fundamental jealousy" (1986:112, quoting W.S. Scott). Self-determining women who arouse jealousy in men do so largely because they are women occupying cultural spaces defined by men for men. The internalization by women, as well as by men, of male definitions of cultural spaces leads to stereotypical cultural images of femininity and masculinity. Those who reject those images are targets for violence by the jealous. Self-directed women reject the confining cultural images and expect that they, and others like them, will be treated like whole and healthy people.

In biblical history the attempt to eradicate virginal female power is evident since Abraham's covenant with Yahweh. The sign of the covenant is the circumcised penis. It is not relevant to women. The first biblical covenant of circumcision circumscribed women's identity by their relationship to men. From that time forward in the records of history, femininity has been closely associated with dependency. The separation of the 'sacred' from the 'profane' placed women's sexuality outside of marriage in the realm of the profane. Uncontrolled female sexuality took on shades of diabolism. It was considered a threat to social morality, an important factor in the stability of the status quo. Motherhood was deemed sacred, not so much because it had an intrinsic sacredness, but because it served the interests of the church, which was supported by the family and state. The family was recognized as the cornerstone of both the authority of the church and the social order. Independent female sexuality continues to be a threat to the foundations of social order. Family relations continue to be constructed in terms of controlled sexual relations and socialization into appropriate sex role behaviour. The heterosexual family still serves as the symbol of the sacred. That is the place where women's sexuality is not attacked. As the prostitutes and witches both claim, women's sexuality is not free there either.

Free expression of women's sexuality continues to be overlaid with projections of looseness of character, i.e., woman out of control. The patriarchal association of independent female sexuality with trouble continues to be integral to the male morality that governs female sexuality. The alleged profanity of women's bodies has been problematic for the sacredness of men's spirituality. Men have attempted to escape from their own bodies as well as from women through, for example, celibacy. Both men and women try to control the demands of their bodies through restraint of sexual acitivity. Institutionalized celibacy, however, goes hand-in-hand with sexual terrorism, such as sexual abuse of children in boarding schools. The Canadian newspapers report extensive child sexual abuse by priests and other religious leaders. The traumatic experiences of hundreds of Canadian children who were at the mercy of male and female religious authorities are finally being acknowledged. Enforced celibacy and other unhealthy attitudes towards sexuality have taken their toll on both the perpetrators of the crimes and, more importantly, on the children who trusted those who were their spiritual counsellors. Prescribed celibacy is a correlative of negative attitudes towards sexuality. These self-negating feelings can be manifest in extreme form through asceticism, where the existence of the body is threatened through neglect or intentional harmful activities.

Asceticism extends into modern day anorexia for women (95 percent of anorexics are female and girls). Control of one's body allegedly indicates control over one's emotions. The disembodied mind is associated with purity of spirit. The separation of the mind from the body is a correlative of the separation of the spirit from the body. In this dichotomous view of self, embodied spirit is an oxymoron. Active sexuality, outside the 'sacred' institution of marriage, is considered profane. The image of an anorexic woman is not easy to relate to active sexuality. It fits more easily with images of chastity and isolation. Anorexia is one way for women to escape cultural associations of them with profane sexuality. At the same time, the representation of women in popular magazines, movies, and shop windows depicts the anorexic woman as seductive. Consequently four-year-old girls are standing on scales in their bathrooms watching their weight, teenage girls smoke in order to lose weight, and many women spend much of their time and money on diets and in slimming programs. It could be said that the sacredness of women is closely associated with the illusive profanity attributed to their bodies.

Profane utterances toward women are predominantly sexual. Men are slandered more through accusations about stupidity or lack of rational

control. Their 'smartness' is generally associated with their financial fi-
nesse. The close association of women with sexuality underlies sexual harassment of women in the workplace. First of all, their choice to be there
rather than choosing economic dependence on a man is sometimes a trig-
ger for profanity toward them. Second, the presence of a woman often
signifies sexual availability to men. Sexual harassment of women in the
workplace (or any place) is often not thought of as violating their right to
non-interference. In the 1990s some men don't know how to act around
women because they can't comprehend women's right to non-interference. If they claim their right to non-interference, they may be called
uppity women, cold women, or any one of a number of the profanities
that women get socialized into thinking are normal reactions to their
presence. Often the cause of men's confusion is blamed on women not be-
having according to older patterns of behaviour where a woman's presence was an invitation for men to move into her space without an invitation. Women internalized this view of themselves as a place of attraction
for men. If they did not attract men they considered themselves failures as
women. It was (and still is for many women) difficult to differentiate
between being harassed and having a healthy interpersonal encounter.

Sexual harassment has to do with power relations rather than
healthy, playful sexual interest. Sexual harassment is, among other things,
unwanted interference. In most cases of sexual harassment there is a
power differential between the two persons. It is usually the more powerful person who initiates the interaction. Refusal to comply with the advances of the other, if that person is more powerful, might affect job
promotion, recommendations, marks in school, publications, or healthy
working relations, and so forth. When women take themselves seriously
as adults and try to interact with men as full citizens with the corresponding rights of a free individual they often get unwarranted hostility directed toward them. The split between the good girl image and the bad
girl one revolves around the axis of women's independence from men's intrusion into their places, whether they are psychological, social, spiritual,
or physical. Violence and negativity towards women is fuelled by the fear
and jealousy of women's independent power. The pervasiveness of violence towards women today is part of the wake left from the witch persecutions. The historical effect of the persecution of witches was to restrict
women's independent authority and to establish a strong antitype image
of self-directed women.

The witch image absorbed the large-scale negativity associated with
exercise of powers by women that were coveted by men. The witch, as
antitype, was the target of male fear and hostility toward women as creators with independent power. As Hilary Lips (1991) points out, people
get nervous with women of power because of the incongruity between images of power and images of femininity.[8] The witch image represents the
antitype of the woman whose authority is circumscribed by male power.

The witch, like the Gnostics of early Christianity (Pagels 1979), refused to bow to the authoritative yoke of the church. Gnosticism was excluded from the Christian canon for several reasons, including a different under-standing of the Divine (both male and female), the role of women in church leadership, and apostles like Peter denying Mary apostolic author-ity in light of her apparent special relationship with Jesus (Gospel of Mary). The Bible, like other canonical literature, is an androcentric text. The redactive (editorial) process ensured a male-centred biblical history which developed in relation to a single male creator deity.

The categories of sacred and profane are generalizable to secular realities such as the canonical traditions of university disciplines. The "great works" are considered so because "they express the struggles and aspirations of humanity in a compelling and beautiful way" (Christ 1978:261). Or so it is said. Christ claims that this is an unexamined prem-ise. She asks, For whom are these great works a power of life? Where do women find themselves in them? One answer is as causes of wars be-tween men, where the names of the women get lost. Another is as wives and mothers of great men. As tragic lovers. As crazy women in the attic. As courtesans who provide fun for predominantly married men. Rarely do great works depict women as self-supporting authority figures. Feminist literature is required for that. The feminist becomes the antitype as she attempts to create alternative images of powerful women. She stands outside the sacred traditions of great works as a heretic. The feminist belongs to the profane in the same way as the witch does in patriarchal consciousness.[9]

Nancy Jay (1991) makes important connections between the binary structures of "intellectual concepts and social distinctions" in her analysis of the sacred and profane with respect to Emile Durkheim's work *The Elementary Forms of the Religious Life*. She describes Durkheim's project as one of locating the source of original categories of thought which shape social patterns. He was not satisfied with the rationalist account (such as Plato's), namely, that fundamental thought forms exist before experience. Nor did he think the empiricist's view (such as Aristototle's) was satisfac-tory: all thought derives from sensate data. His conclusion was that essen-tial ideas that inform social organization "are born in religion and of reli-gion: they are a product of religious thought" (Jay 1991:89, quoting Durkheim). He chose to study Aboriginal Australian men's rituals because he believed them to be the most elementary of all religious practices. For Durkheim, rituals serve the purpose of bringing into consciousness con-cepts that were previously obscured.

He claimed that Australian men, in performing rituals, represent their own society to themselves, thus making aspects of their society available to consciousness as concepts. This representation and conceptualization in turn reinforces and actu-ally creates and recreates the social structure as represented in ritual. It is in these 'collective representations' that the categories originated. (Jay 1991:90)

Tribal and class organization is seen to derive from totemic rituals. Totems represent different groups of natural phenomena, like animals, with people grouped according to their totemic animal which is thought to symbolize their basic personality characteristics. Through totemic rituals, categories of classification arise and are maintained, according to Durkheim. In his view, as civilization progresses, science and philosophy take over the function of maintaining the fundamental intellectual categories which organize social relations and interaction with nature. The distinctive feature of religion, for Durkheim, is that it separates completely the categories of sacred and profane. Religion sets the binary structure into place; philosophy and science maintain it in more sophisticated and civilized ways. Durkheim says, "This division of the world into two domains, the one containing all that is sacred, the other all that is profane, is the distinctive characteristic of religious thought" (Jay 1991:90). It is seen by Durkheim as the fundamental category of thought from which all else is derived, such as good and bad, health and sickness. All other binary oppositions are opposites within the categories of sacred or profane.

In Durkheim's sociology of knowledge, the categories of sacred and profane provide the rationale for the exclusion of women from men's sacred rituals. In his analysis women belong to the category of the profane. They are necessarily excluded because they supposedly cannot connect to the form of knowledge that is derived from the domain of the sacred, achieved through men's rituals. Jay claims, "For Durkheim, the exclusion of women even provides an identifying sign to distinguish truly religious practices from those that are mere magic. Religion performs its essential function—of establishing conceptual thought—for men only. If it serves women, Durkheim never shows how" (1991:91). In his view, women's sexuality is associated with profanity, while men's intellectual acumen belongs to the sacred. This difference is enlarged as civilization progresses, according to his earlier work *The Division of Labor in Society*. Before he began to search for the essential categories of thought, he had already decided on the incommensurate natures and functions of women and men. In light of such a presupposition, a hermeneutics of suspicion is appropriate with respect to his 'discovery' of the foundational importance of men's religious rituals and the incommensurateness of the gendered sacred and profane.

Jay suggests, "Suppose he had set out to account for the origin, not of the categories of understanding, but of something quite similar: the basic laws of formal logical thought" (1991:92). These were formulated by Aristotle, just as were the essential categories of thought. Although I outlined them in Chapter Three, I shall restate them here. "They are the principle of Identity (if anything is A, it is A); the principle of Contradiction (nothing can be both A and Not-A); and the principle of the Excluded Middle (anything, and everything, must be *either* A *or* Not-A)" (Jay 1991: 93). Rationalists say that these logical categories are given to us from a reality apart from the changing phenomenal world, i.e., they are a priori. As Jay points out, however, if we look at the phenomenal world we see change, overlap, inconsistencies, ambiguities. For example, we see water changing to ice, blood coagulating, dry ice, deer antlers bending under heat, wax dummies in windows melting in the heat of the sun, peoples' hair changing from black to white along with their convictions. We don't see anything remaining unchanged and completely unambiguous. If there is any truth to the laws of logic, it must be, as the idealists say, located in a reality that is separate from the world in which we are born and die. Durkheim, however, claimed to reject the idealist's account of truth. His aim was to show that empirically observable religious rituals provide the source of the categories of the understanding which shape social organization. He did not recognize that his basic categories of sacred and profane were assumed intellectual categories that shaped his investigation into the basic categories of the understanding. His sacred/profane distinction entails the basic laws of logic of exclusive categories. They are self-contained categories, without permeability. The excluded middle is the vacuum between the exclusive categories of sacred and profane, which he assumes to be sex-specific. Truth is assigned to what is designated as sacred, while the profane designates the realm of the unreliable. The equivalence between sacredness and truth, as defined by church theologians, was appropriated by secular scientists in their re-interpretation of sacredness as non-emotive rationality. There is an underlying assumption of non-bias in the notion of rational. The bias against women as normative persons with reliable truths is denied. This denial is exemplified in Durkheim's search for the basic categories of human understanding which shape social organization.

Nancy Jay's analysis shows that Durkheim's search for the origins of the categories of understanding that shape social organization is basically an argument for the laws of logic which support exclusive categories. The assumed exclusiveness of sacredness and profanity interacted in his investigation with the assumed exclusiveness of maleness and femaleness. His research depicts the 'hermeneutical circle.' His assumptions determine his findings which, in turn, reinforce his assumptions. Empirical 'discoveries' often reveal hidden assumptions that the researcher was "already always" listening to. If the hermeneutical circle is to be broken, the basic assumptions of the two dimensions of knowledge (philosophical and sociological) have to be examined. Durkheim's assumptions of the profanity of women are part of the wake that remains in patriarchal consciousness as a consequence of the persecution of women as evildoers.

When I was studying Durkheim as a young woman majoring in Sociology in the 1960s, I sensed there was something wrong with his theory of knowledge, but I didn't know where. As is often the case, I attributed the problem to myself as a woman. I was in the wrong category. It seemed that the only way to redeem myself was to try to overcome my femaleness. Fortunately, feminism has changed that kind of self-defeating consciousness for me and many others. The distinction between sacred and profane continues to influence attitudes towards women's sexuality and, accordingly, towards women's identities. As Barstow says, "it is theologically only one step from scorning a woman to believing that she is a servant of the devil" (1988:13). The association of women with the domain of the profane renders women's thoughts and activities suspicious. It makes their connections with the cycle of birth, life, and death slightly dreadful and, hence, feared. Control of women's sexuality and reproductive rights is one way of controlling the fear of women subverting a social order dictated by the basic rules of logic in which men are socially on top. In light of recent scholarship, it is reasonable to conclude that the folk wisdom and healing practices of women threatened, and continues to threaten, the power of the church, universities, and the state.

Social/Sexual Contract

I agree with Martha Reineke when she says, "if our ancestors had thought in the same mode as do today's masters, they would never have put an end to the witch trials" (1990:117, quoting René Girard). Following Adrienne Rich's critique of history as a selective process which excludes many important and determining events, Reineke says, "history is forged in a struggle for consciousness waged against the forces of amnesia" (1990:117). Neglecting the witch persecution as a determining force of history is a striking example of patriarchal reproductive consciousness. History is created and reproduced in part through overlooking the violence directed against women to keep their productive and reproductive powers from claiming their place in history. Because of exclusionary politics, the scapegoating of women as sources of evildoing is a theme that was forgotten in the interests of those who were writing historical "tales of our finest hours" (Reineke 1990:117).

The emergence of social contract theory and the focus on civil rights and freedoms occurred within the context of fraternal patriarchy, i.e., the rule of the brothers. According to Carole Pateman (1988) paternal patriarchy, i.e., the rule of the fathers, was overthrown by the sons who declared equal power among themselves, based on equal rights and freedoms. During the seventeenth century many of the cords were cut between the men of science and God the Father. Following the split between science and religion, reason and faith were either rendered compatible or faith was rejected in the interests of science.[10] Just as the seventeenth century ushered in the scientific revolution against patriarchal religious authority, the eighteenth century was a period of political revolution against monarchical rule. God and kings were toppled in favour of civic brotherhoods. Fraternal patriarchy brought with it social contracts: civic, employment, and marriage which were to institutionalize liberty, equality, and fraternity among civic members of the brotherhood. Civil rights included employment and civic (public) contracts (public rights) as well as the private marriage contract. Pateman points out that the institution-alization of contractual rights was aimed at public rights, while private rights in the marriage contract were ignored. The consequence was that the rights of those in the private sector were controlled by the political rights of those in the public sector. This means only those who were members of the fraternity had independent rights in both realms. The political right over women as members of the private sector was institutionalized in social contracts. Women were part of the property that the men (brothers) had rights over. The marriage contract legalized "orderly access by men to women's bodies" (Pateman 1988:2). Conjugal duty was a wife's obligation which was part of the exchange for protection by her husband against other men. The contract did not, however, protect her or her children against her husband. Continuing family violence attests to that lack of protection. Family violence, however, is becoming a significant public concern. The Canadian government recently set aside grants to help establish three centres in Canada to study and work on family violence. An important aspect of changing family patterns is revealing cultural assumptions that contribute towards male violence in families. This is not to say that female violence does not exist but rather that the vast majority of family violence is perpetrated by men, as I discuss in the last chapter. For that reason, it is important to consider Carole Pateman's claim that the sexual contract is the basic and hidden contract in all social contracts, especially the marriage contract. In her view, the original patriarchal right was man's right over a woman. That right, i.e., the male sex-right, precedes a man's right as a father. That right is believed to be basic and hidden in all social contracts. It was institutionalized in the marriage contract, after which the relations between the sexes in employment and civic contracts was modeled.

Pateman says the marriage contract "is the means through which modern patriarchy is constituted" (1988:2). She persuasively argues that it normalized the original patriarchal right, namely, men's right to women's bodies. In the marriage contract, women were subordinated to men *as men* who largely controlled the couple's income and thereby their place in the social order. The woman gained access to the man's power; however, it was derived power rather than independent. Social contracts of employment and civic rights, like the marriage contract, institutionalize dominant-subordinate relations, even though they ostensibly ensure protection of the rights of the principal parties. Contractual subordination is believed to be part of all forms of systemic domination where, for example, Black people are subordinated to White people *as* White people; where Aboriginal people are subordinated to White people *as* White people; and where non-English and/or non-White Canadians are subordinated to White, English-speaking Canadians *as* White English-speaking Canadians. There is an exchange of service by the subordinate for protection by the dominant. Contracts between individuals of unequal social power assume the legitimacy of the dominant-subordinate contractual relation. While each of the parties can be said to have the freedom to enter into the contract or refrain from doing so, coercive social realities like poverty or fear constrain freedom. Consequently, the rights of subordinated groups are not necessarily protected in contracts which allegedly ensure such protection. Freedom to make choices is influenced by group identity. Individual rights within social contracts are shaped by the power relations of the groups with which the principal parties are identified. Identity politics is a form of politics that is designed to challenge systemic discrimination against the group with which one identifies or is identified by others. Political activism often is characterized by identity politics. Sexual politics is intrinsic, in this view, to social contract theory and the implications that social contracts have for the relations between the sexes.

Pateman says, "political right originates in sex-right or conjugal right" (1988:3). She refers to Adrienne Rich's claim (1980) that the law of male sex-right is intrinsic to prescriptive heterosexuality and underscores all forms of social organization. A consequence of taking the heterosexual marriage as the politically correct model for the relations between the sexes is the negation of the rights of homosexuals. According to Rich, attitudes toward lesbianism and gay rights are shaped by the law of male sex-right. Restrictions on lesbian and gay rights are part of institutionalized forms of domination in the workplace as well as in the home. While both lesbians and gays reject cultural sexual-orientation prescriptions, lesbianism more obviously includes rejection of male authority. Because the male sex-right is interrelated with male authority in patriarchy, lesbianism is a powerful form of insubordination with respect to male authority. Another powerful form of insubordination is autonomous female spirituality. The relatively successful circumscription of women's independent authority in social/sexual contracts in fraternal patriarchy can be attributed, to a large extent, to the severe attacks on women during the witch craze.

The persecution of women as witches was a large-scale effort to restrict women's independent authority. While most women who were murdered were local village healers, some were considered heroes before they were burned as witches. As I mentioned earlier, Joan of Arc is a particularly notable instance of a woman who was a culturally inscribed national hero-turned-witch, who was made a saint centuries later. She is a good example of the arbitrariness of the 'good girl/bad girl' distinction that can be made by others who have the power to identify according to their own interests. From the perspective of Carol Christ's analysis of women in religious traditions, Joan was an exemplary heretic/outsider.[11] She is usually depicted as proud, independent, and strong. There is little doubt that she embodied those qualities. Images of her sitting astride her horse as the Maid of Orleans depict her as the incarnation of Athena, the goddess of war. While the warrior image of her is inspiring and causes indignation at the thought of her murder, it reflects only one image of Joan of Arc. Such a singular image does not acknowledge her vulnerability in the face of the unspeakable tyranny of the ecclesiastical tribunal at her trial and burning in 1431.

In contrast to the indomitable will of the leader of the seige on Orleans, poet H.D. (Hilda Doolittle) writes of the portrayal of Jeanne d'Arc by Carl Dreyer in his film *The Passion and Death of a Saint* (Friedman 1990). In his film, Dreyer shows Jeanne before the tribunal. She is sturdy but broken. Inner strength and extreme vulnerability characterize the broken warrior, as depicted by Dreyer. In the words of the poet H.D.:

This is a real, real, Jeanne (poor Jeanne) little mountain Newfoundland puppy, some staunch and true and incomparably loyal creature, something so much us, the very incarnation of loyalty and integrity . . . dwarfed, below us, as if about to be trampled or kicked into a corner by giant soldier iron-heeled great boots. Marching boots, marching boots, the heavy hulk of leather and thong-like fastenings and cruel nails . . . no hint of the wings on the heels of the legions that followed the lily-banner; the cry that sang toward Orleans is in no way ever so remotely indicated. . . . [T]his is an Athene stripped of intellect, a Telisila robbed of poetry, it is a Jeanne d'Arc that not only pretends to be real, but that is real, a Jeanne that is going to rob us of our own Jeanne. (Friedman 1990:131, quoting H.D.)

Our own Jeanne, according to H.D., is one that walks in chains towards the judges and who is both "intolerably sturdy and intolerably broken" (Friedman 1990:130). She claims that we each have this Jeanne in "the secret great cavernous interior of the cathedral . . . of the subconscious" (p. 130). This Jeanne inside us is the source of our indignation. We don't like to be seen as so compromised. But when the real, real Jeanne walks in there is a lack of comprehension. The "overwhelming bulk of ecclesiastical political accusation" confronting the beaten puppy figure is "sprung" on the viewer in such a way that the picture "doesn't link up straight with human consciousness. There is a gap somewhere" (p. 133). The spiritual power of the small, physically broken child-like woman was the "something in something, something behind something" (p. 133). H.D. says that Joan of Arc was kicked towards the angels by the big boots. Afterwards she was burned at the stake as a witch because she refused to recant her claim that she was guided by a spiritual awareness that was not authorized by the church. It was only centuries later that she was revered as a saint. Today she is being uncovered as an important figure in women's history. Joan of Arc serves as a good study for the demystification of mystics, shamans, heretics, and women in general. The image of Joan of Arc as a beaten puppy trampled by iron-heeled boots is an important counterbalance to that of the proud and independent warrior leading her troops into battle. In both cases she depicts the virgin: one-unto-herself. Her broken physicality was not a manifestation of a broken spirit. The spirit which "is something in something, something behind something" was alive in both sets of circumstances. It was that spirit which makes Joan of Arc indomitable and a model of independent female spirituality.

The murder of women as witches because of their feared power was a lesson to women. It was well learned. The success of the mass murders of women during the burning times was a factor in the apparent reasonableness of excluding women from the social contract fraternities. Women were to be controlled through "protection" by men whom they contracted to marry. Uncontrolled women need not expect protection in the patriarchal model of male-female relations of authority.

Ideally, contracts were intended to regulate free action. They were to be entered into by free agents. With respect to women, however, there was little, if any, allowance for free agency within social contract theory. They were part of what was to be organized by the free agents, the brothers. They were by definition outsiders. Their status as respectable members of civil society relied on their exclusion from public politics and their quiet acceptance of their dependency as wives or daughters. Women outside of marriage who claimed an independent status as working women with their own earned income and ideas were sometimes labelled "hyenas in petticoats."[12] They were outsiders from the perspective of contract theory. Women within marriage were in the ambiguous position of being respected as the producers of citizens and reproducers of cultural values, while they were virtually excluded from full participation in citizenship. The political rights of citizens were the rights of men who owned property, worked in civil society outside the home, contributed to the welfare state, and received benefits from it. The rules of civic order and government rule were established by the citizens and internalized in the form of social morality. Social morality and male morality looked pretty much the same. Women internalized and reproduced it in the home under the authority of the father who took pride in the obedience of both his wife and children.

The structural division between the categories of public (civic) and private (domestic) is assumed in classic contract theory (such as that of Jean Jacques Rousseau and John Locke). It parallels the assumed relation between the sexes. The relation between the sexes in the private sphere, in Pateman's view, established the hierarchical relationship between the public and private spheres. I agree with Pateman's evaluation and conclude that analysis of social organization in the public sphere requires attention to the underlying sexual politics in the private sphere. In my view, sexual relations in the private sphere are intrinsic to politics in the public sphere, such as in the workplace or in electoral politics. Severing the public sphere from the private enables such authorities as social analysts, political theorists, and economists to ignore the influence of the hidden sexual contract in workplaces, politics, and economics. Pateman says, "The structure of relations between the sexes is ignored and sexual relations stand as the paradigm of all that is private or non-political" (1989:3). Politics is constituted in political theory within the public sphere where men rule according to the assumption that their maleness separates them from family obligations and frees them to participate democratically in the management of work, politics, and the economy, without interference from family obligations.

Women's entry into democracy is different from men's because of their association with the private sphere where affective interpersonal connectedness is the priority. The alleged impartiality, i.e., 'professionalism' or loyalty to the workplace that is expected in the public sphere are perceived to be at odds with the partiality of deeply felt personal relations. While men's greatest demonstration of loyalty, i.e., obligation, is to go to war for their country, women's greatest obligation to the state is to have babies (Pateman 1989:11). John Rawls' claim that justice is the first virtue of social institutions is constructed on the suppressed assumption that the family is not a social institution but belongs to the natural realm of biology and corresponding loving relations. Because of women's mandated role to perform the labour of love in the home, a woman who enters the public realm is suspect. She comes without complete consent because she is suspected of divided loyalties. While women's identities are closely associated with the labour of love in the home, men's identities more often develop in relation to their work in the paid labour force. Their integrity is aligned with loyalty to the workplace. It is assumed that men can more often be relied on to internalize the rules of the civic order which give priority to work and politics in the public realm over domestic events and relations. It is also sometimes assumed that men would rather have the power and prestige that comes with paid work rather than attend to the well-being of their children.

I attended a women's law forum where an esteemed male judge was on the panel. The discussion was about promoting equal opportunities and effects in law practices for women lawyers. The male judge suggested that women lawyers might take two or three afternoons off a week to be with their children. The receptionists in their law offices could tell clients that the women lawyers were out of the office, implying that they were in court. There was no mention of the same 'preferential' treatment for men lawyers. I noted that such a solution would merely reinforce existing stereotypes with respect to women being solely responsible for child care. Unless men lawyers were to take equal responsibility for the care of their children, the women lawyers who were to be given 'special' consideration would be penalized because they wouldn't be there as much as the men to receive clients. They would be on the 'mummy track,' without the existence of an analogous 'daddy track.' The judge retorted that I was talking about 'pie in the sky' if I thought men lawyers were going to take time out to care for their children in the middle of the day.[13] This was a man who claimed to be in favour of equality for women. Rousseau's arguments for natural differences between the sexes with respect to nature/women and society/men remain embedded in patriarchal liberal views of social and individual equality in the 1990s. Men will be citizens and women will be mothers. Nevertheless women are increasingly assuming their rights as full citizens. The cost is high, however. Juggling their roles as mothers and citizens has resulted in excessive stress for women, with related illness like cancer, heart failure, arthritis, and so forth. Women's entry into so-called democracy has required a certain amount of effort in overcoming their own femaleness. The kind of democracy that characterizes social contract theory neglected to include sexual democracy, which would take women's sexuality as a normative aspect of half the adult population. Menstruation and menopause are part of all healthy women's sexuality. Pregnancy, childbirth, and lactation are part of many women's sexuality. If women's status in the public sphere is to be normalized, these facts have to be recognized and incorporated into social policy and planning.

Women's sexuality in patriarchal social order has been seen as subversive of order. Pateman cites Rousseau from his *Politics and the Arts*: "disorder of women engenders all the vices and can bring the state to ruin" (Pateman 1989:17). Freud's *Civilization and Its Discontents* reflects the same suspicion of women's position as oppositional to civilization. In addition to the view of women as less capable of sublimating sexual energy into something useful for society, he perceptively adds that women are hostile because they are sidelined. In Freud's view, women's hostility is subversive and, therefore, ought to be controlled. The uncontrolled woman is the 'woman-out-of-order.' The opposition between nature and society with women on the side of nature has served to undermine consent for women to participate as competent citizens. They enter the public realm against the forces of limited consent of both women and men. Families, schools, media, the "great works" all conspire to reproduce the image of woman as subversive. Women who wish to actualize their potentials in a so-called democratic society are faced with achieving consent from women and men to do so. They are presumed to be guilty of divided loyalties and need to prove they are not. It is little wonder that many feminists today are nervous about sex-specificity and prefer gender neutrality. In my view, however, it is precisely the issue of women's sexuality that is at the heart of women's subordination in democracy. In order to evolve toward a democracy that includes sexual democracy it is important to normalize women's sexuality. That requires a change in the social order with respect to the boundaries between the private and public spheres so that women's sexuality is not restricted to the private realm. In addition, it means that men must take their own sexuality into account in the construction of their identities. Their roles as fathers need to be incorporated into social policy and planning. The alleged subversiveness of female sexuality is constructed alongside the denial by men of the importance of their maleness in their self-identity and place in the social order. Underly-

ing the privatization of the socially respectable role related to female sexuality (i.e., motherhood) is the assumption of the dichotomy between
nature and culture.

The great divide between nature and culture hovers as a reminder of
the fear of female power in Western civilization and the attempt to limit it
through exclusionary tactics. Prejudice against women in the public
sphere, which is related to this fear, lead to the occlusion of women's
achievements as well as to slandering them as 'women-out-of-order.' Uncovering the activities of women is an important method of overcoming
suspicion of women's authority and of acknowledging their contribution
to socially defined standards of excellence. For example, Amy Dahan
Dalmédico writes about Sophie Germain, a nineteenth-century mathematician. Dahan Dalmédico says, "we should recognize the analogies between the life of Sophie Germain and our own, and they should lead us to
strive for excellence in the face of prejudice" (1991:122). She was not recognized as an important mathematician largely because she was a woman. Her identity as a mathematician was severly limited by the fact that
she was a woman with the associated characteristics of staying in her
place and not attracting attention to her achievements. Consequently, she
was easily ignored. Any protestations on her part would have likely elic-
ited accusations of making a spectacle of herself. Her choice was to be the
best mathematician she could be, while accepting the cultural limitations
of being a female. The idea of striving for excellence is admirable. To attempt to do it, however, without addressing the prejudice that exists
against women using their skills in influential cultural places is like struggling mightily to roll a rock uphill, knowing that it will roll back down
before it can be secured. Prejudice against women is supported by 'patriarchal procreative power,' i.e., the consent granted to men to be imaged
as self-sufficient creators and maintainers of public and private forms of
social organization. Images of men as all-powerful procreators are found
in various places, such as the birth of Athena from Zeus's head, the spiritual fathers of Locke who tenderly care for their progeny,[14] and the biblical God as creator, nurturer, mother.[15] Women were not granted the same
procreative power, even though they are the ones that can be said to pro-
create in the usual sense of the term. Their procreative power was trivialized in the private sphere. By contrast to the marginalization of women's
procreative power, consent was granted to men to generate meaningful
history. The generative 'individuals' described by social contract theorists
were fraternity brothers, supported by women whose loyalty was to be
directed more towards their men than toward each other. In the democracy of social contract theory, men have the loyalty of each other in the
public domain and the loyalty of their womenfolk in the private domain.
Women, on the other hand, are subordinated to the rule of men in both
places. While their place in the home is clearer to them than their place in

the public workplace, in both places men's procreative power is often exercised at the expense of women.

The overthrow of paternal patriarchy and institutionalization of fraternal patriarchy with social contract theory in the seventeenth and eighteenth centuries did not remove the original, covert male right: to women's bodies. The sexual contract[16] continues as a hidden assumption in modern patriarchy. It means, among other things, that patriarchal reproductive consciousness controls women's reproduction. Patriarchal reproductive consciousness is required for the exercise of paternal procreative power. It assumes an original claim to ownership in the production of offspring through the control of women's bodies. The male sex right and paternal procreative power are entangled with the assumed right to ownership of children who are produced through women's bodies. The right to control women's bodies is a condition for the right to own the women's children, which is illustrated by the children taking the father's name. Reproductive freedom is not a right that women automatically have when they do not have rights over their bodies. The absence of women's rights over their bodies contradicts the principles of a morality of rights. It also contravenes the reality of women as ontologically independent persons, that is, as beings with their own power of directing their desires in relation to their communities.

The control by men of women's reproductive power is exercised in disconcerting ways in contemporary society in new reproductive technologies (e.g., Gena Corea 1985; Susan Downie 1988; Margrit Eichler and Phoebe Poole 1988; Martha Field 1988; Larry Gostin 1990; Renate P. Klein 1989; Judith Lasker and Susan Borg 1987; Deborah Poff 1987; Ann Rule 1987; and the Royal Commission Report on New Reproductive Technologies 1993). In particular, preconception arrangements (surrogate motherhood) are often established on the basis of contract law. In genetic-gestational arrangements, the commissioning man agrees to donate his sperm and the carrying mother provides the ovum. Often a broker acts as a middleman to bring the two principal parties together. He or she may be, for example, a lawyer, a specialist in reproductive endocrinology and infertility, or a psychotherapist.[17] Their business is to bring together men who want to extend their biological stock with women who are willing to help them out. The commissioning man agrees to pay the broker a fee to find a carrying mother and a fee to the carrying mother. The average fee for the carrying mother is from ten to twelve thousand dollars, extending up to sixteen thousand dollars. The average age of carrying mothers is between twenty-five and twenty-seven. The average age of commissioning men is forty-two years. While commissioning men are usually at least middle class and well educated, carrying mothers are generally of a lower socioeconomic class, with less education. Fee for service is the stated condition of the contract. A market model of production shapes the details of the contract. The health of the baby is often a factor in the final payment to the carrying mother. Amniocentesis is usually a requirement in the contractual arrangement in order to check the health of the fetus during pregnancy. Ownership of the healthy baby by the father is assumed. The possibility of mother-child bonding is ignored.[18] The carrying woman must abdicate the integrity of her body and her relatedness to the foetus when she signs a contract with a commissioning man (or woman) to gestate a baby for a fee.[19]

The usual rationale that is presented for justifying the use of relatively disadvantaged women to provide babies for middle-class White men is that the carrying mothers are eager to help out infertile couples who want to care for a child. As Deborah Poff (1987) notes, however, there is more interest in caring for one's own stock than merely caring for a child. Adoption is an option if the issue is merely the desire to care for a child. The desire to pass on his genes cannot be overlooked as a reason for a man donating his sperm to the procreative process where neither his wife nor the carrying mother are seen as 'owners' of the product, i.e., the child. Women's procreative power is appropriated by commissioning men in preconception arrangements. The added feature of a broker strengthens the market production character of the contractural agreement between the commissioning man and the carrying woman. Brokers are legal in the U.S. and are usually paid between $11,000-$16,000.[20] The broker is paid by the commissioning man and therefore would likely serve his interests more than those of the carrying mother, although he or she ostensibly acts in the interests of both principal parties. The welfare of the woman after the delivery of the baby to the commissioning man is not generally of much interest to either the broker or the commissioning man.

The effects on the carrying women, as well as the wives of commissioning men, can be devastating. Wives are not party to the preconception arrangements in many of the legal agreements used by brokers. Their infertility is sometimes used to humiliate them into agreeing with their husbands that they should arrange with another woman to have a baby. In genetic-gestational arrangements where a commissioning husband obtains a baby from the union of his sperm with another woman's ovum, his wife is the outsider. His genes, but not hers, are perpetuated. In other gestational arrangements, it is possible for both wife and husband to contribute to the procreative process. The woman's ovum and the man's sperm are united in vitro (in a glass dish) and the embryo is injected into the carrying mother's uterus. Such in vitro fertilization provides the wife with the possibility of participating while reducing the carrying mother strictly to the function of external gestator. While this form of in vitro fertilization is carried out in some clinics, the standard form of preconception arrangements is that which involves donor insemination of the carrying woman.

Apart from the relative exclusion of the commissioning man's wife from the procreative process, the effects on the carrying mother can be dreadful. For example, Ann Rule (1987) describes a woman who saw an infertility practitioner discussing his brokerage house on the *Phil Donahue Show*. The woman decided to carry a child for ten thousand dollars. She was relatively poor, with three children. She was a victim of incest and was described by a psychiatrist in her required examination as noticeably unstable. After the pregnancy she was described by others as having enjoyed the pregnancy, with no postpartum depression, and only felt a sense of joy and well-being as a result of participating in their program. A year after she gave the baby to the commissioning husband, however, she took her three children to the woods and shot them. No one can say with certainty that there was a connection between the slaying of her children and her participation in the preconception arrangement. At the same time, it makes one wonder about the effects of the surrogacy experience on herself as a person, and on her expectations of her childrens' futures. The representation of carrying women as 'altruistic angels' who happily help out wealthy, infertile couples who desire to care for a child has to be evaluated within the context in which carrying mothers choose to enter into preconception arrangements. In addition to financial considerations, their need for attention appears to be a significant motivating force for their participation. The drastic drop in attention to them after the commissioning man has his child can lead to disastrous consequences. Gena Corea (1985) points out that a woman's lack of expression of her disappointment as well as of her difficulties with emotionally separating from a baby with whom she has bonded during pregnancy and, perhaps, early infancy should not be taken as a sign of her happiness. Her lack of speaking out may be due more to her inability to do so than to her satisfaction with the arrangement.

Carrying mothers, like prostitutes, are most often part of an organized entrepreneurship. Women's bodies in these cases serve the interests of those who can buy their services, whether it is the womb or the genitals. It can be argued that the women choose to enter freely into contracts of fee for service. A closer look at the conditions in which they do so, however, indicates a strong possibility that social factors shape their choices. They may be factors such as money, the desire for attention, the desire to please, possibly the desire to overcome previous involuntary losses such as miscarriages by engaging voluntarily in the process of loss, or the desire to cleanse the body of incestuous impurities. It is not clear whether many women who agree to carry babies for commissioning men do so with a good understanding of the potential emotional difficulties involved in acting merely as a 'mother machine' in the procreative process, as it is designed by entrepreneurs.

The cultural legitimization to use women's bodies for the service of others is the milieu which makes such exploitative practices possible. Current cultural patterns allow and even give explicit permission for individual acts of exploitation. This is not to absolve individuals of responsibility for exploitative activities. Rather it is to say that individual responsibility and cultural values must be understood in relation to each other. The larger cultural patterns need to change in order to support more humane social relations. Social contract theory, for example, gives permission for commercialized preconception arrangements. Rejection of their legality, as demonstrated in the United Kingdom, Australia, and some American states, is an encouraging indication of a shift away from contract law in consideration of human well-being.

It is worth noting a report by the New York State Task Force on Life and the Law (1988). It states that the biological components of gestation cannot be separated from the psychological dimensions of the self. If they are, it is argued, a dehumanizing process occurs. The task force report rejects the market production model in favour of the growth model, where bonding between mother and child, as well as other emotional factors, are taken into consideration in the conception, gestation, and birth process. The New York task force report is to be contrasted with the Ontario Law Reform Commission's *Report on Human Artificial Reproduction and Related Matters*, which endorses the practice of preconception agreements. Margrit Eichler and Phoebe Poole's study (1988) shows that preconception arrangements by Canadians are more widespread than is suspected. The contractual use of women's bodies for profit and the satisfaction of another's interest is often not regarded as problematic in a market production model of procreation. Human well-being is not the primary consideration. Apart from the carrying mother, negative effects are often felt by the commissioned child, the carrying woman's other children, her partner, as well as those from the side of the commissioning man and commissioning woman (if she is party to the arrangement). Most brokerages only work with heterosexual couples, mainly for political reasons. The emotional hook, in a heterosexist society, of providing a much-wanted baby for a heterosexual couple is relatively difficult to argue against. The success of that hook reinforces its use. Consequently, individuals and couples who do not fit with the stereotypical model of deserving parents are usually not accepted into the brokerage clinics. In North America most of the commissioning men or couples are White, middle class, and English-speaking.[21]

The separation of the psychological self from physical parts of the self is necessary for social contracts which depend on renting out parts of the body in a contract of fee for service. Preconception arrangements require a separation of self from body in a woman's consciousness if they are going to be successful. The fact that many women subsequently refuse to give up their babies despite the contract indicates the degree to which they live with an integrated consciousness. The stress that is endured by many when they give up their babies is an inhumane consequence of the agreement. The terms of the agreement are credible only if one assumes a basic separation of body from mind in consciousness. If one includes body consciousness in a view of consciousness, then the acceptability of such contracts are incredible. Using women as 'mother machines' is a consequence of not only the separation of mind from body but also of nature from culture. The natural process of procreation is used by others for their own purpose. It is not lived with in an organic way. Procuring babies through preconception arrangements is an illustration of the orientation toward 'having' rather than 'living with.' The control of women's bodies in this way is an extreme form of the control of nature for the purpose of owning the produce from it as well as profiting from it. It reinforces the hidden sexual contract in social contract theory, which gives permission to men to access women's bodies for their own purposes independently of the well-being of the women whose bodies are being used. Women's procreative power is subsumed under the power of money that can buy the use of women's procreative power. Patriarchal procreative power is demonstrated unequivocally in surrogate motherhood. The possibility for preconception arrangements depends on a perspective that reduces maternal procreative power to a service function. The intrinsic value of carrying women is not a major concern in these arrangements.

If damaging social practices toward women are to be stopped, it is important to re-evaluate underlying beliefs about the nature and purpose of women as self-determining persons. Attitudes toward women's independent authority with respect to reproductive issues, sexual relationships, freedom from sexual harassment, and related authority in social leadership are intertwined with images of women from an ontological perspective. Epistemologies that reflect women's authoritative knowledge require assumptions about women's normality as adult persons and images which reflect a congruity between femaleness and power-full-ness, including maternal procreative power. A morality of justice depends on accepting ontological normativeness for women. The rights of women *as women* in social contract theory are not equal to the rights of men. Social contract theory developed within the context of exclusive and hierarchical epistemological categories that assumed exclusive and hierarchical ontological categories. The basic dualistic category in nature is female/male. It established the model for binary dualisms in social organization. The hierarchical nature of the basic dualism entails the male sex right which is hidden in the marriage contract, employer-employee contract, and in the citizen-state contract. The unfortunate, logical conclusion of the male sex-right in social contract theory is illustrated in preconception arrangements.

While situations of surrogate motherhood can include extreme forms of the exploitation of women's bodies which are experienced by only a minority of women, the issue of control of their bodies is part of the majority of women's lives. In order to establish women's control over their bodies, and corresponding social rights, it is necessary to change the underlying sets of images and associated attitudes towards women as ontologically authoritative persons with respect to their own person as well as the communities in which they participate. Because women are always persons of identifiable communities such as Aboriginals, Blacks, immigrants of various cultural heritages, Whites who work as textile workers, domestic workers, support staff, or professionals, the experience of living as a woman in these different places is different for each woman. At the same time each woman lives in relation to the largely invisible sexual contract which institutionalizes sexual harassment, keeps money for day care out of reach for most women, directs the majority of women into low paying jobs, and causes women to drop out of high-ranking corporate positions where independent authority is mandatory. The "chilly climate" that women experience when they choose to enter male-dominated positions is largely a consequence of viewing women as heretics and outsiders. The attitude that "If you don't like it here, you can go back to where you came from" excuses sexist jokes, sexual harassment, excluding women from social gatherings after work or at lunch time, ignoring women's suggestions in the board room but listening when a man repeats it. I don't mean to say that men have it easy in the workplace. Any person working in a hierarchical workplace suffers from the restricting effects of being dominated that limit a person's energy and creativity. Sexual domination-subordination is, however, an additional form of domination for women.

Recognizing the oppressions of men in the workplace or the lack of rights of disempowered men is as necessary as recognizing the problems for women. A major difference, though, is the added complication of the basic hierarchical relation between the sexes which has not been part of the analysis of individual rights but which has structured the separation between private and public and the corresponding division of labour within each sector and between them. Rights for women and men are translated into different realities because of the hidden sexual contract which puts men at an advantage with regard to domination. Women's work and economics reflects belief in a dependent ontological and, accordingly, social status in ways that men's does not. The struggle between the labour of love and paid labour is an everyday struggle for many women in a more pervasive way than it is for men.

Work and Economics

Structuring social relations in terms of public and private was devastating for women's participation as citizens in the public realm where pay for work is the single most important indicator of social status and authority. The public-private division corresponds to the culture-nature binarism. The work of nature is not calculated into statistics pertaining to national economies (e.g., Estor 1987; Waring 1988). Work in the private sphere is considered work that is natural to women's natures. Giving birth is perceived largely as a natural event, with no real agency on the part of women. In this view of women their pregnancies, childbirths, and nursing are not considered to be illustrations of power, which is associated with achievement and rewarded with social authority. Women's elemental power such as giving birth and producing milk to maintain the life of the child are part of nature. Because women's bodies have this power that is largely exempt from the controls imposed by culture, it is very often excluded from consideration of work activities. Child care is carried out mostly by women, largely because it is generally believed that women have a natural talent for it and men do better competitively in the paid labour force. The reduction of women's natures to their natural functions and the trivialization of nature contributed to the devaluation of women's activities in both the home and in the paid labour force. Because women were assigned the position of nature in the social order, their assigned work was considered to be natural to them, namely, caretaking activities. With respect to a woman's work in the home, Marita Estor says, "because her labour fits her nature it requires no recognition, and receives no attention. It is carried out within a domestic family space, is invisible, is unpaid, and bestows no honour or power on her" (1987:3). Women's work in the paid labour force is often seen as an extension of what is natural to women's natures, as expressed in the home. That is sometimes taken as a justification for not expecting women to either demand or to receive fair payment and employment opportunities.

According to Marilyn Waring (1988) work is defined by the International Labor Organization (ILO) as activity that is paid, productive, and of value. If it cannot be included in the statistical accounts of the national economy then it is considered of no real value, i.e., non-productive work. Women's work in the home, women's work in subsistence farming, and women's volunteer work are all non-productive within the ILO's definition of work. Accordingly, their activities are not part of social policy considerations that are based on productive labour. It is not "economically active" work and is not part of an economic model used for "factual predictions." Women's work that is "non-productive" is not included in economic theory that influences how national accounts are organized and which work is supported, encouraged, and granted power and prestige. Waring claims that if women's work counted as productive work, national systems of accounts would necessarily have to redistribute budget allocations to work that supports the life flow of human beings in relation to nature. In economic theory, as discussed by Waring, labour refers to "those activities that produce surplus value" (1992:518). Surplus value is market value. Preconception arrangements have market value. In contrast, subsistence farming, which might include walking for several hours carrying water, labouring in the fields on a crop that does not go to market, searching for wood, fixing tools, or caring for sick animals is not considered production in the market production models used by members of the United Nations that shape economists' and politicians' social policy decisions.

Because child care in Canada is not visible in a market production model of work, it receives little attention in the national budget or in social policy formulation. For example, in March 1992 the federal government eliminated its proposed child care program and revised the existing baby bonus program. Plans for a national day care program were withdrawn after the government canvassed the population and found that allegedly only 25 percent were in favour of the proposed program. The wording of the question to the public helped to illicit the answer the government wanted. The people surveyed were asked "to rank the priority of a national child care program alongside programs which dealt with issues like drugs and child abuse" (Madden 1992:3). Joanne Oberg, president of the Canadian Day Care Advocacy Association (CDCAA), says that "Pitting child care against other essential children's programs is a shameful tactic. It's like asking whether it's more important to treat a broken leg or smallpox" (Madden 1992:3, quoting Oberg). The Canadian budget, like those of most other United Nations members, does not give priority to child-rearing expenses.[22] It is expected that the family organize their family-work relations so that they can manage their own child rearing. The problem with this solution is that women continue to be the primary caretakers even when they work outside the home (for example, see Arlie Hochschild, 1989).

Waring claims that the question which eventually led to the development of the United Nations System of National Accounts (to which all United Nations member subscribe) arose in the mind of John Maynard Keynes in Britain soon after the outbreak of the second world war. It was How do we pay for the war? Richard Stone joined Keynes in writing the paper, "The National Income and Expenditure of the United Kingdom, and How to Pay for the War." Waring says, "this document formed the foundation of Stone's further work, during peacetime to develop the uniform accounting system subsequently adopted by the United Nations" (1988:54-55). Members of the United Nations then measured their nation's economic health in terms of war and defense budgets. In the United Nations System of National Accounts, social welfare programs are secondary to war and defense programs. Productive work is that which contributes to a national budget. The emphasis in a market production model of work is on economic growth. The orientation toward economic growth motivates the more centralized countries such as Canada, the United States, Britain, France, Germany, and Japan to exploit the natural and human resources of Third World countries. The Gross Domestic Product (GDP) is a measure of economic growth. According to Waring, it has replaced the Gross National Product (GNP) in most countries, but not in the United States. She says that the "GDP supposedly measures production that generates income in a nation's economy, *whether the resources are owned by that country's residents or not*" (Waring 1988:71). Non-resident ownership was not part of GNP but is included in GDP. That allows owners from outside a country to contribute to its GDP. Measuring economic growth in terms of the GDP justifies foreign ownership. The combination

of foreign ownership and low wages in agricultural-based economies contributes to global manipulation of the economy by a few owners, with the
majority working for poverty level wages.

Work that does not contribute to economic growth measured in the
GDP is considered non-productive work. Because men's work contributes
more to the GDP, it gets more attention in development policies. As Waring notes, however, women, do most of the work in Third World agricultural economies. When they have no place to work in their home countries they often become part of the international distribution of Third
World women as domestics and service industry workers. They are slotted
into the lowest end of the economies of centralized nations. When reces-
sions occur in those countries, such as in Canada currently, immigration
barriers become more obstructionistic. The use of women for the profit of
others, whether they are working in their own home, in the homes of others, or in the public sphere as support staff or cleaning staff is widespread
and usually taken for granted. One reason for such exploitation is that
women's work is closely associated with their alleged natural abilities or
inabilities.

Power relations between the sexes manifests itself most clearly in the
form of oppression of women. There is no area of work that escapes the
hierarchal power relations between men and women. When the focus is
on women in the professions, rather than on women at the bottom end of
the labour force or on those who are not counted in the evaluation of productive labour, systemic limitation of women's power continues to be
widespread. A 1992 study conducted by Catalyst, a New York-based non-
profit research organization reveals that it is not only the "glass ceiling"
that women have to contend with but also "invisible walls" (Lopez
1992:B1). Moving up the ladder to high-level management positions
requires moving laterally to gain necessary related work experience. "According to the report, women tend to be placed in staff or support positions in areas such as public relations and human resources and are often
steered away from jobs in core areas such as marketing, production and
sales" (Lopez 1992:B1). At lower levels women get directed into support
positions. Lopez points out that "women account for as many as half of
the professional employees in the largest industrial and service companies, yet they hold fewer than 5 per cent of the senior management positions. And most of the senior jobs they do hold are in areas such as human resources, finance or public relations" (Lopez 1992:B4). Women in
business, like women in the service sector, function primarily to support
men in power over them. The segregation of women through construction
of glass walls is the modern version of occupational segregation, according to Myra Strober, a labour economist at Stanford University (Lopez
1992:B4).

Women in the medical profession in Québec practise less medicine
than their male colleagues, according to a study undertaken at the

Université de Montréal's medical school. The study looked at trends between 1978 and 1988 with respect to women in medical school and the medical profession. During that decade there was a greater increase in the percentage of female physicians in Québec than in the rest of Canada or in the United States: from 11 percent to 22 percent. Nicole Dedobbeleer, who led the study, reported that women now outnumber men in medical schools in Québec. Yet, they "devote fewer hours to their practice, earn less money, opt for general practice rather than specializing, choose the more traditionally female and less lucrative specialities, work in wage-earning institutions rather than self-employed private practices" (Ruvinsky 1992:A12).

A study of women in the legal profession was conducted at the University of British Columbia because women were ceasing to renew their memberships in the Law Society of British Columbia at greater rates than men. The society wanted to know why. A 1991 study results show that the high drop-out rate contrasted sharply with the increase in women entering the profession. "Between 1986 and 1990 the number of women in the profession increased by 58 percent (the increase in men was 12 percent). For the past ten years almost half of the law school graduates in B.C. have been women" (Young 1991:5). The study shows that more women than men are employed in Government or in staff positions; 80.1 percent of males and 62.7 of females describe themselves in private practice; 8 percent of women and 2.7 percent of men are not actively employed. Two broad areas of concern for women were identified: (1) flexible work hours and periods of paid and unpaid leave; and (2) discrimination in hiring, remuneration, promotion and advancement, as well as in sexual harassment (p. 9).[23] The study reveals disproportionate power relations between the sexes in the most prestigious professions. A possible skewing factor of this study is that it focusses on large firms in high-density areas rather than in smaller communities where lawyers might have greater flexibility. It is reasonable to expect to find more women in less stressful law practices in smaller centres. The 'reasonableness' of this assumption, however, cannot be separated from the widespread pattern of women seeking jobs that are compatible with child rearing. A more recent study of women lawyers was conducted by the Law Society of Alberta (Brockman 1992:74). The findings were similar to those of the British Columbia study. Nearly all the women lawyers surveyed and more than three-quarters of the men lawyers believe there is bias against women in the profession. With respect to 'Remuneration and Job Security,' the overall mean income for women per year was $63,518, while for men it was $94, 314. The average hours worked per week for women was 50.9 and for men it was 50.6. Salaries were not commensurate with hours worked. The 1992 Alberta study indicates that the vast majority of both female and male lawyers live in Calgary or Edmonton. Almost 91 percent of the female lawyers and 83 percent of the male lawyers live in one of the two major Alberta cities. The findings from the smaller centres were not obviously different from those in the larger ones.

I do not intend to go into every profession or area of work to illustrate the imbalance in power relations that is connected to the view of women as being closer to nature and therefore of less monetary value. An academic who chooses to have babies or who merely is female has the same kind of concerns as women doctors and lawyers. If a woman rejects the option of trying to "be one of the boys" and lives out her life as a woman who is not ashamed of that fact but rather enjoys her femaleness, then she has to do something about the systemic undermining of women's work and, accordingly, their well-being because they are women.

The dominating power of men is intrinsic to patriarchal reproductive consciousness. In Mary O'Brien's view (1989), reproducing the world is about two things: thinking about the world and acting in it. She claims that males have the power to both define the world as they experience it and act in it according to their epistemological assumptions which exclude the power of women to do the same. She points out five ways in which male power is exercised in patriarchal reproductive consciousness. In O'Brien's view (1989: 11) men have power to (1) regard their relation to the natural world as antagonistic; (2) define women as part of nature; (3) divide public from private life; (4) insist that men must rule each of these domains; and (5) define the continuity of the species as a 'motherhood issue,' which has more to do with nature than culture and is more suitable to women's intellectual interests than men's. Because of the asymmetry in power to reproduce the world, women are caught inside a cage constructed by patriarchal reproductive consciousness.

Marilyn Frye (1992) examines the meaning of oppression by focussing on the notion of 'press' inside the term 'oppression.' When something is put into a press it is "caught in a bind, caught between systematically related pressures" (1992:53). She defines oppression of women as "a network of forces and barriers which are systematically related and which conspire to the immobilization, reduction and molding of women and the lives we live" (1992:55). She differentiates oppression from suffering. In her view, suffering has to do with certain limitations in the system. Oppression, by contrast, is systemic. She describes men's suffering in patriarchy, such as not being able to cry in front of other men, as a limitation of patriarchal culture. It does not prevent men from participating as full citizens in the running of the nation. It is not, therefore, regarded as an aspect of systemic discrimination. I agree with her view that unless we differentiate between isolated limitations and systemic oppression, discussion of women's oppression within the context of pervasive male domination gets obscured by male concerns. That is not to deny ways in which patriarchal culture restricts self-determination for men. Rather it is to bring into focus the pervasive strands of oppression that keep women from full citizenship participation. Men's difficulties in patriarchy are important considerations. They are, however, of a different order than those of women. Frye claims that the multitude of barriers that confront women function to protect men's superior citizenship. Sometimes the same barriers that were constructed to exclude women from full citizenship also negatively affect men. For example, some men suffer from not being free to be househusbands. There has, however, not been a rush of men into the home in the same way as women have gone out of the home to work. I do not believe that economics is the only reason why men have not readily left their positions of power and prestige to do low valued work in the home.

In Frye's view, which I support, men often have legitimate complaints of limitations but not of systemic oppression. I do not intend to imply that Native men, Black men, Coloured men, and so forth do not experience systemic oppression. My claim is restricted to saying they do not experience oppression because they are men. Marilyn Frye uses the bird cage as a metaphor for women's oppression in patriarchy. When the focus of attention is limited to one wire, the cage as a whole is not seen. The pervasiveness of oppression is invisible unless the cage is seen. The bird in the cage cannot get out unless several of the wires are broken. Seeing the wires as part of a complex whole is a condition for breaking the wires and dismantling the cage.

The bird in the cage is only part of the metaphor of oppression of women, from Frye's point of view. Another aspect has to do with the kinds of birds in the cage. Inhabitants of the cage are there because they are members of a social category (race, class, ethnic group, sexual orientation, age, ability, etc.). A person is not oppressed *merely* as an individual. That is not to say that individuals are not oppressed as individuals. Rather, I mean to say that each person is seen by others to have a group affiliation, regardless of whether or not that particular person identifies with the group. For example, a Canadian of Japanese heritage may identify himself as a Canadian rather than a Japanese. During World War II, however, Canadians and Americans of Japanese heritage were interned in prisoner-of-war camps because Japan was at war with Canada and the United States. The self-identity, as Canadian or American, of those interned was of no consequence in the decision to declare them Japanese and barricade them in camps. Group identification is a condition for oppression of any person. Just as an individual is identified in terms of nationality, skin colour, age, and so forth, females and males within every group are identified in terms of their sex.[24] Frye says, "to recognize a person as oppressed, one has to see that individual *as* belonging to a group of a certain sort" (1992:56). The invisibility of women as a group and women's oppression as a social fact are due largely to the membership of women in different groups, each with different immediate concerns. For example, some Native women in Canada are struggling with their communities for more equitable participation in their male-dominated communities as well as struggling alongside their men for more equitable participation in Canadian society. Women from the Philippines who come to Canada as domestic servants and send their money back home (which contributes to their own country's GDP) often live in fear of being deported because of their expendability during a recession.

Apart from employment issues, immigrant women in their own homes sometimes live in fear of being deported by their husbands if they don't satisfy his interests. The majority of immigrant women (from countries other than England and United States) enter Canada as dependents of their husbands.[25] They are disadvantaged in the language because they do not qualify for free English-language courses as their husbands do if they are working. In addition, some husbands do not want their wives learning English because that will increase their independence and threaten the husband's control over his wife. Immigrant women have begun to organize around their rights. Their membership in the category 'immigrant,' however, keeps them in a cage in ways that White, English-speaking, professional women do not experience. The combination of categories is unlimited and the complexity of oppression of women is extensive. Interacting structures of oppression are experienced differently by each woman. I agree with Frye that differences among women do not invalidate the category 'woman.' Both women and men are oppressed as members of races, classes, ethnic groups, and so on, but within these different groups "women are oppressed *as women*, [whereas] men are not oppressed *as men*" (Frye 1992:61). I share Frye's bewilderment about how we could be confused about so simple a thing.

Lack of access to resources is intrinsic to the oppression of women. Women and children occupy the category of 'poorest human beings.' The widespread poverty of women and their children is both an indication of lack of power and a cause of it. In a California study, Ruth Sidel (1992:493) notes that when women get divorced they become, on average, 73 percent poorer than they were in marriage, while men become 42 percent richer. There are few incentives for women to live as full-fledged citizens, i.e., as independent women. Women's wages are lower than men's (they average around seventy cents to each man's dollar in estimates of comparable worth—work of equal value); most jobs are segregated so that women do not move laterally or vertically as easily as men; work in the public sphere is often organized as if it were independent of the workers' private lives. While an increasing number of men are taking more responsibility in the home, most child care work as well as housework is done by women (e.g., Hochschild 1989). An important component of child care is emotional work. This is often more part of the mother's relationship with the children than of the father's. It is a main reason why there is scepticism towards women with respect to their loyalty to their paid workplace. Women take more time off from work than their husbands to stay home with a child who is ill. They generally spend more time thinking about the well-being of their children. Women's private lives often are not as easily separated from their public lives as men's are. A positive consequence is that women usually stay more connected to their families than men do. Men more often sink into a quiet desperation of loneliness because of their patterns of separating their private and public activities. The cultural emphasis on men's financial success in the public domain has resulted in men paying insufficient attention to their families in favour of cultural achievement. This has been supported by women. The asymmetry between cultural expectations of women and men in work achievement levels has inhibited opportunities for men to participate more in home responsibilities and has inhibited rewards for women who wish to have families and to work in their chosen capacity outside the home. Because women are so often stretched between the home and their paid workplace they have little energy to organize themselves to gain more satisfactory salaries.

Workers in unions fare better generally than non-unionized work-ers.[26] Women often do not participate in union activities, however, be-cause of their double work shifts outside and inside the home. The femini-zation of the labour force (more women than men entering the work-force) goes hand-in-hand with the feminization of poverty (many more women than men living in poverty). According to a Canadian Labour Con-gress report (1989), two thirds of Canada's labour force is not unionized. Part-time work is a large category that is non-unionized. It is done largely by women, without any benefits gained by unionized pressure on man-agement. Benefits won by unions such as grievance procedures, regular hours, overtime conditions, holidays, job security, paid leave, and health benefits are not available to part-time workers. Of part-time workers in Canada, 70 percent are women, most of whom are immigrant women. The need to unionize part-time employees is obvious in light of the pover-ty strata that the majority of women occupy because of their low wages, accompanied by no job security. Between 1980 and 1986 female mem-bership in unions grew six times as fast as men's, according to Andrea Waywanko (1989).

The issue of pay equity (equal work, equal treatment, equal pay) is gaining greater visibility as a result of women's political activity in unions. The effects of pay equity legislation introduced in Minnesota, Manitoba, and Ontario since the early 1980s, however, have not yielded the results that were hoped for (Waywanko 1989:8). Revisions are required with re-spect to how job worth is measured. The Ontario Public Service Employ-ees Union (OPSEU), for example, suggests that a pay equity formula be developed that is free of the gender bias which currently privileges male-associated qualities.[27] Rather than excluding casual worker positions and all-women job categories in their selection of job samples, it is suggested that all employees be included in the formula for evaluating work. As it is, the male component in the workplace is required for establishing "comparative worth." It is as if it is impossible to evaluate women's work, such as most child care, when it can not be compared to a man's job. If women's work is to be evaluated as a normal form of work, then it is important to stop taking men's work as the only viable standard from which to measure the value of women's work.

Non-unionized, ghettoized women's work that does not fall under the guidelines of pay equity is further problematized by privatization. Privatization is "the selling or giving up of public services or companies to the private sector" (Farkas 1989:10). Services are market driven rather than policy driven. Service workers do not thrive in an economy driven by profit. Rather than improving services because of competitiveness, corporate consolidation often occurs. This means less competition and more centralized employer control of wages. Unions lose power through corporate consolidation, whether it occurs through internal national privatization or international trade relations.[28] The feminization of the labour force and the feminization of poverty are part of the world market in which women's work at the bottom of the structure in general, and in each workplace in particular, characterizes much of women's institutionalized oppression. The systematic restriction of power constitutes the nature of institutionalized oppression. Male power to describe and organize the world is asymmetrical with women's power. That asymmetry is the basis for oppression that restricts women to alleged non-productive 'natural' places and devalues their contributions to defined productive 'social' spaces. In order to deconstruct patriarchal reproductive consciousness it is important that women experience their power-full-ness in reproducing the world.

Hilary Lips describes power as "the capacity to have an impact on one's environment, to be able to make a difference through one's actions" (1992:500). Power has to do with change. Feminists aim to change the world through the redistribution of power in gender relations. Those women and men, on the other hand, who wish patriarchal reproductive consciousness to remain intact are right to worry about the effects of feminism. The backlash against feminism during the 1980s and early 1990s (e.g., Faludi 1991) is an indication of resistance to feminists' attempts to dismantle the bird cages. Lips points out that there is incongruity between images of femininity and images of power. One set of images has to do with weakness and the other with strength. As Lips claims, helplessness is the opposite of power. In her view, crucial resources for power come with employment. They include income, status, knowledge, and social networks. Because men's income, status, knowledge, and social networks add up to more power than women's, their lifestyles are usually emulated by both women and men. They are at the top of the charts while women are at the bottom. Power is often associated with being right. Accepting the 'rightness' of men's lifestyles leads to the perpetuation of the status quo. Women, as well as men, strive to be like the men at the top. This way of thinking and acting reinforces economic theories built around men's experiences of "productive" lifestyles and perpetuates patriarchal reproductive consciousness. It supports the defined antagonistic relation between culture and nature. What needs to happen instead, suggests Lips, is a critique of a system that defines men's lifestyles as right. In order to deconstruct the belief that men are right because they are on top, it is important to look at the relation between 'right' and 'smart.'

In April 1992, a study of perceived gendered intelligence conducted in Edinburgh, Scotland was reported in Canadian newspapers. Male students generally estimated their intelligence to be higher than it actually was, while female students estimated theirs to be lower. Both generally viewed their mothers' intelligence to be lower than their fathers.' These findings are consistent with those from a Canadian survey on young women (Holmes and Silverman 1992), which was released the same month. Along the same lines, Gloria Steinem (1992) wrote her popular book on self-esteem because she sees it as a fundamental issue in the feminist struggle for freedom from the cage. Women's self-esteem and confidence to take on challenging activities is seriously undermined by the pervasiveness of denigrating cultural attitudes towards women's intelligence.

The pervasive and unfair association of women with stupidity is painful. I will refer to my mother's experience as an example. My mother, Dora, read the April 1992 report in the newspapers about the students believing that their fathers were more intelligent than their mothers. It brought back memories from home when she was raising four children, working in the 'bush' every day with her husband, cooking for hired men, keeping the house in order, and making sure the cow, pigs, geese, chickens, horses, sheep, dogs, and cats were looked after by either herself or one of the children. Sometimes looking after the animals included bringing sick ones into the kitchen so they could stay warm behind the cookstove. She cooked everything on the wood and coal stove. She heated water on it for washing the members of the family, dishes, and clothes. The water had to be packed in buckets from the creek about two hundred metres from the house. The coal-oil lamp chimneys had to be cleaned from soot so we could see across the room. The fly droppings on the windows had to be scraped off periodically so we could see out the windows, especially towards the west in the evening. The plastic that covered the windows in the winter had to be carefully removed and stored, minimizing the rips so the same plastic could be used the next winter. That meant, among other things, carefully extracting the small nails from the thin pieces of wood that were hammered into the window frames each fall. The nails were saved and straightened so they could be used in the fall to put the plastic back over the windows.

In addition to the endless work that was required for everyday living, Mom lived with a sense of self-worth. Her own strength of character provided a model for all of us, two girls and two boys. She had grown up in Eagle Butte, the southern part of the Cypress Hills in Alberta on a ranch.

Her parents had come from England to be pioneers. Or rather, her father wanted to be a pioneer. Her mother came because she was his bride. The move to Canada was a mistake for my grandmother. She rejected the pioneer life but could not escape it. She arrived in the 'God-forsaken' countryside of Eagle Butte at the beginning of the twentieth century. She cast her eye around the lonely landscape, took her big London hats out of their boxes, stomped on all of them, and declared that she would never need them again as long as she lived. As her life wore on in the lonely hills of Eagle Butte, she bore five children, three of whom survived. She died when Mom (Dora) was sixteen. Later that year Dora married a handsome man from Winnipeg who came to work on her father's ranch. He was regarded by the neighbours as an intelligent man.

The funny thing about intelligence is how it is measured. Dad could read and critique in clever ways, but he couldn't put the harness on the horse so it would stay put. He couldn't figure out which end was supposed to go by the horse's neck and which was to go under the tail. He also didn't seem to be able to figure out how to organize money so that it would be available when needed. But he was known around the countryside for his wit and congeniality. He knew how to use words to have the effect he wanted. For example, late one afternoon when I was a teenager I was standing outside the house talking with a friend. Dad thought I had been talking to him long enough and wanted me to come inside to get dinner ready. He came out of the house and said in a very endearing and amusing way, "Winnie, come on inside and fry the lettuce." If I hadn't gone inside the next remark would not have been so amusing. It definitely wouldn't have been endearing. His message was conveyed emphatically but cleverly in a way that one couldn't help but love him for it. He was considered a smart man by almost anyone who had anything to say about him. He had big dreams that he attempted to fulfill. People around him had to put considerable energy into the practical matters of living. Mom was the central character in that drama. Her intelligence was manifest as common sense intelligence (which isn't to say she didn't also have the kind which is measured more abstractly). Common sense intelligence rarely gets much credit.

When my mother read the recent report in the newspaper about students evaluating their fathers' intelligence to be higher than their mothers,' she said it reminded her of when people used to say, "your children are all like their father, except for one who is dumb like his mother."[29] My sister had a doll that we called Dumb Dora because Dad said she was like Mom. As soon as you laid her down her eyes closed and she went to sleep. Mom's tendency to go to sleep immediately after she lay down was likely due to exhaustion; however, it was blindly associated with stupidity.

The association of women with stupidity contributes to the ethos that women do not need education. The illiteracy rate of women in the world is considerably higher than that of men. According to a 1992 United

Nations report about two thirds of the illiterate people of the world are women (reported in *The Globe and Mail*, April 29, 1992:A2). The same report states that boys are twice as likely as girls to go to secondary schools in Africa and many other countries. Third World women, with the highest rate of illiteracy, are at the very bottom of the world power system. The pervasive privileging of boys over girls in family decisions about where the money goes for children's education is reinforced by youths' demeaning attitudes towards their mothers' intelligence, as described in the Edinburgh study. Family scripts perpetuate stereotypes about gender and intelligence. These scripts support the marginalization of women in workplaces and feed into the increasing poverty of women and their children throughout the world.

Just as there is something askew with a system in which men are generally located at the top of the power structures and women generally at the bottom, so there is something off-balance when common sense intelligence is valued less than abstract reasoning, whether it pertains to women or men. There is also a perniciousness in assuming that intelligence, in whatever form, is gendered. It is a self-fulfilling prophecy. In a system in which it is normal for men to have greater resources, men's power of authority is experienced as natural, while women's is more often regarded with scepticism. This imbalance of gendered power relations is reinforced by, for example, family scripts that rate the father's intelligence higher than the mother's and by public institutions that allocate more resources and visibility to men's activities. Women's place in both private and public activities is often characterized by derived power that they claim through their shaded place alongside the men who occupy positions of power in the sunshine of cultural achievement.

There are different ways of realigning the relations between gender images and power images. One is to get more women into positions of power where they can serve as models of women with their own power. Another way is to change the cultural orientation of power from domination to one in which power is used to bring together in a balanced way the kinds of work that people do as members of social communities. The latter approach involves new economic theory that is focussed on realigning the relations between power and gender images. It includes restructuring the distribution of wealth, changing the ways of measuring work value and productivity, and developing new images of female power in which women as reproducers are experienced as active agents in post-patriarchal reproductive consciousness.

A model for the development of new economic theorizing is found in the work of Hilkka Pietilä, a Finnish economist working on a 'new model for global economics' (Waring 1988:299). The model is oriented toward the maintenance of well-being in a community rather than market price that can be statistically recorded. Pietilä's model makes the household economy visible in the records of productive work. In her paper, "Tomorrow Begins Today,"[30] Pietilä suggests three circles of economic productivity, based on Finland's economy in 1980. The central and most dominant circle is the "Free Economy." It refers to non-monetary work and production that people do to maintain the well-being of the community. According to Pietilä, 54 percent of the people's time and 35 percent of the money of the national economy belongs to the "Free Economy" at the centre of three concentric circles. The second circle (the middle one) is called the "Protected Sector." It consists of home market and public service work such as the construction of houses, food production, schools, health, and other community services which are not tightly controlled by the world economy. The legislation for these community services is local or national, but not internationally directed. This sector accounts for 36 percent of the total amount of work time and involves 46 percent of the national accounts. Compared to the "Free Economy," work in the "Protected Sector" occupies 18 percent less working hours but 11 percent more of the money in the national budget. The third circle, the outer ring, is called the "Fettered Economy." It is concerned with large-scale production and is fettered to the world market. Prices, competiveness, and demand are determined by the international market, according to Marilyn Waring's account of Pietilä's schema (1988). Of the total number of working hours, 10 percent are devoted to this part of the economy, while 19 percent of the budget is allocated to work that is determined by the world market. From Pietilä's and Waring's point of view, the United Nations System of National Accounts is organized so that the "whole life of society is geared to support this sector [Fettered Economy] while it accounts for a modest proportion of total production in any one nation and in the world" (Waring 1988:301). Given current values, the Fettered Economy is the heart of the formal economies. It is the aspect of production that is directed at the export market, driven by the demands the world economy.

In contrast to the formal economy, Third World countries depend heavily on an informal economy, which "meets the requirements of the domestic market" (Harrison 1991:177). The informal economy can be related to Pietilä's Protected Sector, as well as to her category of Free Economy, where prices are regulated locally or work is done without payment. Harrison found in her study of Jamaican women that workers in the informal economy are usually 'surplus' population: "the dislocated peasants, displaced and landless wageworkers, and the marginally self-employed" (1991:177) who are casualties dating back from "the consolidation of the capitalist mode at the turn of the century" (p. 176). Harrison states that the women who occupy the lowest strata of Jamaican society are "women who represent some of the most marginal segments of the working class and aged dependents" (p. 174). She says that because women in Third World countries generally earn less than men, "Third World women represent a *cheaper than cheap* segment of the international work force." The interaction of class and gender, along with racism, in the face of imperialism and colonialism yields the situation of "superexploitation" of all Third World workers, but especially of women.

The formal economy of each country as well as the world market depends on the informal work to balance the payments. In Jamaica, for example, the informal economy dealing in ganga (marijuana) carried the national economy through the economic crises of the 1970s. Harrison points out that "While it may be clear that informal economic processes are subordinate to and dependent upon formally recognized economic sectors, it is also important to realize that capitalist accumulation itself is dependent upon the subsistence-oriented and other petty-scale activities of the informal sphere" (1991:178). The fettered economy is not fettered exclusively to the world market but also to the free economy as well as the protected sector. Without exploitation of the majority of the world population that exists in the margins, it would not be possible for the countries at the centre (industrialized ones) to be so 'developed.'

Mexico is a good example of a country where the informal economy is essential to the functioning of the formal economy.[31] After World War II, development projects were initiated in many communities to replace subsistance existence with services that facilitated better living conditions for the local people. The population of Mexico City increased from three million in 1964 to between sixteen and twenty million in 1992. The most marginalized communities missed out on the development of new services that were built by the central bureaucracy during the period of rapid expansion. Because they could not satisfactorily exist at a decreasing subsistence level they set up a 'new commons' system. The old European 'commons' system was organized around community squares where members of the communities controlled their local affairs. With the rise of capitalism in Europe the commons were appropriated by centralized governments. The idea of the 'new commons' is not that they will be appropriated but that they will be recognized for their contributions to the formal economy and incorporated into the national accounting system and policy-making decisions. Residents living in the 'new commons' communities work together to develop services that they need, such as houses, toilets, schools. Gustavo Esteva believes that money from locally organized businesses and modes of production outweighs the formal economy in its contribution to Mexico's national budget. In his view, the formal economy would benefit from incorporating the so-called informal economies into its own system rather than ignoring their contributions or blocking them through bureaucratic obstruction. In his view, development would surge ahead if it was grounded in the needs of the local communities and used the labour resources of these communities. The value of work in terms of its contribution to the well-being of the community is basic to the 'new commons' approach. As it is, the 'new commons' are marginalized in the development programs in Mexico. The programs which are funded are most often shaped by the suggestions from a central directorate that might be out of touch with the needs of the diverse communities. As indicated by Esteva, the viability of the Mexican economy depends on the success of the 'new commons' approach, which gives priority to the needs of the particular communities in the development of work projects.

A similar kind of approach is found in British Columbia, Canada in the WomenFutures Community Economic Development (CED) Society (Alderson and Conn 1988). "The goal is to gain greater community control over the resources of the community through the creation of stable employment, the investment of capital and the utilization of local resources" (1988:1). They established a WomenFutures loan guarantee fund. It guarantees loans to selected proposed businesses controlled by women. The rationale behind the organization is the recognition that women often cannot secure financing because "they have difficulty meeting the security requirements of financial institutions" (WomenFutures Loan Guarantee Fund brochure). Examples of eligible activities are (1) the establishment of an income-generating agricultural business by a rural-based non-profit society; and (2) renovating a retail outlet shared by a group of craftswomen. The idea is to facilitate women working together for the well-being of the community in addition to making a living from their work. Members of the Society can make returnable contributions or donations to the fund. In that way many people can contribute to the development of a variety of businesses. This type of local economic development around the needs of the community is an example of work that is productive while it strengthens the well-being of the community through participation.

The work of Esteva from Mexico and the WomenFutures Community Economic Development Society of British Columbia fit well into the economic model posited by Hilkka Pietilä. Pietilä suggests that value of work with respect to its contribution to the well-being of a community can be measured by using *volume* of work as an evaluative criterion. Volume refers to labour power (number of workers and number of hours). It might be expressed in physical units or in the number of people cared for. From the use of volume as a criterion for the value of work, economic theories and social policies would flow more from value of services for the well-being of the community than from statistics which serve the interests of those who are working with a budget that does not take the informal economy into account. Work takes on a different meaning if its value is also assessed in terms of caring rather than exclusively in relation to market value which can be recorded statistically.

Qualitative measurement of productive work expands the possibilities for economic models and theorizing. Waring suggests that activities count as work when "there is a market equivalent, where obvious skills are involved, where there is obvious production . . ." (1988:142). Productive work would then include giving birth, volunteer work, studying, mowing the lawn, painting the trim on one's house, or on a neighbour's house. She suggests that on the census form the term "main activity" should replace "work" when citizens are asked what they do. Her activism in New Zealand to get the census form changed to be more representative of what people actually do has led to the inclusion of the following list in the 1986 New Zealand census. The question asked was: "What is your main work or activity?" The list of choices is as follows: (1) home duties—looking after children; (2) home duties—not looking after children; (3) full-time student; (4) retired; (5) unemployed; (6) paid job, business, farming, profession; (7) unpaid work in a family business; and (8) other (such as hospital patient). Please state _____ (Waring 1988:142-43). Waring did not get the term "work" exchanged for "main activity"; however, the phrase "main work or activity" was accepted in the place of "work" alone. The new phrase allows for both criteria (volume and market value) in the assessment of work.

In addition to integrating different kinds of work activities, it is important to connect these activities to the well-being of the ecology. I agree with Waring's view that in order for work to be related sensitively to the ecosystem, it is necessary that information about renewable and non-renewable resources be used as guidelines for productive work that is compatible with the survival of the planet. Two different accounts of non-renewable resource depletion are offered by Waring. Excessive resource depletion occurs when "the exploitation of these resources is greater than their carrying capacity measured by their natural rate of regeneration" and/or "if it results in relatively diminished levels of well-being for future generations" (Waring 1988:303). If neither the natural environment nor the human environment can replenish or recycle sufficiently to overcome the damage caused, then use of resources is excessive and unjust. The abuse of the earth in these accounts resembles burnout or severe exploitation in people such as Blacks, the household labour of women who sustain the market value of work of others, or the labour of Chinese indentured immigrants to Canada who worked on the railroad and died anonymously, largely for the benefit of White Anglo-Saxon Canadians. The orientation towards exploitation is an important concern with respect to the well-being of everyone in relation to the ecosystem. It is of particular concern to women because of the sexual exploitation that is often integral to their economic exploitation.

Pietilä's and Waring's economics reflects the concerns of women's reproductive consciousness with respect to themselves as women as well as the relations between human beings and the earth. The well-being of communities, including women, children, and men, in this view depends on integrating the public and private spheres in the lives of each person. Redefining work as one's main activity and, thereby, including the work of caring in the evaluation of productive labour is an important move toward realigning images of power and gender images. In this schema, all the images are transformed through reinterpretation of power as well as of femininity and masculinity. It is a move in the direction of power-full-ness through connectedness to others. The labour of love is counted into the evaluation of work. The status quo organization of work as exclusively a paid, public activity is no longer appropriate. Accordingly, the exclusively paid work-oriented lifestyle of men is not the esteemed paradigm to be applied to women's lives, or to be perpetuated in men's lives. Pietilä's model from Finland, Esteva's 'new commons' approach in Mexico, and the Vancouver WomanFutures program are examples of organizing the economy around local needs. Among other things, these models and programs serve to bridge the gap between work in the paid labour force and work in the family.

Working in the Family

Katherine Mansfield wrote in her journal in New Zealand in 1922: "Risk—risk anything. Care no more for the opinion of others, for those voices. Do the thing hardest on earth for you to do. Act for yourself. Face the Truth" (Waring 1988:14). For women who are socialized into mediating family relations, acting for themselves is, indeed, often the hardest thing to do. In addition to a belief that their interests are secondary to those of their mates and children, women generally have to risk poverty if they choose to act as citizens with independent rights. Waring says, "women are a Third World wherever we are: low on capital, low on technology, labor intensive, and a source of raw materials, maintenance, and underpaid or unpaid production for the more powerful" (1988:xix). The situation is not the same for all women. In some sense the equation between all women and the Third World trivializes the desperate conditions of Third World workers in the world economy and, in particular, Third World women's work. Even the practice of clustering Third World workers in one category obscures the vast differences encountered in various countries and periods in history.[32] Despite that caveat, there is value in stating the equation between women and the Third World. It underscores the systemic oppression of women that restricts their ability to act in their own interests.

The relations of families to the global economy are coextensive with the psychology of women's identity within the context of family relations. Ann Ferguson cites the 'mediation problem' as a factor in women's disempowerment in family relations (1989:94). In her view the construction of femininity includes the 'triangular gender identity.' The wife/mother is the mediator between children, mate, and self. She usually has more emotional investment in the children than the man has and acts as a mediator between the children's desire for nurturing and the man's desire for partnering. Ferguson suggests that masculinity is largely defined by possessing a wife or lovers as well as by male bonding. In light of that, a man (who is socialized into patriarchal masculinity) is usually more interested in connecting to the woman than to the young child. He is often jealous of the woman's time with the child. Ferguson describes the "emotional logic of this incorporative triangle" in the following way. The woman sacrifices her interests which are not defined through the child/mate/self bond. That leads to a bargaining imbalance which supports male dominance. She is less likely than the man to fight for her rights as an independent citizen because of her socialization into the role of mediator. Her position is weakened further if a strong father/son bond implicitly, or explicitly, includes depreciation of the mother.

This 'incorporative triangle' is illustrated in the film *Kramer vs Kramer*. The woman leaves the household one evening in a state of psychological turmoil. She leaves their seven-year-old son with his father because she thinks the boy would be better off with his father than with her, for the time being, because of her emotional state. The reason she left the household was that she could not bear to continue to live in the alienated relationship she had with her husband. She believed that it was driving her crazy. After being treated in therapy for nearly a year and a half and then securing a well-paying job, she informed her husband that she would be getting a divorce from him and claiming custody of their son. Although she won custody, she could not take their son out of his home, where he lived with his father. It was the home she had decorated with their interests at heart. She decided, painfully, to give up custody of their son for his sake. During her fifteen-month absence from the home, a healthy father/son bonding developed. The fact that the father finally took an interest in his son during those fifteen months had a strong emotional persuasiveness that was portrayed more vividly than the much longer period during which the mother was the primary caregiver. The court granted custody to the mother largely because she had a well-paying job and, therefore, could provide for the son better than could the father. Despite this court decision, the mother put the son's interests ahead of her own, not a unique situation, and allowed the son and father to remain together. She quickly became relatively peripheral in the lives of both the husband and the son, despite her marriage of eight years and mothering activities for five-and-a-half years. A message that could be drawn from the film was that the woman was good because she subsumed her own interests under those of others, especially her son.

The popular appeal of *Kramer vs. Kramer* is due partly to the fact that it conveys more than one major message. In addition to illustrating the 'incorporative triangle,' it also conveys the sensitivity of both parents to the well-being of the child. While the mother gave up custody of her son for his sake, the father gave up his job for the boy. A consequence of the departure of the mother was the bonding between the father and son. The father lost his job because he could not sustain the double shift , i.e., looking after his son as well as satisfying his boss in his paid job. He chose his son over his job, even though his boss had selected him for a privileged position. He took a lesser-paying job with another company so he would have more time with his son. It is possible that if he had done that before his wife left him, the family might have remained intact. The film highlights the stress that leads to personal and family collapses when the lust for power and ambition overshadows the well-being of people.

It could be argued that economics played an important part in the court's decision to award the mother custody of the boy. Although the mother in *Kramer vs. Kramer* won custody of her son, it was not only because of the argument for maternal rights. She had a well-paying job. One can speculate about whether she would have gained custody if she had a low-paying job, as most women do. The psychology of power relations in a family is connected to structural power relations in the economy. Widespread low wages of women in the paid labour force is connected to women's roles in the family. As women have significantly moved into waged work during the past twenty years, their rate of poverty has escalated. It has been increasing since the 1970s. According to Ferguson, over half of poor families in the United States are headed by women. While 50 percent of children in single White mother families are poor, 68 percent of children in single Black and Latin mother families live in poverty. Race, among other factors, compounds the gendered discrepancies in wages.

The majority of all single mothers are overburdened with respect to economic and labour responsibilities. While single mothers are overburdened in regard to both economics and work, mothers with partners are subject to overwork even though they may not be poor. Stress from working inside and outside the home is a serious consequence for many women, following the trend in the 1970s to work for pay. Arlie Hochschild (1989) conducted her influential study of young, employed couples with children after she experienced the problems of trying to teach in a university and look after her baby. She wondered where the children of her male colleagues were. Her study shows that only about 20 percent of the fathers spent as much time as the mothers looking after children and working in the home. Hochschild's study reveals that there is a wage gap between women and men in their paid jobs and a 'leisure gap' between them at home. Hochschild claims that studies indicate that "working mothers have higher self-esteem and get less depressed than housewives, but compared to their husbands, they're more tired and get sick more often" (1989:4). When Hochschild focussed on the feelings of women and men trying to juggle work inside and outside the home, she found that women in the more traditional couples did not want to complain about their heavy work loads because their husbands were 'helping them out.' Among the egalitarian couples (20 percent of the total), work in the home was assumed to be the responsibility of both parents and they spent equal time caring for the children and doing housework. In 80 percent of the families, however, the woman assumed more responsibility for both child care and housework.

Since the 1970s women have been moving into the paid labour force faster than men, but men have not moved very much into the unpaid labour force of the household (e.g., Jenson, Hagen, and Reddy 1988). During the 1980s a backlash to the feminization of the workplace emerged. The backlash to feminist attempts for reciprocity of wages and home responsibilities (Faludi 1991) has led to increased 'Momism' in the media.[33] 'Momism' is an ideology that assumes the naturalness of women as mothers in the home. It has moral implications, namely, that a good woman is a mom in the home. The corollary, 'Dadism,' does not have the emotional persuasiveness of 'Momism' because identities of fathers are more associated with cultural achievement than 'natural' functions. 'Dadism' did not take hold during the 1970s and 1980s, even though there was an increased awareness of the need for men to participate more in household work and childrearing activities. One reason for the reluctance of men to leave their jobs can be attributed to the wage gap between women and men. The one earning the most money is likely to be the one remaining in the paid job, while the lesser paid one cares for the children in the home, if it is economically possible for either parent to remain in the home. In the majority of families both parents work outside the home, with the consequence of 'the second shift' for both parents to some degree or one parent to a greater degree. Ironically, the women's movement is sometimes blamed for the plight of women today suffering from disproportionate work loads in their families.

Blaming feminists for the excessive stress felt by women as they attempt to juggle home and paid work is a way to avoid making the changes that need to be made if women are to assume their rights to participate fully in democracy. Part of a person's democratic rights is the right to work for pay. If that right is to be actualized in egalitarian ways, it is necessary to reconstruct paid work and family relations so there is more flexibility for both mothers and fathers to participate both outside and inside the home. Furthermore, it is possible that women's leadership styles will contribute to more humane working conditions outside the home. For example, Sally Helgesen (1990) studied the lives of four American women executives and concludes that women's ways of leadership can be good for both the office and the home. She found that the structural organization of their respective workplaces was characterized more by a 'web-like' structure than a 'chain-of-command.' Information flowed more easily along horizontal lines among various levels of employees in the web-like network. The women executives were noticeably receptive to enquiries and suggestions from their employees. Family problems that arose during the day were dealt with, not as interferences but as important things to do. The connectedness among the employees in the office was paralleled by the connectedness between the office and the home. Helgesen's study is supported by a more recent survey of employee attitudes towards women 'bosses' (Taylor 1992). Taylor found that the personal concern of women in their leadership styles was noted by men as well as by women employees. Rather than blaming feminists for excessive stress among women, a more useful approach would be to integrate the activities of paid work and work in the home, taking the health of the workers into consideration, as recommended by feminist social analysts.

Ann Ferguson coined an important expression with respect to analyzing women's positions in both the paid labour and unpaid labour force: sex/affective production. It refers to "ways of organizing, shaping and molding the human desires connected to sexuality and love, and consequently to parenting and social bonding" (1989:77). In Ferguson's view, male dominance and other forms of dominance are initiated and maintained through these "systems of sex/affective production." She uses the term 'production' to mean 'work.' Sex/affective work is activity that satisfies human needs (in contrast to market value). It is used to support the market economy. Sex/affective work is seen to be evaluated in terms of the goals of the socio-politico-economic structures of the society.

Ferguson's discussion of sex/affective work is embedded in a theory of sexuality as 'social energy.' Sexuality as social energy is sex/affective energy. It is bodily social energy that expresses the desire to unite with social others. She does not claim an a priori desire, but rather an empirically observed one that exists 'cross-culturally.' Ferguson says that the desire to unite with others socially "has always been harnessed to motivate people to engage in the other sorts of human labour necessary to meet human needs" (1989:79). In her view, people's desires to connect with each other are interwoven into the social fabric of any given society. Social goals shape the ways in which those desires are legitimately expressed. Labour that is devoid of any form of bonding is, in this view, not productive. Productive labour, then, includes sex/affective labour.

Sex/affective labour is gendered labour. Marriage institutionalizes the relations of sex/affective work in the family according to the social goals of the society. In the global economy, where only market valued work counts, sex/affective work doesn't count. Women's work inside and outside the home is disproportionately characterized by sex/affective activity. David Alexander cites four categories of women's sex/affective work in the home which is designed to serve the needs of husbands, children, and other members of the family (including 'chosen family members' who may or may not be biologically related). The four categories are: (1) physical maintenance labour; (2) personality labour; (3) nurturance labour; and (4) sexual labour (cited by Ferguson 1989:97). Physical maintenance refers to health care such as feeding, cleaning, and nursing people. Personality labour utilizes mediating skills directed towards keeping family relations functional. Nurturing skills include listening, advising, supporting. Sexual labour may be explicit sexual servicing, flirting, physical appearance for the satisfaction of the male observer, and other activities that enhance the man's sense of self-worth.

It is worth noting that many women enjoy work that involves looking after others and facilitating their well-being. Some men also enjoy doing sex/affective work. The point here is not whether particular individuals enjoy subordinating their own interests to those of more dominant others. Rather it is about mandating sex-specific work roles and their moral implications. If nurturing roles are mandated for women, then women do not feel good if they do not perform those roles. This is not merely a psychological issue. There is a close fit for most people between feeling good and doing what is prescribed by societal norms. Self-determination for women (just as for men) requires feeling good about actualizing their potentials. This may or may not mean working primarily as a caregiver inside or outside the home. Women, as well as men, have a right to actualize their passions, intellect, and moral strength in ways that do not depend on their ability to subordinate themselves to others. Ideally, caregiving would be part of everyone's work rather than mandated to one sex.

As it is, the sex/affective work of women in the home is often taken as their natural function. Their 'goodness' is usually measured in terms of the skills they employ to mediate family relations and facilitate the growth of others. These same kinds of skills are often expected of women in the paid labour force, although they are not rewarded financially. The low pay of the majority of women reflects, in part, the attitude that women's work does not include a great deal of achievement. It is often perceived as a matter of natural skills, namely, those related to sex/affective work. While it is not self-evident that the workplace is modelled after the family, the resemblance between women's work inside and outside the home is there. It is possible that women's place in the home is modelled after women's place in the paid labour force. My own view, like that of Carole Pateman, is that the home situation, specifically the relation between the man and woman, is the model for employer-employee relations, with the workplace reinforcing the woman-man relations in the home. The home and paid workplace are mutually reinforcing with respect to the construction of women's identities. The particular ways in which sex/affective work is conducted depends on the social conditions in which women live.

There are no general patterns which can be used to describe sex/affective work for women of different races, classes, ages, ethnicities, religions, or any other social category which is part of the construction of a person's identity. There is, however, a general principle that can be applied with respect to the asymmetrical power relations associated with sex/affective work of women in different contexts. As Ferguson points out, the sexual division of labour in the marketplace and in the home is intrinsic to male dominance. The ideology of "Momism" reinforces male dominance because it maintains the view that women's main job ought to be that of "Mom," whose unpaid job is characterized by sex/affective labour that maintains the ideology of male proprietorship of women and children. Further, it perpetuates the position of the husband/father breadwinner as 'alienated proprietor,' which fuels his anger and jealousy and contributes to family violence.

The asymmetry between women and men's roles in families corresponds to the patterns in the paid labour force. Individual, structural, and symbolic factors affect the construction of identity through work in the household and outside of it. Motherhood is closely associated with female identity. That is not surprising. One need not ascribe the desire of women to have babies exclusively to patriarchal cultural prescriptions to reproduce for individual men and the male-dominated economy, although it is tempting to do so in light of cultural rewards for 'good' women who have babies within heterosexual marriages and 'bad' women who do not. Male morality with regard to motherhood and women's sexuality is driven by an ethos of proprietorship on the part of patriarchal men. Possessing women and their children is manifested in the corporate family in which the man's name identifies the woman and children. Even when 'head of household' on formal documents is no longer used, it is difficult to get away from the implicit sense of it when the man's name covers over the name of the woman and indicates ownership of the children to which she gave birth.

The psychology that is intrinsic to the backlash against feminism includes the part played in both the economy and the family by 'homosocial sex/affective energy' (Ferguson 1989:80). Homosocial energy may or may not be homosexual. Bodily sexuality is part of social sexuality and is defined according to the way in which it serves other social needs. As Ferguson points out, sex-segregated work serves as a means for homosocial bonding for both women and men. When women enter male-dominated workplaces they often forego the bonding that is experienced in women-dominated places, either in the home or outside it. It is not uncommon, for example, for women to choose nursing over medical school for that reason. Men's resistance to women entering previously exclusively men's clubs, where male bonding occurs and strengthens business and professional relations, is understandable, although not justifiable if one believes in the free citizenship of women. Ferguson points out that the feminist threat to the sexual division of labour, among other things, is a threat to "male-bonding sexual energy" (1989:80). It is the same for women, even though women's bonding has not been associated with networks of power in ways that men's have. In most cases women-bonding occurs in enclaves such as household economies, pink collar ghettos, and the informal economy such as crafts and small businesses inside or outside the home. Women's bonding is not closely connected to market value work. It is, however, important for the maintenance of individual identity, despite the fact that it often inadvertently maintains male dominance.

An example of positive homosocial bonding among women is found in the film *Steel Magnolias*. Very few would deny the strength that the

women in the movie derive from their associations with each other, especially in the hair salon. It is a place where women exchange important
information and receive significant personal affirmation. It is a safe and
lively place to be. My own experience at the Hair Hut in Invermere, British Columbia, while I was writing the first draft of this book, reminded me
of *Steel Magnolias*. Although the Hair Hut is not an exclusively female
workplace (it is partially owned and operated by one man as well as several women), it has the same nurturing atmosphere as that depicted in
Steel Magnolias. The social climate of the Hair Hut is conducive to the
health of clients and appears to be conducive to the well-being of those
working there. There is an atmosphere of enjoying the presence of each
other. It is not likely that women are going to readily abandon work
among women with whom they can bond in important ways. The warm
climate of the Hair Hut, for example, is a noticeable contrast to the chilly
climate of workplaces where patriarchal 'professionalism' enervates the
life force of the workers by minimizing interpersonal bonding.

I discussed earlier the distinction, used by Carole Pateman, between
paternal and fraternal patriarchy. Both forms of patriarchy include the
domination of women by men through an unexamined assumption of
male sex right to females and corresponding proprietorship of them. Ann
Ferguson suggests a third form of patriarchy that she believes characterizes North American society today: public patriarchy. As doubled-waged
families became the norm in the latter part of the twentieth century, individual male control in the family weakened. Male control of females
shifted to the state and media, in Ferguson's view. Control of women in
the family continues, however, through unequal division of family wages,
unwaged household labour, volunteer work, domestic violence, and family decision-making power. Ferguson cites these contemporary public
mechanisms of controlling women: gender segregation of wage labour,
state controls over women's physical and mental health and biological reproduction, exploitation of all mothers' unpaid childbearing and rearing
labour, and the mass media's gender stereotyping and sexual objectification of women in a context of sexual consumerism (Ferguson 1989:104).

Ferguson's analysis of contemporary patriarchy is close to that of
English sociologist Sylvia Walby (1990). Walby claims that contemporary
patriarchy can be theorized according to six categories: (1) waged work;
(2) housework, (3) sexuality, (4) culture, (5) violence, and (6) the state.
Culture includes representations in the media, education, religious institutions, and so forth. The state refers to laws which control individual and
group rights, such as abortion, mother and father rights, legalization of
midwifery, pharmaceutical regulations, immigration laws, medicare benefits, definitions of families, pay equity programs, and tax laws. Each woman is a member of many different social categories. The combination of
factors affecting their identities makes it so that each woman is a unique
mixture of determining factors such as age, colour, sexual orientation,

state of health, language, etc. Yet, throughout the interweaving factors which yield a unique composition for each woman, an identifiable self, there is the reality of woman *as* woman.

Susan Moller Okin points out (1989) that gender is an issue of justice in the family. In her view, which I support, it is impossible to even theorize about a just society when the primary socializing agent, the family, is the location of widespread violence against children and women. The devaluing of mandated sex-specific nurturing and subsistence work in an economy which is structured around market labour is a form of injustice. The rationale for this injustice includes the often unexamined assumption that work in the home is not productive work and, therefore, is devalued. The value of work done by women in the public realm is often measured according to the same presuppositions as their work in the home. Family relations and global work relations are constructed along gender lines, which makes gender an issue of justice in both the family and the economy.

In the United States only 15 percent of families are composed of a male breadwinner and a female homemaker. In Alberta over 70 percent of mothers with young children work outside the home. New family relations are necessary to make it possible for women to bear children and to extend their identity beyond their reproductive capacities. Just as I do not wish to reduce women's identities to reproductive capacities, I reject attempts to ignore women's reproductive capacities in theorizing about the constuction of women's identities. The increasing existence of different kinds of family relations facilitates the possibility of moving beyond either extreme.

Ann Ferguson describes six types of 'countercultural' families that are organized according to principles of gender justice. They include: (1) communal family households (members may or may not be biologically related); (2) reconstructed nuclear family (blended family); (3) lesbian or gay couples with children; (4) heterosexual couples living together but not married, with children; (5) divorced or separated but co-parenting; and (6) revolutionary family as community (non-kin or a combination of the above) (1989: 181-82). Pooling resources, incomes, domestic work, and childrearing reduces the liability of motherhood in a world organized around the principles of a formal market economy. These family lifestyles do more, however, than make life more humane within the existing economic structures and local labour markets. They contribute to reorganizing the economy so that household work, community work, and international exchange are given different importance than they are in a market economy analysis. Among these families there is likely to be more emphasis on family and community work and less willingness to participate in work that is organized exclusively around the principle of profit.

The emergence of complimentary family structures is coextensive with alternative definitions of work, evaluations of work, as well as a move away from an ideology of 'having' to one of 'living with.' Increased attention to the well-being of individuals, communities, and global structures is consistent with a change in the underlying intentionality from domination to partnership. The construction of new symbolic meanings with respect to the normativeness of femaleness as well as of maleness is important within that social and cultural shift. In particular, new sexual coding regarding women's bodies free of the male sex right is required. A move toward sexual democracy in the family is part of the shift away from the dominator model of evolution. It is supported by a view of reality as essentially a process of interrelatedness, maintained through respectful interaction with each other and with our environments.

The shift towards more integrative participation among people, as well as with the ecosystem, is slowing undermining the exclusionary boundaries that separates insiders from outsiders. Self-identification and other-identification are becoming more congruent in narrative identities (stories about a person's identity) and social places of individuals and groups. The integrity of persons is a basic requirement for the notion of 'living with.' Women's integrity depends to a large extent on opportunities to integrate and live with their various kinds of personal strengths that characterize their self-identification. They require cultural space to act out their strengths and participate in the construction of images of power to which they can identify and claim as their own without fear of making spectacles of themselves. Fair salaries for valued work are an important correlate of female cultural images of power. In addition, there needs to be increased cultural value attached to work activities that facilitate home, community, and global bonding. Homosocial, as well as heterosexual, bonding is part of living with each other in ways that promote productive activity in all social places. Valuing the contribution of women's energy in social production is a healthy approach to moving out of a patriarchal consciousness and into a partnership model of enhancing existing resources for greater human and natural development.

Notes

1 The dates of the witch persecutions vary with authors. I am adopting the dates of 1450-1750 that are stipulated by Martha Reineke (1990), as they approximate the majority of views.

2 See Anne Llewellyn Barstow (1988) for an important analysis of witch persecution as a focus for studying the history of women.

3 The phrase "the burning times" was coined by Starhawk (1982:183-84). Reineke claims that this phrase is inaccurate because many women were killed as witches by methods other than burning, such as hanging. I shall continue to use the phrase because it has evocative power that unites people in protest against the persecution of witches. In my view, the point is not whether women were burned or hanged but the fact that they were murdered because of exercising their own spiritual healing powers.

4 An analogy can be made between the interpretation of Joan of Arc as a saint and the legacy of Florence Nightingale as an angel of mercy. Florence Nightingale rebelled against her prescribed role as an idle Victorian lady. She rejected marriage and decried

the mindless chatter of most women of her class. She defined herself according to her work, which placed her in the position of outsider in her society. Her essay, *Cassandra* (1979), is an example of her outrage towards the restrictions placed on women's passion, intellect, and moral activities. Florence Nightingale, like Joan of Arc, was an autonomous woman who would not, and could not, accommodate to the restrictions placed on women's self-determination. The need to re-interpret these women as servants of the medical profession or the church reflects their powerful contributions, despite the fact they were female outsiders.

5 The term 'antitype' is borrowed from Howard Eilberg-Schwartz (1989).

6 See Rita M. Gross (1987) for a helpful account of Vajrayana insights into the importance of body in spiritual consciousness.

7 Sexual violence against children is a serious and widespread social sickness. Evidence of its pervasiveness is increasingly emerging. Its importance cannot be underestimated. My focus on violence against women is not intended to imply any lack of significance of the reality of child abuse.

8 For an argument for the pervasive, albeit invisible, power of women in Canada, see Sherrill MacLaren (1991). MacLaren begins her book with a quotation from Madame Jeanne Sauvé, who says, "Women need to stop being afraid of power. They need to take it and use it." MacLaren's book is largely about gaining power within existing structures. Although there is some attempt to critique the use of power as a dominating force within the dichotomous model of cultural achievement versus nature, the book is mainly an account of women's power within the existing dominator model.

9 Mary Daly's *Wickedary* is a brilliant attempt to reclaim names like hag, spinster, crone, witch, lust which are negatively connoted in patriarchy and keep women afraid of choosing independence and expressing their power of creation, of healing, of accepting death in the birth, life, death cycle. Turning profane terminology into sacred images for women is a gift of Mary Daly's.

10 The compatibility of reason and faith was rejected, however, by fideists like Kierkegaard and Pascal who argued that they are incommensurate with each other. In Kierkegaard's view, for example, faith goes beyond reason and requires a leap into the unknown. He cites the irreconcilable claim about the divinity and humanity of Jesus as the basic faith claim of Christians. It cannot be rendered reasonable. Men of science, such as Hume, rejected Christianity for precisely the same reason as fideists embraced it: its lack of rationality. Others attempted to show that reason depended on faith, such as Descartes.

11 Ann L. Barstow develops a helpful analysis of Joan of Arc as a spiritual healer in her *Joan of Arc: Heretic, Mystic, Shaman* (1986).

12 Mary Wollstonecraft was called a hyena in petticoats when she published her *Vindication of the Rights of Women* (1967).

13 The issue of integrating child care and paid work may eventually become more of a "lifestyle" issue than a gender issue. My brother-in-law, a lawyer with three young children, chooses to work less time in order to be with the children. He claims that the choice is more between working in a high-pressure firm or a more low-key practice rather than between mothers or fathers caring for their children. Still, he is speaking from the position in the family of being the major breadwinner while the mother of the children works very much part time in order to be home with their daughters most of the time. In my view, the sexual division of labour is still obvious.

14 See John Locke 1967:II, Sect. 110.

15 Arguments for the inclusive nature of God, within the context of patriarchal biblical history, are useful to get beyond patriarchal interpretations. At the same time they might reinforce the patriarchal image of God in terms of the procreative power of the Father. While I admire the imagination of Sallie McFague's (1987) imaging of God as Mother, Lover, and Friend, the danger of extending the image of a male God as everything looms at the edges of her creative exploration.

16 Carole Pateman's *The Sexual Contract* (1988) provides an extended analysis of the ways in which men's assumed sex right, i.e., access to women's bodies, makes the issue of

women's consent to sexual relations in marriage irrelevant; the same can be said for consent to sexual advances in the workplace.

17	Examples of brokers in the United States are Mr. Noel Keane (lawyer), Dearborn, Michigan; Dr. Richard Levin (specialist in reproductive endocrinology and infertility), Louisville, Kentucky; and Ms. Betsy Aigen (psychotherapist), New York City.

18	The 'Baby M' case in the U.S. about ten years ago is an example of a birth mother who agreed to carry a baby for a couple and then changed her mind when the baby was born. After two court cases the birth mother won the right to keep the baby. This case served as an example of arguing for the rights of the purchaser (property rights) over the rights of the mother who developed a human bond with the baby during gestation (human rights). I have discussed this case more extensively in Tomm 1990. For an extensive account of this case see the book written by her mother, Mary Whitehead (1989).

19	Phillip Parker (1984) argues that commissioning men pay a fee for service, not for parental rights and responsibilities. The importance of this distinction is to attempt to avoid the impression that commercial arrangements between commissioning men and carrying mothers are distasteful and inhumane.

20	See the Royal Commission Report on New Reproductive Technologies (1993) for a more comprehensive discussion of the use and payment of brokers in the U.S, especially pp. 528ff.

21	Three studies which describe the social categories of both commissioners of babies and carrying women are the following: Phillip J. Parker (1984); Eichler and Poole (1988); and the Office of Technology Assessment (OTA) study (1988).

22	Canadian women have been organizing to protest the tax arrangements which allow absent spouses to deduct support payments from their taxable income while counting support payments by the absent spouse as income for the parent who has custody of the child. According to Marsha Erb (lawyer), 72 percent of children are cared for by their mothers after divorce (*Calgary Herald*, May 6, 1992). A study by the federal Justice Department in 1985 indicates that two thirds of women and children were living below the poverty line after divorce. The current tax laws aggravate the reality of poverty for divorced women with children. Since June 1992, when Susan Thibaudeau's case was heard before the Federal Court, there has been increased awareness of the asymmetrical effects of support payments on the father and mother's taxable incomes. In this precedent-setting case, Thibaudeau's support payments were not counted as taxable income, thereby opening the door to changing the law.

23	*Women in the Legal Profession: A Report of the Women in the Legal Profession Subcommittee* (Young 1991), conducted within the Law Society of British Columbia, is an in-depth analysis of many of the same kinds of work issues which affect women in all the professions and industry. In addition, it includes a valuable bibliography.

24	See Alice Kehoe (1989), for example, for a discussion of the *Berdash*, a category which is neither strictly female nor male.

25	This may change soon in Canada because the government is discussing the idea of decreasing the number of dependents allowed to enter the country and permit a higher percentage of independents, i.e., those who earn their own living.

26	See, for example, the detailed study of the history of women in unions in relation to the history of The International Labor Organizaton (ILO) that is described by Carol Riegelman Lubin and Anne Winslow (1990).

27	The Hay system used to define job worth is considered biased in favour of, for example, male strength.

28	See Marjorie Cohen (1987) for a lucid analysis of the possible effects of the The Free Trade Agreement between Canada and the United States.

29	That particular brother became a successful businessman who frequently occupies the position of Master of Ceremonies and speaker on behalf of the family at social gatherings. His intelligence is lively and impressive.

30 Hilkka Pietilä's paper was presented at the 1985 UN Conference for Women in Nairobi. Marilyn Waring (1988) uses Pietilä's paper as a turning point in the search for a new economic model which will serve to stimulate more appropriate economic theories that take women into account in the evaluation of productive labour and the formulation of social policy.

31 The Canadian Broadcasting Corporation (CBC) broadcast a series of two lectures on the Informal Economy (Esteva 1990). The second lecture explored the 'new commons' being practised in Mexico. The 'new commons' system, as described by Gustavo Esteva 1990 (a 'deprofessionalized' intellectual who left a high position in the Mexican government in 1975 to work with the peasants and urban marginals), is a variation on the informal economy.

32 For discussions of differences in Third World economies see, for example, Schüssler Fiorenza and Carr (1987); Ward (1990); Mohanty, Russo, and Torres (1991); and Jayawardena (1986).

33 In May 1992, when I was writing the first draft of this book, CBC *Morningside* called to discuss the issue of "Momism" in the media. *Morningside* researchers are planning a panel to discuss the recent trend in Canada to return to traditional family and religious values. The woman caller from *Morningside* and I discussed the importance of speaking from the heart (as is associated with traditional values) while not mandating individuals into socially prescribed roles because of their sex. For example, "Momism" undermines possibilities for "Dadism" because the father's role in "Momism" is to bring home the bacon. It doesn't include cooking it.

Six

Towards 'Living With'

Living with Uncertainty

IN THE FIRST chapter I referred to the doctrine of *pratityasamutpada*, i.e., life as a continually changing process of interacting conditions. It is a basic metaphysical doctrine about the temporality of everything that exists. An important implication of this view of reality is that everything is characterized by uncertainty. In this chapter, I wish to emphasize this view of reality in my discussion of living with changing circumstances. It contrasts with the view of 'having' a life or set of circumstances in which expectations will be satisfied as anticipated according to previous experiences. Living according to the doctrine of *pratityasamutpada* is expressed well in a song by Leonard Cohen: "Anthem." In his gravelly voice, he sings about the benefits of the unwelcomed and unexpected occurrences in our lives. This view is summarized in one sentence where he sings, "There is a crack in everything. That is how the light gets in."

In my view, the challenge is to stay present enough to oneself to move through the cracks and come out stronger on the other side with more insight into the relatedness of oneself to the rest of the network of interacting conditions. Staying present to myself in the face of life-threatening circumstances is confusing because when I think about who I am I experience myself as no thing with which I can identify. There are no expectations on which to rely. I live with uncertainty. It is the quality of my life that is most present in my consciousness.

Living with oneself in the cracks and emerging with strength from them depends a great deal upon paying attention to the conditions that support the health of one's life system. This includes self-relatedness, connections to other people, to other species, and to the larger ground of support found in the ecosystem. Living with cracks that are life-threatening provides important opportunities for centring oneself in the reality of interdependency and changing circumstances. It significantly reduces the tendency to have a strong attachment to the image of oneself as a self-sufficient, independent person. There is a greater inclination to live in a mode of interdependent relatedness, which entails a large degree of

Notes to Chapter Six are on pages 318-19.

uncertainty. At the same time, paradoxically, one can experience greater security in the peace that comes from letting go of self-centred importance. Life-threatening experiences provide an opportunity to shift from self-centredness to a centredness of the self. As I discussed in Chapter One, the latter kind of centredness emerges in the context of relatedness. This kind of subjective and intersubjective energy allows for increased receptivity and responsiveness within the life system as a whole. The experience of one's integrity in relation to connective energy that allows for the life system to move toward living more comfortably with continual uncertainty is sometimes felt as grace.

An example of living gracefully with uncertainty is found in a particular Tai Chi movement that I was taught recently. It resembles the movement of a large bird landing on a branch. When the bird lands it places one foot gently on the branch to determine whether it is stable. If it is, the bird gradually increases the weight on the foot until it rests easily on the branch. The bird's security comes from balance. In Tai Chi, the practitioner places one foot gently in front, with the heel touching the floor softly. The weight remains on the back foot that rests directly underneath the person's body. After feeling the security of the floor with the front foot, the person shifts the body weight forward from the back to the front foot. The hands are moved gracefully in various patterns that coincide with the shifting weight of the feet from back to front. There is a strong emphasis on bodied mindfulness in this practice. The purpose is to find one's balance in a context of constant movement. The challenge is to do it with grace. In my situation, Tai Chi is a concrete way to become mindful of what I am living with and to maintain some level of balance within a context of radical uncertainty.

When uncertainty about one's own existence is lived with it can be experienced as a crack that allows in light with respect to the tenuous nature of all existence. This is especially true with regard to the ecosystem, which has deteriorated rapidly due to widespread human self-centredness and lack of a cultured orientation of living with nature. Living with oneself with greater mindfulness is integrally connected to living with the earth in a healthy way. Living mindfully with oneself in a healthy way requires a healthy environment. Lawrence LeShan[1] eloquently connects personal health with the environment when he says: "Over and over again I have seen one of two things happen when the total environment of the person with cancer is mobilized for life and his or her inner ecology is thereby changed in a positive way" (LeShan 1990:xi). The two things to which he refers are prolongation of life with a fuller experience of the self and, secondly, miracles of turning one's life around, making the cancer a facilitator of life rather than a signal of the end of it. His approach to working with people living with cancer is primarily psychological, citing feelings and attitudes as important factors in the presence or absence of cancer. I agree that these subjective qualities are paramount in a person's way of living with themselves. It is as important, however, to connect inner ecology with the external ecosystem which significantly influences the way each person is able to live with themselves both in cultural spaces and in the more natural environment. One must focus exclusively on developing positive attitudes within an environment that undermines the health of much of the lifesystem.

A useful summary of unhealthy environmental agendas is provided by Rosemary Ruether (1992) in her discussion of "New Narratives of World Destruction." She cites overpopulation and poverty, illiteracy, the greenhouse effect, deforestation, dwindling biotic diversity, air pollution, toxic wastes, militarism and war, and nuclear arms (1992:85-111). She condenses this list to "four horsemen of destruction": population, pollution, poverty, and global militarization. Social issues and psychological states are inseparable in a view of reality characterized by interdependent origination. The historical pattern of domination, of being in control through destructive means, is not conducive to living gracefully with oneself or with the environment. Changing our collective direction toward a more healing world includes reducing exploitation and developing a greater balance so the natural integrative energy can emerge.

According to the doctrine of *pratityasamutpada*, to which I subscribe, living with uncertainty is intrinsic to participating in the process of changing conditions in the ecosysytem. It is important, however, to distinguish between healthy uncertainties that are integral to the mysteries of life and those which are created by cultural programs that are pathological, such as listed above. From a spiritual point of view, personal and ecological well-being depend on living the mysteries of nature as a welcome part of cultural development. Science was largely initiated around the motivation to control nature's secrets (e.g., Keller 1992). Most societies in the world are plagued with illnesses that derive from such things as pollution, toxic waste, and dessication of renewable resources. As a consequence, many of us experience ourselves as chemical refugees. It is difficult to find a place to be healthy.

Environment, Ecology, and Ecofeminism

Jane L. Collins provides a helpful working definition for environment: "ecosystems on which production depends" (1991:36). Ecosystems are historically and socially specific. Urban dwellers sometimes think of the environment with reference to recreational activities such as hiking as well as the healthy beauty and peacefulness found among wild flowers, animals, and mountains. Among this population there is generally a moral sense of preserving the natural environment for the reproduction of depletable resources and the protection of animals. Agricultural people, on the other hand, who depend on the land directly for their livelihood, organize themselves around particular resources that they use to maintain their households. Whether one is looking for water, wood, fertile ground for sowing seeds, or grazing land for animals will affect the social issues pertaining to the environment. Agricultural people generally do not use the word 'environment' when discussing things like water, wood, or useable land. They live too closely with the land to distance their relationship to it. A chief of a local Aborigine band in Alberta said in conversation that Aborigines use the term 'land' rather than environment. They live with the land, not the environment. I use the term 'environment' because it is a widely used term in the literature and in the media and, therefore, can serve as a general term, referring to the context in which human activity occurs.

According to international studies of agricultural societies (e.g., Gallin and Ferguson 1991), women are the main householders concerned with providing their families with food and water directly from the land. Environmental issues, therefore, may be seen as gendered issues. The term "sustainable development" in Third World development describes a shift away from profit-orientation in the short-term production of the 1960s and 1970s to a long-term perspective aimed at renewing finite resources. Environmental programs have been initiated throughout the world to mitigate overuse of raw materials and devastation of the land. Good intentions and actual changes have to compete, however, with the profit-motive: the bottom line which dictates that the maximization of profits is the purpose of development.

International competitiveness determines whether a country is First World or Third World. Studies show, however, that economic success as indicated in the GNP or GDP, is historically inseparable from the view of environment as something 'to have' rather than 'to live with.'[2] The evaluation of work solely in terms of market value often forces rural families to aim for short-term profits rather than long-term gain. Subsistence farmers are usually not financially able to preserve the conditions for reproduction of depletable resources that is important for continued use of the land. For example, rotation of crops is a necessary condition for long-term production from a piece of land. When preservation conditions are not satisfied, the land becomes poor. The consequences are that families experience scarcity of food. Women, the majority of the householders, are forced to spend more time with less results in their attempts to provide the necessities for their households.

Most of the householders (main functioning adult members of households) in many agricultural communities in Third World countries are women. The men migrate to the cities in search of waged labour for First World corporations. This outward migration of the men from the farms means, among other things, that women are left to do all the work on the subsistence family land. Walking for water and/or wood may take up many hours a day. Taking care of children, the elderly, or relatives and neighbours who need things done for them is labour intensive. Preparation of meals is time-consuming. United Nations studies show that women do two thirds of the world's work (e.g., Schaum and Flanagan, 1992). Jane Nandwa, a former Kenyan Ph.D. student at the University of Alberta,[3] told a Women's Studies class at the University of Alberta (1990) that wives are valuable commodities in most rural African communities because they are needed to work. Men often don't know where the water source is or where to look for wood. When men leave the household in search of migrant work, the women are left with a vast overload of work. Their concern for preserving the conditions of reproduction of primary resources decreases as their workload increases while their access to resources decreases.

Ironically, Third World rural women's access to resources often decreases as technology is introduced into their communities. This is often accompanied by a decrease in their authority. Women usually pack water in rural communities. Because it is so time-consuming and labour intensive, it would seem that the installation of pipes to carry the water into the community would be good for everyone. The consequence for women, though, is a decrease in their social power. The management of the pipelines and the organization of the distribution of water is taken over by the village men as they work with the developers from First World countries. The idea that the developers were making life easier for the communities ignored the power relations in families and communities that had developed within the context of access and control of resources. The main users of water are still women in these communities; however, the main decision-makers are men.

The struggle for control of the resources is not just an issue between women and men. It also interacts with class and caste. In India, for example (Jane L. Collins 1991), a poor community had a water well that continued to function during the 1985 drought in Aurangabad district. The women of the community were the main users of the well to supply the water needs for their families. Because of the drought, wells in other communities dried up. Rich farmers appropriated the well, had a priest 'purify' it and refused to allow the rightful owners of the well to use it (Collins 1991:43). Just as increased mechanization marginalizes women's access to necessary resources, scarcity of resources leads to the exclusion of poor women from access to their primary source of livelihood. The consequence is increased sickness and disease. This is exacerbated when women's use of healing plants is eliminated through deforestation and the destruction of the plants. Pharmaceutical replacements are often too expensive to buy. The situation is sometimes compounded when women herbalists are accused of being witches and are persecuted, leaving no accessible health resources available to the community. This is an example of how environmental and health issues interact in relation to gender and economic concerns. Rural women as householders, especially in countries such as Africa and India usually live with the environment as a means for survival. They organize social movements to preserve the environment in order to survive.

The goal of survival often places 'peasants' against 'environmentalists' in social movements to save the environment. Those who live with the land and survive from its production are often interested in the issue of sustainability of the resources. Environmentalists, on the other hand, are motivated by a desire to overcome the industrialized orientation of using nature for profit. There is overlap between the two approaches to development, but there can also be conflict. Examples of conflict between the two views in Canada are the conflicts over seal hunts and over trapping in northern Canada by Aborigines. Conflict arises between the exploitation of nature for profit and the right of people to use it in a sustainable manner. Negotiations between those who live with the environment in terms of survival and those who are consciously attempting to change the industrial orientation from proprietorship of nature to partnership are part of the 'back to the land' movement that is occurring in Canada, as well as other industrialized countries.

Poverty is concerned with short-term survival. This often leads to decreased concern about the long-term. Poverty among rural householders, of which women are the majority, is caused largely by the marginalization of subsistence farming methods and products. This devaluing of small family farms is largely a result of centralized control of marketing by foreign countries such as Canada, the United States, and European countries. As products are increasingly geared to international markets and innovative techniques are used to produce what these countries desire, the control by men of processing and marketing increases. This underscores the global feminization of poverty and contributes to the further marginalization of women.

The feminization of poverty is not restricted to agriculturally based economies. In industrialized countries women have entered the wage labour force in increasing numbers. They have gained independence and political rights. Women on their own is an increasing global phenomenon (Folbre 1991). In Canada, the United States, and northwest Europe, over 20 percent of householders (replaces head-of-household) in all households are non-married females. In the Caribbean, Latin America, and Sub-Saharan Africa women are the main reference persons in 14 percent of all households. The levels are lower, however, in most Asian countries. Pakistan ranks the lowest of all countries studied, with almost no female-headed households (Folbre 1991:99). This does not mean that Pakistani women are completely controlled by the men in their families. It merely means that by formal Western methods of evaluating power within families they rank the lowest. Other methods of determining power relations may well elicit different conclusions. Nancy Folbre notes, "In general, women have gained new rights and men have resisted new obligations, thereby reinforcing a traditional sexual division of labor in which women take primary responsibility for the costs of social reproduction" (1991: 106).

Folbre points out that the incidence of children born out of wedlock is part of the increasing phenomenon of women on their own. In 1984 in Sweden, 45 percent of births occurred out of marriage, while in 1983 in the United States, the statistic was 20 percent. A significant difference in living styles between Swedish and American single mothers is that in Sweden most women who have children without being married cohabit, usually with men. By contrast, half of the American single mothers live alone. In light of this difference, children of American single mothers are more likely to live in poverty than the Swedish children. This is because the majority of fathers do not support their children economically when they do not live with them. Earlier I cited statistics which show that in America more Black and Latin children live in poverty than White children of single mother families. One of the reasons for the high degree of mobility of Black and Latin men in America is similar to the outward migrant phenomenon of Third World men. Black and Latin men in America are marginalized in the workforce with a high percentage of them working in casual labour jobs. The expendability of their jobs contributes to their migratory work and living patterns. Women with children cannot move as readily, consequently they work in marginalized jobs which allow them flexibility to work at home as well. They perform the double tasks of productive labour for their employer and unpaid reproductive social labour at home (reproducing cultural values and practices). They also often work at other part-time jobs to supplement their low wages. The intersection of gender, class, and race often shapes women's social reproductive work in patriarchy. This can contribute to women having a patriarchal social consciousness in which their own marginalization is accepted without much question.

Poverty is a central issue in an analysis of women and the environment. In agricultural economies women are the ones who most often need access to resources like water, wood, and subsistence produce. At the same time they are the ones with the least power to control the resources when development projects exclude them from management of the resources. As mentioned earlier with reference to the work of Marilyn Waring, if women's work counted in the constitution of the United Nations System of National Accounts women would not be excluded from social planning that would give financial support and social status to their work. In order for the cycle between profit motive and poverty to be broken, it is necessary to re-evaluate work, to recognize its contribution to the stability of communities. Social policies and the organization of labour might, then, reflect the significance of work in the home and the community as well as in the international market.

Why does it seem to be "natural" that women are generally poorer than men? Why is it acceptable that women are increasingly marginalized in Third World development projects? For example, when bicycles are sent to women in an African community to help them get to the market more easily, why is it that their menfolk feel justified in taking the bikes away from them and eventually wrecking them?[4] While economics is one of the most significant determinants of the construction of a person's identity, it does not explain why it is women rather than men who end up at the bottom of the social strata and who are generally considered to lack intelligence as well as strength of character. Using nature for serving profit interests, without regard for replenishing natural resources or preserving conditions for their renewal, is a noticeable feature of the dominator model of evolution. The association of nature with women underlies the economic domination of women in a cultural evolutionary orientation that separates culture from nature and inscribes its particular form of cultural values onto nature in general and woman's nature in particular. Because woman's nature has been defined by cultural inscriptions which dishonour women's sexuality, an important task is to re-inscribe women's sexuality from a transformed symbolic coding system. Ecofeminism contributes towards the achievement of this goal. An element of ecofeminism is its focus on honouring women's bodies with regard to their sexuality.

The issue of sex underlies the genderedness of economic structures and social policies. This is also true with respect to environmental issues. Ecofeminism developed within the larger ecological social movement. The ecology movement gained momentum in reaction to the exploitation of nature for profit. Similarly, social movements developed in reaction to exploitation of those who have been considered of less value than the dominant group. The pervasive hierarchy of men dominating women is grounded in the close association of women with nature. Correspondingly, women's thoughts and activities are closely associated with their nature as allegedly primarily sexual beings, an identity that has generally been devalued in both the home and outside it. I am not saying that women should not be identified with their bodies. I wish to make it clear that the problem is not with women's bodies, but rather with the denigrating attitudes towards them, extending to the whole female person. The view of both women and nature as raw material to be used according to the desires of others underpins exploitation of both. A consequence is an unhealthy environment and often a dangerous place for women. While environmental issues are not restricted to those pertaining to women's bodies, there is considerable overlap.

According to Carolyn Merchant, the term 'ecofeminisme' was coined in 1974 by the French writer Françoise d'Eaubonne. Its original meaning referred to "women's potential for bringing about an ecological revolution to ensure human survival on the planet" (Merchant 1990:100). While ecofeminism emphasizes connections between the earth and the female body, it does not need to exclude the activities of men or their bodily connections to the ecosysytem. The main point is that there are similar ways in which women's bodies and the earth provide the starting point for life. This is not the case with men's bodies. In my view, the body as source of life is central to both the female body and the earthbody. The association between the exploitation of nature and of women in the socio-politico economies that were shaped by war budgets of aggressive militaristic nations gave rise to ecofeminism. Merchant notes different ecofeminisms according to the feminist theoretical framework in which ecofeminism is embedded.

The three main ones are liberal, radical, and socialist ecofeminism. Liberal ecofeminism is centrally concerned with changing laws and regulations within existing structures, such as acid rain regulations or chlorofluorocarbon production which is used in fast food containers. Chlorofluorocarbons deplete the ozone layer and contribute to changing environmental conditions to produce 'the greenhouse effect.' One possible consequence is that as temperatures warm, ground water levels decrease, causing, for example, drought and loss of wetland areas for bird breeding. Another one, in other geographical locations, is that as polar caps melt there is an increase in sea levels. Because each ecological change affects the rest of the ecosystem, depletion in one area leads to lack of sustainability in others. Liberal ecofeminists focus on preventive measures which will help to sustain existing resources and avoid future disasters.

The central focus of radical ecofeminism is to address exploitation of nature and women. In this perspective, gender issues are understood as deriving from sexual (biological) differences. Disregard and denigration of the earth is seen as analogous to the denigration of women's bodies and their functions. Merchant's description of radical feminism is too restrictive in my view. She does not connect her concern with sexuality to gendered division of labour in the socio-politico-economic areas of analysis. In light of the gendered division of labour and related discrepancies in pay, hiring, and promotion policies, and the chilly climate in the workplace experienced by many women, economic issues must be seen as directly related to sexual differences. That is not to say that other differences aren't as important or even more important for particular individuals.

An important reason to focus on rewriting the meaning of women's sexuality is to move beyond the restricted associations which identify women primarily with reproduction and as less-than men in intelligence, moral integrity, or authority. Women need to be considered normal adult human beings, without bodily stigma that come from comparing them with men as the norm. Attention to the normativeness of both femaleness and maleness is a path to creating social justice for both. I agree with Charlene Spretnak that all forms of daily exploitation of women are functions of an unhealthy infrastructure of attitudes, values, and beliefs about women (1990:9). There is a need to address the multidimensional ecosystem that corresponds to the way in which women and men's identities are constructed. Radical feminism is directed at changing the infrastructure.

Socialist ecofeminism, the third category, directs its attention at the market economy of a society and its exploitative functions with regard to women and environmental resources. Merchant believes that socialist ecofeminism has the most potential for transforming relations of production that affect ecological systems. She believes that socialist ecofeminism incorporates the important insights of the other two and goes beyond them. I disagree with her position. It places a socialist feminist standpoint at the centre of analysis and more or less trivializes the insights of the other two main perspectives. I believe that socialist feminism is flawed at the root because it does not address the infrastructure on which the various patterns of social organization are constructed. I do not wish to go into a discussion here of the conflicts between socialist feminism and the other forms. Rather, I wish to emphasize that categorizing the various feminisms in exclusive categories is problematic and does not reflect the complexity of most feminist positions. Merchant differentiates socialist feminism from radical feminism essentially in terms of how they envision social change. She says that for socialist feminists "materialism, not spiritualism, is the driving force of social change" (1990:103). This kind of separation of economic concerns from a spiritual and sexually specific understanding of human nature is unhelpful in the development of an integrated approach to the issue of domination and exploitation. In contrast to Merchant's fragmenting approach to ecofeminism, Spretnak connects liberal, radical, and socialist concerns in her more comprehensive account. In Spretnak's view, ecofeminism is evolving through the interaction of all feminist perspectives that include a concern for both women and the ecology. They include ecopeace, ecojustice, economics, ecopolitics, ecoeducation, ecophilosophy, and ecotheology (1990:6).

Spirituality is an important component of ecofeminism. This is not often mentioned in socialist feminism. A notable exception is the Owenite movement in England in the early part of the nineteenth century and associated religious communities which developed later, including those in America.[5] The domination of science over religion during the industrial revolution, however, led to the marginalization of socialist praxis that included attention to both women and nature. Barbara Taylor notes that "Exactly a century ago Engels consigned the ideas and hopes of the first British socialists, the Owenites, to a utopian prehistory of scientific socialism, a period of 'crude theories' and 'grand fantasies' which had to be superseded by historical materialism before the communist struggle could be waged on a sound, scientific basis" (1991:360). Since the industrial revolution and the developing ethos of scientific control of nature, attention to a holistic basis for social organization has been largely deemed utopian and has been widely disregarded. I agree with Ynestra King (1990) that our 'technological, industrial culture' has been characterized by a split between spiritual interrelatedness within the ecosystem, on the one hand, and socio-economic-political analysis, on the other. The feminist traditions developed their platforms within that binary divisive context, with some forms of spiritual feminism on one end of the spectrum and militant socialist feminism on the other polarity.

In contrast to the split between spirituality and socialist concerns, Robert Owen's spiritual socialism included the development of a number of trade unions for women in 1833-34. Both middle-class and working-class women agitated for reforms against men's greater wages for the same work. It was a long-standing practice for men to agitate against their bosses, but until unions were formed women generally had no recourse for grievances. With the development of unions, the more aggressive women resisted their poor working conditions and wages and rallied against "those who style themselves the lords of creation" (Taylor 1991:361). A major contentious issue was the lack of adequate provisions for women to work for a wage and for their families simultaneously. The issue of sexed-identity was crucial to changing working conditions for women. It was not sufficient for women to be given lower wages than men for the same work and, at the same time, be responsible for the well-being of their families. As the industrial revolution emerged with greater force, however, these issues got pushed aside by Marxists in favour of economically based class issues exclusively. In 1896 Clara Zetkin told a Social Democrat rally that "It is not women's petty interests of the moment that we should put in the foreground, our task must be to enroll the modern proletarian woman in the class struggle" (Taylor 1991:362). This attitude that women's concerns are to be made invisible within the rubric of social concerns that revolve around men's experiences continues today. This is a major reason why women's social movements emerged within the various existing social movements. Each feminist perspective picks up the flavour of the movement of origin.

Since the second wave of feminism in the 1960s, Marxism has been modified by socialist feminists to reintroduce the 'Woman Question.' It remains, however, subsumed under the 'Class Question.'[6] Sex and class are perceived as interactive issues and not exclusive of each other. Sex, however, is defined in gender terms (ie., femininity and masculinity) that are more sociologically oriented than the biological reference of sex-specificity (i.e., female and male). This emphasis on sociological determinism and avoidance of biological facticity is a well-intentioned attempt to distance feminist analysis from biological determinism (e.g., the view that women's nature as baby producers is their destiny in life). I agree with the desire to eliminate the tendency to use biological determinism to justify women's lower wages and the 'naturalness' of their unpaid reproductive work. I do not, however, agree with the separation of economic-socio-political issues within ecofeminism from the more holistic approach of taking sexuality and spirituality into account, as well as determining factors in the health of the ecosystem.

Socialist feminism makes an important distinction between the environmental concerns of women in their roles as householders (main provider for their families) and in their relation to the earth as life-givers as mothers. It is important to not romanticize the connectedness of women to the earth because of their reproductive capacity and nurturing activities. This tendency is in the same category as romanticizing poverty. It obscures the wretchedness of it. Poor farming women, whether in Third World countries or industrialized countries, are mostly concerned with providing for their families. Just as women in such poverty stricken agricultural communities might not be interested in long-term sustainable planning of the earth, they might also not be interested in connecting the reality of their own (re)productive bodies with the earth as a (re)productive body. The immediate practicality of livelihood issues occludes more imaginative associations.

My own experiences growing up in the Cypress Hills form an example of practical economics obliterating conscious spiritual connections to nature. Our family had a timber business. We all worked in "the bush" cutting down trees, limbing them, "snaking" them out (a horse pulling the trees out of the forest with a chain tied around them), loading them onto a truck in the summer or a horse and sleigh in the winter, and moving them on down to the stack in the yard by the house where we peeled them with a hand drawknife so they could be used by local farmers and the telephone company in southern Alberta. We raised animals for food. We packed water from the creek and cleaned debris from it. In the summer we sometimes shared the crock of drinking water in the kitchen by the front door with the horse who would occasionally sneak his head in for a drink. Coyotes had to be kept at bay so we could have the chickens for eggs and Sunday dinners.

Hours were spent in the summer looking in the woods for the horses. They always went as far away as the fence would allow them to go. Because we used the Provincial Park for grazing rather than our own restricted land, they could go a great distance. The time in the woods was usually welcomed because then I didn't have to pack water, wood, coal, clean out the barn, or do the dishes. It was a good time to let my imagination develop and to have thoughts that didn't fit in anywhere else. If I should mention any private thoughts about the mysticalness of the woods to anyone back at the house when I returned with the horses, I was told to get my head out of the clouds and was assigned a practical task to keep me out of mischief. Emptying the chamber pots generally brought each of us back to the material world in a hurry. At the same time, this chore increased my desire for the clean air of nature.

The focus on material conditions for survival dominated our existence in one of the most beautiful and spiritual areas of Alberta. It is true that spiritual consciousness can get subsumed under material consciousness in survival conditions. It is not true, however, that the two are incompatible. In ecofeminism, historical, material consciousness and spiritual consciousness are interrelated by those who participate in feminist spirituality. The differences between the practical concerns of women who are trying to live with the land and the spiritual interests of feminists engaged in feminist spirituality need not cancel each other out in the development of feminist approaches to ecology. Recognizing the differences as part of the larger concern of the relation of the human species to the earth and the social relations of women and men within that context will help to overcome exploitation of both the earth and women. Insights from all the feminist perspectives are required for the success of that revolutionary development.

Ynestra King notes that any revolution needs a cultural foundation and a utopian vision (1990:115). Imagination is part of innovative change. Lack of imagination, on the other hand, leads to reductionist thinking such as disqualifying descriptions of attempts to highlight the strengths of sex-specificity rather than gender neutrality as 'feminist essentialism."[7]

In my view, socially constructed historical agency cannot be separated entirely from subjective spiritual agency. The vitality of spiritual agency is part of the cultural foundation that provides for a utopian vision which drives social change. An example of spiritual vitality motivating social action is depicted in the *Chipko Andolan* (the hugging movement) organized by Indian women who were living in poverty but who had a social conscience that was grounded in their spiritual connection to the forests in their communities that they were trying to save from destruction by developers (Caufield, 1984). They wrapped themselves around the trees when the men came with axes and bulldozers. They vowed to die before they would allow the trees to be cut down. In that way they saved their forests and inspired other women throughout India to do the same. Part of their inspiration came from the Gandhi movement that emphasized passive resistance to British Imperialism in India in the 1940s. Gandhi's social movement was motivated and maintained by his spiritual/social vision of the people of India governing themselves in ways that were more congruent with their holistic spiritual heritage and self-identities.

In addition to saving the forests as part of the local ecology, these women were also determined to keep them for the purpose of sheltering the various medicinal herbs they found in the forests. They used herbs from the forests for treating ailments among the poor in rural areas. When the forests were destroyed the healing plants were also lost. Pharmaceuticals which replaced the plants were too costly for the people to buy. A consequence was the increase in disease and deaths. When the women resisted deforestation in the interests of continuing with their healing practices, they were accused of witchcraft. This is an example of the interwoven nature of the environment with the social organization of communities and technological, industrial cultural values.

Women's health issues are centrally connected to social, economic, and political issues.[8] The United Nations report on women as 'wasted asset' links women's illiteracy to their health as well as to their ability to produce from the land, benefit from the family economy, and their awareness of social and political issues. "Women's inability to read instructions on a packet of contraceptive pills or a diarrhea remedy, a seed catalogue or an invoice, a will or a newspaper, bars them from the full benefits of development and prevents them from making their full contribution" (*The Globe and Mail*, April 29, 1992:A2, a newspaper report quoting from a United Nations health report). Their inability to read labels or to purchase health remedies limits their role as healers. The association of women healers with ignorance (because of their illiteracy) is a further justification for marginalizing them.

It is a short step from the association of women healers with ignorance to the more extreme negative connotation of evilness. Witchcraft (as an evil practice) is a charge that is not far from the minds of those against herbal treatment and midwifery performed by women who are not trained according to Western medical standards. Herbal treatment for abortions is another long-standing pagan practice throughout history which is still widespread in India today. Paganism means 'from the country.' It was given a denigrated meaning by urban- and university-trained doctors and priests who wished to discredit spiritual and healing practices that took no notice of formal religion or other kinds of education. The domination of nature by culture is analogous to the domination of rural by urban, of Third World by First World, and of women by men. Ecofeminism, as part of ecology, is a path toward living in a balanced way with the ecosystem and is an important means by which women's interests can become visible and valued.

Ecology is defined by Judith Plant as "the study of the interdependence and interconnectedness of all living systems" (1990:155). She says that "Ecology teaches us that life is in a constant state of change, as species seek ways to fit in particular environments that are, in turn, being shaped by the diversity of life within and around them. Adaptation is a *process*" (1990:156). Ecology brings together issues relating to ontology (being), epistemology (knowing), and ethics (living humanely). A person's ontological reality is the central point of their Identity, which is constructed within the process of ontological interrelatedness. From a holistic perspective of being, each person's identity is inseparable from their way of participating in the changing world. This includes their own changing identities.

This philosophical view of oneself as a process of changing reality is experienced with remarkable clarity when one lives with a life-threatening illness. There is no security in the most basic aspect of being, namely, continuing to breathe. At the same time this stark reality of possible imminent death seems to provide the impetus to get free of patterns of eating, thinking, working, and relaxing that diminish personal and ecological energy. Facing extinction of one's identity as a separate person enhances the experience of identity as an energy field interacting in a larger network of fields. When this dynamic reality becomes part of one's identity, there is a feeling of being free. It includes greater awareness of the inseparability of the life system. This feeling of ontological connectedness reduces the insecurity that is part of self-identity in which personal resources are depleted. In my own case, I find that as I work with health professionals to move my energy through my body I become increasingly sensitive to the energy of other people and non-human animals or things around me. Living more fully with my own energy helps to facilitate closer connectedness to my environment. In this process, my identity becomes more integrated with that of other life forms around me.

With respect to the interactive process of human identity and participation in the ontological process of changing reality, Plant says that "Social ecology seeks ways to harmonize human and nonhuman nature, exploring how humans can meet their requirements for life and still live in harmony with their environment" (1990:155). Environmental ethics is coextensive with the ethics of human relations. Social justice entails ecological justice. Ecological justice is part of ontological justice: respect for non-interference in the right to the sustainability of human resources and environmental resources as they interact in the life-giving process. The time is passing when virgin forest (uncut by man), virgin oil (uncontaminated by manmade preservatives), virgin soil (untilled by man), or virgin girl (untouched by man) can be used as metaphors by the 'lords of creation' who defined nature, nature's products, and women as resources to be used for economic profit or personal gratification. An ironical twist with regard to these metaphors is that they were devised by men who are also largely the destroyers of this so-called virginity.

The analogy between nature and woman within the mindset of exploitation is poignantly characterized in the oft-used phrase "used up" with reference to depletable resources. Just as resources get used up so they are no longer available to the profiteer, so women as wives and mothers get used up as they produce children, get older, and no longer bear any resemblance to the patriarchally defined virgin. Aging prostitutes are another example of women being used up. Their value on the market usually declines rapidly as they move beyond the teenage years. The view of women as valuable only when they are young is part of the technological, industrial orientation to the land. Old women and old land get scarred from use. Their use-value becomes negligible in the view of exploiters. The search goes on for other resources to use to satisfy the greed behind profiteering and domination. This practice is, however, now being called into question and actively opposed by environmentalists, ecologists, and ecofeminists.

A new understanding of relations between humans and the environment increasingly informs social analysis of power relations between women and men. This combined perspective contributes to the construction of an alternative intentionality that positively affects social change. Intrinsic to this shift toward greater ecological sensitivity is the spiritual vitality of life-giving power that is an integrative force within the life system. Every social revolution needs a cultural foundation and a vision which relies on imaginative construction of new symbols. We need to construct symbols that bring together the 'natural' with the historically constructed in a way that they are understood to be constructively interactive rather than oppositional. In this view, ontology is the ground for ethics. Our connectedness to the environment is the bridge to experiencing reality as an adaptive process. Recognizing the sacredness of the earth is a step toward acknowledging our bodies as sacred and our activities as part of a mystical and rational process of life-giving directedness. The new stage of evolution ('living with') requires imaginative construction of a new symbolic order (system of giving meaning) which is founded on the belief that nature and culture are interactive energy fields that are grounded in the earth and in our bodies. Living with this belief facilitates possibilities for tapping into energy that expands individual self-identity and more powerful cultural constructions of positive body-based female imagery.

New Images

One way to represent women as independently powerful is through depicting them carrying briefcases as they climb the ladder through the glass ceilings in professional workplaces. Juxtaposing images of women's bodies that integrate materiality and spirituality is another pathway into new conceptions of female power. Both sets of images are about woman-power.[9] They are both needed for a revolution to occur in the equalization of power relations between the sexes. While the briefcase-carrying woman is a useful image for some, it has the potential of supporting the status quo view that women need to minimize the reality of their female bodies in order to succeed in the move towards more social power. A second problem with this representation of women is that most women do not live that way. The vast majority of women are not professionals. This is not to say that the professional image should not be used to represent women as significant participants in the social realm. I believe it is very important. It is also important, however, to work toward changing underlying negative attitudes toward women *as* women which often prevent them from being taken seriously and willingly accepted as social leaders. Without wanting to emphasize the view of women as victims, I wish to emphasize the importance of recognizing the reality of women's relative exclusion from cultural positions of power because of scepticism towards women's authority. This withholding of consent to grant women social authority is closely connected to the worry about them disturbing long-established patterns of male social relations of power. At the centre of this worry is the reality of woman's sexuality that is manifested in her female body.

As mentioned earlier, exclusionary practices toward women are maintained mostly by constructing women's identity in ways that are incongruent with images of power. Their sexuality is denied or controlled in attempts to maintain a social order characterized by positions of power that are largely established through male bonding. It is unlikely that the goal of equality between the sexes will be reached without new and positive images of women living with their own power in whatever circumstances they live in. This means that it is not enough to project images of female power primarily through the briefcase-and-high-heel model.

The framework of greed and domination that typifies technological, industrial culture cannot be changed fundamentally by trying to fit women into it at higher levels. This is not to say that women shouldn't be getting into positions they deserve. It is necessary that women get into positions of decision-making in order to change work structures and social policies. At the same time, the struggle to get women into positions of social authority is hampered by underlying attitudes which are suspicious of independent women. This cultural suspicion is deeper than social practices. Eliminating such suspicion, or at least reducing it, requires imagery that brings forth new ways of seeing and living with a sexed body. Images of women living power-fully in relation to themselves and to what else they are near to forms the big picture in which the theorizing in this book occurs. Through such images, new social meanings can emerge.

Social meaning is inextricable from symbolic meaning, which is closely connected to imagery. Theories of self have usually developed within the framework of a separate intellectual and body consciousness. Indeed, the notion of body consciousness is an oxymoron if consciousness is defined solely with reference to the intellect. Separation of the body from rational consciousness has been a major reason for its denigration, with certain parts of the body such as the two lips being unspeakable. Speaking through the body is a relatively new idea that integrates intellectual and body consciousness in self expression. Rationality becomes a more holistic concept. Its meaning is redefined to include imagery and feelings as well as propositions that can be deemed true or false. Truth and falsity give way to how each person experiences the reality in which they participate. Each person's imagination is part of their rationality as an epistemological subject. Imagination includes imagery. Body imagery is required to put flesh on the anorexic concepts of self as a conscious being living with self-determination.

Irigaray (1985a) claims that women's lack of autonomy, i.e., lack of self-determination, comes largely from fear of losing approval, especially the father's approval. Fear often prevents people from envisioning something and believing they deserve to have it. It undermines one's capacity to take risks. Consequently, it restricts the imagination and makes one 'hearing impaired.' In her view, women live in the 'zone of silence' (1985a:113) with respect to the discourse of the fathers. The 'fathers' discourse' in the global economy leaves most women silent as they work like mules in agricultural communities to provide for their children. That discourse does not restrict only women and their children to silence and poverty in the global economy. It applies to marginalized men as well. For example, in the May 4, 1992 issue of *Newsweek* the article, "Slavery," reports on indentured bondage of families in various countries such as Pakistan, the Dominican Republic, Haiti, Mauritania, South Africa, and other countries. Employers lure desperate workers to their plantations, brick-making factories, or whatever their line of work is, pay them wages that they cannot live on and then lend them money to live. The longer they work the more debt they incur. The debt is passed on from one generation to the next. Children in those families are born into slavery. Within that system of illegal slavery, women (more than men) serve as sexual slaves as well as field and household slaves. The realities of women in whatever material conditions shape their existence is importantly affected by the fact that they are women. This is not intended to undermine the significance of how men's sexed identity affects their lives. It is not, however, as normal for men to be reduced to their body functions as it is for women, nor for their authority to be restricted merely because they are men.

In light of the need to develop new images pertaining to women's bodies, the work of Luce Irigaray is important for thinking about the vaginal lips, for example, as a model for the concept of self-in-relation. Her emphasis on *nearness* of the lips fits with the notion of *permeable self*. The image of the two lips near to each other capitalizes on the view of self as present to oneself through presence to another. Grounding a theory of self in the image of the two lips is helpful for overcoming the embarrassment that is generally felt by both women and men about this material aspect of women's sexuality. Irigaray's work is ground breaking because she theorizes about new and helpful cultural meanings that arise from female imagery that has generally been excluded from acceptable academic discussion. The emerging social and cultural evolution toward 'living with' rather than 'having' is closely connected to the development of positive images of women's bodies that reflect the body as sacred. An attitude of sacredness toward one's body is coextensive with an attitude of sacredness toward the earth in feminist spirituality. While Luce Irigaray's philosophy of the female body could be construed as being so abstract that it appears to have nothing to do with 'earth matters,' the implications of her philosophy are clearly applicable to feminist spirituality. Her work is enhanced when it is conjoined with that of spiritual feminists who work with goddess imagery in holistic ways. It is important to note that neither Irigaray nor most spiritual feminists discuss their evolving body-based imagery of women as definitive. In my view, the important point here is to develop a theory of women as selves in which their independence as women and their permeability as participants in the ecosystem are made visible and applauded.

The fact that a woman inhabits a female body makes a great deal of difference to how she experiences the material conditions of her social existence. Her sex is never an irrelevant fact. Similarly, the fact that a man inhabits a male body is never irrelevant to his thought or activities in the conditions of his existence. While the conditions of existence vary for each person according to race, class, ethnicity, sexual orientation, age, religion, ability, etc, the fact of being a woman or a man is central in the composition of the self within a community. To assert the centrality of sexuality is not to assert an unchanging essence about the reality of femaleness or maleness. The social meaning of one's sexuality is invariably constructed within the network of social meanings associated with the other aspects of the self.[10]

I wish to differentiate between the view of self as socially constructed through the needs and desires of others (i.e., appropriated) and constructed in relation to others. Appropriation of the self by others' needs, including those of the state (such as birth rates), requires a soluble self. By contrast, the permeable self is constructed in relation to others without losing oneself to their agendas because of an impermeable aspect of self. The impermeable aspect of self is the self in solitude. The capacity to be alone in the presence of oneself or in the presence of others is the feature of self-identity that differentiates the permeable self from the soluble self. It is what protects self-loss in relation. The presence of self to self or to others entails body consciousness in the enunciation of self as subject. Self-consciousness is awareness of self as embodied person. Embodiment includes sexuality. The point of focussing on sexuality here is to bring women's sexuality into the symbolic structuring of meaning from a positive female-imaged imaginary. As Irigaray notes, in the 'fathers' discourse' women's sexuality is seen as the excess factor (1985a:110-11). The task is to give women's sexuality equal space in the symbolic system of meaning. Imagery of women as spiritually powerful, sexual adults is important for the accomplishment of that goal.

The image of the two lips touching is an effective reference for identity because it 'smacks' of excitement about the eroticism of one's own being. One of the reasons it is such a stimulating image is that it has been largely forbidden in most forms of discourse, especially academic. When something is excluded from discourse it is not part of a person's consciousness. It sounds outrageous to ground identity in the two lips and it is embarrassing to many people, both women and men. It is an erotic image that draws attention to itself, something that 'good' women are not supposed to do or they make spectacles of themselves. Their speech is supposed to reflect their felt modesty. Images of women's bodies or body parts usually conform to what men feel comfortable with. Women tend to see themselves in relation to those images, and their social acceptability largely depends on a close correlation between how they see themselves and how they look from an outsider's perspective. With an emphasis on identifying ourselves according to prescribed acceptable images that are visually available to others, what cannot be seen is not discussed.

Irigaray connects the 'optics' of discourse with how eroticism is viewed. Since the time of Plato's *Republic*, seeing has been closely associated with knowing in Western culture. The metaphor of light is used to express the presence of knowledge. By contrast, the darkness of ignorance is something to avoid. It is like being in Plato's cave where appearances are mistaken for reality. In this epistemology, where light and dark symbolize knowledge and ignorance respectively, touching serves little purpose in the discourse. When discourse is grounded in a body, the emphasis on seeing rather than touching reflects the priority of male auto-eroticism over female. Further it gives more reality to heterosexuality and male homosexuality than it does to lesbianism. From outside the body, women's vaginas are generally perceived as holes, as nothings. By contrast, men's erect penises are very visible. Their presence is extended when facsimiles of the penis are erected in parks, in front of buildings, or as the very buildings. In addition, one only has to glance at the shape of defence missiles to make the connection between the shape of the male sex organ and highly valued cultural constructions. Cultural discourse is inseparable from social meanings constructed in relation to emotionally laden body parts. Strong erections and their social counterparts have an optical effect that contrasts sharply with holes which need to be filled up for completion.

Discourse that privileges sight over touch, grounded in male morphology, is intrinsic to self-identity as separate self. Seeing the self as strong and separate, as the ideal form of the male organ, corresponds with the belief in the right to intrude into the space of others and to conquer them. The alleged passivity of the hole, like the presence of an unused field, is seen to invite intervention. The right of women to protection from male intrusion is becoming more of a reality. Freedom from intrusion, however, is not automatically assumed to be either a right or even desirable by those who live predominantly with the assumption of the male sex right. Because of the pervasiveness of the presupposition of the male sex right in patriarchal cultures, it requires considerable effort to alter our ways of discussing reality to include references to female morphology that emphasize touching. Grounding discourse in the female body facilitates a shift from a dominator model that revolves around identity in terms of separate self to a more egalitarian one in which the notion of permeable self is central. The image of the two lips helps to concretize this view of the self as 'living with,' through touch. When a person is present to themselves or to other people the experience of 'nearness' is felt. This does not necessarily mean physical nearness, rather it can be a feeling of being near because of living with a receptive and responsive consciousness. It is a liveliness of being connected. I believe living with this kind of presence is invariably erotic in the sense that the person's energy is positively awakened. This is sometimes referred to as charisma. The effect is to stimulate life-giving energy for the self as well as for others. In order that women can live with their eroticism it is important that there be accepted cultural images of women's bodies that can be internalized and lived with energetically.

The nearness of the two lips brings to mind the notion of pleasuring oneself. It could also be a motivating image for men to reflect on what the two lips open into and how they might be welcomed into a relationship. In this respectful view of women, pleasure derives not from penetrating the other, filling up what is perceived to be a gap, but rather it is experienced as being near the other. It is the presence of both to each other that stimulates the liveliness of each. In this view of the self as permeable, mutuality is built into the notion of identity. Irigaray says "Woman 'touches herself' all the time, and moreover no one can forbid her to do so, for her genitals are formed of two lips in continuous contact. Thus within herself, she is already two—but not divisible into one(s)—that caress each other." This model of the touching of two or more things near to each other is useful not only for centredness of oneself but also for interrelatedness to outside centres of energy. Whether or not one agrees with Irigaray's emphasis on female sexual organs as a basis for a philosophy of self, it helps us to listen to something different from what we have already been listening to. I do not mean to say that different is automatically better. I do believe, however, that it is better for women to listen to how their language reflects their experiences of their bodies than to continue to deny the aspect of reality that their bodies provide in their identity.

Because of their anatomy (i.e., vagina seen as lacking a substantial reality), women have often been defined in terms of lack: lack of intelligence, lack of initiative, lack of personal integrity, lack of social authority. As pointed out by Irigaray, there is an alternative way of seeing women's vaginas. By looking at the vagina with a speculum one sees a cave-like structure. Rather than looking at it from the flat surface of the exterior as a depression, it can be seen from within as a mysterious source of wonderment. It is a place of erotic excitement that is alive with energy which vitalizes consciousness of self as an embodiment of sacred mysteries. Women's bodies historically have been denigrated more than men's, partially because they have more juices. A more helpful way of experiencing the juices is to think of them as a metaphor for imaging the fluidity of reality. The juices merge with the flesh through mucous, which is neither juice nor flesh. In this view of the body, mucous is positively connoted. It is no longer symbolic of bodily matter as abject. Experiencing one's body positively as a metaphor for the ambiguity of life—neither completely one thing nor the other—is a beginning for new linguistic forms that reflect the fluidity and plurality of ontological reality. If this were the case, then the social "I" would reflect the specular "I" as a source of wonder and an opportunity to engage in the mysteries of living more fully in the presence of oneself within a network of interrelated and changing contextual circumstances.

I think that Irigaray's focus on female body parts such as the two lips, the vagina, and mucous violates current sensibilities in, at least, North American discourse. She makes a spectacle of herself when she evokes the speculum as a way for women to develop a new subjectively based form of discourse about themselves. Central in her view of the self as subject is 'wonder': the feeling of awe. I agree with her that this is the main passion that creates the desire for self-determination. The wonder of one's body and the desire to live fully with it are key to thinking of eroticism as a form of both sexual and spiritual self-expression. Wonder leads each of us to the magnetic poles inside us and between us as whole persons.

Using images which crack the veneer that covers the 'wild side' of women's bodies is a way of opening up possibilities for women to affirm themselves and to create linguistic meanings which bring female morphology more into the realm of acceptable discourse. This emphasis on women's anatomy is intended as a strategy to get out of a symbolic order constructed exclusively on male morphology in which women's bodies and their whole persons are defined by 'lack.' It is a strategy to develop new forms of discourse which include women-centered ways of enunciating subjectivity. I do not see this strategy as an end in itself. By this I mean that my goal is not to contribute to another reactionary view of women and men as not being able to think like each other because their anatomy is different. There is little point to developing sex-specific theories of the self that construct further barriers to communication between women and men. The point is to facilitate better modes of interaction in which both women and men participate as full citizens. It is important not to equate anatomical differences with personality and role differences. At the same time, in social contexts where maleness is generally associated with intellectual and moral superiority it is important to establish a way of thinking about women as self-governing persons in their own right, including female sex rights. The image of the nearness of the lips and their presence to each other is a powerful model for self-identity as pluralistic within an interrelated ecosystem.

While Irigaray's work is revolutionary with respect to the uses of images pertaining to women's morphology, her writing is restricted in its spiritual implications. Her images connect well, however, with female imagery found in, for example, goddess spirituality and shamanism. Because I do not find satisfactory spiritual sustenance in the monotheistic traditions, it is of considerable importance to me to be able to trace my British heritage to traditions in which independent, powerful female imagery is available. From my reading of the literature and in discussions at several conferences, I believe this is an interest of many women. It is not a matter of trying to reconstruct an earlier period of history and transplant it into the contemporary period. Rather, pagan images and mythologies provide inspirational resources for increasing numbers of women in their drive for 'sexual democracy.'[11] Cultural mythologies underscore social realities. As Carol Christ noted (1987b), symbols are embedded in consciousness. In times of crises or transition we revert back to deep-seated beliefs, values, and attitudes which are associated with symbols that reflect our culture's most entrenched beliefs. These symbols are religious symbols which reflect the ultimate meaning of life in terms of our origins, natures, and destinies. Even a predominantly secular society is founded on such cultural symbols.

This happens specifically with women who have rejected symbols which restrict their power and independence but they have not replaced them with new images. In periods of upheaval, the void is filled with old images and meanings. They provide few, if any, resources for envisioning a way out of the crisis. Alternative images are required to fill the void. Images are more powerful if they have an historical trajectory. Because of this, it is important to connect one's own spiritual life today with the spirituality of women in the past. I am not positing an ancient matriarchal society to be used as a model. Furthermore, it is arguable whether one ever existed (e.g., Lerner 1986). If patriarchy is defined as male control of women's economics, legal status, and sexuality, and matriarchy is the opposite of patriarchy, then it appears that there has never been a matriarchy.

I am not looking for a matriarchal model but rather for communities where women are respected spiritual leaders. The best models we have today come from some Native communities where women's spiritual contributions are highly valued (e.g., Gunn Allen and Talamantez). There is plenty of evidence for the existence of more egalitarian lifestyles and societies which exist(ed) in conjunction with pagan mythology, practices, and belief systems.[12] Goddess imagery is associated with the materiality of living-in-relation. It is not the female counterpart of God imagery, the distant manipulator of creation and events. Goddess energy is about bringing reality into existence through participation. It is about 'living with' one's own energy and simultaneously with that of other sources such as spiritual guides. There are a variety of ways to depict goddess presence as a transforming energy that lifts a particular person into a broader reality and at the same time brings the universal energy into the individual's consciousness. Goddess presence might be experienced in the presence of friends, as an image of a single woman or as an image of an interactive community of women. It might appear as part of nature or as a felt state of grace within one's own consciousness.

Goddess spirituality can be closely related to shamanism, although this is not necessarily so. In my own experiences, the images in shamanism are more related to animals and natural objects. Nevertheless, at the beginning of each shamanic journey the recurring goddess image of three women's heads on a single bosom comes into consciousness to guide me. This image is joined by another one of an actual Inuit shaman whom I have never met or seen a picture of but from whom I have received treasured gifts. Vision quests or journeys are common practices among those who train in and practise shamanism. They exist outside the paradigm of normative consciousness which is defined from within the constrictions of empiricism and rationalism of our Western heritage.

Occasionally, conferences are organized to facilitate communication between mystics and scholars. I attended one of these in 1975 at the University of Calgary. The belief that mystics have experiences that stand apart from those of scholars is widely held by most scholars. The term 'mystic' is a description applied to those who have experiences that cannot be defined within empirical or rational parameters. The so-called mystics at the particular conference referred to above did not define themselves as mystics. Their 'mystical' experiences were not mystical to them. The same thing is said about visions or quests by those who have them. They are real experiences which involve an alternate form of consciousness. The expansion of consciousness through the incorporation of alternate consciousnesses is not regarded as problematic or mystical by those who enter into these forms of consciousness, but rather is experienced as increased knowledge of oneself and other aspects of reality. I believe that the knowledge derived from these experiences can be applied directly to everyday life. This is especially true with respect to self-knowledge as well as experiencing the ecosystem as interchanging energy fields. The experience of shape-shifting is particularly poignant here. I believe that shape-shifting is a profound way of learning about the changing reality of oneself. It creates a strong awareness of the arbitrariness of the boundaries we use to separate things into categories. Shape-shifting also is an excellent means of realizing the tentative nature of one's own identity.

Images from spiritual experiences can be great forms of empowerment for women, whether it is from goddess spirituality, shamanism, or any other form of spirituality. A goddess image that is particularly relevant today in the drive for women's sexual democracy is that of Kali, who symbolizes the 'antitype' woman. In any culture where death is life's enemy, Kali has generally had bad press. For example, she is classically portrayed as ferocious, black, with many hands, and her tongue hanging out of her mouth as she stands on the body of Shiva, the symbol of the warrior in mythology. Racism and sexism in the traditional depictions of Kali gives her a definite 'outsider' status. Re-interpretaion of Kali, however, is occurring. She is newly depicted by feminists as the goddess who represents the power to destroy what needs to die so that new creation can occur. She represents the power of transformation. Invoking Kali on vision quests or journeys is a powerful way of feeling the strength to let go of destructive energy and thought patterns and allow new ones to emerge in one's consciousness.

Recently while on a journey I had an experience of Kali coming into my consciousness. The fiery energy that was part of her image turned into a fire. I experienced myself as the flame that was Kali. As the flame burned I felt lighter. When the journey was over I no longer experienced the confusion and inertia that were there prior to the experience. They were 'burned up.' The heaviness had disappeared. I returned to my work with new energy and motivation to create. That experience is one of many in which Kali's transforming energy has informed my consciousness. She represents death to that which should die so that new creation can occur. She is an appropriate goddess image for the social and cultural shift away from fear of nature to one of living with it. Kali is an image that helps us to say 'no' to victimization and 'yes' to creating new forms of social organizations. Her image represents creative power through the destruction of oppressive forces. Her presence can facilitate the possibility of breaking free of ideas of powerlessness, of beliefs about mandated roles, and of notions of goodness which are self-effacing. Connecting to Kali's power enables a person to make space for new developments by weakening the grip of previous negative realities. These negative forces in a person's consciousness can be referred to as the demons with which one struggles, without attributing an external existence to them. In classical representations, Kali was usually depicted as a demon, whereas in women-centred interpretations of her, she symbolizes the destroyer of demons.

The image of Kali as the goddess who has the power to give and take life can be related to images from other cultures where female spirits are depicted in creation stories. Creation stories are basic to a culture's beliefs about the origins, natures, and destinies of its people. Creation stories that feature female images are associated with cultures which value the contributions of women. For example, Dhyani Ywahoo describes a creation story of the Tsalagi people (Cherokee). In this story, life as it is known today comes from Star Woman, the mother of all. She fell through a hole from 'the Seventh Heaven' (the world of light) downward. Animals conspired to create a place for her to land. Water Spider (or Muskrat, depending on the myth) put 'firmament' from the bottom of the ocean on the back of Turtle. Buzzard flapped his wings to raise mountains with valleys between. The 'earth' was made on Turtle's back as a safe place for Star Woman to land. She landed safely. "Her breast gave forth corn, beans, and squash; her tears, rivers of fresh water. All humans may trace their roots to the mother of all, Star Woman. Through her blessing the spark of mind was emblazoned within us as a sacred fire, that the mystery of life might be understood as the many in the One" (Ywahoo 1987:30). As Ywahoo notes, this story is about how thought shapes 'hard' reality. The inseparability of ontology and epistemology is reflected here.

Belief in the inseparability of mythology and 'hard' reality is further depicted in the story about the contents of Star Woman's womb. She "carried in the emptiness of her womb twelve potential characteristics of humankind," which symbolized the twelve original clans of the Cherokee. The twelve crystals that Star Woman carried in her womb correspond to twelve aspects of human nature. They are quartz (will), ruby (compassion), topaz (building intelligence), orange jasper (manifestation of beauteous form), emerald (wisdom of particulars and science), rubillite & rose quartz (energy of devotion to manifesting the ideal), amethyst (energy of transfromation), pearl (luminescent planetary mind), fire opal (individuated mind awake in the solar stream), tourmaline (awakened mindfulness of relationships beyond rings of solar system), azurite (energy of reconciliation), and aconite (cycle's completion, systems unwinding, returning to emptiness). These twelve dimensions of human potential are taken as the bases for twelve different clans. They are each identifiable, yet they are part of the same source. The many are divisible yet unified. The contents of Star Woman's womb have much in common with the development of integrated vision that Buddhist meditation is designed to facilitate. In this case, 'seeing' is not merely an isolated source of sense data. Seeing is knowing that is achieved through living with integrative power. It creates out of the return to emptiness. Emptiness is not nothing. It refers to consciousness which is free from restrictive ideas. Star Woman's "decaying body brought forth grasses, grains, beans, squash, all good things for the people to eat, and her tears springing forth in her time of birthing became fresh waters to drink" (Yhawoo 1987:32). Birth and death belong to the same moment.

Tsultrim Allione points out that in Tibetan Buddhism *prajnaparamita* (the perfection of wisdom) is associated with femaleness (1984:21). It is "the principle of cosmic structure" and is neither female nor male, but is regarded as the feminine principle because of "its quality of fertility or potentiality" (p. 21). Allione compares the Buddhist view of the feminine principle of creativity to that described by Starhawk with reference to goddess-imaged creativity. Starhawk says that in goddess-centred creation, "The world is born, not made, and not commanded into being" (Allione 1984:22, quoting from Starhawk). In goddess imagery, spirit and matter are woven together in things and thoughts, in ontology and epistemology. Creative power is not restricted to biological reproduction. Neither is biological reproduction restricted to concrete things or to humans or animals as separate from the continual reproduction of reality. The reproduction of reality is not restricted to cultural or social reproduction. Nature is not reduced to everything outside culture. Indeed, there are powerful myths in Western culture that could be used today to affirm birth-life-cycles in which the reality of nature and cultural beliefs are congruent with each other. In addition, it is possible to bring together in a spectrum a variety of female images that integrate the various dimensions of women's power. Kali's kind of power to take away old life and create new beginnings can be connected to a more motherly image, such as Demeter's, that evokes the same birth-death dynamic but with a different representation of it.

For example, in her article on the nature religion of Demeter and Persephone, Mara Lynn Keller claims that "The Mother Earth religion did not glorify the sacrifice of her children, but celebrated their birth, enjoyment of life, and loving return to her in death" (1990:41). In this, Demeter mourns the absence of her abducted daughter Persephone, who has been taken to the underworld. Demeter refuses to let the sun shine until Persephone is restored to her. Eventually a plan is negotiated in which Persephone is returned for half the year and returns to the underworld for the other half. The crops grow during the time the mother and daughter are together. The quiet time of renewal occurs when they are apart. These times reflect the meaning of summer and winter. The elemental power of Demeter, as mother, that is connected to the life system of the earth can be related to the power of Kali that is used to transform dying life patterns into creative beginnings. Her power to give life is inseparable from the power of death of which she is also a part. Her connection to Persephone while she is in the underworld represents the power of life that remains unactualized but full of potential in death. This view of death as being integral to life is analogous to the latent period of winter that is necessary for the germination of new crops each spring. Living with the elemental power of nature includes having faith in its restorative power. Images such as Kali and Demeter are helpful for women to experience their own power to transform energy that would normally lead them into death into life-affirming ways of living. This is not to advocate avoiding death, but rather to not be overcome by negative energy that serves only to destroy, without hope of opening new pathways for positive energy to actualize the seeds of potentiality within them. Power-filled female images that reflect the dynamic of grounding one's energy within oneself in relation to the social and natural realities that co-construct a person are vital to women's vitality.

Faith as reflected in the Demeter mythology is most importantly faith in the power of cyclical regeneration in which birth, life, and death are part of the continuous process of transformation. Sexuality is central to that process. Bodied spirituality is represented in the myth of Demeter through fertility. She is the exemplary mother figure. Demeter gives a different sense of women's power than Kali does; however, they both represent passionate self-expression as well as strong participation in what is going on around them. Kali's passion is to bring about the truth, more in a cultural sense. She stands up for her own views and destroys what she perceives to be false beliefs. Her energy passionately burns off inappropriate ideas and opens up possibilities for new ones to emerge. Demeter, on the other hand, is passionate about her connection with her daughter

Persephone. As goddess of fertility of the land, she refuses to bring forth the crops while Persephone is lost. She represents the importance of harmony within the ecological system and her own power to throw it out of balance. At the same time she does not have complete control over the mysteries of the cycles of nature. She must negotiate a balance between being with her daugher (the time of the crops) and living apart from her (the latent winter period). Because the myth of Demeter is about fertility, it is more congruent with pervasive cultural images of femaleness than that of Kali. Kali is the antitype while Demeter is the stereotype with regard to projecting female power in terms of normal female identity.

As the image of Kali illustrates, however, fertility is not limited to material reproduction. It can be a process of generating beliefs or activities that make space for new developments. Fertile thinking, for example, is required to escape the grip of life-negating thoughts that make many of us ill or keep us marginalized in the cultural constructions of meanings that would strengthen our self-images. Sometimes this process is relatively peaceful but at other times it is expressed in angry acts of resistance. Kali represents the latter with her many hands flailing wildly as she wears skulls around her waist and carries a sword. The image of her as a warrior is frightening if it represents a crazy woman from exile who has burst illegitimately into a civilization where there is no place for women to be big, black, and threatening. She is the image of woman-out-of-control. Her passion burns like a flame. It quickly destroys the deadwood, i.e., things without generative possibilities. If one is concerned about being part of what will likely be destroyed in her flame, there is reason to fear the power of Kali. On the other hand, having her on your side can be very energizing. She represents the power to resist the network of cultural constraints that many women live with. Rather than succumbing to them, she passionately destroys them and gives birth to her own truths. In this way she serves as a powerful model for women.

Demeter's passion is more in terms of elemental power that links a mother's relation to her daughter with the presence or absence of the sun. In her story, the presence of Persephone is analogous to the warm sunshine of the summer. Her absence is like the cold darkness of winter. Her rage is about having her daughter taken away from her. Her elemental power of connectedness was challenged. Her angry response was to withhold the crops until Persephone was returned. Demeter's mother image is helpful in a similar way to the image of the independent woman that Kali represents. They both represent moral outrage at perceived injustices to their freedom to live with their own power. They effectively direct their energy to stopping what they perceive to be an injustice. For this reason they are helpful images to cultivate for women who wish to live with their own power to resist domination and to actualize their potential. The juxtaposition of Kali, the social activist, and Demeter, the mother, brings together different polarities in a portrayal of integrated female power.

When these disparate forms of passion are experienced by women as part of an integrated energetic participation in a cultural shift toward living with their own power, then it is possible that women will increasingly know themselves as a plurality of identities.

In this way, the barriers between culture and nature will be less real in each person's self-identity and in their other-identification that comes from cultural inscriptions. In this depiction of Kali and Demeter, Kali is more symbolic of living with the cultural laws of renewal, while Demeter represents the power of governance through living with the mysteries of nature, yet each includes the depiction of the possibilities of social and biological power with which females can live. The images of both Kali and Demeter are strong with respect to depicting women either expressing their power or withholding it in the face of adversity. In both myths, death is depicted as a point of breakthrough into a welcomed development. It is not regarded as a dreadful event to be avoided at all costs. In this way, they both provide a positive interpretation of change. Shifts in patterns of thought and action come out of the flame of passion from this kind of energy. An aim is to move toward a cultural paradigm in which female images are interpreted more in terms of women's legitimate strengths and are not marginalized through rhetoric that depicts powerful women as women-out-of-control and, therefore, to be feared. Along with new images, a more positive interpretive model is needed to shift from the view of women's power as threatening to one in which it is valued and lived with as a normal part of each person's ongoing reality. An initial step toward a paradigm shift in the construction of women's identities is to begin with an 'interpretive drift' away from the view of women's power as threatening to a more friendly one.

Interpretive Drifts

I will use a study of magic to illustrate how an interpretive shift might occur. Magic is a form of power that is often, although not necessarily, associated with women. Men as well as women practise magic; however, I will use it here with reference to women since women's power is the focus of discussion. T.M. Luhrmann, an anthropologist, studied magic in England to determine how 'normal' people come to accept magic as rational. Her account of how they do provides a helpful understanding of how experiences shape beliefs about reality. Reality is described as "dynamic flux shot through with subtle forces and unknown energies" (1989:119). She defines interpretive drift as "the slow drift in someone's manner of interpreting events, making sense of experiences, and responding to the world" (1989:12).

Because magic is generally thought of as a practice that is opposed to scientific reasoning, it is a good place to examine how so-called rational people believe in the power of magic. Luhrmann points out that the core belief of magic is that the mind affects matter. A humorous, but apt, example of this claim is the one I saw recently on a birthday card for someone who is fifty years old. It said, "age is a matter of mind over matter, if you don't mind it doesn't matter." This depicts the attitude that we create our own realities according to our interpretations. That is not to say that nothing exists outside of interpretation, but rather that our interpretation shapes it. What matters with regard to magic is that mind affects matter. It is as though you'll see it when you believe it. Rituals are devised to train the mind for that purpose. Repeated practice leads to new understandings. New understandings lead to increased involvement, which supports the new interpretations. The consequence is that the practices become rational to those who do them often enough. This is to say that after sufficient repetition the activity is congruent with the practitioner's way of thinking about the world. When something is rational to a person, the experience and view of reality are mutually reinforcing.

In the process of interpretive drift, new ways of describing events emerge. The new experiences take on a significance that motivate the person having them to talk differently about them than they would have initially. The person begins to fit the experiences into a new way of talking about them which gives them a coherence that they previously didn't have. In doing so, there is a shift in the way that person describes meaningful reality. New descriptions get integrated with existing perceptions; as they do, however, there is a shift in perceptions. A shift in perceptions coincides with an interpretive drift. As this occurs, old perceptions are modified or jettisoned in relation to the newly emerging ones. Coherence is required for an experience to be rational. In order for coherence to prevail there needs to be coherence among the prevailing set of perceptions in a person's consciousness. There needs to be a fit between the old perceptions and new ones. This means that the lived experience and the ability to describe it must cohere. Incoherence is a misfit between a person's experiences and the interpretive framework into which it is placed in a person's consciousness. This is a form of craziness and happens when new experiences are radically different from previous ones or when one does not have sufficient interpretive skills to render an experience coherent. Women often live with incoherence when they live within a linguistic framework that does not allow for adequate expression of their experiences. For this reason they are sometimes associated with ignorance. It is similar to living in a culture where you don't speak the language. This is a good reason for why it is important that women, especially in their own culture, participate more fully in the development of the language in which they may describe their own experiences more adequately. Furthermore, because new experiences are the basis for new ideas, it is important to listen to those who have experiences that are outside the normal parameters used to describe reality. Paying attention to marginalized activities in one's own culture is helpful in expanding the evidential basis of its reality. In order for them to be taken as culturally acceptable they need to be connoted positively in the language. This process of inclusion is facilitated by understanding the underlying rationality behind the activities.

According to Luhrmann, there are four basic assumptions of magic: (1) the physical universe is only a part of reality; (2) human willpower can change the environment; (3) willpower must be directed by the imagination; and (4) the universe is an ordered system of correspondences which can be used for good or evil (1989:121). The people practising magic whom Luhrmann studied believe that you receive back seven times what you send out. Accordingly, they practise good magic. This same belief is characteristic of modern witches as well as of shamans, such as those trained by Michael Harner and his associates in The Foundation for Shamanic Studies in Connecticut. There is a corresponding belief among spiritual healers throughout the world that an integrative energy exists from which everyone can benefit if they are receptive to it. In North America, the most notable spiritual healers are found among Native healers who have retained the tradition and from whom non-Natives have learned their skills.[13]

In Luhrmann's study, most of the witches (including wizards) she studied in London were middle-class urbanites. Women and men, including unpaid householders, scientists, university students, and professors, constituted the members of the six covens she studied. Very few came from the country. Luhrmann postulates that rural witches likely had their own covens or were more likely to be 'lone witches.' The members of the covens in which she participated generally separated their identities as witches from their conventional identities such as computer analyst, professor, graduate student, commercial artist, or tradesman. Fear of ridicule was cited as a strong deterrent to 'going public.' She discovered that the kinds of people engaged in witchcraft are generally those who are taken to be ordinary, sensible people who look and act 'normal.' The importance of her work here lies in her analysis of the shift in thinking that allows a 'normal' person to 'make sense' of magic. Her study is largely about the process by which intellectual habits are altered during the transformation to magician.

She suggests that there are three basic steps in the transformative process to magician. They are (1) shifts in basic perceptions and analysis of events; (2) basic experiential changes and increased use of symbolism in language and practice; and (3) shared intellectual strategies to bridge magic ways of knowing with scientific ways of knowing (Luhrmann 1989:11-12). Interpretations of everyday experiences change. They change because new habits develop with regard to paying attention to things, organizing what is noticed into new meanings, and remembering it in ways that support a particular interpretation. An example of an event that could be interpreted either as a mundane or a significant one is when two people meet on a street after not having seen each other for many

years. One way of interpreting the meeting is to say it was merely a coincidence and to pay little attention to it. It then becomes one more item
that dims quickly in one's memory without having much effect. Another
way of interpreting it is to regard it as a sign of 'synchronicity,' i.e., meaningful coincidence. That interpretation disposes one to pay more attention
to it, to organize it into the larger framework of interpretive meanings,
and to remember it as indicative of something that is happening on a
larger scale in one's life. In this interpretation there is an orientation to incorporate it into the existing relations of events in which one is engaged.
As a person gives this particular event an interpretation of synchronicity,
there is an element of taking magic seriously in the otherwise mundane
event.

Believing in synchronicity is a condition for performing rituals that
create effects at a distance, such as sending love to someone who is not
present at the ritual or assisting a friend in another country to overcome
an illness. Luhrmann found that all the rituals performed by people in the
covens that she studied were positively directed, based on belief in an integrative universal power. They were attempts to draw on the integrative, healing power that is available to all if they are disposed to train in
its use. The basic belief that mind controls matter shapes the training process of mindfulness. Rituals are believed to facilitate concentration of the
mind so it can direct positive energy to a designated place, either the self,
somebody else, or an environmental situation such as disbanding nuclear
weapons (as in the Greenham Common sit-in several years ago in Britain). Successful rituals are believed to have effects. Part of the interpretive
drift of the person becoming a magician is to learn what rituals count as
successful.

Counting something as evidence is largely a matter of interpretation,
of making connections which would not be made by an outsider. Confidence in the new connections between events depends a great deal upon
agreement among group members about their efficacy. A shared body of
knowledge among members of a coven and between covens gives legitimacy to the new set of categories and distinctions made in the transformation to magician. As the body of knowledge gets established among the
groups, new assumptions are taken for granted and are not questioned.
Luhrmann notes that insider/outsider interpretations differ more because
of the process of becoming knowledgeable than from the peculiarities of
magic (1989:115). Connections between rituals, their effects, and the
formation of new conceptual relations largely characterizes the changes in
intellectual habits in the transformation to magician. As a person develops
a magician's consciousness, a new view of 'life-back-at-the-office' emerges.
According to reports from practising magicians, one effect of participating
in magic is to see everything outside of it as "dull and uninspired"
(Luhrmann 1989:247). Because of their tendency to see things more from
the perspective of magician, even their so-called dull activities at the

office take on more significance than they otherwise would have. They claim that participation in magic tends to make everyday activities more imaginative. Events that are connected synchronistically are given more meaning and make apparently random daily occurrences more intelligible.

The changes in intellectual habits that occur during the transformation to magician are changes that could be said to occur in any specialized training. Luhrmann says that "Becoming a specialist often makes an activity seem sensible" (1989:116). That is true of academic disciplines as well as of magic. Selection of evidence, interpretation of the results of methods, and communication about their value are all determined by the training process to which one is subjected. Meaning is always locally defined by the dominant interpretive framework, i.e., belief system. Understanding develops from coherent structuring of experiences (Lakoff and Johnson 1980). While understanding is required for coherence, it is difficult to be entirely coherent about a reality that is continuously changing. While it is plausible to say that everything is always changing, it is the case that some things are more radically different from their immediate cultural context than other things. Magic is one of those things.

Along with such experiences as shape-shifting or having a vision when one has never had one before, magic is often described through 'half-baked' ideas. Because of lack of clarity of these descriptions of new experiences they are often disregarded. It takes imagination to give them coherence. Albert Einstein, among the most highly developed people, was a great advocate of imagination. Part of his posterity is a postcard of him with his hair flared out from his head, eyes popping out of their sockets, exclaiming, "Imagination is everything." Understanding without imagination is unlikely to effect a great deal of change. Sometimes unexpected experiences occur which opens one's understanding to include what was previously categorized as the unimaginable. When the unimaginable stimulates the imagination, new 'experiential gestalts' (Lakoff and Johnson 1980) emerge in one's consciousness, and a person's understanding takes a leap.

When a radically new experience enters into an existing interpretive framework, it dislodges the existing set of perceptions that constitute one's consciousness, or 'field of meaning' (Gerhart and Russell 1990). New experiences create disturbances in a person's mind set. Just as 'reader-reception' of a text depends upon a certain mind-set, so experiencer-reception is limited by the existing perceptual tools of an individual's consciousness. Limitations of new interpretations are exacerbated by training that emphasizes memorization, repetition, devotion to canonical texts, as well as cultural practices of slander and ridicule of the unfamiliar which is often equated with the unimaginable.

Luhrmann's study of witchcraft in England is a good example of how allegedly irrational beliefs become rational to those who take part in the practices of the craft. It also illustrates how the author attempts to receive new 'esoteric' information while remaining faithful to her specialist training as an anthropologist. There is tension throughout the book between interpretations of experiences by the practitioners, on the one hand, and Luhrmann's interpretations of their interpretations, on the other. The author's scepticism with respect to talking about personal experiences in a way that does not reduce them to complete subjectivism is prevalent throughout the book. However, if one follows her account of an interpretive drift, she achieves her goal of showing how magic is reasonable.

Radically new experiences are often regarded with scepticism. This is true not only for the one who has the experience, but even more so for those who have not had such experiences and who doubt their reality base. When I had my first radical spiritual experience, it was too different from what I already knew about reality to fit into my own knowledge framework. I couldn't explain it and didn't mention it to anyone for about a year, until I spent an evening with a friend who I thought might be able to give it some meaning. I was lucky with her friendship and have benefited greatly from her expertise in the meaning of symbols. Her friendly reception made it relatively easy for me to describe that experience as well as several following it. There was a different response, however, at a conference where I referred to spiritual experiences to partially ground the theory of self that I was presenting. For example, at lunch following my presentation, I overheard an influential academic, who was sitting at the same table, comment that she finds such experiences interesting, but is relieved that everyone doesn't attempt to construct a theory from their personal spiritual experiences. The idea was that personal spiritual experiences are idiosyncratic and have little or no generalizability. Reporting one's own experiences as a basis of reliable knowledge has yet to find acceptance in the academy.[14] Academic training instills the assumption that it is better to act as an interpreter of the experiences of others than to interpret one's own experiences. Although this assumption remains dominant with respect to grounding theory in personal experience, there is some movement toward writing our own stories in scholarship. I hope to contribute to this shift toward an expansion of the evidential basis for reliable knowledge.

The relation between knowledge and metaphor arises when discussing spiritual experiences. I shall briefly discuss metaphor and then proceed to connect the discussion to spirituality. In this way I aim to contribute toward the connection between reliable knowledge and spirituality. There is tension between two ways of interpreting metaphors: metaphor as objectivity (literal meaning) and metaphor as subjectivity (figurative meaning). According to Gerhart and Russell, this tension is the hallmark of myth. Metaphor includes ambiguity between the figurative meaning of an utterance and its literal meaning (1990:115). Lakoff and Johnson suggest that a new metaphor replace the old two: the metaphor of 'experiential truth' (1980:179). This is congruent with my own work and is admirably depicted in Young and Goulet (1994) where they describe their methodology as 'experiential' and refer to unusual experiences as 'extraordinary.' Lakoff and Johnson claim that the metaphors of objectivity and subjectivity were intended as ways of rendering unusual experiences coherent. Rituals are described as repeated structural practices that minimize the otherwise chaotic nature of experiences. They, along with symbols, help in organizing one's thoughts by constructing an experiential gestalt: the organization of particular experiences into a coherent whole. The purpose of symbols is to make thoughts visible. They are required to communicate the meaning of everyone's experiences. The use of new symbols is part of an interpretive drift into a new way of experiencing any aspect of reality. New experiences often depend upon the possibility of new symbols being accepted as meaningful expressions of those experiences to make them valid for both the ones who have the experiences and for others with whom they attempt to communicate. It is not acceptable to perpetuate the Cassandra syndrome, where she was given the blessing to see and speak clearly, but was cursed with the reality of not being listened to. This syndrome is like the 'woman in the attic' image. It is important to shift away from this view of women's knowledge of the unusual. Accordingly, it is important to theorize from personal experiences. Metaphor has an important part to play in theorizing from the unspeakable. It must not be confused, however, with mistaking the reality of experiences with language about them. This confusion does not help to bring more experiences into the symbolic system of meaning, but rather continues the process of making language the reality and obscuring the facticity of lived experience.

Metaphor is defined as "imaginative rationality" in which one thing is understood or experienced in terms of another (Lakoff and Johnson 1980:5, 235). Gerhart and Russell refine the meaning of metaphor by claiming that there is an identity relation between the two terms of the metaphor that are likened to each other. For example, "The chairman plowed through the discussion" is an example of metaphor if both the author and the reader understand the two items which are identified (i.e., chairman and plow). Gerhart and Russell also use the example of "God is love" as a metaphor which identifies two items. If the reader cannot give any meaning to God, for example, then the utterance has no meaning. If it has meaning then it serves as an expression of identity that is not questioned. The task of many communicators is to get linguistic expressions culturally accepted in ways that their real meaning is not questioned. Metaphor is intrinsic to language as the main cultural symbolic system of meaning.

The model of language described by Gerhart and Russell distinguishes between the use of language and the form of language. The cognitive model of language constructed by Gerhart and Russell is helpful here to explain how change occurs in meaning and, consequently, how new experiences contribute to interpretive drift. They develop Ferdinand de Saussure's view of language as form: a system of relations of concepts. Language as a meaning system is characterized by shifting relations of concepts. The construction of language as a system of nodes (concepts) and branches (relations between the concepts, the 'logical distance' between them) is imaged like Buckminster Fuller's geodesic domes. Changing the lengths of the struts changes the shape of the dome. Concepts (nodes) are "the things that 'come to mind' when words or signs are encountered" (1990:118). The relations between the concepts (branches) vastly outnumber the concepts. They adopt Ricoeur's (1978) notion of 'logical distance' as the length of the branch between concepts. A meaning field is constructed with a particular 'topology,' according to the various lengths of the branches. Changing the relational distances between concepts brings about a different surface on meaning field. Meaning emerges in terms of the arrangement of concepts in the meaning field. Communication of meaning depends upon understanding the meaning field, which is culture-bound.

Change in the topology of the meaning field occurs with new experiences. They stimulate concept changes, shifts in the relations of concepts, and relocation of old concepts. Metaphorically speaking, the effect of new experiences on the metaphoric cognitive process is like the construction of another geodesic dome. Speech is the manifestation of concepts, while non-linguistic thought processes flick around the field of meaning (Gerhart and Russell 1990:119). New experiences, accompanied by their half-baked concepts, disturb the meaning field and cause changes in meaning. Lack of conceptual clarity occurs in the advent of new experiences.

Clear thinking, in Gerhart and Russell's model, comes from analyzing the relations between the concepts. Understanding these relations has predictive value. One can deduce the meaning of a concept in the meaning field because of its relation to other concepts, which one presumably understands. Science is described as the process of understanding empirical evidence in terms of existing relations of concepts. Worlds of meanings are constructed within localized cultures or sub-cultures. Metaphor helps to communicate across culture-bound meaning fields. According to Gerhart and Russell, metaphor "forces relations in one field to be isometric with those in another . . ." (1990:121). The similarity that is created allows for understanding across boundaries of difference. It is necessary, however, that there is some understanding of both sets of meaning fields in order for metaphor to work (e.g., like the metaphor of the chairman plowing through the meeting). If both sets are understood by one person, but only one set is understood by another, then the utterance is a metaphor for one (identity relation) and a simile for the other (where one thing is like the other). Metaphor, in Gerhart and Russell's view, provides a stronger connection than simile between the two mean-ing fields. The 'metaphoric cognitive process' is the activity of gaining understanding through relations of concepts in a single meaning field and then between meaning fields. It facilitates a shift in understanding through the development of alternative conceptual relations. This is a use-ful way of understanding how interpretive drifts occur within a flexible language system of meaning fields. It does not, however, address the reality of lived experience.

The driving force behind the 'metaphoric cognitive process' is described as the "ontological flash." It is recognition of possible new topological arrangements of meaning fields, of alternative geodesic domes. So long as tension between the sets of relations of concepts inheres in the meaning field, it has a metaphoric quality. When the tension diminishes it no longer has the metaphoric quality. It takes on the quality of 'reality.' A shift in meaning has occurred. The interpretive drift culminates in an established set of relations which are taken for granted. The cumulative effect of inter-pretive drifts in a large number of meaning fields may be regarded as a paradigm shift. Metaphor is a tool which allows us freedom to move beyond fixed meanings of concepts and culture-bound meaning fields. Metaphor is a mode of "presentational symbolizing" (Culpepper 1986). Symbols present an integrated image that crosses over categorical boundaries. Metaphor uses symbolic presentations to integrative separate, linguistic meanings that go beyond discursiveness. Metaphor allows us to dispel the myths of objectivity as well as complete subjectivity. It allows us to 'flick about' in the meaning field and remain open to 'ontological flashes.' While the value of metaphor is inestimable in the understanding of language as a process of constructing meaning through changing relations of concepts, it remains limited by its place in language and is different from lived experiences that are beyond any linguistically framed meaning.

The reference to 'ontological flash,' however, seems to allow an open-ing into an experiential, prereflective aspect of consciousness that is a dis-tinguishing feature of radical spiritual experiences such as visions or shape-shifting. It is this aspect of spirituality (or magic) which can only be dubiously interpreted by a non-experiencer. Normative consciousness excludes the 'reality' of alternate consciousnesses referred to by those who have these spiritual experiences that do not fit the experiencer's perceptu-al or cognitive framework. Metaphor has to do with imagination and with identity relations between concepts. I, along with others who have had such experiences, wish to claim that radical spiritual experiences go beyond either of these features of metaphor. We do not wish to say that our experiences were "as if" experiences. In shape-shifting one might become, for example, a tree, a cougar, or a flame. In my own experiences, it is not "as if" I was these things, but rather that I was. As a flame I feel heaviness burning off. After the experience I feel lighter and enjoy more clarity of thought. When I experienced being a tiger I felt the wind blowing my tail and the solidity of my four feet on the ground in the midst of the stormy weather as I stood at the edge of a cliff overlooking a valley in the mountains. These experiences are not unusual among those who live with natural spiritual powers. When we have these experiences we do not go somewhere else geographically or take on a different physical appearance from the perspective of a normative consciousness.

Such experiences are changes in one's consciousness with regard to the way we live with our energy at that time. These changes in ways of being can be seen as normal if one views oneself as an energy field. Representations of different kinds of energy are lived with in terms of shape-shifting or having visions. Spiritual consciousness includes a deeper level of living with oneself and with the rest of reality as interactive and interrelated energies. Increased spiritual training and frequent ritual practice facilitates expansion of one's experiences of reality as energy. This view of reality can be spoken about metaphorically; it is, however, beyond metaphorical representation. One needs to say it 'as it is' rather than using the phrase 'as if.' These experiences do not lend themselves to representation in terms of 'quasi experience' as suggested by 'as if.'

Returning to normative consciousness includes changes in one's knowledge and identity that emerged during the spiritual experience of becoming a different form. I find that the spiritual experience is not a flash of insight into a new relational set of concepts; however, it usually leads to that. The metaphor is secondary, in this view, to the experience of altered consciousness. Consciousness is defined here as the interrelatedness of prereflective felt awareness and reflective meaning. Within this view of consciousness, one can understand in a felt sense, without the accompanying meaning that is given through reflection. There is no interpretive framework available to give them meaning. Each experience that I have had over the past eight years brings new meaning which requires reflection. Sometimes I do not have any understanding of the experience at first. I gradually gain understanding through reading about experiences of others, the meaning they have attributed to symbols and images which were part of my experiences, and by listening to how others analyze their experiences (spiritual or ordinary, everyday ones). I begin to make connections between the images in my experiences and the world around me in ways that I did not prior to the experiences.

Metaphors and myths are valuable tools for communicating meanings across boundaries of meaning fields where precise, literal meanings are difficult or impossible to communicate. If they are used, however, to represent radical spiritual experiences in terms of 'as if' experiences, then they diminish and misrepresent those experiences. They do not allow for the distinction between normative consciousness and alternate consciousness in which identity changes. The change in identity between normative consciousness and alternate consciousness is not like a split personality. The two forms of consciousness are continuous with each other.

Normative consciousness, from my perspective, is one that keeps me functioning in my culture. Within it I stay out of the way of oncoming buses and pay attention to what my tasks are as a co-creator of reality. Alternate consciousness, however, provides the greater source of spiritual insight that informs my everyday living. It is fundamentally about living with various kinds of energy that shift and change form continuously. In light of these experiences, it is sometimes difficult to take normative consciousness seriously. After sufficient reflection, the identity experienced within alternate consciousness becomes part of the new set of relational concepts that constitute a pluralistic identity. The self is understood differently. The concept of self is changed in part through the expansion of identity as a tree, a cougar, a snake, and so forth. It is also changed in part because of the new experience of the self in relation to such things as the earth, trees, fire, animals, and other people. In Gerhart and Russell's manner of speaking, new things "come to mind" with regard to the concept of self. Using the geodesic dome model, the relational distances which connect self to the environment, to other people, to different aspects of the self, change length. The topology of the meaning field of the self shifts. It shifts in relation to the topology of the field of meaning of community, of society, of the direction of social and cultural evolution. Alternate consciousness of radical spiritual experiences can serve as powerful contributions to an expansion of normative consciousness in an understanding of interpretive drift. They help to understand how the 'unimaginable' becomes part of the imagination which informs metaphorical cognitive consciousness.

Outstanding changes in intellectual habits occur in many meaning fields. Transformed to magician, one 'sees' the continuity between spiritual experiences and everyday activities. Transferring from teaching chemistry to teaching women's studies, or developing a philosophy of disability after becoming disabled are other forms of transformed knowledge. In each of these cases, among an infinity of others, the topology of the meaning fields changes in relation to a multitude of other meaning fields. Metaphor helps us to understand the content of each field and the relations among them after experiences have taken shape through conceptualization. When interpretive drifts within and between fields develops into a crescendo, a paradigm shift in the worlds of meanings occurs. Metaphors help us to stretch our minds. "A mind that is stretched to a new idea never returns to its original dimensions" (Ackerman 1990, insertion at the front of her book, quoting Oliver Wendell Holmes).

Transformation of knowledge occurs through the interaction of experiences and reflections (e.g., Code 1991; Minnich 1990; and Zalk and Gordon-Kelter 1992). Knowledge from the margins changes the dimensions of meaning fields (e.g., see any issue of *Kinesis*, a Canadian newspaper that publishes "News about Women that's Not in the Dailies"). Knowledge from the margins enlivens "mainstream" knowledge. There is little doubt that feminist writing is affecting the topography of knowledge with regard to philosophical thinking, scientific knowledge, and social activism directed at sexual and social democracy. As the margins increasingly affect the constituency of more widely held beliefs, there is more receptivity of experiences which have been previously designated outside the realm of philosophical, scientific, or other socially important meaning fields such as those relating to economics, politics, and social stratification. Feminist spirituality and ecofeminism are now major fields in ecological and environmental landscapes (e.g., Spretnak 1986). The global economy currently is sometimes examined in relation to women, the environment, colonialism, and cultural assumptions as interlocking aspects of a connected process of injustice (e.g., T. Minh-Ha Trinh 1989). The shift in topography of knowledge is due, in part, to including women's experiences and reflections in the re-interpretation of concepts and the relations between them. Spiritual experiences such as those involving female imagery, animals, trees, fire, water, earth, as well as male imagery, are inspirational experiences which enlarge the imagination and remove inertia as they provide motivation to work for a more humane and connected community.

Paradigm Shift Toward Integrating Spiritual and Social Realities

Interpretive drifts can contribute toward a more inclusive knowledge paradigm. This shift includes accepting a greater variety of lived experiences as an evidential basis for normal reality. Part of this process toward a more inclusive knowledge paradigm is to think more carefully about assumptions that we have taken for granted with respect to events like 'mystical' experiences and the practice of magic. Fear and scepticism toward these activities often arises more out of ignorance and learned biased attitudes than from the reality of the activities themselves. Conventional wisdom tends to be an accumulation of cultural and related family scripts that are difficult to analyze because we can't distance ourselves sufficiently to see them. As Carol Christ (1987b) notes, cultural assumptions often seem so obvious that we don't know how to start to think differently. It is only when hidden assumptions are questioned, however, that inertia is removed and the conditions for change are created.

In an attempt to explain how change occurs within vast cultural systems of entrenched beliefs, Thomas Kuhn (1962) initiated the notion of paradigm shift. It refers to a major alteration in the topography of meaning fields. It emerges from changing the basic assumptions around which received wisdom is based. Feminist scholarship contributes toward a paradigm shift with respect to diverse cultural assumptions about the origins, natures, and purposes of women. It attempts to alter cultural inscriptions that are written onto women's identities in their particular places in history, in geographic locations, and in social categories. Feminist perspectives are part of social and evolutionary drifts that are intended to bring about more egalitarian and ecologically friendly global interaction (see, for example, Eisler 1987 and Maturana and Varela 1987).

A basic assumption of a feminist paradigm is that women are full citizens with sex-specific identities who have a right to self-determination. A second assumption is that self-determination for the expression of wholeness requires social justice. Justice is impossible, however, in a social system that assumes a hierarchical, ontological, and/or social relation between the sexes. Structured dependency (as hidden in the notions of femininity and contemporary chivalry) is a sign of injustice. The existence of systematic economic, emotional, and intellectual dependency is connected to the basic assumption of ontological dependency. The chivalrous notion of protecting women by treating them as if they are the property of their protectors is part of the mindset that restricts women from acting on their own without fear of being attacked, exploited economically, slandered, or intellectually bullied. Many women live with these fears and some men regularly perpetuate the bases for them.

Both women and men internalize many of the same assumptions about these normalized unhealthy relations between the sexes which promote psychological and social distortions for both sexes. Because many cultural assumptions about what is normal female and male behaviour are invisible, they unconsciously reinforce social injustice even in the lives of those who are well intentioned. The circularity of hidden assumptions and social realities contributes to inertia with regard to eliminating injustices in personal relationships, families, local communities, regions, nations, and globally. A paradigm shift occurs when basic assumptions in a multitude of locations are questioned and interpretive drifts begin to break down established meanings in the conceptual fields which organize the reality of lived experiences.

Interpretative drifts are socially constructed. They are also partially individually determined. Each person's desires contribute to the larger social reality which simultaneously shapes individual desires. Feminist spirituality and feminist social critical analysis both revolve around the axial slogan 'the personal is political.' It is equally true that 'the political is personal.' There is invariably an interactive process between individual subjectivity and social influences in such places as families, community organizations, schools, various employment places, religious institutions, legal institutions, and political organizations. Feminist spirituality generally focusses more on the psychological dimension, while feminist social analysis targets political and economic factors. Both tend to pay attention to ecological issues, which are readily connected to both individual and collective ways of living with, for example, waste, chemicals, and war.

Self-determination is also a point of intersection between spiritual and social analysis. There is a difference, however, in the way in which it is discussed. From the spiritual point of view, it is more a question of 'mind over matter,' whereas from a socialist view the issue is to a larger extent 'matter determining mind.' Both of these perspectives highlight important truths. Spiritual beliefs about one's connectedness in the life-system can positively affect a person's attitudes about possibilities for self-determination, even when the social conditions are not very supportive.

Despite the shared concerns of feminist spirituality and social critical analysis, a tension exists between the two orientations. They both aim to bring about a more inclusive way of living with ourselves and our chosen communities. The tension lies in the tendency of one perspective to pay insufficient attention to the importance of economics for well-being and the other to largely disregard the contribution from spiritual knowledge that provides a stabilizing effect in the midst of all circumstances. This is not to affirm Marx's view of religion as an opiate for those who live in constant misery. Rather it is to say that an orientation to being centred in oneself as part of an integrative network of relationships can provide a basis of connectedness rather than divisiveness when working for change in political and economic realities. In case I am misunderstood, I am not advocating that there should be less emphasis on improving pay cheques for women's work. On the contrary, economics is a major point of contention in most women's lives. Raising women's standard of living globally is a central feminist concern. Social activism toward that end is vital for the well-being of women. The qualification that I wish to add, however, is that this necessary activity can be carried out in ways that include more attention to personal feelings of connectedness.

My goal is to work toward integrating these two perspectives more fully. I do not wish to overemphasize the 'heartfelt' side of the dilemma and ignore the factor of exploitation. There is little point, for example, in developing a trusting disposition without also recognizing ways in which structured power relations erode trust. Trust may be almost unconditional between friends and lovers or, ideally between parents and children. Trust between colleagues who work in a hierarchically structured organization, however, often has a different basis. It depends more on assumptions associated with the relations between the positions that each colleague occupies. Unconditional trust is unwarranted in such places. The chilly climate (i.e., one that is not friendly to minorities) in which previously marginalized people often work when they take up positions in an established hierarchy often affects their ability to do their best work. Many women from all social categories and men from marginalized places experience a chilly climate in higher ranking positions in their workplaces more often and more intensely than White, middle-class men. Affirmative action is intended to mitigate the problem. The idea behind affirmative action is to open up spaces in the mainstream for the more marginalized, thereby changing the structure of the mainstream. This evolutionary process of change through the breakdown of exclusive boundaries is an important consequence of both seeing reality as connected and continuously working to eliminate social injustice.

   Overcoming inertia in the evolutionary process can be understood, in part, by seeing how it might operate in the life of an individual. Susan Wendell's account of the different perspectives a person might have with regard to oppression and responsibility, as discussed earlier, helps to understand this. In situations of domination and subordination, one might have an oppressor's interpretation. Structural discrimination, in that perspective, is explained in terms of the victim's problem. Blaming those who are without access to resources such as money, education, and emotional support for their lack of motivation, without attention to social determinants, is characteristic of an oppressor's perspective. It may be held by a privileged person and internalized by a victim. The one without access to resources often has low self-esteem. A lack of self-regard contributes to self-blame, which feeds into a lack of motivation and reinforces inertia and blame by others. As Wendell points out, inertia is often overcome when anger at the oppressive conditions and/or oppressor motivates action. The victim sees their own victimization as caused by institutionalized injustice. Justified anger moves one out of inertia and toward change. If one gets stuck in the anger, however, it reduces one's ability to see the interaction between self-responsibility and other-responsibility. In Wendell's view, which I support, blocked anger characterizes the victim's mentality. It becomes a pervasive negative consciousness that inhibits self-determination and sets up a negative cycle between self and others. A constructive, alternative perspective suggested by Wendell is that of responsible actor. One learns to differentiate between that for which one is personally responsible and that which can be attributed to others. The responsible actor perspective requires an understanding of causal interrelatedness. Wendell labels that understanding the perspective of the observer/ philosopher. As she notes, one needn't be a professional philosopher to understand how things are related to each other. It is important, however, to be able to stand back and observe oneself within the context in order to see the structured power relations and one's collusion in it.

   For a major shift to occur with respect to social justice and women, it is important that self-determination, or responsible action, be understood within social contexts in which three loci of power can be identified. Hilary Lips' (1991) discussion of power in terms of individual, collective, and institutionalized power is relevant here. In the event of systemic injustice, it is necessary that collective power function for the benefit of individuals and groups. Every individual is part of an other-identified group, whether they want to be or not. They are a particular colour (e.g., pink, brown, black, tan), are situated in a certain economic strata, are urban or rural, native or immigrant, and so forth. Group rights are inseparable from individual rights. When individuals are treated apart from their groups they become tokens which usually serve to inhibit changes that might improve the conditions of their group (e.g., Patricia Hill Collins 1991). One Black woman, for example, may be hired as a political strategy which is seen to "take care" of the discrimination of Black women. She is seen to represent all Blacks and her differences, as well as those of her group, can be ignored. In Canada, Native women occupy the lowest economic strata in the workforce. Hiring or befriending one Native women without paying attention to Native rights, such as land rights and self-government rights, is another form of tokenism. As mentioned earlier, within Native rights is the issue of Native women's rights. It is a divisive issue among the women as well as between the women and men. Individual rights and powers of self-determination cannot be extricated from the group context. Collective power is a condition for a paradigm shift in structural power relations. Institutionalized power relations are challenged through collective bargaining and political activism. Identity politics is part of the paradigm shift with regard to social justice. Affirmative action is motivated by the desire to base justice on collective, as well as individual, rights. The government of Iceland serves as a model for legislating social policies which promote the rights of women and children. Before a piece of legislation is passed it is evaluated for its effects on children and women. Rather than describing such action as reverse discrimination, it is more appropriately described as a mechanism for resisting and overcoming existing discrimination toward children and women. Affirmative action can only be described fairly as reverse discrimination if there is no existing discrimination which it is designed to counteract.

Despite the inseparability of individual and social issues, it is possible to look specifically at the individual to get a handle on the way in which responsible social action can be grounded in personal power. Gabrielle Roth (1989) authoritatively shows how emotional and spiritual balance within oneself is important for effective action against social injustice. She claims there are five basic emotions which constitute each person's consciousness. They are fear, anger, sadness, joy, and compassion. Her shamanistic understanding of self-determination closely resembles a Buddhist approach to mindfulness. She claims that "everybody has a shaman inside, waiting for a wake-up call" (Roth 1989:2). Her wake-up call is dance.

Roth teaches dance in New York City to people from every social category imaginable. She believes that regardless of each person's unique combination of personal abilities and social determinates, everyone is a dancer. For Roth, dance is movement. I agree with her claim that the deepest movement occurs in stillness. Compassion comes from stillness. Stillness is congruent with emptiness. Emptiness is the absence of distorted or blocked emotions. It is a dynamic stillness which is the source of movement as self-determination. Grounding movement in stillness is akin to grounding knowledge in silence. In her affirmation that there is a centrality of stillness in all movement, Roth supports Alice Walker's claim that silence is the source of all truth. I believe that this view of knowledge and action provides a visionary basis for feminist work.

Walker's account of truth and Roth's theory of movement resemble the Buddhist focus on wisdom and compassion in the development of mindfulness. Wisdom and compassion are described metaphorically as the two wings of a bird which enable it to fly. A bird flies, it seems, for the same reason it sings. "A bird does not sing because it has an answer—it sings because it has a song" (Ackerman 1990:193). The song is a metaphor for individual power. According to Roth, dance is a good way for people to access their song. The inside flows outward through dance. To be a whole human being is to express the sacred powers which are part of each person's identity and are necessary for survival. These powers are the power of being, loving, knowing, seeing, and healing. Shamanic consciousness involves purposeful attention to the development of powers that are integral to everyone as a human being. Each person has their own songs which express the integration of these powers if they are flowing. Our individual task is to sing our songs. Dancing opens up the flow of energies, the sacred powers. A condition for the flow of energies is the transformation of our relationships to the five basic emotions (fear, anger, sorrow, joy, and compassion). Self-determination is a matter of learning to relate to our emotions in ways that facilitate the possibility of integration of personal power.

Fear, anger, sadness, joy, and compassion are part of consciousness. We are never without these emotions. Spiritual training is not a matter of learning to overcome them, but rather to live with them in a way that expresses their power in a healthy way. Individual power is developed through transforming our relationships to these emotions so they are expressed directly and effectively. Their balanced presence is constitutive of a responsible actor who has an observer/philosopher perspective and acts appropriately for constructive consequences. Appropriate behaviour is grounded in being present to these emotions. Understanding emotions as kinds of energy that are interrelated to other forms of energy in the lifesystem helps to put oneself into perspective and to focus on balancing self-knowledge with the dynamics of the larger system.

In this view of the emotions as levels of energy that are invariably present to us, fear is closest to the surface. Fear is a protective mechanism. Feeling afraid leads to defensive behaviour or flight from that which is feared. Fear is a necessary condition for survival. Feeling fear allows one to survive in relation to the source of fear. It is necessary to feel afraid in order to survive frightful conditions. When, however, fear becomes an overriding emotion in one's consciousness, it is no longer a healthy mechanism for survival. It becomes maladaptive and surfaces inappropriately as paranoia or other pathological ways of interpreting things and events. It is often experienced in such ways as fear of dying, of aging, of losing one's current state of health, of losing approval of others, of losing citizenship, of losing one's job, or of loss of anything with which one is familiar. Fear of loss, of the unknown, lies at the heart of hostility as in, for example, men's fear of women's power or women's fear of men's authoritarianism. The more fear there is, the more likelihood there will be violence by the dominant as well as furtive manipulation by the subordinate. Overcoming distorted fear is a condition for interrupting patterns of domination-subordination. An initial condition for overcoming fear is getting in touch with it. One way of getting in touch with oneself is through moving with the energy in dancing rhythms that open energy fields.

Following Roth, there are five basic rhythms corresponding to the five emotions. They are: flowing, staccato, chaos, lyric, and stillness. For those who are interested in following this, Roth has a tape that includes those five rhythms (*Initiation*). Fear is a flowing rhythm, anger is staccato, sadness is chaos, joy is lyrical, and compassion is stillness. Feeling rhythms is part of feeling emotions. Bodied consciousness is necessary, in this view, for clear thinking and responsible acting. Anger is a reaction to injustice. Violation of one's sacred powers of being, loving, knowing, seeing, and healing is appropriately responded to by anger. Anger at systemic discrimination is justified anger. As a defense mechanism of individual sacred power, it is necessary for spiritual and personal survival. When the individual is supported collectively in their response to injustice, there is a better chance for survival. Social movements constitute resistance to violation of the powers of individuals who are identified with oppressed groups. Social support for individual oppression is a powerful motivator for a person to move out of a state of inertia. Many women have found the women's movement and women's studies to have this effect on their lives. The close connection between personal health and social (including family) conditions cannot be overstated. Personal responsibility for one's well-being is vital. The same is true for social responsibility for personal health. In order for the lifesystem to be balanced, there needs to be congruency between the interactive dimensions of internal subjectivity and social conditions. The goal of self-determination, in my view, is to move out of stuckness and towards freedom of movement.

The path out of anger is described by Roth as a movement from a lack of initiative to intuitive well-being. The five stages that she discusses are: inertia, imitation, intuition, imagination, and inspiration. Her view of anger as an agent for liberation is compatible with Wendell's. For Wendell, anger moves one from debilitating self-blame to placing responsibility with those who restrict one's movement. Likewise, Roth claims that anger moves a person from inertia to the second stage in her model, namely, imitation. Anger can motivate a person to start paying attention to some of the causes that determine the limiting conditions of a person's life. While anger is not always the emotion that serves as the stimulating energy, it often is. The corresponding musical rhythm of anger is staccato. It is sharp and forceful. Staccato rhythm helps to unblock stuckness. Stuckness is characteristic of psychological depression and/or social oppression. When the oppression is revealed and anger can be expressed, often the depression is reduced. That is not to say that oppression and depression are identical, but rather that there is an important overlap between them. Letting go of pent-up anger and learning to focus it on deserved targets frees up positive energy for other pursuits. When anger is focussed and not displaced into a pervasive negative orientation, new possibilities for loving arise.

The power of love is sacred to the wholeness of being human. The likelihood of self-love is greater as anger is unloaded from the heart. Self-love is usually developed within an experience of love from another, such as parents, children, friends, and lovers. Projection of one's own strength onto a loved one is not an uncommon experience. In the process of moving from inertia to imitation, that projection generally is onto the role model. A teacher, a book, or something else might provide insight into the causes for one's disempowerment, while simultaneously opening a possible way out. As the person moves out of inertia, they might begin to imitate the external source of insight, usually a role model. Imitation is a first step out of inertia. Imitation of another person is part of most people's journey into fuller self-expression. It is, however, only a transition phase. Personal creativity requires moving through the stage of imitation and into what Roth calls intuition. It is a way of being, loving, knowing, seeing, and healing that relies on unreflected felt awareness. It is the aspect of consciousness which is uninformed by reflection. It is a gut reaction. Letting go of rules of observation and reflection allows a person to pay attention to gut reactions. Such abandonment is associated with chaos. The musical rhythm for intuition is chaotic. Letting the body go wild in dance helps to get in touch with the untamed aspect of the self. Hidebound egocentricity, and the caged bird feeling are emptied from consciousness in chaotic dancing. An individual's personal style of movement emerges. A new flow of energy develops and creates more opportunity for a deeper emotion to be felt.

The third level of emotional energy that is always present to some degree in one's consciousness is sadness. If one is not overcome completely by despair, the embrace of deep-seated sadness can lead to new ways of knowing. Embracing sadness constructively depends upon support from others. A function of accepting sadness is to open a person to receiving loving support from others. Many people who have lost a loved one comment on how compassionate they have felt since the loss. That is due partly to the keenness of the pain of loss. Another factor is the response of others to their felt pain. I can relate well to this feeling. After my surgery for lung cancer and the ensuing infection, which was followed by another operation, I have been keenly aware of people in physical pain. The sadness of being in such pain and the corresponding isolation I felt at that time has left me with a continuing sensitivity to others in similar conditions. I believe that I live with a sadness that is more present to me than it was before. This increased presence of sadness, however, is counterbalanced by a greater feeling of compassion for others in pain. Embracing sadness is, among other things, accepting one's vulnerability. To open oneself up to the loss that sadness denotes is to permit oneself to be more open to oneself and to others. This is often referred to negatively as losing control; however, I experience this loss as a gain of part of myself. I believe that some of the feelings that I attempted to control are now more present to me. I agree with Roth that attempts to remain in control make the body stiffen up. Chaotic dance helps the body to loosen up. I support her view that illness is in large part an indication of energy blocked as a result of inappropriate control of the emotions. Release from tension is necessary for the next step in Roth's helpful model of movement toward health: joy.

Joy is energy that allows a person to see with their own eyes. Consciousness moves from the level of imitation to imagination. The mirror is no longer used to reflect the cultural inscriptions that women often perceive through the eyes of men or their own male-identified eyes as they look into the mirror and imitate. Rather, the mirror can be used to see oneself as she is present to herself. It provides an opportunity for reflecting back one's imagination of new bodily expressions of internal creative energy. The mirror becomes a personal tool for constructing the self imaginatively. Reflections of vital energy are seen in place of wrinkles. The body, whichever part that is reflected in the mirror, is the signifier of uniquely organized embodied spiritual power. The joy of seeing oneself with new eyes after being released from unfocussed fear, anger, and sadness allows the spirit to sing. When a person sings their own song it is a reflection of a groundedness in themselves. They see that groundedness reflected in the mirror. Seeing themselves with new eyes allows them to listen to themselves with new ears. They can listen to new concepts rather than to the ill-fitting ones to which they used to accommodate themselves. They can see their bodies as expressions of sacred powers. They can dance that power and feel their groundedness as connectedness to the sacred power of others and to the earth. The body is a map which choreographs our energy. It is a pattern of energy that connects us to other human bodies, animal bodies, and the earth body. The joy of seeing these patterns of connectedness can be accessed through rhythmical dance and used to transform daily life into a sacred art. The attitude of joy expressed through dance can be taken into the workplace, the kitchen, and the bedroom. Audre Lorde is an inspiration to us all as she lived out her joy while struggling against cancer, even though eventually she succumbed to it. Joy is one of the five basic emotions in this model of emotions. All five are thought to characterize every person's consciousness. Having the emotion of joy does not mean that fear, anger, and sadness are overcome. It exists in relation to them. Each has its time of expression.

The deepest emotion is compassion. It is the strongest healing emotion. Compassion depends on a person's power of being, loving, knowing, and seeing in ways that are empty of obstructions. The Buddhist doctrine of *Sunyata* is about the emptiness of egocentricity. Blocked emotions are constitutive of egocentricity. They are the negative side of self-interest. The positive side of self-interest is based on respect for oneself, the self-love that is intrinsic to loving others. It is the eros that is necessary for agapé. Self-love and benevolence are alternative ways of describing wisdom and compassion. Knowing oneself requires loving oneself. It is the condition for compassion toward others, which is a healing activity. Healing is the process of restoring calmness to the soul. In shamanic discourse, healing is associated with soul retrieval (e.g., Ingerman 1991, 1993). It is directed towards activating a person's spiritual power by retrieving parts of their soul that have broken away, thus depleting its power to keep the energy field of the person in balance. Soul retrieval aims to restore health by bringing back lost energy resources and restoring balance in the flow of emotions. This allows for stillness of being where the inside flows outward. It is a centredness of an inner balance that can be described as ecstasy. It is the blissfulness of graced consciousness, as described earlier. Ecstatic dance, T'ai Chi, chanting, meditation, prayer, or dreams and visions are ways of achieving this state.

The calm centredness from where one's energy flows outwards is a valuable resource for imaginative and constructive social participation. Compassion is the felt emotion of this stillness of being. It is experienced as inspired by others who benefit from such a person's compassion. I am fortunate to have known a person who lived with inspired compassion. He died recently. Even as his death was approaching with an inevitability of which he was aware, his compassion for others was an inspiration to those around him. His energy remained in balance through regular meditation, which he had practised for his lifetime as a Tibetan spiritual leader. When he knew that I had cancer he urged me to keep meditating and phoned long distance to support my energy level and discuss meditative practices. I learned from him that conscious effort is not required to be compassionate when one's actions come from one's spiritual power centre. The power of healing is a sacred power. It can be experienced in many ways such as the power of animal spirits, spirit guides in the form of goddesses and gods, natural objects like trees and water, or more abstractly as Spirit. Compassion is the power that is the spirit at the centre of a human being.

Spirituality is about compassionate healing. Feminist spirituality is about healing women as individuals, as groups, as responsible actors, while working toward greater social justice and ecological sensitivity. Responsible action in the face of injustice is about resisting it and working toward creating living conditions that are more conducive to healthy lifestyles that support the energy fields of the whole ecosystem. It is reasonable to suggest that living in balance with nature and with other people is greatly facilitated by keeping in touch with the spiritual energy at the deepest level of one's being. This is especially poignant for active feminists who live with many tensions in their lives. Many of us live with fear of punishment for claiming our own authority, anger at the violence done against women, sadness about the missed opportunities for women to be whole human beings, joy in the shared celebration of women, and compassion for others who challenge one's own assumptions. Roth says that "Living love, living powerfully through love involves getting into the rhythm of the basic life energies that sustain us" (1989:88). The core of spirituality is being connected to these basic life energies.

A useful way to experience myself as part of these energies is through shape-shifting. The doctrine of *pratityasamutpada* is lived during these times. These experiences of knowing myself as changing realities have helped me live with critical illness differently. The changing nature of self-identity that I have experienced during shape-shifting opens up new ways of experiencing myself as part of a lifesystem of energies that are interdependent. Through these experiences it becomes less reasonable to restrict my identity to that which belongs to normative consciousness. Because of experiencing myself more as shifting energy within a network of interactive energies, my view of death as transformation has been enhanced. My Buddhist training many years ago started me on a significant interpretive drift regarding death as a transformation rather than the end of something. This drift has been strengthened through work with goddess spirituality and shamanic journeying. In light of this interpretive drift, my recent encounter with near death has included more of a tendency toward thinking about it in terms of transformation rather than exclusively as possible loss of life. This is not to say that I haven't felt frightened, alone, exhausted from pain, and confused. Rather I merely wish to say that my own spiritual training and practices have contributed significantly to making spirituality a reasonable resource for feminist social activism.

Whether one resonates with a spiritual understanding of human nature or with a secular view, human-ness is generally understood to have something to do with compassion. David Hume (1978), for example, rejected a spiritual understanding of human nature. Yet his theory of morality depended on his claim that human beings have a tendency toward benevolence as well as selfishness. His theory of the calm passions is an attempt to reconcile selfishness with benevolence. The result is that, in his view, the morally developed person acts on the basis of calm passions. Selfish desires are considered in light of the interests of others. In Hume's view, when that relation is purposefully analyzed, one discovers that one's own interests are inseparable from those of others in the community.

While spirituality is obviously not necessary for morality, it is a powerful source of morality. The orientation of spirituality toward balance and integration makes it an important resource for those concerned with social justice. Recognizing the body as an expression of spiritual energy is helpful, especially for women. Celebrating the body through transforming images, dances, music, art, theatre, and so forth is both imaginative and inspiring. These avenues for new thought and expressions promote the well-being of women. They provide inspiration for new ways of imagining women's creative participation in society. Spiritual consciousness such as Buddhist meditation, shamanic consciousness, and goddess consciousness provide possibilities for transforming consciousness from a state of inertia to one that is imaginative and even inspired. Spiritual consciousness provides new input into the imaginative infrastructure which supports the linguistic symbolic ordering of meaning.

Meaning fields in the structuring of language change their shape as new concepts enter the field and old ones are altered. It is not just a matter of logical distance between the concepts in the structuring of meaning, it is also an issue of changing the logic in the construction of the meaning fields. Increasing emphasis on fluidity would help to remove the staticness of the "geodesic dome" structure of each world of meanings. Luce Irigaray's use of mucous is a good start in the movement from staticness to fluidity. It is neither fluid nor flesh. Using the image of mucous as neither one thing nor another has a similar intention as the Buddhist four-pronged negation. It is a claim about the nature of reality as neither this nor that. The four prongs include the following four statements: it is not the case that an utterance is true; it is not the case that an utterance is false; it is not the case that it is neither true nor false; and it is not the case that it is true and false. The point of both the mucous image and the four-pronged negation claim is to reduce categorical thought from limiting our experiences. The four-pronged negation argument has the same logic to it as the Zen koan which asks about the sound of one hand clapping. The impossibility of answering this question jars us out of the inertia of old thought patterns and creates possibilities for new meaning fields to develop in which the ecstasy of living with paradoxical knowledge might be more adequately reflected. The expression of ecstasy usually brings to mind the movement of uncontrolled energy. I agree with Roth, however, that ecstasy is the exquisiteness of stillness. To image ecstasy as stillness is paradoxical. Paradoxes provide opportunities for breakthroughs in our ways of thinking. They open space for interpretive drifts and ultimately for paradigm shifts in what is believed about the nature of reality and the preferred ways of living with it. New experiences, images, and language provide alternative meaning fields in which we can develop new interpretations that form a broader evidential basis for reliable knowledge about the mysteries of reality.

The development of more integrative interpretations of reality goes hand-in-hand with constructive and innovative social action. A notable example of such social action is the WomenFutures Community Economic Development Society of Vancouver.[15] In conjunction with the Social Planning and Research Council of British Columbia, WomenFutures received a grant from the Department of Health and Welfare Canada for their project on "Women and Community Economic Development" (CED). The purpose of the study "is to gain a better understanding of all dimensions of women's participation in Community Economic Development activity, with particular focus on identifying and analyzing how women's participation effectively integrates both the social and economic objectives of CED to achieve community well-being" (WomenFutures 1991:10). Their project is motivated by a desire to understand how women analyze the economy, how they participate in it, and how they are empowered by their participation. They have recently published a handbook in both French and English entitled *Counting Ourselves In: A Woman's Community Economic Development Handbook*. It is available to women across the country. The focus is on work that contributes to the well-being of community members as well as to the sustainability of natural resources. The orientation is towards living with each other in community and with nature in a way that sustains the whole system.

The paradigm shift toward 'living with' rather than 'having' is occurring in many places. The drive toward increased literacy, especially of women from largely agricultural economies, is a welcomed part of the shift. Affirmative action that promotes better working opportunities for women throughout the world is another significant activity. Overcoming the association of women with stupidity, with workhorses, with environmental decorations, and with images that reflect powerlessness is in each case integral to the shift toward egalitarianism. The shift toward greater balance requires a celebration of women through new images that reflect the many possibilities for their strong presence in the cultural construction of their own identities, in socio-politico-economic activities, and with respect to their own self-identification as subjects with full citizenship. Spirituality is a rich renewable resource for supporting women in their activities for social change. Their work for greater social justice and ecological integration can be significantly enhanced when it comes from the stillness at the centre of their beings, where positive energy motivates their activities. Social change arising from the compassion of the spirit characterizes a paradigm shift toward 'living with' both spirituality and critical social analysis in a balance that creates supportive conditions for women's spirits, bodies, and the places where they are.

Notes

1 Lawrence LeShan has done research and teaching for over thirty-five years with thousands of cancer patients, members of their families, and professional health care workers.

2 For example, see Lourdes Benería (1982); Peter D. Little and Michael M. Horowitz (1987); Irene Dankelman and Joan Davidson (1988); Louise Fortmann (1985); Carolyn Merchant (1990); Carol Riegelman Lubin and Anne Winslow (1990); and K. Sharma (1984).

3 Unfortunately Dr. Nandwa succumbed to cancer shortly after she returned to Kenyatta University where she planned to teach and to help rural women become more literate and socially active in gaining more freedom to expand their education and professions.

4 This was an example cited by Jane Nandwa when she was discussing the genderedness of the use of technology in Kenya. The introduction of technology to ease women's burdens almost invariably presented an opportunity for a man to take over control. In her view it was taken as a male right.

5 For an extended analysis of Robert Owen's form of socialism see Barbara Taylor (1983).

6 Socialist feminist authors such as Dorothy Smith, Alison Jaggar, Nancy Hartsock, and Michèle Barrett, to name only a few, are beacons in the development of feminist social criticism. Their contributions, and those of other socialist feminists, are critical in the analysis of social injustice and the move toward social egalitarianism. While their analyses have been ground-breaking for changes for women in the workplace, any analysis that focusses almost exclusively on economics largely misses the component of sex/affective labour in any kind of work, especially in the home. Mia Campioni and Elizabeth Grosz address this issue in a helpful way in their article "Love's Labours Lost: Marxism and Feminism" (1991).

7 For a longer discussion of this, see Joyce McCarl Nielsen's section on "Feminist Essentialism" in Nielsen 1990. Sociologists tend to be wary of sex-specificity and prefer to refer only to gender in the interests of avoiding biological determinism. In my view, sociological determinism is the obverse of biological determinism and rests on the same dualistic mind/body assumption.

8 For a clear and well-organized presentation of women's health issues, see Nancy Worcester and Mariamne H. Whatley (1988).

9 For an actual image and account of womanpower in the sense of climbing the corporate ladder, see Uma Sekaran and Frederick T. Leong (1992).

10 For a socialist account of this view of the pluralistic self, see Ann Ferguson (1991), who describes the theory of the pluralistic self as 'aspect theory' of self. The self is constructed from various aspects that are given their social meaning according to the ways in which they serve the goals of the community in which they are constructed.

11 This term was gratefully borrowed from Ann Ferguson (1991).

12 The evidence comes mainly from archaeological findings such as graves, cave drawings, and the organization of ancient community structures. For example, graves of male leaders which included the rest of their household are dated since the period in history when the northern invaders conquered European, Asian, Persian, and Mesopotamian countries where pagan symbolism influenced social practices of living with the earth and each other with less aggression. Cave dwellings depict the fluidity of human and animal presence, such as bird heads on women's bodies and snake-women as symbols of perspective on the process of birth, life, and death as cyclical and regenerative. Community structures show the centrality of the kitchen, around which are living quarters for communities of people.

13 A good example of this is the story of a Sioux holy man, Frank Fools Crow, in Thomas E. Mails (1991).

14 Fortunately, reporting one's own experiences is becoming more acceptable as an alternative to the usual anthropological method of describing other people's. The anthology edited by David Young and Jean-Guy Goulet (1994) is a good example of anthropologists who write about their own experiences in the field or at home. These scholars are writing in the wake of the questionable reputation of Castaneda, the most notable anthropologist who writes about his own radical personal spiritual experiences. In my view they face criticisms of Castaneda's work in a critical and constructive way that adds strength to their own accounts. I applaud the courage of these writers.

15 For further information, the office is: WomenFutures, Community Economic Society, 217-1956 West Broadway, Vancouver, B.C. V6J 1Z2.

Bibliography

Ackerman, Diane. 1990. *A Natural History of the Senses*. New York: Random House.

Adler, Margot. 1986. *Drawing Down the Moon: Witches, Druids, Goddess-Worshippers, and other Pagans in America Today*. Boston: Beacon Press.

Agarwal, Bina, ed. 1988. *Structures of Patriarchy: State, Community, and Household in Modernising Asia*. London: Zed Books,

Alderson, Lucy, and Melanie Conn. 1988 (December). *More than Dollars: A Study of Women's Community Economic Development in British Columbia*. Vancouver: Womenfutures Community Economic Development Society.

Allen, Jeffner, and Iris Marion Young, eds. 1989. *The Thinking Muse: Feminism and Modern French Philosophy*. Bloomington: Indiana University Press.

Allen, Paula Gunn. 1991. *Grandmothers of the Light: A Medicine Woman's Sourcebook*. Boston: Beacon Press.

_____. 1986. *The Sacred Hoop: Recovering the Feminine in American Indian Traditions*. Boston: Beacon Press.

Allione, Tsultrim. 1984. *Women of Wisdom*. London: Routledge & Kegan Paul.

Andolsen, Barbara Hilkert, Christine E. Gudorf, and Mary D. Pellauer, eds. 1985. *Women's Consciousness/Women's Conscience: A Reader in Feminist Ethics*. San Francisco: Harper & Row.

Atkinson, Clarissa W., Constance H. Buchanan, and Margaret R. Miles, eds. 1987. *Shaping New Vision: Gender and Values in American Culture*. Ann Arbor: UMI Research Press.

Atwood, Margaret. 1985. *The Handmaid's Tale*. Toronto: McClelland & Stewart.

Baier, Annette C. 1987. The Need for More than Justice. In *Science, Morality & Feminist Theory*, edited by Marsha Hanen and Kai Nielsen. Calgary: University of Calgary Press.

_____. 1985. What Do Women Want in a Moral Theory? *Noüs* 19 (March): 53-63.

Barstow, Anne Llewellyn. 1994. *Witchcraze: A New History of the European Witch Hunts*. San Francisco: Pandora.

_____. 1988. On Studying Witchcraft as Women's History: A Historiography of the European Witch Persecutions. *Journal of Feminist Studies in Religion* 4, no. 2:7-19.

_____. 1986. *Joan of Arc: Heretic, Mystic, Shaman*. Lewiston: E. Mellen Press.

Bateson, Mary Catherine. 1990. *Composing a Life*. New York: A Plume Book.

Beauvoir, Simone de. [1953] 1961. *The Second Sex*. Translated and edited by H.M. Parshley. Reprint, New York: Bantam Books.

Belsey, Catherine. 1991. The Metaphysics of Desire. Paper delivered at the University of Alberta, September.

Benería, Lourdes, ed. 1982. *Women and Development: The Sexual Division of Labor in Rural Societies: A Study Prepared for the International Labour Office within the Framework of the World Employment Programme*. New York: Praeger.

Benjamin, Jessica. 1988. *The Bonds of Love: Psychoanalysis, Feminism, and the Problem of Domination*. New York: Pantheon Books.

————. 1986. A Desire of One's Own: Psychoanalytic Feminism and Intersubjective Space. In *Feminist Studies/Critical Studies*, edited by Teresa de Lauretis. Bloomington: Indiana University Press.

Bepko, Claudia, and Jo-Ann Krestan. 1993. *Singing at the Top of Our Lungs: Women, Love, and Creativity*. New York: Harper Collins.

————. 1990. *Too Good for Her Own Good: Breaking Free from the Burden of Female Responsibility*. New York: Harper & Row.

Berger, Pamela C. 1985. *The Goddess Obscured: Transformation of the Grain Protectress from Goddess to Saint*. Boston: Beacon Press.

Bleier, Ruth. 1986. Lab Coat: Robe of Innocence or Klansman's Sheet? In *Feminist Studies/Critical Studies*, edited by Teresa de Lauretis. Bloomington: Indiana University Press.

Bolen, Jean Shinoda. 1984. *Goddesses in Everywoman: A New Psychology of Women*. San Francisco: Harper & Row.

————. 1979. *The Tao of Psychology: Synchronicity and the Self*. San Francisco: Harper & Row.

Bordo, Susan. 1990. Reading the Slender Body. In *Body/Politics: Women and the Discourses of Science*, edited by Mary Jacobus, Evelyn Fox Keller, and Sally Shuttleworth. London: Routledge.

Brock, Rita Nakashima. 1989. On Mirrors, Mists, and Murmurs. In *Weaving the Visions: New Patterns in Feminist Spirituality*, edited by Judith Plaskow and Carol P. Christ. San Francisco: Harper & Row.

Brockman, Joan. 1992 (March). *Identifying the Issues: A Survey of Active Members of the Law Society of Alberta*. Calgary: Law Society of Alberta.

Brown, Karen McCarthy. 1991. *Mama Lola: A Vodou Priestess in Brooklyn*. Berkeley: University of California Press.

————. 1989. Women's Leadership in Haitian Vodou. In *Weaving the Visions: New Patterns in Feminist Spirituality*, edited by Judith Plaskow and Carol P. Christ. San Francisco: Harper & Row.

Browning, Janisse. 1992. Women's Theatre: Surfaces that Need Breaking. *Kinesis* (February): 18.

Burstyn, Varda, and Dorothy Smith. 1985. *Women, Class, Family and the State*. Toronto: Garamond Press.

Butler, Judith. 1990. *Gender Trouble: Feminism and the Subversion of Identity*. New York: Routledge.

Campioni, Mia, and Elizabeth Grosz. 1991. Love's Labours Lost: Marxism and Feminism. In *A Reader in Feminist Knowledge*, edited by Sneja Gunew. London: Routledge.

Canadian Labour Congress. 1989. Report in "Why Unions." *Challenging the Barriers: Edmonton Working Women Newsletter* (Spring/Summer): 4-6.

Cannon, Katie G. 1988. *Black Womanist Ethics*. Atlanta, GA: Scholars Press.

Card, Claudia, ed. 1991. *Feminist Ethics*. Lawrence, KA: University Press of Kansas.

Carson, Anne. 1992. *Goddesses & Wise Women: The Literature of Feminist Spirituality, 1980-1992: An Annotated Bibliography*. Freedom, CA: The Crossing Press.

Caufield, Catherine. 1984. *In the Rainforest*. Chicago: University of Chicago Press.

Chernin, Kim. 1981. *The Obsession: Reflections on the Tyranny of Slenderness*. New York: Harper & Row.

Chodorow, Nancy. 1978. *The Reproduction of Mothering: Psychoanalysis and the Sociology of Gender*. Berkeley: University of California Press.

Christ, Carol P. 1991a. Mircea Eliade and the Feminist Paradigm Shift. *Journal of Feminist Studies in Religion* 7, no. 2:75-94.

————. 1991b. Why Women Need the Goddess: Phenomenological, Psychological, and Political Reflections. In *A Reader in Feminist Knowledge*, edited by Sneja Gunew. London: Routledge.

————. 1989. Rethinking Theology and Nature. In *Weaving the Visions: New Patterns in Feminist Spirituality*, edited by Judith Plaskow and Carol P. Christ. San Francisco: Harper & Row.

————. 1987a. *Laughter of Aphrodite: Reflections on a Journey to the Goddess*. San Francisco: Harper & Row.

————. 1987b. Toward a Paradigm Shift in the Academy and in Religious Studies. In *The Impact of Feminist Research in the Academy*, edited by Christie Farnham. Bloomington: Indiana University Press.

————. 1978. Heretics and Outsiders: The Struggle over Female Power in Western Religion. *Soundings: An Interdisciplinary Journal* 61, no. 3:260-80.

Christ, Carol P., and Judith Plaskow, eds. 1992. *Womanspirit Rising: A Feminist Reader in Religion*. 2d ed. San Francisco: HarperSanFrancisco.

Cixous, Hélène. 1991. The Laugh of the Medusa. In *A Reader in Feminist Knowledge*, edited by Sneja Gunew. London: Routledge.

Code, Lorraine. 1991. *What Can She Know?: Feminist Theory and the Construction of Knowledge*. Ithaca: Cornell University Press,

————. 1987. *Epistemic Responsibility*. Hanover, NH: University Press of New England.

Cohen, Marjorie. 1987. *Free Trade and the Future of Women's Work: Manufacturing and Service Industries*. Ottawa: Canadian Centre for Policy Alternatives.

Cole, Eve Browning, and Susan Coultrap-McQuin, eds. 1992. *Explorations in Feminist Ethics: Theory and Practice*. Bloomington: Indiana University Press.

Collins, Jane L. 1991. Women and the Environment: Social Reproduction and Sustainable Development. In *The Women and International Development Annual*, eds. Rita S. Gallin and Ann Ferguson. Vol. 2. Boulder, CO: Westview Press.

Collins, Patricia Hill. 1991. *Black Feminist Thought: Knowledge, Consciousness, and the Politics of Empowerment*. New York: Routledge.

Condren, Mary. 1989. *The Serpent and the Goddess: Women, Religion, and Power in Celtic Ireland*. San Francisco: Harper & Row.

Conner, Randy P. 1993. *Blossom of Bone: Reclaiming the Connections between Homoeroticism and the Sacred*. San Francisco: HarperSanFrancisco.

Cooey, Paula M., William R. Eakin, and Jay B. McDaniel, eds. 1991. *After Patriarchy: Feminist Transformations of the World Religions*. Maryknoll, NY: Orbis Books.

Corea, Gena. 1985. *The Mother Machine: Reproductive Technologies from Artificial Insemination to Artificial Wombs*. New York: Harper & Row.

Culpepper, Emily. 1991. The Spiritual, Political Journey of a Feminist Freethinker. In *After Patriarchy: Feminist Transformations of the World Religions*, edited by Paula M. Cooey, William R. Eakin, and Jay B. McDaniel. Maryknoll, NY: Orbis Books.

————. 1986. The Politics of Metaphor: A Feminist Philosophy. Paper delivered at the annual meetings of the American Academy of Religion.

Currie, Dawn H., and Valerie Raoul, eds. 1992. *Anatomy of Gender: Women's Struggle for the Body*. Ottawa: Carleton University Press.

Dahan Dalmédico, Amy. 1991. Sophie Germain. *Scientific American* (December): 117-22.

Daly, Mary. 1989. Be-Friending. In *Weaving the Visions: New Patterns in Feminist Spirituality*, edited by Judith Plaskow and Carol P. Christ. San Francisco: Harper & Row.

————. 1987. *Websters' First New Intergalactic Wickedary of the English Language/Conjured by Mary Daly in Cahoots with Jane Caputi*. Boston: Beacon Press.

————. 1984. *Pure Lust: Elemental Feminist Philosophy*. Boston: Beacon Press.

————. 1978. *Gyn/Ecology: The Metaethics of Radical Feminism*. Boston: Beacon Press.

————. 1973. *Beyond God the Father: Toward a Philosophy of Women's Liberation*. Boston: Beacon Press.

Dankelman, Irene, and Joan Davidson. 1988. *Women and Environment in the Third World: Alliance for the Future*. London: Earthscan Publications.

Davaney, Sheila Greeve. 1987. The Limits of the Appeal to Women's Experience. In *Shaping New Vision: Gender and Values in American Culture*, edited by Clarissa W. Atkinson, Constance H. Buchanan, and Margaret R. Miles. Ann Arbor: UMI Research Press.

————. 1986. Radical Historicity and the Search for Sure Foundations. Unpublished paper presented at the American Academy of Religion.

Derrida, Jacques. 1987. Women in the Beehive: A Seminar with Jacques Derrida. In *Men in Feminism*, edited by Alice Jardine and Paul Smith. New York: Methuen.

Devor, Holly. 1989. *Gender Blending: Confronting the Limits of Duality*. Bloomington: Indiana University Press.

Dexter, Miriam Robbins. 1990. *Whence the Goddesses: A Source Book*. New York: Pergamon Press.

Diamond, Irene, and Gloria Feman Orenstein, eds. 1990. *Reweaving the World: The Emergence of Ecofeminism*. San Francisco: Sierra Club Books.

Dinnerstein, Dorothy. 1976. *The Mermaid and the Minotaur: Sexual Arrangements and Human Malaise*. New York: Harper & Row.

Dourley, J.P. 1990. *The Goddess, Mother of the Trinity: A Jungian Implication*. Lewiston: Edwin Mellen Press.

Downie, Susan. 1988. *Babymaking: The Technology and Ethics*. London: Alden Press.

Downing, Christine. 1988. *Psyche's Sisters: Reimagining the Meaning of Sisterhood*. San Francisco: Harper & Row.

————. 1981. *The Goddess: Mythological Images of the Feminine*. New York: Crossroad.

Durkheim, Emile. 1915. *The Elementary Forms of the Religious Life: A Study in Religious Sociology*. Translated by Joseph Ward Swain. London: G. Allen & Unwin.

Eichler, Margrit, and Phoebe Poole. 1988 (September). *The Incidence of Preconception Contracts for the Production of Children Among Canadians*. Toronto: Ontario Institute for Studies in Education.

Eilberg-Schwartz, Howard. 1989. Witches of the West: Neopaganism and Goddess Worship as Enlightenment Religions. *Journal of Feminist Studies in Religion* 5, no. 1:77-95.

Eisler, Riane Tennenhaus. 1987. *The Chalice and the Blade: Our History, Our Future*. Cambridge, MA: Harper & Row.

Eliade, Mircea. [1951] 1964. *Shamanism: Archaic Techniques of Ecstasy*. Reprint, New York: Pantheon.

Esteva, Gustavo. 1990. The Informal Economy. *Ideas*. CBC, 28 November.

Estor, Marita. 1987. Women's Work Is Never at an End: Paid and Unpaid Labour. In *Women, Work and Poverty*, edited by Elisabeth Schüssler Fiorenza and Anne Carr. Edinburgh: T. & T. Clark.

Falk, Nancy Auer, and Rita M. Gross, eds. 1989. *Unspoken Worlds: Women's Religious Lives*. 3d ed. Belmont, CA: Wadsworth.

Faludi, Susan. 1991. *Backlash: The Undeclared War Against American Women*. New York: Crown.

Farkas, Kris. 1989. Women and Privatization. *Challenging the Barriers: Edmonton Working Women Newsletter* (Spring/Summer): 10-13.

Fatona, Andrea. 1992. Black Women in Nova Scotia: From a Site of Resistance. *Kinesis* (March): 7.

Felder, Cain Hope, ed. 1991. *Stony the Road We Trod: African American Biblical Interpretation*. Minneapolis: Fortress Press.

Ferguson, Ann. 1991. *Sexual Democracy: Women, Oppression, and Revolution*. Boulder, CO: Westview Press.

————. 1989. *Blood at the Root: Motherhood, Sexuality and Male Dominance*. London: Pandora.

Feuerbach, Ludwig. 1967. *Lectures on the Essence of Religion*. Translated by Ralph Manheim. New York: Harper & Row.

Field, Martha A. 1988. *Surrogate Motherhood*. Cambridge, MA: Harvard University Press.

Finson, Shelley. 1987. Feminist Spirituality Within the Framework of Feminist Consciousness. *Studies in Religion/Sciences Religieuses* 16, no. 1:65-77.

Fiorenza, Elisabeth Schüssler. 1983. *In Memory of Her: A Feminist Theological Reconstruction of Christian Origins*. New York: Crossroad.

Fiorenza, Elisabeth Schüssler, and Anne Carr, eds. 1987. *Women, Work and Poverty*. Edinburgh: T. & T. Clark.

Fletcher, John, and Andrew Benjamin, eds. 1990. *Abjection, Melancholia, and Love: The Work of Julia Kristeva*. New York: Routledge.

Folbre, Nancy. 1991. Women on Their Own: Global Patterns of Female Headship. In *The Women and International Development Annual*, Vol. 2, edited by Rita S. Gallin and Ann Ferguson. Boulder, CO: Westview Press.

Fortmann, Louise. 1986. *The Role of Local Institutions in Communal Area Development in Botswana*. Madison, WI: Land Tenure Center, University of Wisconsin–Madison.

Foucault, Michel. 1980. *Power/Knowledge: Selected Interviews and Other Writings, 1972-1977*. Edited by Colin Gordon and translated by Colin Gordon et al. Brighton: Harvester Press.

————. 1972. *The Archaeology of Knowledge and the Discourse on Language*. Translated by A.M. Sheridan Smith. New York: Pantheon.

Fraser, Nancy, and Sandra Lee Bartky, eds. 1992. *Revaluing French Feminism: Critical Essays on Difference, Agency, and Culture*. Bloomington: Indiana University Press.

Freire, Paulo. 1970. *Pedagogy of the Oppressed*. New York: Herder and Herder.

Freud, Sigmund. 1975. *Civilization and Its Discontents*. Translated by Joan Rivière. London: Hogarth Press and the Institute of Psycho-analysis.

————. 1973-74. *The Standard Edition of the Complete Psychological Works of Sigmund Freud*. Translated and edited by James Strachey. London: Hogarth Press.

Friedman, Susan, ed. 1990. H.D. (1886-1961). In *The Gender of Modernism: A Critical Anthology*, edited by Bonnie Kime Scott. Bloomington: Indiana University Press.

Frye, Marilyn. 1992. Oppression. In *Gender Images: Readings for Composition*, edited by Melita Schaum and Connie Flanagan. Boston: Houghton Mifflin.

_____. 1983. *The Politics of Reality: Essays in Feminist Theory*. Freedom, CA: The Crossing Press.

Fuss, Diana. 1992. "Essentially Speaking": Luce Irigaray's Language of Essence. In *Revaluing French Feminism: Critical Essays on Difference, Agency, and Culture*, edited by Nancy Fraser and Sandra Lee Bartky. Bloomington: Indiana University Press.

_____. 1989. *Essentially Speaking: Feminism, Nature & Difference*. New York: Routledge.

Gadon, Elinor W. 1989. *The Once and Future Goddess: A Symbol for Our Time*. San Francisco: Harper & Row.

Gallin, Rita S., and Ann Ferguson, eds. 1991. *The Women and International Development Annual*. Vol. 2. Boulder, CO: Westview Press.

Gallop, Jane. 1988. *Thinking Through the Body*. New York: Columbia University Press.

Garry, Ann, and Marilyn Pearsall, eds. 1989. *Women, Knowledge, and Reality: Explorations in Feminist Philosophy*. Boston: Unwin Hyman.

Gatens, Moira. 1991. A Critique of the Sex/Gender Distinction. In *A Reader in Feminist Knowledge*, edited by Sneja Gunew. London: Routledge.

Gerhart, Mary, and Allan Melvin Russell. 1990. The Cognitive Effect of Metaphor. *Listening* 25, no. 2:114-26.

Gilligan, Carol. 1982. *In a Different Voice: Psychological Theory and Women's Development*. Cambridge, MA: Harvard University Press.

Gilligan, Carol, Janie Victoria Ward, and Jill McLean Taylor, with Betty Bardige, eds. 1988. *Mapping the Moral Domain: A Contribution of Women's Thinking to Psychological Theory and Education*. Cambridge, MA: Harvard University Press.

Gilman, Charlotte Perkins. 1979. *Herland*. New York: Pantheon.

Gimbutas, Marija Alseikaite. 1982. *The Goddesses and Gods of Old Europe: Myths and Cult Images*. Berkeley: University of California Press.

Goldenberg, Naomi R. 1990. *Returning Words to Flesh: Feminism, Psychoanalysis, and the Resurrection of the Body*. Boston: Beacon Press.

_____. 1982. *The End of God: Important Directions for a Feminist Critique of Religion*. Ottawa: University of Ottawa Press.

_____. 1979. *Changing of the Gods: Feminism and the End of Traditional Religions*. Boston: Beacon Press.

Golub, Sharon. 1992. *Periods: From Menarche to Menopause*. London: Sage.

Gostin, Larry, ed. 1990. *Surrogate Motherhood: Politics and Privacy*. Bloomington: Indiana University Press.

Gould, Glenn A. 1968. A Conversation with John McClure. *The Glenn Gould Legacy: J.S. Bach*. Compact Disc. CBS Records.

Govier, Trudy. 1990. Trust and Distrust: A Conceptual Framework. Unpublished paper, The University of Calgary, Calgary, Alberta.

Greenberg, Blu. 1981. *On Women & Judaism: A View from Tradition*. Philadelphia: Jewish Publication Society of America.

Gross, Rita M. 1993. *Buddhism after Patriarchy: A Feminist History, Analysis, and Reconstruction of Buddhism*. Albany: State University of New York Press.

_____. 1989. Menstruation and Childbirth as Ritual and Religious Experience among Native Australians. In *Unspoken Worlds: Women's Religious Lives*, edited by Nancy Auer Falk and Rita M. Gross. 3d ed. Belmont, CA: Wadsworth.

_____ . 1987. I Will Never Forget to Visualize that Vajrayogini Is My Body and Mind. *Journal of Feminist Studies in Religion* 3, no. 1:77-89.

Grosz, Elizabeth. 1990a. The Body of Signification. In *Abjection, Melancholia, and Love: The Work of Julia Kristeva*, edited by John Fletcher and Andrew Benjamin. New York: Routledge.

_____ . 1990b. Irigaray's Notion of Sexual Morphology. Paper delivered at the Spring Conference on Imag(in)ing Women: Representations of Woman in Culture, University of Alberta, Edmonton, Alberta.

_____ . 1989 (Spring). Bodies and Knowledges: Feminism and the Crisis of Reason. Paper delivered at the University of Alberta, Edmonton, Alberta.

Guenther, Herbert V., trans. 1975. *Kindly Bent to Ease Us. Part One: Mind*. By Longchenpa. Emeryville, CA: Dharma Publishing.

Guenther, Herbert V., and Leslie S. Kawamura, trans. 1975. *Mind in Buddhist Psychology*. By Ye Shes rgyal-mtshan. Emeryville, CA: Dharma Publishing.

Hamilton, Roberta, and Barrett, Michèle, eds. 1986. *The Politics of Diversity: Feminism, Marxism and Nationalism*. London: Verso.

Hampson, Margaret Daphne. 1990. *Theology and Feminism*. Oxford: Basil Blackwell.

Harding, Sandra. 1986. The Instability of the Analytical Categories of Feminist Theory. *Signs: Journal of Women in Culture and Society* 11, no. 4:645-65.

Harner, Michael. 1980. *The Way of the Shaman: A Guide to Power and Healing*. San Francisco: Harper & Row.

Harrison, Beverly Wildung. 1989. The Power of Anger in the Work of Love. In *Weaving the Visions: New Patterns in Feminist Spirituality*, edited by Judith Plaskow and Carol P. Christ. San Francisco: Harper & Row.

Harrison, Faye V. 1991. Women in Jamaica's Informal Economy: Insights from a Kingston Slum. In *Third World Women and the Politics of Feminism*, edited by Chandra Talpade Mohanty, Ann Russo, and Lourdes Torres. Bloomington: Indiana University Press.

Hartsock, Nancy. 1990. Foucault on Power: A Theory for Women? In *Feminism/Postmodernism*, edited by Linda J. Nicholson. New York: Routledge.

_____ . 1983. The Feminist Standpoint: Developing the Ground for a Specifically Feminist Historical Materialism. In *Discovering Reality: Feminist Perspectives on Epistemology, Metaphysics, Methodology, and Philosophy of Science*, edited by Sandra Harding and Merrill B. Hintikka. Dordrecht: Reidel.

Hekman, Susan J. 1990. *Gender and Knowledge: Elements of a Postmodern Feminism*. Cambridge: Polity Press.

Helgesen, Sally. 1990. *The Female Advantage: Women's Ways of Leadership*. New York: Doubleday Currency.

Hersh, Richard H., Diana Pritchard Paolitto, and Joseph Reimer, eds. 1979. *Promoting Moral Growth: From Piaget to Kohlberg*. New York: Longman.

Heyward, Carter. 1993. *When Boundaries Betray Us: Beyond Illusions of What Is Ethical in Therapy and Life*. San Francisco: HarperSanFrancisco.

Hick, John. 1966. *Evil and the God of Love*. London, Macmillan.

Hochschild, Arlie Russell, with Anne Machung. 1989. *The Second Shift: Working Parents and the Revolution at Home*. New York: Viking Press.

Hoffmann, Yoel. 1980. *The Idea of Self, East and West: A Comparison Between Buddhist Philosophy and the Philosophy of David Hume*. Calcutta: Firma KLM.

Holmes, Janelle, and Eliane Leslau Silverman. 1992 (March). *We're Here, Listen To Us!: A Survey of Young Women in Canada*. Ottawa: Canadian Advisory Council on the Status of Women.

hooks, bell, and Cornel West. 1991. *Breaking Bread: Insurgent Black Intellectual Life*. Boston: South End Press.

Huang, Agnes. 1992. WomenFutures: Money to Build. *Kinesis* (March): 5.

Hume, David. [1888] 1978. *A Treatise of Human Nature*. Edited by L.A. Selby-Bigge. 2d ed. Reprint, Oxford: Clarendon Press.

Ingerman, Sandra. 1993. *Welcome Home: Following Your Soul's Journey Home*. San Francisco: HarperSanFrancisco.

_____. 1991. *Soul Retrieval: Mending the Fragmented Self*. San Francisco: HarperSanFrancisco.

Irigaray, Luce. 1992. Diotoma's Speech. In *Revaluing French Feminism: Critical Essays on Difference, Agency, and Culture*, edited by Nancy Fraser and Sandra Lee Bartky. Bloomington: Indiana University Press.

_____. [1977] 1985a. *This Sex which Is Not One*. Translated by Catherine Porter with Carolyn Burke. Reprint, Ithaca, NY: Cornell University Press.

_____. [1974] 1985b. *Speculum of the Other Woman*. Translated by Gillian C. Gill. Reprint, Ithaca, NY: Cornell University Press.

_____. 1984. *Éthique de la différence sexuelle*. Paris: Éditions de Minuit.

Jaggar, Alison M. 1983. *Feminist Politics and Human Nature*. Sussex: Harvester Press.

Jay, Nancy. 1991. Gender and Dichotomy. In *A Reader in Feminist Knowledge*, edited by Sneja Gunew. London: Routledge.

Jayawardena, Kumari. 1986. *Feminism and Nationalism in the Third World*. London: Zed Books.

Jenson, Jane, Elisabeth Hagen, and Ceallaigh Reddy, eds. 1988. *Feminization of the Labor Force: Paradoxes and Promises*. New York: Oxford University Press.

Johnson-Odim, Cheryl. 1991. Common Themes, Different Contexts: Third World Women and Feminism. In *Third World Women and the Politics of Feminism*, edited by Chandra Talpade Mohanty, Ann Russo, and Lourdes Torres. Bloomington: Indiana University Press.

Kant, Immanuel. [1785] 1981. *Grounding for the Metaphysics of Morals*. Translated by James W. Ellington. Reprint, Cambridge: Hackett.

Kehoe, Alice B. 1989. *The Ghost Dance: Ethnohistory and Revitalization*. Fort Worth, TX: Holt, Rinehart and Winston.

Keller, Catherine. 1986. *From a Broken Web: Separation, Sexism, and Self*. Boston: Beacon Press.

Keller, Evelyn Fox. 1992. *Secrets of Life/Secrets of Death: Essays on Language, Gender and Science*. London and New York: Routledge.

Keller, Mara Lynn. 1990. The Eleusinian Mysteries: Ancient Nature Religion of Demeter and Persephone. In *Reweaving the World: The Emergence of Ecofeminism*, edited by Irene Diamond and Gloria Feman Orenstein. San Francisco: Sierra Club Books.

Kelly, Joan. 1984. *Women, History & Theory: The Essays of Joan Kelly*. Chicago: University of Chicago Press.

King, Sallie B. 1991. *Buddha Nature*. Albany: State University of New York Press.

King, Ynestra. 1990. Healing the Wounds: Feminism, Ecology, and the Nature/Culture Dualism. In *Reweaving the World: The Emergence of Ecofeminism*, edited by Irene Diamond and Gloria Feman Orenstein. San Francisco: Sierra Club Books.

Kirby, Vicki. 1991. Corporeal Habits: Addressing Essentialism Differently. *Hypatia: Special Issue, Feminism and the Body* 6, no. 3:4-24.

Klein, Anne Carolyn. 1987. Finding a Self: Buddhist and Feminist Perspectives. In *Shaping New Vision: Gender and Values in American Culture*, edited by

Clarissa W. Atkinson, Constance H. Buchanan, and Margaret R. Miles. Ann Arbor: UMI Research Press.

Klein, Renate P., ed. 1989. *Infertility, Women Speak Out about Their Experiences of Reproductive Medicine*. London: Pandora Press.

Kohlberg, Lawrence. 1971. Stages in Moral Development as a Basis for Moral Education. In *Moral Education: Interdisciplinary Approaches*, edited by C.M. Beck, B.S. Crittenden, and E.V. Sullivan. Toronto: University of Toronto Press.

Kohlberg, Lawrence, and R. Kramer. 1969. Continuities and Discontinuities in Childhood and Adult Moral Development. *Human Development* 12:93-120.

Kuhn, Thomas S. 1962. *The Structure of Scientific Revolutions*. Chicago: University of Chicago Press.

La Belle, Jenijoy. 1988. *Herself Beheld: The Literature of the Looking Glass*. Ithaca: Cornell University Press.

Lacan, Jacques. 1977. *Ecrits*. Translated by Alan Sheridan. New York: W.W. Norton.

Lakoff, George, and Mark Johnson. 1980. *Metaphors We Live By*. Chicago: University of Chicago Press.

Lasker, Judith N., and Susan Borg. 1987. *In Search of Parenthood: Coping with Infertility and High-Tech Conception*. Boston: Beacon Press.

Leacock, Eleanor, Helen I. Safa, and contributors. 1986. *Women's Work: Development and the Division of Labor by Gender*. South Hadley, MA: Bergin & Garvey.

Lerner, Gerda. 1986. *The Creation of Patriarchy*. New York: Oxford University Press.

LeShan, Lawrence L. 1990. *The Dilemma of Psychology: A Psychologist Looks at His Troubled Profession*. New York: Dutton.

Lips, Hilary M. 1992. Women and Power in the Workplace. In *Gender Images: Readings for Composition*, edited by Melita Schaum and Connie Flanagan. Boston: Houghton Mifflin.

––––––––. 1991. *Women, Men, and Power*. Toronto: Mayfield Publishing.

Little, Peter D., and Michael M. Horowitz, with A. Endre Nyerges, eds. 1987. *Lands at Risk in the Third World: Local-Level Perspectives*. Boulder, CO: Westview Press.

Lloyd, Genevieve. 1984. *The Man of Reason: "Male" and "Female" in Western Philosophy*. Minneapolis: University of Minnesota Press.

Locke, John. 1967. *Two Treatises of Government*, edited by Peter Laslett. 2d ed. Cambridge: Cambridge University Press.

Lopez, Julie Amparano. 1992. Women Also Faced with Invisible Walls. *The Globe and Mail*, 4 March: Sec. B, pp. 1 and 4.

Lorde, Audre. 1988. *A Burst of Light: Essays by Audre Lorde*. Ithaca, NY: Firebrand Books.

––––––––. 1984. *Sister Outsider: Essays and Speeches by Audre Lorde*. Freedom, CA: The Crossing Press.

Lubin, Carol Riegelman, and Anne Winslow. 1990. *Social Justice for Women: The International Labor Organization and Women*. Durham: Duke University Press.

Luhrmann, T.M. 1989. *Persuasions of the Witch's Craft: Ritual Magic in Contemporary England*. Cambridge, MA: Harvard University Press.

Lyons, Nona Plessner. 1988. Two Perspectives: On Self, Relationships, and Morality. In *Mapping the Moral Domain: A Contribution of Women's Thinking to Psychological Theory and Education*, edited by Carol Gilligan, Janie Victoria

Ward, and Jill McLean Taylor, with Betty Bardige. Cambridge, MA: Harvard University Press.

MacIntyre, Alasdair. 1981. *After Virtue: A Study in Moral Theory*. London: Duckworth.

MacLaren, Sherrill. 1991. *Invisible Power: The Women Who Run Canada*. Toronto: Seal Books.

Macquarrie, John. 1983. *In Search of Humanity: A Theological and Philosophical Approach*. New York: Crossroad.

Madden, Signy. 1992. Federal Budget Blows: Child Care, Baby Bonus Lost. *Kinesis* (April): 3.

Mahowald, Mary Briody, ed. 1983. *Philosophy of Woman: An Anthology of Classic and Current Concepts*. 2d ed. Indianapolis: Hackett.

Mails, Thomas E. 1991. *Fools Crow: Wisdom and Power*. Tulsa: Council Oak Books.

Markale, Jean. 1986. *Women of the Celts*. Translated by A. Mygind, C. Hauch, and P. Henry. Rochester, VT: Inner Traditions International.

Maroney, Heather Jon, and Meg Luxton, eds. 1987. *Feminism and Political Economy: Women's Work, Women's Struggles*. Toronto: Methuen.

Massey, Marilyn Chapin. 1985. *Feminine Soul: The Fate of an Ideal*. Boston: Beacon Press.

Maturana, Humberto R., and Francisco J. Varela. 1987. *The Tree of Knowledge: The Biological Roots of Human Understanding*. Boston: Shambhala.

McClung, Nellie L. 1915. *In Times Like These*. Toronto: McLeod & Allen.

McFague, Sallie. 1987. *Models of God: Theology for an Ecological, Nuclear Age*. Philadelphia: Fortress Press.

McGillivray, Don. 1992. The Proof Is Not Always in the Pudding. *Calgary Herald*, 27 January: Sec. A, p. 4.

Merchant, Carolyn. 1990. Ecofeminism and Feminist Theory. In *Reweaving the World: The Emergence of Ecofeminism*, edited by Irene Diamond and Gloria Feman Orenstein. San Francisco: Sierra Club Books.

Minnich, Elizabeth Kamarck. 1990. *Transforming Knowledge*. Philadelphia: Temple University Press.

Mitchell, Juliet. 1974. *Psychoanalysis and Feminism*. New York: Pantheon.

Mohanty, Chandra Talpade, Ann Russo, and Lourdes Torres, eds. 1991. *Third World Women and the Politics of Feminism*. Bloomington: Indiana University Press.

Mookerjee, Ajit. 1988. *Kali: The Feminine Force*. New York: Destiny Books.

Moraga, C., and G. Anzaldúa, eds. 1981. *This Bridge Called My Back: Writings by Radical Women of Color*. Watertown, MA: Persephone Press.

Morrison, Toni. 1987. *Beloved: A Novel*. New York: New American Library.

———. 1974. *Sula*. New York: Knopf.

Morstein, Petra von. 1988. Self and Two Varieties of Self-Loss: Disconnected Moments. *Atlantis* 13, no. 2:93-99.

Morton, Nelle. 1985. *The Journey Is Home*. Boston: Beacon Press.

Murdoch, Iris. 1967. *The Sovereignty of Good Over Other Concepts*. Cambridge: Cambridge University Press.

Murphy, Julien S. 1989. The Look in Sartre and Rich. In *The Thinking Muse: Feminism and Modern French Philosophy*, edited by Jeffner Allen and Iris Marion Young. Bloomington: Indiana University Press.

Murry, J. Middleton, ed. 1954. *Journal of Katherine Mansfield*. London: Constable.

Nagao, Gadjin M. 1978. "What Remains" in Sunyata: A Yogacara Interpretation of Emptiness. In *Mahayana Buddhist Meditation: Theory and Practice*, edited by Minoru Kiyota, assisted by Elvin W. Jones. Honolulu: University Press of Hawaii.

Nielsen, Joyce McCarl. 1990. *Sex and Gender in Society: Perspectives on Stratification*. 2d ed. Prospect Heights, IL: Waveland Press.

Nightingale, Florence. [1852] 1979. *Cassandra*. With an Introduction by Myra Stark and an Epilogue by Cynthia Macdonald. Reprint, Old Westbury, NY: The Feminist Press.

Noble, Vicki. 1991. *Shakti Woman—Feeling Our Fire, Healing Our World: The New Female Shamanism*. San Francisco: HarperSanFrancisco.

_____. 1983. *Motherpeace: A Way to the Goddess through Myth, Art, and Tarot*. San Francisco: Harper & Row.

Noddings, Nel. 1984. *Caring, A Feminine Approach to Ethics & Moral Education*. Berkeley: University of California Press.

Northrup, Christiane. 1990. Honoring Our Bodies. *Woman of Power: A Magazine of Feminism, Spirituality, and Politics* 18 (Fall): 16-19.

Nye, Andrea. 1990. *Words of Power: A Feminist Reading of the History of Logic*. New York: Routledge.

O'Brien, Mary. 1989. *Reproducing the World: Essays in Feminist Theory*. Boulder, CO: Westview Press.

Office of Technology Assessment. 1988. *Infertility, Medical and Social Choices*. Washington, DC: U.S. Government Printing Office.

Okin, Susan Moller. 1989. *Justice, Gender, and the Family*. New York: Basic Books.

Pagels, Elaine Hiesey. 1979. *The Gnostic Gospels*. New York: Random House.

Parker, Phillip J. 1984. Surrogate Motherhood, Psychiatric Sciences, and Informed Consent, Baby Selling and Public Policy. *Bulletin of the Academy of Psychiatry and Law* 21.

Partnow, Elaine, comp. and ed. 1977. *The Quotable Woman, 1800-1975*. Los Angeles: Corwin Books.

Pateman, Carole. 1989. *The Disorder of Women: Democracy, Feminism and Political Theory*. Cambridge: Polity.

_____. 1988. *The Sexual Contract*. Stanford: Stanford University Press.

Pellauer, Mary D. 1985. Moral Callousness and Moral Sensitivity: Violence Against Women. In *Women's Consciousness/Women's Conscience: A Reader in Feminist Ethics*, edited by Barbara Hilkert Andolsen, Christine E. Gudorf, and Mary D. Pellauer. San Francisco: Harper & Row.

Penelhum, Terence. 1970. *Survival and Disembodied Existence*. London: Routledge and Kegan Paul.

Plant, Judith. 1990. Searching for Common Ground: Ecofeminism and Bioregionalism. In *Reweaving the World: The Emergence of Ecofeminism*, edited by Irene Diamond and Gloria Feman Orenstein. San Francisco: Sierra Club Books.

Plaskow, Judith. 1990. *Standing Again at Sinai: Judaism from a Feminist Perspective*. New York: Harper & Row.

_____. 1988. Toward a New Theology of Sexuality. Paper delivered at the annual meetings of the American Academy of Religion.

Plaskow, Judith, and Carol P. Christ, eds. 1989. *Weaving the Visions: New Patterns in Feminist Spirituality*. Translated by Allan Bloom. San Francisco: Harper & Row, 1989.

Plato. 1968. *Plato's Republic*. New York: Basic Books.

_____. 1894. *Plato's Theatetus*. Translated by Benjamin Hall Kennedy. Cambridge: Cambridge University Press.

Poff, Deborah C. 1987. Content, Intent and Consequences: Life Production and Reproduction Technology. *Atlantis* 13, no. 1:116-24.

Presley, Elvis. 1987. *The Number One Hits*. Scarborough, ON: BMG Music Canada.

Probyn, Elspeth. 1991. This Body which Is Not One: Technologizing an Embodied Self. *Hypatia: Special Issue, Feminism and the Body* 6, no. 3:111-24.

Rawls, John. 1971. *A Theory of Justice*. Cambridge, MA: Belknap Press of Harvard University Press.

Reineke, Martha. 1990. "The Devils Are Come Down Upon Us": Myth, History and the Witch as Scapegoat. In *The Pleasure of Her Text: Feminist Readings of Biblical and Historical Texts*, edited by Alice Bach. Philadelphia: Trinity Press International.

Rich, Adrienne. 1980. Compulsory Heterosexuality and Lesbian Existence. *Signs: Journal of Women in Culture and Society* 5, no. 4:631-60.

Ricoeur, Paul. 1978. The Metaphoric Process in Cognition, Imagination, and Feeling. *Critical Inquiry* 5, no. 1:143-59.

Rorty, Richard. 1979. *Philosophy and the Mirror of Nature*. Princeton, NJ: Princeton University Press.

Ross, Herbert. 1989. Director of film *Steel Magnolias*. With Julia Roberts and Sally Field.

Roth, Gabrielle, with John Loudon. 1989. *Maps to Ecstasy: Teachings of an Urban Shaman*. San Rafael, CA: New World Library.

Roth, Gabrielle, and The Mirrors. 1988. *Initiation*. Audio dance cassette tape.

Rousseau, J.J. 1979. *Emile: or, On Education*. Translated by Allan Bloom. New York: Basic Books.

————. 1968. *Politics and the Arts: A Letter to M. d'Alembert on the Theatre*. Translated by Allan Bloom. Ithaca, NY: Cornell University Press.

————. 1968. *The Social Contract*. Translated by M. Cranston. Harmondsworth: Penguin Books.

Royal Commission Report on New Reproductive Technologies. 1993. *Legal and Ethical Issues in New Reproductive Technologies: Pregnancy and Parenthood*. Ottawa: Canada Communications Group-Publishing.

Rubin, Gayle. 1984. Thinking Sex: Notes for a Radical Theory of the Politics of Sexuality. In *Pleasure and Danger: Exploring Female Sexuality*, edited by Carole S. Vance. London: Routledge and Kegan Paul.

Ruether, Rosemary Radford. 1992. *Gaia & God: An Ecofeminist Theology of Earth Healing*. San Francisco: HarperSanFrancisco.

————. 1985a. *Womanguides: Readings toward a Feminist Theology*. Boston: Beacon Press.

————. 1985b. *Women-Church: Theology and Practice of Feminist Liturgical Communities*. San Francisco: Harper & Row.

————. 1983. *Sexism and God-talk: Toward a Feminist Theology*. Boston: Beacon Press.

————. 1974. *Religion and Sexism: Images of Woman in the Jewish and Christian Traditions*. New York: Simon and Schuster.

Rule, Ann. 1987. *Small Sacrifices*. New York: Signet.

Ruvinsky, Maxine. 1992. Women MDs Practise Less Medicine—Study. *The Edmonton Journal*, 16 January: Sec. A, p. 12.

Saffire: The Uppity Blues Women. 1990. *Hot Flash*. Chicago: Alligator Records & Artist Management.

Sanday, Peggy Reeves. 1981. *Female Power and Male Dominance: On the Origins of Sexual Inequality*. Cambridge: Cambridge University Press.

Sayers, Janet. 1991. *Mothers of Psychoanalysis: Helene Deutsch, Karen Horney, Anna Freud, Melanie Klein*. New York: W. W. Norton.

Schaum, Melita, and Connie Flanagan, eds. 1992. *Gender Images: Readings for Composition*. Boston: Houghton Mifflin.

Schüssler Fiorenza, Elisabeth. 1983. *In Memory of Her: A Feminist Theological Reconstruction of Christian Origins*. New York: Crossroad.

Schüssler Fiorenza, Elisabeth, and Anne Carr, eds. 1987. *Women, Work and Poverty*. Edinburgh: T. & T. Clark.

Scott, Bonnie Kime. 1990. *The Gender of Modernism: A Critical Anthology*. Bloomington: Indiana University Press.

Sekaran, Uma, and Frederick T. Leong, eds. 1992. *Womanpower: Managing in Times of Demographic Turbulence*. London: Sage Publications.

Shannon, David T. 1991. "An Ante-bellum Sermon": A Resource for an African American Hermeneutic. In *Stony the Road We Trod: African American Biblical Interpretation*, edited by Cain Hope Felder. Minneapolis: Fortress Press.

Sharma, Kumud, with Sahba Hussain and Archana Saharya. 1984. *Women in Focus: A Community in Search of Equal Roles*. Hyderabad, India: Sangam Books.

Sheehy, Gail. 1991. The Silent Passage: Menopause. *Vanity Fair*, November/December: 222-27 and 252-63.

Sheffield, Carole. 1992. Sexual Terrorism. In *Feminist Philosophies*, edited by Janet A. Kourany, James P. Sterba, and Rosemarie Tong. Englewood Cliffs, NJ: Prentice Hall.

Sidel, Ruth. 1992. The New American Dreamers. In *Gender Images: Readings for Composition*, edited by Melita Schaum and Connie Flanagan. Boston: Houghton Mifflin.

————. 1990. *On Her Own: Growing Up in the Shadow of the American Dream*. New York: Viking.

Silman, Janet. 1987. *Enough is Enough: Aboriginal Women Speak Out*. Toronto: Women's Press.

Smith, Andy. 1991. For All Those Who Were Indian in a Former Life. Manuscript. November/December: pp. 44-45.

Smith, Dorothy E. 1987. *The Everyday World as Problematic: A Feminist Sociology*. Boston: Northeastern University Press.

Smith, Lynn. 1989. What Is Feminist Legal Research? In *The Effects of Feminist Approaches on Research Methodologies*, edited by Winnie Tomm. Waterloo, ON: Wilfrid Laurier University Press for the Calgary Institute for the Humanities.

Spelman, Elizabeth V. 1988. *Inessential Woman: Problems of Exclusion in Feminist Thought*. Boston: Beacon Press.

Spinoza, Baruch. [1677] 1982. *The Ethics and Selected Letters*. Edited with an Introduction by Seymour Feldman. Translated by Samuel Shirley. Reprint, Indianapolis: Hackett Publishing.

Spretnak, Charlene. 1991. *States of Grace: The Recovery of Meaning in the Postmodern Age*. San Francisco: HarperSanFrancisco.

————. 1990. Ecofeminism: Our Roots and Flowering. In *Reweaving the World: The Emergence of Ecofeminism*, edited by Irene Diamond and Gloria Feman Orenstein. San Francisco: Sierra Club Books.

————. 1986. *The Spiritual Dimension of Green Politics*. Sante Fe, NM: Bear & Company.

————. [1978] 1981. *Lost Goddesses of Early Greece: A Collection of Pre-Hellenic Myths*. Boston: Beacon Press.

_____, ed. 1982. *The Politics of Women's Spirituality: Essays on the Rise of Spiritual Power Within the Feminist Movement*. Garden City, NY: Anchor Books.

Starhawk. 1982. *Dreaming the Dark: Magic, Sex & Politics*. Boston: Beacon Press.

Statistics Canada. 1993. *Earnings of Men and Women/Gains des hommes et des femmes*. Annual Report. Catalogue 13-217. Ottawa.

Steinem, Gloria. 1992. *Revolution from Within: A Book of Self-Esteem*. Boston: Little, Brown.

Stone, Merlin. 1978. *When God Was a Woman*. New York: Harcourt Brace Jovanovich.

Streng, Frederick J. 1967. *Emptiness: A Study in Religious Meaning*. Nashville, TN: Abingdon Press.

Talamantez, Inés. 1989. The Presence of Isanaklesh: A Native American Goddess and the Path of Pollen. In *Unspoken Worlds: Women's Religious Lives*, edited by Nancy Auer Falk and Rita M. Gross. Belmont, CA: Wadsworth.

Taylor, Barbara. 1991. Lords of Creation. In *A Reader in Feminist Knowledge*, edited by Sneja Gunew. London: Routledge.

_____. 1983. *Eve and the New Jerusalem: Socialism and Feminism in the Nineteenth Century*. London: Virago.

Taylor, Charlotte. 1992. Report on Leadership Styles among Men and Women, in *The Entrepreneurial Woman*, as reported by Gerald Graham in an article entitled Leadership Styles Differ between Men, Women Bosses. *The Edmonton Journal*, 23 May.

Teilhard de Chardin, Pierre. 1970. *Hymn of the Universe*. English translation, London: Fontana Books.

Thomson, Judith Jarvis. 1990. *The Realm of Rights*. Cambridge, MA: Harvard University Press.

Tickner, Lisa. 1988. *The Spectacle of Women: Imagery of the Suffrage Campaign 1907-14*. Chicago: University of Chicago Press.

Tomm, Winnie. Forthcoming. Embodied Spiritual Consciousness: Beyond Psychology. In *Psychoanalysis, Feminism and Religion*, edited by Mary May Downing.

_____. 1993. Otherness in Self-Disclosure: A Woman's Perspective. *Studies in Religion/Sciences Religieuses* 22, no. 4:487-502.

_____. 1992a. Ethics and Self-Knowing: The Satisfaction of Desire. In *Explorations in Feminist Ethics: Theory and Practice*, edited by Eve Browning Cole and Susan Coultrap-McQuin. Bloomington: Indiana University Press.

_____. 1992b. Knowing Ourselves as Women. In *Anatomy of Gender: Women's Struggle for the Body*, edited by Dawn H. Currie and Valerie Raoul. Ottawa: Carleton University Press.

_____. 1991. Goddess Consciousness and Social Realities: The Permeable Self. In *The Annual Review of Women in World Religions*, Vol. 1, edited by Arvind Sharma and Katherine K. Young. Albany, NY: State University of New York Press.

_____. 1990. Sexuality, Rationality, and Spirituality. *Zygon* 25, no. 2:219-38

_____. 1987. Gender Factor of Metaphysics in a Discussion of Ethics. *Explorations: Journal for Adventurous Thought* 6 (Fall): 1-27.

_____. 1984. Spinoza, Hume, and Bazubandhu: The Relation between Reason and Emotion in Self-Development. Ph.D. dissertation, The University of Calgary.

_____, ed. 1989. *The Effects of Feminist Approaches on Research Methodologies*. Waterloo, ON: Wilfrid Laurier University Press for the Calgary Institute for the Humanities.

Trinh, T. Minh-Ha. 1989. *Woman, Native, Other: Writing Postcoloniality and Feminism*. Bloomington: Indiana University Press.

Ulanov, Ann Belford. 1981. *Receiving Woman: Studies in the Psychology and Theology of the Feminine*. Philadelphia: Westminster Press.

Vasubandhu. 1933. *Trimsika*. Commentary by Sthiramati (Trimsika-bhasya). Edited by Enga Teramoto. In Tibetan. Kyoto: Association for Linguistic Study of Sacred Scriptures.

Vogel, Karen, and Vicki Noble. 1981. *The Motherpeace Round Tarot Deck*. Berkeley, CA: Self-published by Karen Vogel.

Walby, Sylvia. 1990. *Theorizing Patriarchy*. Oxford: Basil Blackwell.

Walker, Alice. 1982. *The Color Purple*. New York: Washington Square Press.

Walsh, Heide, Betty Loughe, and Shashi Assanand. 1992. Immigrant Women at the Doctor's Panel. *Kinesis* (March): 4.

Ward, Kathryn, ed. 1990. *Women Workers and Global Restructuring*. Ithaca, NY: School of Industrial and Labor Relations, Cornell University (ILR Press).

Waring, Marilyn. 1992. A Woman's Reckoning: An Introduction to the International Economic System. In *Gender Images: Readings for Composition*, edited by Melita Schaum and Connie Flanagan. Boston: Houghton Mifflin.

――――. 1988. *If Women Counted: A New Feminist Economics*. San Francisco: Harper & Row.

Waywanko, Andrea. 1989. Who Pays for Pay Equity. *Challenging the Barriers: Edmonton Working Women Newsletter* (Spring/Summer): 8-9.

Weaver, Mary Jo. 1989. Who Is the Goddess and Where Does She Get Us? *Journal of Feminist Studies in Religion* 5, no. 1:49-64.

Weems, Renita J. 1991. Reading *Her Way* through the Struggle: African American Women and the Bible. In *Stony the Road We Trod: African American Biblical Interpretation*, edited by Cain Hope Felder. Minneapolis: Fortress Press.

Wendell, Susan. 1990. Oppression and Victimization: Choice and Responsibility. *Hypatia: A Journal of Feminist Philosophy* 5, no. 3:15-46.

――――. 1989. Toward a Feminist Theory of Disability. *Hypatia: A Journal of Feminist Philosophy* 4, no. 2:104-24.

Wheeler, Anne, dir., with Kenneth Walsh and Tantoo Cardinal. 1987. *Loyalties*. Canadian National Film Board, Studio B.

Whitaker, Kay Cordell. 1991. *The Reluctant Shaman: A Woman's First Encounters with the Unseen Spirits of the Earth*. San Francisco: HarperSanFrancisco.

Whitbeck, Caroline. 1989. A Different Reality: Feminist Ontology. In *Women, Knowledge, and Reality: Explorations in Feminist Philosophy*, edited by Ann Garry and Marilyn Pearsall. Boston: Unwin Hyman.

Whitehead, Alfred North. 1925. *Science and the Modern World*. New York: The Free Press.

Whitehead, Mary Beth. 1989. *A Mother's Story*. New York: St. Martin's Press.

Whitford, Margaret. 1991a. *Luce Irigaray: Philosophy in the Feminine*. New York: Routledge.

――――. 1991b. Irigaray's Body Symbolic. *Hypatia: Special Issue, Feminism and the Body* 6, no. 3:97-110.

Wilson, Marie. 1988. Native Peoples. *New Internationalist* (August): 18.

Wittig, Monique. 1982. The Category of Sex. *Feminist Issues* (Fall): 63-68.

Wolf, Diane L. 1990. Linking Women's Labor with the Global Economy: Factory Workers and Their Families in Rural Java. In *Women Workers and Global Restructuring*, edited by Kathryn Ward. Ithaca, NY: School of Industrial and Labor Relations, Cornell University (ILR Press).

Wolf, Naomi. 1990. *The Beauty Myth*. Toronto: Random House.

Wollstonecraft, Mary. [1792] 1967. *A Vindication of the Rights of Woman*. Reprint, New York: W.W. Norton.

WomenFutures. 1991. Women and Community Economic Development. A project of the Social Planning and Research Council of B.C. and Womenfutures Community Economic Development Society, proposal written in 1991. Address is WomenFutures, Community Economic Development Society, 217-1956 West Broadway, Vancouver, B.C. V6J 1Z2.

Worcester, Nancy, and Mariamne H. Whatley. 1988. *Women's Health: Readings on Social, Economic, and Political Issues*. Dubuque, IA: Kendall/Hunt Publishing.

Young, David, and Jean-Guy Goulet, eds. 1994. *Being Changed: The Anthropology of Extraordinary Experience*. Peterborough: Broadview Press.

Young, Katharine P., et al. 1991. *Women in the Legal Profession: A Report of the Women in the Legal Profession Subcommittee*. Vancouver: The Law Society of British Columbia.

Ywahoo, Dhyani. 1987. *Voices of Our Ancestors: Cherokee Teachings from the Wisdom Fire*. Edited by Barbara DuBois. Boston: Shambhala.

Zalk, Sue Rosenberg, and Janice Gordon-Kelter, eds. 1992. *Revolutions in Knowledge: Feminism in the Social Sciences*. Boulder, CO: Westview Press.

Index

A